Mooring Against the Tide

Mooring Against the Tide

WRITING FICTION AND POETRY

SECOND EDITION

Jeff Knorr
Sacramento City College

Tim Schell
Columbia Gorge Community College

PEARSON
Prentice
Hall

Upper Saddle River, NJ 07458

Library of Congress Cataloging-in-Publication Data
Knorr, Jeff.
  Mooring against the tide: writing fiction and poetry / Jeff Knorr, Tim Schell.
    p. cm.
  Includes bibliographical references and index.
  ISBN 0-13-178785-3
  1. English language—Rhetoric. 2. Creative writing—Problems, exercises, etc.
3. Poetry—Authorship—Problems, exercises, etc. 4. Poetry—Authorship—
Problems, exercises, etc. I. Schell, Tim. II. Title.

PE1408.K6886 2006
808.1—dc22

                                                              2004017081

Editorial Director: Leah Jewell
Acquisitions Editor: Vivian Garcia
Editorial Assistant: Melissa Casciano
Production Liaison: Joanne Hakim
Executive Marketing Manager: Brandy Dawson
Marketing Assistant: Mariel DeKranis
Manufacturing Buyer: Brian Mackey
Permissions Specialist: Mary Dalton Hoffman
Cover Design: Robert Farrar-Wagner
Manager, Cover Visual Research & Permissions: Karen Sanatar
Cover Illustration/Photo: Salvador Caballero, "Placidez," Sunset on Lake, oil on canvas,
    76 cm × 60 cm (29.9" × 23.6"). Decorative Expressions Inc.
Composition/Full-Service Project Management: GGS Book Services, Atlantic Highlands
Printer/Binder: The Courier Companies

Pearson Education LTD., London
Pearson Education Singapore, Pte. Ltd
Pearson Education, Canada, Ltd
Pearson Education—Japan
Pearson Education Australia PTY,
  Limited

Pearson Education North Asia Ltd
Pearson Educación de Mexico, S.A. de C.V.
Pearson Education Malaysia, Pte. Ltd
Pearson Education, Upper Saddle River, New Jersey

10 9 8 7 6 5 4 3 2 1

ISBN 0-13-178785-3

Contents

II Fiction 151

Preface

The first edition of *Mooring Against the Tide* was comprised of the two genres of poetry and fiction, and modeled after a creative writing workshop wherein the students read and critique work of their peers in an effort to discover what is working in a story or in a poem and what is not working, and thereby apply these lessons to their own work. In this second edition, we have maintained the workshop-oriented structure, but we have made many changes as well: we have replaced two guest essays with two new essays; we have increased the number of exercises in each chapter; we have added a section of selected readings of both fiction and poetry along with short essays on how to read a story and how to read a poem; and after each chapter we have directed the students to these selected readings as examples of what was discussed in the chapter. We hope these changes will further enhance the students' experience in the challenging and rewarding art of writing fiction and poetry, and to that end, help them more clearly examine the human heart in its constant state of turmoil.

The book is organized by genre with each respective genre organized by chapters defining the elements of fiction and poetry. Each chapter is followed by workshop sections wherein student stories and poems are presented.

In the chapters covering the elements of fiction and poetry, we have presented utilitarian definitions for the reader followed by essays by guest writers. For example, in the chapter on "Sound in Poetry, "we present a definition of that element followed by an essay on sound by Alberto Rios who addresses the quality of sound in his own students' work. In the fiction section of this book, we define the various uses of "setting" in the chapter so-named. Following that definition is an essay by the novelist Valerie Miner who writes about the role of setting in one of her own student's story.

In the workshop sections of the book, we present first the student poem and student story without notations, followed by questions the reader is asked to consider. Following this is the same story and the same poem, this time with our notations and then our critiques of the student work. Finally, student revisions are presented with critiques.

It is our hope that the structure of this book will allow the readers to witness the creative evolution of poems and stories, and that they will see the process of writing as inherently dynamic as the writers go through draft after draft in the effort of crafting the finest fiction and poetry they are capable of. Whether used by a student-writer in a creative writing class or by a student-writer at home alone, this book will serve as a guide to steer through sometimes rough and unsure waters until the writer is safely moored against the tide.

ACKNOWLEDGMENTS

I would like to thank my wife Sachiko, and my daughter, Maya, for their patience and support during the writing of this book. I would also like to thank my friend and colleague, Jeff Knorr, who, as ever, was a pleasure to work with.

—*Tim Schell*

Great thanks is due my wife Diane and my son, Gabriel for giving me time, support, and patience while writing this book. Also, thanks to Tim Schell, colleague and friend, who is great to work with and always an inspiration.

—*Jeff Knorr*

From both of us, special thanks is due our editor, Vivian Garcia, for her belief in the project, patience, and energy. Also, thanks to Karen Schultz at Prentice Hall for her support and dedication to the project. And to all of the reviewers who offered their vital support and feedback in order to make this edition even better than the first.

Reviewers:

Julie MacDonald, Southeast Community College
Joe Davis, NIACC
Christian Michener, Saint Mary's University
Peter Donahue, Birmingham-Southern College
Amy Sage Webb, Emporia State University
Michael Heffernan, University of Arkansas
Jenny Brantley, University of Wisconsin-River Falls
Sharon Oard Warner, University of New Mexico
Aaron A. Abeyta, Adams State College
Amy Fleury, Washburn University
Jane Hallinger, Pasadena City College
Christopher Davis, University of North Carolina at Charlotte
Margo Williams, Cape Fear Community College

Richard Johnson, Kirkwood Community College
Stephanie Mood, Grossmont College
James Cervantes, Mesa Community College
Sidney Watson, Oklahoma Baptist University

—Jeff Knorr,
Tim Schell

Mooring Against the Tide

PART ONE

Poetry

CHAPTER
1

GETTING STARTED

WHERE ARE THE POEMS HIDING?

There are poems hiding all around us—they are in corners of the room in spider webs, they are in the smooth handle of my grandfather's hammer in the garage, they are in the French toast for breakfast, and on the lawn of the old lady who lives across the street.

Finding subject matter we think is worthy enough for a poem can be one of the most difficult tasks we encounter. This very notion of finding worthy subjects is problematic because we tell ourselves that a poem deserves something better than we have come up with. This, unfortunately, is a losing battle. So, how do we win? We find subject matter that is accessible and human. People like to read about the world they live in, and, as writers, we ought to write about it.

James Wright, when asked about his poem "Lying in a Hammock on William Duffy's Farm in Pine Island, Minnesota," explained that he was not trying to do anything heroic in that poem, but rather he was trying to capture a moment in his life in which he felt a sense of delight. What he meant by not being heroic was that the poem need not work on a grand level. A poem does not need to

There is in one room in one day in one man's life, material for a lifetime.

John O'Hara

conquer us; it just needs to show us something and capture a moment. In doing so, the poem moves us. Sometimes a student writer comes up with a "great idea" for a poem only to miss what is really the great, moving moment at the middle of it. Why? These moments are often the smallest and most nonheroic moments, but for this reason they are also the most human. Over the years it has been put into our heads that poems must be larger than life and must have something great to say. And they do have great things to say. But poems are only great when they touch us. So I often say to students who are searching for subject matter, "Find a simple moment, a moment that is normal to you or a part of your life, and figure out what is important at the center of that."

One of my students was on a road trip in Alaska with his long-time childhood friend when their truck broke down. So they slept in the back of the truck in a gas station parking lot in a very small town in Alaska. This is what came later.

North of Anchorage an Hour

Here, there is an amount of option;
Fashion stays on
the "Outside,"
where priority-mail
arrives sooner than   5
seven days.

Tonight, bars named after
guns and rabid animals
blink signs and
tomorrow, just as many   10
churches open at
eight and eleven.

JACKOB CURTIS

When Jake brought the poem to class, I was struck by how much he had accomplished in the poem by keeping it simple. He had created a poem that seemed to mirror the place. Moreover, this is not a poem that is larger than life; it *is* life. Note how much he says with small details like *priority-mail* or *bars named after / guns and rabid animals / blink signs.* To close the poem, he contrasts the bar image against churches—giving them opening times like bars—and the idea of "options" that he begins with. Simplicity has given Jake some fine mileage.

On the first day in my writing workshops, or even introduction to literature courses, we go around the class and each of us tells one thing we've noticed in the last two weeks that we didn't notice before. Of course the answers range from "The lady across the street uses a cane," or "I have a little spot of rust on my car door just below the lock," to "I noticed over the holiday that I really appreciate my family," and "I always go out with my dad to split wood. I never split it; I just go and talk with him." Once we have done this, we talk about these observations as topics for poems. (We usually agree that observations like "appreciating my family" has the least strength of the four because it is so abstract). For some reason we've missed these things previously, walked right by them. But now, simply because we've noticed them, they've touched us and held us tightly for a moment. And that makes them ready to be subjects for poems.

Seeing Your World as Poetic?

So now that we've figured out how to find the poems, to know their hiding places—at least sometimes—we need to figure out how to make this a regular event. Consider this the "off-the-page" writing process. This is where we begin to use the process of writing to interpret everyday events. In order to do this, we have to be open to redefining our world and to be ready to view it and define it at any moment. This should please anyone with writer's block because it means we are always writing.

Let's step back for a moment. When we went through the process of noticing something we hadn't noticed before, what was happening was that, for one instant, we stopped or slowed down long enough to see it. And in doing so, we allowed that thing to take hold of us. So, what is the key?

First, slow down. Years ago when I walked with my two-year-old, a walk around the block might take forty minutes because every few yards he said, "Look, Papa, a bug." Or "Look, Papa, a leaf." The list of things he noticed was endless and most of them were rather exceptional findings, especially for him—he was two and he had never seen some of these things. To define them in new ways, for example, to watch the way a caterpillar moves, is to see them as fresh. And to couple these with feelings, to put the concrete with the abstract, is to begin to make poetry. So I began to note these things on our walks around the block—how many poems live on our block.

After we've slowed ourselves enough to notice possible subject matter, the next step is to let it work on us. We may not do this at the moment, but then again, we may. In this equation—slowing down and noticing things + feeling them = a good subject—the second part is not so separate from the first. In fact, the two parts often happen simultaneously. But allowing ourselves to perceive a moment or thing as important, significant, tragic, delightful, or harrowing, for instance, will let the moment (or thing) blossom into some semblance of a poem later; these words themselves mean little because they are abstracts. Without **images** to represent them, it is hard to relate to them or attach to them. And because we naturally perceive a moment as concrete when we create and notice subject matter, we need to recreate it for our readers when we write poems. Creating concrete images and allowing abstracts to remain below the surface is one of the most important tools in the craft of writing poetry. Take for instance this image—holding someone. The image itself is concrete, but the emotion and the desire for connection are left below the surface of the image.

> How I want to reach you;
> slip my hands past your canvas
> coat and hold you in the barn light as
> night folds its dark clench over us.

Look at the following poem. This student found that something that was in front of her all the time was actually poetic. Lynne is a pretty creative person and she has a knack for finding good subject matter. But really, what Lynne does well is to simply write about things that are constantly in front of her. She figures out how to squeeze the poetic moment out of something "normal." Here, she has not only explored her identity and the tension that we all face, but also the tension she faces particularly.

How to Pretend You are not You

> Make fun of your parents
> who cannot go to the store
> without tripping over the word, "grocery."
> Lie about where you were born.
> Mock the kids
> at school who look like you
> and think you will help them.
> Stab them in the back
> without the knife.
> Hammer on their spines
> with your closed fist.
> Spit on them at the back
> of the Blue Bird school bus.
> Wish you were at least half
> and had a name like Jenni or
> Randi with an i, so you can
> dot them with hearts.
> Complain about the smell of moth balls
> because it exposes you.
> Insist on drinking milk instead of soy—
> eating potatoes instead of rice.
> Dye your hair hot pink or seaweed green.
> Curse your ancestry for not giving

you big, double-lidded eyes
with sunflowery flecks.
Refuse to play the piano, clarinet
or violin well.
Fail calculus and physics.
Tell everyone you would rather
die than become a doctor.
Tell your mother who raised you
on nirvana and plums
that Buddha is a fat, gold statue
and incense burning is a pagan tradition.
Tell her you love eating meat
regardless of that line about
animals being sentient beings.
And when you can no longer
face yourself for the things
you have done and said
ask for forgiveness.

LYNNE YU-LING CHIEN

This was an important poem for Lynne because it caught the deep emotion she felt about many days in her house and her life. And she projected those feelings through the images she portrayed. The subject matter had literally been sitting in front of Lynne for a long time. The trick that Lynne so aptly shows us here is to find the moments in our lives that many can relate to because of their normalcy and yet turn them in a way that causes their emotional resonance to rise off the page.

Keeping Notes: Mining for Poems

Once we have a handle on finding poems and subjects and seeing our world as a poetic place, the next step is writing things down. But this is hard. Students often say that it's hard to find the time to write, and we all understand this. Too often there are just too many things to do in one day, so we have to find time to write when we can. We squeeze it in because it seems like a luxury, and everything else seems like a necessity. Nobody is going to make time for us to write, however, so we need to find ways to make time for ourselves. Ultimately, we must always be writing. I've written notes or pieces of poems in my head at the fair, on a napkin in a restaurant, on a piece of wood in the garage, on a leaf page of a cookbook in the kitchen. This is part of the process that comes before actually sitting down and writing the whole poem. This is the art of note-taking.

These moments of writing things down are extremely important. One object or occasion may not turn itself into a poem immediately. It may need some fermenting and aging like wine. But we need to get the initial note down—the same as putting young wine in the barrel so it can age—before we can ruminate on its possibilities. Later, when we sit down to work on a poem, to try and write the whole piece, we can pull out these notes and work them in step by step.

What is important about taking notes is figuring out how you'll manage them. Maybe you take notes on scraps; that's fine, but collect them somewhere—a shoebox, a shopping bag, a desk drawer, or a bulletin board above your desk. Have them somewhere where you can find them when they're needed. This is your wine cellar of ideas. If you're not a scrap person or need a more disciplined approach, buy a notebook or journal book to keep notes in. Buy something you like, something that contains paper that is friendly. I believe Garrison Keillor in his assertion that a blank eight-and-a-half-by-eleven sheet of paper looks as big as Montana when you don't have anything to write. So if Montana isn't your landscape, go with Rhode Island and get the pocket-sized notebook. If you want something a bit more classy and with some hospitality, go with Georgia and get the hardbound journal with fine pages. Whatever you decide, be comfortable with it and have it close by. And make yourself write notes.

Sometimes sitting down and forcing ourselves to write can be difficult, but sitting down to write notes can ease the pressure. Try some exercises. Write down five things from yesterday that you noticed that seemed poetic. Make a list of poems you want to write. Write an abstract word—sad, for example—and under it write a one-sentence image that illustrates that abstract. Write down five or ten one-sentence similes or metaphors. Later, these things will find their ways into poems and in some cases may be the driving forces behind the poems.

These exercises and taking notes are the cornerstones of your poems. It is rare that a whole poem just comes, already formed, already packaged as a poem—it takes shaping and crafting. When we have a reserve of images and ideas that we can work with, whole poems come more easily. A craftsperson in a woodshop, for example, needs to know what kind of wood to use for the frame, sides, front, and the door of the cabinet he is building. And in the shop he has these different woods available—maybe some plywood, maybe clear-grain maple. Over time he collects more and more wood and more and more tools. Consider this as you build your note supply. Even if you don't put together whole poems each day, you will be collecting the substantive pieces that will make up your poems later.

NOTES FOR SELECTED READINGS

Note how something as simple as attending a friend's wedding was what inspired Lisa Chavez's poem "At a Wedding in Mexico City." It can help illustrate that activities we take part in regularly are good subjects for poems.

Exercises

1. Think of something concrete that you have noticed in the last two weeks (e.g., the old lady across the street walking slower than usual, a rust spot by the lock on your car door, the fineness of the coffee grounds, etc.) and use those for the concrete launch point of a poem. Make that the opening image that drives the poem.
2. From your past school days as a child, think of a student in one of your classes who was always made fun of, was the subject of ridicule and the object of cruel jokes. Write a poem, from the adult perspective, looking back on the actions that were heaped on that child by you and your peers.
3. Take some animate object in your world (e.g., a bird, a baseball player, a dog, a fish, a mother, a roommate, etc.) and describe its action. Be sure to portray in the description what the magic of the action is.

2

IMAGERY

As writers, we strive to arrest the reader, to hold him in a moment. This is no easy task, but when we do it, and when we do it well, we achieve something powerful. But how do we do this? One of the ways we do this in poetry is through **imagery**. Put simply, an **image** is a picture created by our words. Through imagery we turn **abstracts**—feelings and ideas—into part of our physical, concrete world. Most often, when we speak of images, we mean something that we can see. But don't forget that we use the term image when we discuss those words that also touch our other senses. When we use images in our poems, we give the reader a heightened perception of our world, we turn on his senses, and we allow our world to become part of his. We let the reader see a fountain of grasshoppers springing out of tall grass. And then he is there with us.

Often in poetry there is more to an image than meets the eye. Under or behind the image is a feeling or an idea. This may simply be one feeling or idea attached to the image, or the feeling may rise from the context of the poem. Images should stand in front of abstracts and veil them. When we make this happen, we create provocative images that show something rather than tell about it. This is when our language begins to take

Poetry always endeavors to arrest you, and to make you continuously see a physical thing, to prevent you gliding through an abstract process.

T.E. Hulme

on power and become something much more than mere reporting. If we want reporting, we can subscribe to our local paper. But when we want to be swept away in a poem we need language that turns in on us or that steals our hearts, ears or sight.

HOW DO WE CREATE THEM?

Images can be created in a number of different ways, but no matter how we create them or what types of images we create, images are a poet's best friends. I once had an instructor/mentor say two things that have hung around as two of the best basic pieces of advice I may have ever been given. First he told me, "It is too much to ask of readers to give them abstracts in the first sentence of a poem—give them images." And he told me (however harsh it was at the time, it held on as good advice), "I don't really care if you tell me how you feel in the poem—show me something and I'll figure out what I'm supposed to feel." As a reader and a writer of poems over the years, I've found both of these to be true. And there are ways to do this.

One of the ways we create vibrant images in a poem is to use **metaphors** and **similes**. These types of images are based on comparisons and allow us to relay abstract ideas to the reader in very concrete terms. What's more, we use these all the time in our daily speech without consciously thinking about it. A metaphor is a comparison that says one thing *is* another. For example, I might turn to my friend and say "Luis *is* the moon." This is a very basic metaphor, but it serves the purpose for the moment. The thing to remember in this example is that now Luis is no longer Luis; rather, he has taken on the qualities of the moon. The effect is that the metaphor now causes the reader to think about the image, to think about Luis having the qualities of the moon ascribed to him, and ultimately the reader is pushed to a deeper level in the poem.

Metaphors can function at various levels in a poem. At times, they function within a line or a small number of lines. Maybe a metaphor serves to power a stanza and is the overriding image. There are two types of metaphors commonly used: the **implied metaphor** and the **extended** or **controlling metaphor**. An implied metaphor does not actually state in the comparison what the main object is being compared to; rather, it implies the comparison, usually through action or by ascribing attributes. For example, we can compare a man to a fish by saying *he finned his way across the room / eyeing the bait*. In the following image, the implication applies to both people: *Mother squawked at me as I fluttered out the back door*. These metaphors work on a very subtle level but their impact should not be taken lightly. When we use them, they can offer great resonance and depth to our images.

The extended or controlling metaphor is another useful and powerful tool. It gets its name because this type of metaphor extends itself throughout an entire poem. In other words, it may control the entire poem, pushing it this way or that. One superb example of this is Alice Walker's poem "A Woman Is Not a Potted Plant" wherein the metaphor of a woman being potted, trimmed, watered, not watered, or clipped back serves to illustrate her thoughts on how society treats women. In the following poem a student writer, Dale Nelson, works with an implicitly made metaphor that we don't really see until late in the poem—it has a connective force because he's making images early in the poem (stanza 2) connect to the end of the poem through the sense of scars and weather and cold. Hence, we see that the metaphor works. It is dependent, though, on the reader knowing the particular usage of the term *outlaw* in stanza 2. On the north coast of California, a tree that is not cut down in a clear cut area and is left standing after the cutting, slashing, and hauling is called an *outlaw*.

My People (1969)

Sitting in weather with hats on. Sweatshirts. Nearby
a kettle of crab. Uncle Dud swimming in a gallon
of soft red wine. Someone has already
pissed on the fire.

Skyline a haphazard riddle of salt-burned outlaws;
some cracked by storm, some bent at the middle,
some rising stiff and tall into sharp spikes.

Pepperwoods down in the swale, blond oat grass
from last summer humped along the road.
A blue Studebaker canted heavily against a black stump.

Buckhorns nailed to the shed wall,
fish in the smokehouse. Aunt Sophie fetching an armload
of firewood, swinging an axe, mouthing a cigarette,
she squints down and threatens the dog.

Dad and his cousins arguing politics, tossing
horseshoes which flip in long elegant orbit to iron pins
driven deep in the earth. Everything rustles,
everything looks well-used.

Cousin Stephen cracks an Oly and says the word "Gook."
Crosses his eyes and touches a bullet hole
on his right shoulder.

Uncle Dud swoons over the table. "That ain't shit,
after what I seen." His watery blue eyes examine a crab
on a plate. Wood smoke washes over him and steam
wraps around him. The kettle bubbles and crabs
roll in hot foam.

Cool wind off the ocean catches the essence of rain.

DALE NELSON

A simile works in relatively the same way as a metaphor in that it is a comparison. But in the case of the simile, we either use the word *like* or *as*. For example, "The brown winter river moved *like* molasses." Or, "The horse's flanks were strong *as* alder." In the first example we have details—brown and winter—to give us color and a sense of temperature, depth, and season. But when the writer uses "*like* molasses" we know more about how the river is moving and what the color might be. In the case of the horse, we can draw some conclusions about how strong the horse is or what his flanks might feel like. Alder is a very hard and strong wood; hence, the author has chosen this detail carefully and appropriately. What's more, it's a natural detail that might also lend a hand in describing the horse's setting. Notice in the simile, unlike the metaphor, the horse remains a horse and the river remains the river, but the comparison still serves to add depth and information to the image.

As a younger writer I worked hard to write images. How could I not? All of my professors, instructors, and mentors said to use images—or else! So I worked for the great image. But what I often found myself doing was trying to create strong images by using adjectives, adverbs, and strong active verbs. And I actually did create some good images. These are certainly tools that help create strong images. So after class one day my writing instructor said, "Come by my office tomorrow so we can talk about the poems you've written this semester." Realizing that he had finally noticed all my effort and the improvement in my images, I left class that day elated. When I arrived at his office the next day, ready for some solid praise, he said, "You know, your images have improved, but you haven't used a simile or metaphor all semester. How can you expect to write poems without similes or metaphors?" I was crushed.

The net effect, though, was positive. I adopted two strategies to help me create similes and metaphors in my poems. First, when I sat down to write, I always started by writing five similes or metaphors in my notebook. In a matter of weeks I had collected pages of them. This was like stretching before running—it didn't take long, and when I was writing I felt loose and ready to move around in the poem. The second thing I did was to revise for similes and metaphors. I would go through the poem and look for a place where I might use a simile or metaphor—maybe it was already half created with an image I was using in the poem—and when I found that place I would create or insert a simile or metaphor. This worked well for me and still does today. And I often tell students in our workshops to do the same thing. Let's look at some workshop writing. The following stanza was from a poem by a beginning poetry student.

Today it rains.
The wind blows hard.
I feel the thunder
and know there is lightning.
You look at me with a rigid, gray face.   5

RHONDA ENOS

Now note Rhonda's changes in line 2 using metaphor, and she adds a simile at the end.

Today it rains.
The wind is furious.
I feel the thunder
and know there is lightning.
You look at me with a rigid, gray face,   5
eyes like coal.

While these changes were modest, they served to amplify Rhonda's stanza and add depth to the images. What's more, after she made the changes, she felt that she had captured an emotional sense of the stanza while keeping the poem concrete and image-driven. Her classmates in the workshop had urged a change to line two (*the wind blows hard*), suggesting that it certainly was concrete and active but a bit empty and dull. And they also liked the change at the end, saying that the "eyes like coal" suggested an even darker and colder feel to the relationship between these two people. They liked that the color of coal, as they saw it in their heads, went along with the gray coloring of a thunderstorm.

Another element of metaphor that Rhonda employs in the above stanza is **personification**, which is giving a nonhuman object some human characteristic. For example, *the wind tiptoes through the trees.* Or in another case, *I swatted at air / the wasp laughed and dove again.* The use of personification helps to bring alive those things outside our human world and makes those other realms understandable to us. It also helps add to the zest of images by allowing the author to be original and fresh in her construction.

While we should always strive for fresh, original language use, at times we can bump up against some common pitfalls in constructing images, metaphors, and similes. When working to craft images, we might come up with **clichés**. These are phrases or images that are, and have been, so commonly used that they are not original at all. For example, *her eyes were blue* *pools* has probably been written in just about every adolescent schoolboy's notebook or first love poem. That doesn't discount the emotion behind it, but it's not crafted or original. Avoid clichés at all costs in literary writing unless you are using them for some satirical effect. And even then, triple check to see how effective they really are. Another pitfall is what Donald Hall has referred to as the "dead metaphor." This is tricky to find because a dead metaphor is a metaphor that seems original and crafted but in the end falls flat because it's too close to other metaphors and similes we've already encountered. Don't worry too much about this—even the best of the best writers struggle with this on a regular basis. When it happens, just be able to identify the problem and revise it out of the poem. This takes time, practice, and most of all patience, but in time your sharp eye toward imagery will be well developed.

Imagery is one of the elements most needed by poets and most called upon in the writing process. Remember that images can awaken our senses, stir us, and move us deeply while staying relatively calm on the surface—like a stick that's used to stir what's on the bottom of a pond. And often the best images, those which are concrete and detailed, say more implicitly than they do explicitly. As Ernest Gaines said in a workshop I attended once, "'You know,' I tell students, 'just show me those things—I'm a pretty smart guy; I'll figure it out.'" And that's the way to proceed. As writers, if we worry about showing the world and crafting the details carefully, we can leave the wonder, the shortness of breath, the skip of the heart, to the reader. It's their heart and it's our duty to move it.

LAYING BARE THE BONES: A MEDITATION ON IMAGERY

Lisa D. Chavez

When I was in graduate school—working at that time in literature rather than creative writing—a professor asked us to consider our thought processes.

"What forms do your thoughts take?" he asked. "What do you see in your head when you're writing?"

He answered the question himself, before anyone could reply. "We see words," he said.

I was a stubborn student, already past 30, and not willing to let anyone dictate their notions of my thought process to me. I raised my hand. "I don't see in words," I said. "I see in images. Then I translate those visual images into words."

"That's impossible," he told me. "You're a poet. You work in words. You must think in words."

But I don't. And though I am certainly much less confident than he that one person's thought processes are like another's, I would venture to say that, many of us follow a similar writing process: we think in images. We follow the movie of our mind, and translate those images into words.

Here's an exercise I like to do in my poetry classes, early on. I'll give you some words, and take note of whatever comes into your head when you read these words. Anything at all—don't censor. Ready? Here are the words:

Love.
Justice.
Death.
What did you see?

In my classes, I ask students to close their eyes, and I say the words out loud. The responses vary from person to person, but the most common response is an image, sometimes personal, sometimes a symbol: for love people see hearts or a loved one. For justice scales, or a policeman or a gavel. For the most part, people report seeing a visual image, though some have told me they've seen the word itself. The words I choose are abstract, and most of us move instantly from abstraction to a specific image.

We don't all think alike, but I believe we mostly see the world this way—in images. We see specifics, concrete details. Ask someone what she sees when you say the word grandfather, and she's likely to focus on her own grandfather. Abstractions are meaningless until we translate them into something concrete that means something to us.

Imagery is anything that evokes the senses. It includes simile and metaphor, the bread and butter of poetry. But specific detail also shows us something, and is equally important. An image is anything we see, feel, hear—sensory detail that grounds us in the specific. It is the most important component of writing.

I use a lot of invention exercises in my classes, because I believe they help writers get started and because they help them discover the unexpected. And I find that exercises can be as useful for me as well. One exercise I've found to be particularly successful is not original to me. It's a first-line auction, and it works like this: all students write a first line. Other students bid on these—they bid by telling the author what poem they would write to fit that first line. The author of the line gives it away to whoever has come up with the best bid.

We did this exercise in class, once, and took our first lines home with us to write a poem. I got "I remember the moment I stopped being a child." I didn't like that line, but I took what was leftover because I'm the teacher. It took me a long time to think of anything to write to go with that line, but as I was wrangling over it, an image of a wasp bumping against a window came to me. I don't know where that image came from, but I was fascinated by it and I repeated the lines over and over to myself: a trapped wasp buzzing in an empty room. As I said before, I've always been moved by images, tend to think in images. And I often write to an image in my poems: I see a vivid picture in my head, shape it into a line of poetry, then try to write a poem that will lead me to that end. When I thought of the line about the wasp, I knew I had the end of the poem, but what would it be about? Finally, I remembered a story I was told almost 20 years ago, the story of how a friend had discovered his father's suicide. I kept thinking about that and then I wrote a poem, a dramatic monologue, spoken from the point of view of such a young man.

I needed to work in that first line, but it seemed too easy to me to have the speaker say he remembered the moment he stopped being a child. Instead, I decided to base the entire poem on the opposite premise: this man sifts through a number of tragic memories, all related to his father's suicide, trying to decide at what point exactly he lost his innocence. The poem begins like this:

Lost Country

I don't remember the moment
I stopped being a child. Memories
like a baby's blocks scattered
by a clumsy hand—which is the one?
The moment I saw my father's truck
in the driveway and I went still—hands
twisting to fists in my pockets?
Early autumn, and I was just coming back
from school. I was always home first,
so this could only be bad news:
someone hurt, dead, or him fired
or drunk. Maybe that wasn't it.
Maybe it was the instant I entered the empty
house—no sound except the slow
ticking of the kitchen clock and the bump
of a wasp at a window, wings grazing glass.
I called for my father. No response. Silence
settled like dust.

Well, you can see I changed the first line, but you can also see how it is still an integral part of the poem. I use a great deal of imagery here, both specific detail and metaphor and simile that show a reader the seemingly empty house: the quiet so strong and ominous that the soft sounds of the clock, the buzz of a wasp become loud. I knew that to believe in my character, to sympathize with him, readers would have to be grounded in an actual setting, which I tried to create with details of sight and sound.

The middle of the poem, which I haven't included here, shows how after discovering the suicide, the young man steps into his father's role—even taking a job at the same place and learning to drink hard with his father's friends. He gives over his life to his dead father. I end the poem with this stanza:

> Maybe the moment
> I'm looking for is the one
> I never saw except in dreams:
> My father taking the stairs slow,
> shotgun and shells in his hands.
> He slumps into the kitchen chair
> he brought up from below. Loads
> the gun. Unties his shoe. Then he blows
> my whole life to hell: my childhood
> a distant country, and me
> a trapped wasp buzzing
> in an empty room.
>
> LISA D. CHAVEZ

When I went back to class the next week I read the poem aloud. And I told my students how it came to be written—how the first line unexpectedly led me to an image, and how I recognized that the image would close the poem. How at that point I still didn't know what the poem would be about. Then I told them how I remembered the story I recount here, about a young man whose father killed himself. How he was the oldest son, pushed too early into adulthood, and how he'd felt trapped in a life he'd never chosen. I hadn't seen this man for years, nor thought of that story, but unexpectedly the image and the story came together and I had my poem. (The character and details in my poem, by the way, are made up and do not reflect the real man.) And so my students and I talked about how image can convey emotion and how we recognize the rightness of the image, that precise emotional resonance, even if we often can't articulate why or how the image works. After writing the poem I could go back to it as a critic and unpack the imagery—the threat of the wasp's sting countered by the fact that it is trapped parallels the speaker's own position, his anger and his despair—but in the flush of creating the poem I didn't know that; I only knew that I had an image that felt right.

I often use this poem, and this exercise, as an example of how an image that haunts can be a doorway into poem. How imagery, especially metaphor, can work on an emotional level even before we're able to intellectually understand it.

Here's another exercise I like to do. I give students postcards, the odder the better, and tell them they have a week to write a short poem—one that would fit on a postcard—that is somehow inspired by the image on the card. The poems diverge wildly from the postcards, but what they share is this: they begin in imagery and must contain something specific to ground them.

This is an example of a poem from that exercise. The postcard was a drawing of a skeleton, and it's just coincidental that subject matter is similar to the one my poem:

These are my bones

See? Look closer. You can see
right through that rib cage,
can't you? No heart
and my bones don't have to breathe.

In eighth grade, I had a girlfriend,
a redhead. She boarded horses, liked being
by herself. She was quiet,
beautiful—the kind of beautiful everyone noticed,
my brother included—but she chose me,
said I felt enough for both of us.

They moved out, across town. I learned
to drive, failed anatomy.
Our junior year in high school,
she put a 12-gauge shotgun
in her mouth and squeezed.

At twenty-eight, there are parts
of me that still can't stomach the sound
of her name, the thought of her bones: burned
and scattered by the barn.

—JEFF PROCTOR

This is a revised version of the poem Jeff wrote from the class assignment. It's the kind of poem I admire most: precise language grounded in specific detail, with a strong emotional impact. The first time I heard him read this in class, heard those lines "she put a 12-gauge shotgun/in her mouth and squeezed," I felt the hair rise on the back of my neck, and I knew I had been totally drawn into the world of the poem. I felt the shock of loss. The girl's suicide was unexpected, no doubt as unexpected in real life as it is in this poem. Yet if we look at this poem carefully, we can see the clues that make this unexpected yet not unbelievable: the poem sets up tragedy by the speaker's claim that he has "no heart." In the first stanza, we don't know why the speaker says that—later, when we learn things like he "felt enough for both" of them, we understand the problem is not that he has no heart, but rather that he has too much, that he can't escape his pain.

The poem doesn't tell us any of this. Instead, Jeff uses images of the body to show us what the speaker feels: his body stripped to bone, as if to strip away flesh and heart would strip away the ability to feel loss. This focus on the physical is continued throughout the poem: the speaker "failed anatomy," a simple detail that pulls the imagery of the poem together well, and is an ironic twist to all this talk of the physical body. Then we get to the final stanza, in which the speaker uses more physical imagery to express pain: *there are parts / of me that still can't stomach the sound / of her name.* This colloquial phrase is the perfect addition to the poem here, the way the speaker still can't physically deal with loss. And in a subtle, but wise choice, Jeff chose to say *parts / of me* rather than the more direct *I can't stomach*. This makes a difference because it is a subtle allusion to the body divided into parts, like the bones we have seen in the first stanza and the bones we will see scattered in the next line.

It's the end of the poem that really is really devastating: that image of the girl's bones *burned / and scattered by the barn*. Not only does it tie us back to the bones in the beginning of the poem, the bones we now understand the speaker in some ways wishes he was, so he wouldn't have to feel, but it also gives us a literal of image of the beautiful young girl, now reduced to scattered bones. It is an image of the terrible cruelty of death. If we read it literally, intellectually, we understand that there are not actual bones lying around the barn. The girl has been cremated, her ashes scattered. Yet the way the image is phrased, for a moment we're likely to see literal bones, and be reminded that we are speaking of a person here. Cremation is just what this poem says, the burning of bones (and flesh) and yet our tendency is to turn from that reality, to take comfort in the abstract. This poem does not allow us the luxury of turning away. We are forced to see this girl reduced to bones, to ash. From the beginning the images and details of the poem force us to look at loss and death with clear eyes.

Yet not coldly. This poem is not just about this girl's death, but it is about the speaker's reaction to it, and while we mourn her loss, don't we also mourn the speaker's pain? We applaud him for his sensitivity, and wish, somehow, to protect him, wish for him an armor, so he doesn't have to be stripped to bone himself. It's a complex and beautiful poem, working on a number of levels, and it succeeds primarily because of Jeff's skillful use of metaphor.

In this poem, bones—which remember are never really seen at all, only imagined—become a metaphor for loss, pain, for what is left behind when death has robbed of us of one we love. The speaker of the poem can hardly bear to think of the girl's bones, and yet he shows us his own in the opening of the poem, exposing what is most hidden: not only bones, hidden beneath muscle and flesh in life, but his secret, lingering pain. In a sense, the speaker of this poem is stripping himself to bone, to what is most fundamental: saying here is my pain, look at it and feel your own hidden losses. The poem reminds us of how we go through life hiding our deepest emotions from others. It strips us down to bone.

Beginning writers sometimes leave out images or specifics, because they believe that others will relate better to vagueness. This is a mistake. We identify not with the general but with the specific; we reach the universal through the particular. Though Jeff's poem may be about a specific red-haired girl, the poem succeeds because we can all imagine the shock of sudden loss.

This is what all poets must learn: to pay attention to detail and imagery. Think about the way a photograph of beloved can move us: the image brings back, in a flood of emotion, all we once loved. Think how films can move us: images flicker across a screen, and through the specifics of those characters, we experience emotion.

This is what poetry does best. Through image, through a leap of logic, it strips everything down to bone and thus shows us beauty in what is most hidden. These are my bones. Images are the bones of the poem, a skeleton we must create so others can share in our experience. And I believe that this is the most important lesson to learn, the one that will serve you best in the end: show us something, and let your images move us. Show us what you love, what hurts you, evoke it all with images. Let us experience these images, these fragments of beauty that strip away our doubt and defenses and pare us down to bone.

NOTES FOR SELECTED READINGS

Note the use of concrete images in Tom Crawford's poem "Fish." You might pay attention to how he not only uses the snow in the poem but how the image of the fish becomes connected to the feeling of the persona in the poem.

Note how, in such a short poem, we receive much through the central image of the eagle in Alfred Lord Tennyson's poem, "The Eagle," because of its metaphoric and symbolic quality.

Exercises

1. Take an abstract word and write it on the top of a sheet of paper. Then write three to eight lines using an image to illustrate that abstract concept but do not use that abstract word or any other

abstract words in the image. You may only use concrete details. Use the following example as a guide.

Sad

> The wind howls
> and rain presses against the backs of clouds.
> Leaves run and hide under bushes.
> All this while the bagpipe screams
> a funeral song.

2. Write a poem using one central object in the poem and make the emotional energy in the poem run through this object.
3. Look at a photograph, then write a poem about what is happening just outside the borders of the photo. Be sure to use concrete details in your metaphors and descriptions.

CHAPTER

3

LINES AND STANZAS

One is often able to distinguish between poetry and prose simply by looking at the page. With the exception of a prose poem, we can look at a poem and identify it as such. While this is a very basic tool for identifying a poem, it is not insignificant. It works. The use of **lines** and **stanzas** is a major element in poetics. Hence, this is a very important tool for any poet to know how to use. A line is just that—it's a line of text in a poem. A stanza is a group of two or more lines set together in a poem and often arranged around a metrical or rhythmic pattern. A poem may be all one stanza or it may be divided into, say, six four-line stanzas.

As you rub these words together they spark and whole new combinations happen.

Naomi Shihab Nye

Now that we know what lines and stanzas are, let's talk a bit about how and why we use them to affect our poems. Lines and stanzas often occur in a very natural, organic way. They happen because we have decided to break a line the way we think or feel the words dividing themselves. Or stanzas may occur because we feel a group of lines works well together conceptually. Let's look at lines first.

Lines do a number of things in a poem—both spatially and conceptually. In relation to space on the page—the way words appear—lines provide a spatial context in which the words function. This is initially the way the words look on the page and the way we see them. But as we read the poem it becomes not just how they look on the page but how they work with and against each other in the reading process. And ultimately, as writers, we need to be thinking about how our words are working with and against each other while we write. For example, note the difference in the following lines:

The wind swept
off the dunes and raced
against the waves,
pulling their white hair
out away from shore.   5

Here, we have five lines broken ostensibly to show the images in each line. But note that the lines begin with an article, prepositions, and a present participle. These are not bad choices but consider the possibilities in these lines. Think how many ways we might break them. Let's look at a revision of these lines.

The wind swept off the dunes and
raced against the waves, pulling
their white hair out away from shore.

Notice that in this choice of line breaks we get longer lines. We might also notice a change in the rhythm we feel in the language. Having the words *and* and *pulling* at the ends of the lines doesn't seem natural, as *out* does in line five of the first presentation. But, it may create a sense of tension in the language or a sense that the wind is working against the natural rhythm of the waves. We might also note that this line structure seems to complement the internal rhyme in lines two and three a bit more than the previous line scheme. No matter the changes, notice that the line acts as a frame of emphasis and causes us to focus on different emotions, thoughts, and/or parts of the poem with each change.

This brings us to another point about lines and their function. Lines provide a way to create or control the rhythm and musical sense of the poem. They provide the length of breath we might need or the number of syllables working together in a unit of words. This is very subtle in poems but is the undercurrent to what we hear and feel in a rhythmic sense. One way to play with this, as you think about line breaks, is to simply count syllables in your lines. If you have three lines of roughly six syllables each, how is that different from two lines of nine syllables each? This is something to play and work with. Notice that, as you change the rhythm of a line by making it longer or breaking it to be shorter, you also alter the meaning of the words.

When we begin to notice that the rhythm and meaning play off each other, and we realize that they're connected, we can see how **ambiguity** can form in poems. Ambiguity occurs when something is open to more than one meaning. This can be a positive effect. Remember that, when we write poems, we want and need to get all the mileage we can out of each word—which means we have to write with an expansive view of the way the words work rather than a narrow view. So as you begin to see how rhythm works in your lines, you'll notice that the rhythm changes based on the **syntax**, or word order, of your lines.

> leaning heavy on the dark sky
> the moon crested behind an oak

We can change these lines if we aren't satisfied with the syntax. And sometimes we ought to experiment just to see what is held in the change.

> heavy on the dark leaning sky
> the moon crested behind an oak

The change is slight. So try again and see what you think.

> behind an oak, the moon crested
> heavy on the dark leaning sky

Working with the syntax and seeing options in setting the words will not only open rhythmic possibilities, but will open more doors for meaning. One element of line breaks that affects rhythms is the **caesura**. A caesura is simply a pause *within* a line, and usually occurs because of punctuation—maybe a comma. But a caesura may also happen because of the way two words fall next to each other rhythmically. In this case, don't be fooled into thinking that using caesuras is a difficult technique. Just keep in mind that this is what pauses within lines are called and that they can make all the difference at times. Another element of line structure that is related to syntax, rhythm, and meaning is **enjambment**. This occurs when a line's grammatical sense and meaning carry over into the next line. This, again, is not overly technical, but consider how we pause at the ends of lines in rhyming poetry whether there are periods or not. Enjambment is one of those tools to toss into the box and notice as you use it, so you become more and more aware of it as a force in your writing.

All this can seem overwhelming, but the benefit is that as you become more comfortable and proficient with the tools, your writing becomes sharper and more crafted. So while we recognize poetry on the page because it looks different from prose—that ragged right margin—as writers, we come to know line breaks and structure as important tools. They often seem subtle, maybe even casual, to the reader. But we know differently. We know the power inherent in the crafting of lines and know that the writer works intently on breaking lines for reasons of meaning and sound and the music of language.

THE STANZA

A stanza is a group of lines in a poem separated on the page by a space break from another group of lines. In free verse, these groups of lines do not need to be the same in number, but a stanza usually signifies that there is some type of organizational structure to the poem. A writer often organizes lines into stanzas based on some conceptual coherence. No matter how many stanzas a poem has or how those stanzas occur in the poem (maybe some have three lines, maybe some have four, maybe all have two), the stanza serves to provide some sense of coherence to the lines. The movements between stanzas help to guide us smoothly through the meaning of the poem.

In more formal poetry, or in fixed forms, stanzaic structure is guided by the type of poem (sonnet, sestina, villanelle, etc.), the dominant meter (for instance, iambic pentameter), and the rhyme scheme. For example, a four-line stanza with iambic pentameter, and a rhyme scheme of *a b a b* would be called a quatrain. The use of stanzas and their very fixed structures in fixed forms helps give a framework to the poem as well as a technical context wherein the content functions. But, let's go back to free verse because that's what most of us will probably be writing.

So in free verse, why use stanzas at all? That's a fair question and sometimes we use only one stanza. But that, too, has a history; it comes from the stichic tradition of poetry. This simply means that the lines fall into one unit and are arranged by their rhythmic quality rather than separated into stanzas based on either number or meaning. So why break parts of the poem with white space? One reason we might use stanzas is that they help us control what we want to say. In some ways it's not all that different from a conversation. And after all, in some ways, we, as writers, are having conversations with readers. In conversation, when we change the subject or even alter it by nuance, we note this in some way: a pause, a change in tone, a change in breath. These are all things that can be set off by stanza breaks. Hence, we use the stanza form as a guide. If we want to look at it with a bit more severity, we might even say that we can control both the poem and the reader through stanzas.

What comes of this control, this movement of lines and subject matter, of rhythms and breath, is a control over the dynamics of the poem. With stanzas we take on the ability to bring the poem up to crescendo-like levels and then ease it back down again, to run the poem full-speed like a train, or slow it down. So ultimately we're back to a somewhat rhythmic control over the poem and guidance for the reader. We hope this use of stanzas, though, comes off naturally. When we take the poem up to a high point and bring it down again with the use of stanzas, we ought to do this because the subject matter calls for it. This way the stanzas fit; they're in the right place at the right time, and the readers hardly notice. But they notice how the poem feels. The stanzas, their structure and movement, ought to mirror or enhance either the subject matter or the emotional and intellectual context of the poem.

One of the things we do with lines and stanzas, as Robert Hass points out, is that we put our breathing, our rhythmic nature, into other people's bodies: "When one says somebody else's poem aloud, one speaks in that person's breath." This is where our own physiology becomes part of the language, and this is where line and stanza structure meet and help create our poetic voice. Listen to the movement of the language, hear the rhythms around you and use them to fill the page, to move your lines and guide your poems.

HEY, GOOD LOOKIN', HAVEN'T WE MET SOMEWHERE BEFORE?

Beckian Fritz Goldberg

You're sitting in a bar contemplating your Jagermeister, and the person on the next barstool has just given you this line. What do you do? If you're a woman, you probably give him a withering glance and tell him to buzz off. O.K., let's say you turn to deliver your *buzz off* and you notice he happens to be gorgeous. So you hesitate, thinking, "He's gorgeous, but does he really think that kind of opening works?" So he's gorgeous and stupid. You have your standards. He strikes out. A cheesy line is a cheesy line.

In our parallel universe, you're sitting in a bar contemplating et cetera and you're a man. A woman comes up to you and delivers this line. What do you do? This situation is much more "iffy." If, for example, she's gorgeous *and* stupid, well . . . it pretty much makes your night. After all, guys are easy. If she's not so gorgeous, then you might pass and see if something better shows up.

Which brings up the first two points about the line. One, with the poem you can't always turn around and see the beguiling form of the speaker. You hear "Hey . . . " and you're on your own. And if you're trying to get the reader's attention, generate some interest, seduce a little, it doesn't matter how cute you are. You have to come up with something more likely to spark a little heat than, "Hey, good-lookin' . . . " In fact, *heys* should be avoided altogether until you really know how to follow up, as in: "Hey, Jude . . . na-na-nuh-na, hey, Jude." (See "The '60s" in an almanac or talk to your grandparents.)

The second point—there's a reason the Muse is traditionally thought of as female. Not only because a bunch of white male poets thought her up, but because she has standards for heaven's sake. (See first paragraph.) A poet who relies on a bad line is simply going to strike out. If you're going to approach someone—all those sensitive people at the bar reading Keats, for example—you need to know your audience. They've heard the "Hey . . . " until they simply don't look up anymore. And they've also heard, a hundred times, "Ah, thy beauty is to me as those Nicean barks of yore . . . " and all those other lines Poe used to try out on women. So it's important to use the right line for the right audience

and remember that catchy lines that have been used before, even successfully, are clichés, like the guy in the bar in blue polyester who's still
using, "Hi, I'm Virgo. What's your sign?" (See "The '70s.")

An opening line sets the tone and often determines the course of the
evening—the course of the dusky and alluring poem. Yes, it's a lot of
pressure. That's why poets end up in bars in the first place. If we take a
look at some opening lines by students, we can see the effects of several
different approaches. The first draft of one poem opens this way: "My
grandfather used to shoot them." It's direct and it also makes us curious.
We're likely to read on, at least for a bit. Of course, it's not a line that
works well in bars. (See "Psycho," any decade, any century.) This line
sets up an expectation, generally a nice thing for a line to do, but it also
means the poet has obligated himself not only to let us in on what "them"
means, but to follow through with something significant. If "them" turns
out to be tin cans set up for recreational shooting, we're likely to think "so
what?" The poet has let us down. If it turns out to be something we care
about, then we are further drawn into the poem.

Another poem opens, "The smell of cut grass." Are you going to ask
this one to dance or are you going to wait for something better to come
along? It's a line that names a stock image, the smell of cut grass, the smell
of rain, the smell of baking cookies, the whole long list of "Smells Of . . ."
The second line of the poem is "of grease." O.K., I, for one, like the grease
here because the expectation (if any) set up in the first line is that I was
going to get some lovely springtime poem about grass and clouds and
maybe even love. The grease is not a predictable move, so it helps. But why
is it on its own line? As a *line*, is "and grease" one that works, that gener-
ates interest or moves the poem forward? Does it create a pace or rhythm
that guides or seduces the reader? Here's the complete first stanza:

> The smell of cut grass
> and grease
> takes me back
> to grass piles in the bed of the Ford pick-up.
> My dad standing over a lawn mower   5
> ready for the yellowed stones of his palms
> to push the blade over the victim of his hunger. Me
> with riverock in hand, I aim at the rigid
> back of my asthmatic brother.

The most noticeable thing about the form of the stanza is how different the first three lines are from the rest of the stanza. The opening pace
or rhythm is deliberate, slow, broken into small phrases as if to feed the
reader one small piece at a time. Then all of a sudden the fourth line
rushes out, piles everything together: "to grass piles in the bed of the
Ford pick-up." It's as if the poet got tired and just threw away the rest.

The next lines, however, are a little more consistent in their rhythm which suggests that finally the poet has begun to find a more natural cadence, something closer to her own voice. In revising the poem, reading it aloud and listening to the way the lines break usually helps a poet hear where she hasn't helped the reader move through the poem. At the very least, that's what good use of the line *should* do.

Meanwhile, back to the shooting grandfather. Here are the first five lines of the poem, which runs twenty-seven lines and has no stanza breaks:

> My grandfather used to shoot them.
> I was about sixteen when he told me.
> Ted was long gone, and he'd just come back from shooting Jeff.
> Ted was mine, if a kid can ever call a hunting dog his.
> "See the crooked-tailed one?" Granddaddy said.   5

Aside from scaring us a little with that third line, the poem's use of the line makes it sound stilted and static. There's no variation here, just a string of declarative sentences: "My grandfather used to," "I was," "Ted was," "Ted was." But clearly the poem wants to tell some sort of story about the speaker's past and his relationship with his grandfather and possibly with his hunting dog. The use of the line is getting in the way, probably because the poet, here, isn't sure what the difference is between a line and a sentence or statement. Each line ends with a period. Just like *Dragnet.* (See "The '60s" again.)

The poem continues:

> "That'n's yours."
> He turned out to be the best hunter of the litter.
> I can still hear his, "Wraoooooo!"
> Lady has lung cancer and
> We're having a vet do it.   10
> Even having him come to the house.
> But it's just a useless old dog.
> He used to dig a hole, then stand the dog beside it.

Wait a minute. That's the line we've been waiting for. Make that the first line and it will probably help with revising the whole poem. "He used to dig a hole, then . . . " One of the problems related to the serial-statement technique here is that all things get equal weight; there's no subordination, no emphasis, and no clear indication of time sequences, something a stanza break might help with, for example, between the eighth and ninth lines, where the speaker jumps from past to present.

There's nothing "wrong" or "right" about a particular kind of line: short, long, broken with the breath, flowing with the rhythm of a story, or weaving in and out of one rhythm into another for effect. The challenge is to find the kind of line that works with the subject and mood of the poem, and to guide the reader through it, to make the kind of music a voice makes. The same poet who wrote about his grandfather in this poem, uses the same "brand" of line in a later poem, because he gravitates to narrative poems, but here he uses it much more successfully:

> Your '67 Nova taught you he was right about Chevys.
> This man could do anything.
> Built the lake house in Interlachen by himself,
> From the septic tank to the slab to the blocks to the shingles.
> You two slept there and caught and lost the biggest bass in the lake.   5
> Grass bass, boat bass, log bass—it all depended where you found them,
> But they were always near something . . . .

It's still a line that is direct, breaks with the natural movement of speech, but it has much more variety, different rhythms, and it moves the reader easily along.

In a poem that strives for a more lyric tone, another poet uses a line that moves carefully, attempting to emphasize a particular phrase and to slow down the poem which is usually what short lines do.

> My black rose thrives
> in the moist air
> under the tridge at midnight
> in the shadows.
> I sit cross-legged   5
> on the wet
> picnic table
> watching the fog roll in.
> The match strike blows my silence
> as his Marlboro lights,   10
> across the river the alarm blasts out
> sending thousands
> flooding
> into the rain
> from the Ashman Court Hotel.   15

In these first two stanzas, the poem does benefit from the shorter line—certainly the poem moves slowly, quietly, emphasizing some sort of texture in most lines: the shadows, the fog, the rain, the moisture, the match flame. It is a poem of smaller gestures within a larger context, the relationship between the "he" and the "I" of the poem. What commonly happens with this use of the line is that we tend to break larger phrases into smaller parts, and too many of those parts are prepositional phrases. Just glance down at the first word in each line: *My, in, under, in, I, on, picnic, watching, The, as, across, sending, flooding, into, from.* The problem is first that prepositional phrases don't make very interesting lines: in the shadows / into the rain / in the moist air / on the wet. Additionally, because of the line breaks, the first word of a line gets a little more emphasis than it would otherwise. Placing emphasis on "in" or "at" isn't usually productive. What happens is that these become the "leftovers," the empty phrases you don't know where to put. They are sacrificial lines, so that the poet can have another line such as "My black rose thrives" or "The match strike blows my silence . . . " Unfortunately, it often leads to a predictable pattern of *in the*'s and *of the*'s. A poem can't work up much energy this way. Try:

> My black rose
> Thrives in the moist air
> Under the tridge, midnight,
> I sit in the shadows,
> Cross-legged on the picnic table,   5
> Watching the fog
> Roll in. The match strike
> Blows my silence . . . .

There are, of course, many options here and they will depend, to some degree, on other changes the poet makes (dropping "at" before midnight, for example.) The most "radical" change in this version is the transition between stanzas. Putting "roll in" on the same last line as "The match strike," gives a little more energy to the moment, since the lines read almost as if the speaker is watching the fog roll in in the light of that match strike. In addition, the phrase "blows my silence" has more impact on its own because it's no longer a subordinate moment—it implies not only "blows" as in breeze but also as in "blows my cover." Since this poem does turn out to be about the break-up of a relationship from the speaker's point of view, the new line breaks and stanza break help the poem build to its moment. (See "Breaking Up Is Hard To Do," "The '60s"; "How Can You Mend a Broken Heart," "The '70s"; "You Give Love a Bad Name," "The '80s"; "My Heart Will Go On," "The '90s.")

A stanza break can do more than divide the poem into neat little "poem-paragraphs." It can signal a transition (in time or place), sharpen the impact of the poem's movement, or work as a poem's "cinematography," a change of camera angles. Note the effect in this student poem about a dream:

> I am dressed in the delicate lace gown.
> At the end of the aisle—an old boyfriend
> who fucked me the way a tiger rends prey.
> His sweat splashed against my face
> In the church. I am shaking my head, backing away,   5
> the congregation turns a firm stare,
> *he wants you, don't be a selfish girl.*

Saving "in the church" until the next stanza suspends the reader a moment in time because the sweat splashed against her face seems solely connected with the sexual encounter in the past. Yet, that changes abruptly when the speaker reminds us that, at dream-present, they are in a church—and it's almost as if the present and past blur in that moment, an intentional effect here that matches the movement of dream. It's also an example that shows there are times when a prepositional phrase can be used effectively at the beginning of a line. There may even be times when "Hey, good-lookin'" works.

Nah. Let's not get carried away. You don't want to wake up the next morning in some roach motel with an ugly poem crumpled up next to you and your head pounding iambic pentameter. Next thing you know, you'd end up a fiction writer, and we don't want *that*.

NOTES FOR SELECTED READINGS

Note how Teresa Leo uses line breaks and stanzas in "Anniversary" to create rhythmic movement in the poem and to create a conceptual momentum.

Exercises

1. Write as you would when you normally sit down to write. But write in prose without using any line breaks. Then go back and break the prose into lines. Once the writing is broken into lines, break it into stanzas. Pay close attention to where, when, and why you're breaking the language where you are.
2. Write two to three lines of imagery—something you might use in a poem later. Then rewrite the image five different ways by changing the lines various ways (e.g. the length, the syntax, the order of the lines, etc.).
3. Take a poem you've been working on or write a new one and do some stanza work. First, if your poem is all one stanza, break it into multiple stanzas. If your poem is multiple stanzas, shift lines—see how the stanzas work or don't work when you move the last line of stanza 1 into the first line of stanza 2 and the last line of stanza 2 into the first line of stanza 3. Try moving stanzas around. Try moving a stanza near the end of the poem closer to the start of the poem. When doing this you ought to be able to see the value of the stanza in various places of the poem and its internal strengths and weaknesses will probably stand out.

4

SOUND AND THE POEM

Sound is everywhere. It is around us constantly and we are regularly moved or startled or taken by sound. Take, for example, the crashing together of two train cars coupling at the rail yard, the crunching of a can under a girl's foot, the fast panting of a dog in the shade of a tree, the screech of tires against asphalt, the plunk of a rock in a pond. These sounds we know, and maybe we hear them every day, depending on who we are and where we live. Often we don't think of them as poetic. But we have reactions to these sounds when we do hear them. Sound is something that moves us—it can frighten us, relax us, delight us. And because of this, we can capture the sounds around us in words, and add them to the sensory experience a reader encounters in our poems.

In our daily lives, we have learned to hear sounds and move right past them or through them. But the same magic that is held in imagery is held in sound. We need to slow down and listen momentarily to catch it. And, of course, this is what we're doing in a poem—temporarily slowing the reader in a moment in order to catch what is important. My young son regularly hears noises and looks at me with a furrowed brow and a cocked head and asks, "What's that?" He is hearing the world—in some cases for the very first time—and

You become a conduit for the spirit of language to flow through. At that point you become a musician or an actor. You almost become possessed in that the world flows through you, becomes through you.

Quincy Troupe

sound is a part of the magic in his world. The readers should get nothing less because often they are entering our world through the poem for the very first time. Should they be as captivated as a small child? Absolutely. Should they turn to ask us "What's that?" Probably not. In this case, we should make sure the poem is clear.

So how do we create sound quality in a poem? The first element to consider is **diction**, which is word choice. The words we choose at any moment have much attached to them and sound is one of the qualities to consider. One of the first results of diction is the **tone**, the emotional sense, of the words or poem. We know tones—kind, angry, sympathetic, jealous, ironic, or sarcastic. The emotional sensibility of a word, though not a physical tone like the lingering ring of a bell, is a psychological sound that a reader marks with a voice; essentially it is a psychic ringing of the words. The way in which word choice helps to create these tones is through the **denotation** or **connotation** of words. The denotation of a word is the standard, or dictionary, definition. The connotation of a word is the cultural and contextual definition. As poets we have to be concerned with connotation—in fact, usually more than denotation—because these connotations give a depth and breadth of meaning to the world around us. When choosing words for your poems it's important to consider how they will function in the poem and what meanings will emerge from them. Aside from using denotation and connotation to create a poem's tone and emotional resonance, there are other conventions that affect the actual sound of our poetry within each line—how the poem comes to the ear.

These conventions are largely technical, and they are also tools for creating sound. We need them and we need to know how they work and what they do for us. But when we write, they tend to show up a bit more naturally, or organically, than we might think. So if they show up naturally, why do we need to know them as tools? We need them because when we revise or when they don't just blossom onto the page, it's necessary to know when, where, and how to pick them up and use them.

Let's start by talking a bit about consonant and vowel sounds in words. Alliteration and assonance are two poetic elements that arise from the use of consonants and vowels. **Alliteration** is the repetition of consonant sounds that usually occur at the beginning of words, which produces an echo effect and links words through their sounds. For example, *the Friends Fought*. Or in another case, *the Snake Silently moved away*. Alliteration is a relatively easy tool to use and you should become conscious of it when you write. Next time you sit down to write, think about it and make a point to use it, and you will also begin to see it in the poems you read. **Assonance** is the repetition of vowel sounds in the final syllables of words and produces an effect similar to alliteration. For example, *pretEnd you're a tree and extEnd your arms*. In both cases, this repetition of sounds can cause the words to blend together closely, not only through sound, but in meaning as well. Let's look at a student poem in which alliteration and assonance both emerge very gracefully in the poem.

Sprinkler

On purple nights, when the air is tendered, with no hint of flurry
We might find ourselves on the porch,
Overlooking our lawn.
Perhaps summoned there by the need to relive a gilded hour

When wisps of crabgrass did not litter the yard,
And the car did not milk away our savings
When our roof was more than an umbrella
And the splendor of firecrackers could outshine the stars.

But on this night, I'm as wilted as uncut grass,
And you've never seen me like this,
So when the sprinkler head goes off, you leave me to walk into the hail
Knowing that I might trail you

And as the frigid water plasters our hair
We're cast under an opium daze.
Swaying to keep balance,
We're two moths lost in our fury.

AMY WONG

Notice how many times in this poem Amy has used alliteration, repeating consonant sounds both at the beginnings of words that stand next to each other and those close to each other in words next to each other and on different lines. Moreover, she has employed assonance in the same manner. At times the repetition of the vowel sounds comes from words placed next to each other in the lines and at other times the assonance happens from one line to another. And in this serene setting of the poem, the sound (as well as the word choices and their meanings) does much to create the poem's feel because of the way the words land in our ear. The sounds do much to hold words together and glue concepts and emotions together, and because of the placement of sounds in the mouth—the way we hear and recognize them as soft or hard—the sound assists in building or easing off tensions in the poem.

Another element of sound to consider is **onomatopoeia**, when a word sounds like or resembles what it is. For instance, *a snake hisses* or *the wood fell with a thud onto the ground*. We can come up with a number of examples like *buzz, rattle, squeak*. And this is a very effective tool for sound because we can not only capture the sound an insect may make but we can couple words in very original ways too. Along with these aforementioned tools, it can be important to consider the number of syllables in words that come together in lines and stanzas, next to each other or on top of each other in different lines.

Considering syllables alongside alliteration, assonance, and onomatopoeia can combine to produce **euphony** or **cacophony** in our poems. Euphony is the blending of sounds to produce a pleasurable effect on the ear while cacophony has the opposite effect and produces a noisy or unpleasant effect on us. This may happen from the true sound of the word, or the word's meaning, or it may happen based on line structure and groupings of words—for example, James Wright's lines "the cowbells follow one another / into the distances of the afternoon." These cowbells are not breaking apart our afternoon with their clanging. They are actually producing some sense of relaxation.

While these technical conventions of sound need to be thought about consciously at first, the more you use them the more they will show up in your writing naturally. And, while you use these tools the way a carpenter uses a saw, remember this easy rule that can help you be successful with them: never force or impose a convention on a poem. The language should always be natural and should fit what you write. For example, if you were crafting an image of Grand Central Station in New York City at rush hour, you would want to produce cacophony in the poem. Whatever the case, remember that these effects can help enhance an image as well as a whole poem.

NOTICING SOUND AND GETTING IT INTO POEMS

Sound makes us feel. The sounds of this world are great and abundant. Consider all the cultures, the languages, voice inflections, and cadences and tones we hear from people's mouths in the way they pronounce words based on their cultural or regional backgrounds. If we're not familiar with some specific sound we can find it easily. But we have to hear the sounds in our world and know them before we can use them in our poems.

Go to a place that is unfamiliar to you. If you live in a rural area, go to a place you don't normally frequent, such as a nearby field, or a pond, a farm, a meadow, or a logging road. Maybe go to the next town over, or your own town will do. Sit in front of the barber shop, if you've never sat there before, and then listen. Hear those sounds that you haven't taken in before, those that are new or foreign to you. In a city? Go to an area that is outside your ethnic experience—a Chinatown, Little Italy, Little Tokyo, Northbeach, an Irish district, or an area that is Hispanic or African American. First, just observe all that's going on—maybe markets are open and selling things you don't typically eat. Maybe people shop differently there. Maybe they have to call out to the man behind the meat counter. Maybe there is a small grocer on the sidewalk barking at people to come in and shop or buy from him. The sounds are abundant. Then begin to just listen to them, what they are, how they stir you, and how they cause people to move and react and jump into action. This is when we see that sound can actually be the launching place for so much.

This exercise illustrates for us that sound can bridge many gaps, cause us to cross many boundaries and caverns and come upon some rather startling revelations—some we may understand quite well, maybe even logically. And others we simply feel because the wind sounded a certain way, or the man at the vegetable stand said something in Cantonese we didn't understand but made an old lady smile—and we understood her smile and that's what moved us. In that, we've watched a whole relationship form over sound. These sounds that we come to know and can ultimately place in our poems give richness to our writing and to the world in which we create.

It can be difficult to start a poem at times, and to have to concentrate on sound may seem to make starting even more difficult. But let's use sound as a tool to begin our work. When beginning a poem, there is no need to go in a straight line, to follow a specified path. We don't necessarily need to proceed logically from one place to another. Let connections happen. This can be part of your creative process. One way to allow yourself some room to create in your poems is to let the sound guide you and control the words a bit. You might be surprised how sound can become a driving force behind the language, pushing it forward, making words connect in new, fresh ways, and making people want to read the poem aloud. Listen to the words and let the syllables or letters connect and push you in a direction of choosing words. Take for instance the following lines.

> . . . As I took the stance I had seen my father use
> I saw the milkweed plant
> that grew beside the chopping block.
> Curled maple leaves scratched the ground like claws
> and trees rustled in the wind . . . .
>
> JESSE WOODCOCK

While Jesse's lines are certainly image-filled, they are powered by sound. Notice the way the "s" sound runs throughout the lines, and inside the lines Jesse does a wonderful job with elements such as assonance—his repetition of "a" and "o" and "e" sounds. And we shouldn't forget the power behind the sound of the claws scratching the ground. These sounds propel the image and the poem forward. The sounds roll out of the mouth—these are words meant to be read aloud. We hear the scratching and rustling.

Sound can be one of the major forces behind a poem, the force that propels the language, that helps our sensory experience in the poem come alive. And more, when it's done well, the experience becomes real, the language becomes transparent, and we hear what is happening in the poem. Take note of how things sound and apply them to your use of language and your word choices. Capture the screech of birds, the clanging of crabs against the pot, and the sizzle of rain on the pavement. And most important, weave the sounds into the emotional context of the poem so that the technical function of the words is woven tightly into the emotional or intellectual fabric of the poem. Push open the creaking gate of our minds and make us follow you into your world of sound.

DEGAS IN VEGAS: SOME THOUGHTS ON SOUND IN POETRY

Alberto Ríos

> I rhyme to see myself, to set the darkness echoing.
> —SEAMUS HEANEY

Something that is "sound" is something that is well-made. Sound in poetry is a discussion not simply of what a poem's noises are. It also questions whether those noises are working—whether they help the poem to be well-made. This suggests that a poem's sound operates beyond coincidence, and that the poet is as aware of sound as a musician or composer. Sound, in this sense, is part of the poet's toolbox. It is one more choice that helps the poet to write a better poem.

Sound exists or does not exist in a poem—that is, as a reader you are very aware of it, or else it makes no *particular* difference. These two conditions may be thought of as sonic intensity and sonic distance. Sonic intensity refers to a condition in a poem in which the sound is everything. Sonic distance, on the other hand, occurs when sound is simply one more part of whatever makes the poem successful.

The poet may use sonic intensity for several reasons. First, a moment in a poem may be magnified or trumpeted by sound. This technique may serve to make the reader more aware of the importance of the moment, or it may suggest a complexity that the reader might otherwise have overlooked. Second, sound itself in the mouth of the reader may be the point of the poem. In either case, sonic intensity slows the reader down by making that reader pay attention. In doing this, the poem suggests a lateral, or sideways, movement, rather than simply straightforward movement. This kind of movement in a poem says to the reader, *I know you're in a hurry, but sit down for a moment and have a glass of cold lemonade—it'll make you feel better.*

Sonic distance, on the other hand, suggests forward or linear movement. This technique says to the reader, *Yes, I saw him, Sheriff. He ran thataway—you'll catch him if you hurry.* This approach may be equally important to the poet's intention and may also be used for a variety of reasons. The poet, for example, may not want the reader to linger. The point to be made may be farther down in the poem, or else there may be more to read before jumping to any conclusions. In this case, sound in the mouth of the reader is exactly what the poet does not want. The poet may purposefully use quiet or unpretentious wording in order to avoid drawing attention to the language, which may not be the point of that particular poem. Maybe the poet prefers the reader to consider the whole idea of a poem' may be telling a kind of story.

Sonic intensity often leads to what are called lyric poems. These are poems of substantial, imaginative moment, where the beginning, middle, and/or end—the plot elements—are not as important as the moment experienced. Sonic distance, on the other hand, often suggests what are called narrative poems. In narrative poems, plot elements clearly come into play and have an importance equal to the single moment in a poem. What's happened and what's going to happen are as important to understanding the poem as what's happening in the moment.

These two approaches are not necessarily on opposite sides, and many, even most, poems blend both the moment and the story of a poem. In both sonic intensity and distance, however, sound helps to achieve the greater purpose of the poem. As a result, through the centuries sound has been especially associated with poetry.

But what kinds of sounds create this intensity or distance for the reader? Any single sound will do, but it is not the single sound that produces these results. It is, instead, a careful combination of sounds that creates one effect or the other. If a sequence of syllables, words, or whole lines makes the reader pay attention because of their collective sounds, then sonic intensity occurs. *Peter Piper picked a peck of pickled peppers, picked a peck of*—well, you know the rest. "Peter Piper" is a good, classic example of a group of sounds that make a reader pay attention. A tongue twister is purposefully difficult and challenging in the mouth, using alliteration to produce this effect. Alliteration is the repetition of the same sound at the beginning of a series of words. Much poetry, while more subtle than a tongue twister, exhibits the same attentive use of language, as in the following short examples of Anglo-Saxon prosody from student poems: "wept, awoke. I wandered and slept," "in her gravel garden, again," and "beside him icy saplings."

Rhyme, of course, is another way to make the reader pay attention. This is a time-honored device associated with poetry, and by extension, music. Rhyme is very effective. Like dynamite, it can absolutely do the job. So, the poet's first question when using rhyme should probably be: Is there a job to be done by the rhyme? That is, why is it being used? Rhyme may be pleasing to the ear, but upon entering the ear it reaches the brain, which may have a second opinion. If all it does is bring attention to itself without furthering the poem in any particular way, then things begin to fall apart. Children's poetry or silly poems written purely for fun are often the exception to this standard: *How now, brown cow.* But if the poem is meant to be successful on some greater level, then there has to be a point to the rhyme, in the same way choosing a certain word has a point.

Rhyme is certainly not a bad thing, however. At its best, rhyme's repetition offers to the reader a variety of pleasing sensibilities, including, for example, a sense of completion and recognition, both of which are comforts to the human spirit. Rhyme repeats a sound, which the reader recognizes as having heard earlier in the poem. This suggests a number of reasons for its usage—memory, for one. If a reader recognizes the sound, this means the reader remembers it, and therefore is actively engaged in memory, no matter how slight. But if a poet is writing about the future, then perhaps rhyme is not a congruent choice. Rhyme is certainly one tool in the poet's toolbox, but a good writer, like a good carpenter, does not use only a hammer to build a porch.

And rhyme is not simply one thing. There are many, many forms of rhyme. Too often the word "rhyme" is relegated only to its simplest and most overt association, true rhyme—as in *blue* and *glue*. Rhyme, however, can occur anywhere, and in any sequence, and is often much more elegant and surprising in something other than its true rhyme form. Rhyme may occur at the beginning of a line, for example, rather than at the end. And it may be more jazz-like than straightforward, as in the old wrestler's name, Gorgeous George. Rhyme is clearly there, but it's a little trickier to tame. Our impulse might be to think "Gorgeous Georgeous," but therein is the delight—it doesn't behave itself, and so as a listener you take notice. And therefore, what a brilliant name this becomes for a wrestler who himself would not behave.

Sometimes more than sounds or words get repeated. Whole lines or even whole sections of poems might repeat. In blues poems, for instance, the first two lines are usually the same, while the third is completely different. Repeating the first line focuses the reader, and builds up a dramatic foundation. It sets up the reader, who knows the third line is coming. This is reminiscent of watching Lucy hold Charlie Brown's football, and of the way she moves it every time he comes up to kick. Rhyme often plays a part in this repetition. A blues refrain line, then, is a cousin to the alliterated word. It's a mix of the familiar with the unfamiliar, and that juxtaposition creates energy. The first part is an introduction, a comfort, but the second part sweeps your legs out from under you. It's like: *shake hands*—which we know how to do, familiar and regular—*with the President of the United States!* Or, *with this grizzly bear!* Well, of course blues, and often much literature, is a little more interesting and funny than that. It's more like: *I love my girlfriend, I do I do with all my life / I love my girlfriend, I do I do with all my life / But oh but oh don't tell my wife!*

Many things, then, enhance sonic intensity. But finally, the best is the oldest technique of all, and one which combines all of these practices: reading aloud. You can only put one sound at a time in your mouth, while your mind on the other hand can race between ideas much more quickly, not being hampered by sounding anything out at all. This sounding out slows a poem down, and puts it to the lyric test. This shows, quite easily, how every word ultimately matters.

Sonic distance is the other side of sonic intensity. If in combination the sounds in a poem produce no particular effect, no jolting to the ear, the result is sonic distance. In a poem, this technique may lead to a greater narrative or story, to a consideration of ideas, or sometimes simply to quietude—but it absolutely has an effect as well, and is equally a part of the poet's toolbox. This is a poem without obvious rhyme, without a predictable refrain or structure, without the alliteration. It has no ready clues to offer the reader beyond the words themselves. It asks a small faith from the reader, and must offer something worthy in exchange.

Sonic distance cannot be described, therefore, by any particular characteristics. Rather, as readers, we must consider the whole poetic effect, the sense of genuine response we have in finishing a poem. In this way, *the reader* is the rhyme to the poem. The reader is the third line of a blues refrain, the one that is changed. This is a lot to ask of a reader, and sets the stakes high. "His eyes were his résumé," someone wrote. And I understood. Someone else wrote about "a compass on a lazy Susan," and the sudden science inherent in this image was beguiling, making the idea more forceful than even its carefully placed extra share of "s" sounds.

When thinking about all of this, when reading or writing a poem yourself, beware of instructions and rules and dissections. The best and first thing in trying to understand or write a poem is to listen and think for yourself. Taste the poem in your mouth. Listen to it as it comes out of there. The mouth is its ancient home. Understand too that no single rule or set of rules applies to all poems. The greatest gift a poem has to give is that it is new: Its subject matter and, at least to some extent, its own rules are new.

This does not mean to say that a great poem doesn't talk about old things, or that it ignores the rules that govern language use. A great poem knows, understands, and utilizes those very ideas, but in the same moment finds a way to go beyond them. The best poems, finally, may simply come down to good choices, which may not be consistent or constant at all—good choices, each step of the way, whether by rule or by invention or both. Regarding the words in a poem, have the patience to ask yourself, *Is this a good choice? A sound choice?*

Here is the final, great secret about poems and sound. A great poem is hard to read aloud, finally, because it takes your breath away. But this is a good problem. If by its sounds the poem has rendered you speechless, and if those sounds come to mean something important to you in that moment, then—no matter what rules ought to apply—the poem has done its job.

NOTES FOR SELECTED READINGS

Note the use of sonic element used internally in the lines of Amy Lowell's poem "Winter Ride." Also, note the use of internal rhyme, and the gluing together of concepts and images this creates, in Robert Wrigley's poem "Those Riches."

Exercises

1. Write three to five lines and pay close attention to using alliteration as many times as possible. Then, write six lines and try to use assonance at the ends of the lines.
2. Create a few short images and try to use a word with onomatopoeia in each image.
3. Create an image and in it use a new and original word for a sound. Rather than giving the mother in the image a human voice, apply the trait of some animal. Notice how the sound quality changes because of the power in your original use of language.

C H A P T E R

5

RHYME AND METER, THE MUSIC OF POEMS

I'm going to function under an assumption—that most writers (especially young writers) don't like to use rhyme. And some who do like to use it don't use it well. Excuse me if that's offensive, but I'll clarify it in a minute. So, functioning under that assumption, I'm going to take the role of the used car salesman and see if I can have you driving off the lot in the make and model of rhyme that suits you. That's important—to find the rhyme that suits you. Better yet, we don't have to deal with financing—you just drive away. But once you drive away, it's yours; you live with this one because there's a no-return policy. Let's start looking and I'll try to clarify some things about rhyme.

Some of the things I hear from students in my poetry workshops sound like this: "Rhyme seems too constricting"; "It's hokey—it sounds like a Hallmark card"; "Rhyme is way too conventional and conservative"; "Old poets use rhyme." Here's my favorite: "I don't know why, I just don't like it." These are all fine things to say; I said them once too and most of my colleagues probably did, but somewhere along the line we drove off the rhyme lot with a winner. What I see as common among all these is that poets who say these things about their own work or others' work are not talking about the type of rhyme that works naturally, the kind of

The metric movement, the measure, is the direct expression of the movement of perception. And the sounds, acting together with the measure, are a kind of extended onomatopoeia—that is, they imitate not the sounds of an experience but the feeling of an experience, its emotional tone, its texture.

Denise Levertov

rhyme that just shows up and is unobtrusive. They're talking about the kind of rhyme that is imposed on poems. And that's the first rule of rhyme I want to state—don't impose it; rather, let rhyme happen naturally by having it raise itself in the poem. A quick example: I once had a student who loved rhyme. One day she brought into class a very dark, rhyming poem about a serial killer. Hence, it had a sing-songy meter to it. None of us knew what to say. "Was she writing satire?" we asked. "No," she said, "I just like rhyme." O.K., fine, but that was the wrong time to rhyme. That was a poem that needed tension between the words.

Before we go any further, let's lay down some definitions of rhyme and the types of rhyme we have. **Rhyme** is an echo produced by close placement of two or more words that have similarly sounding final syllables. There are a number of types of rhyme: there is **masculine rhyme**, in which two words end with the same vowelconsonant combination (hand/band); **feminine rhyme**, in which two syllables rhyme (shiver/liver); **end-rhyme**, in which the rhyme comes at the end of the lines (this is probably the most commonly used rhyme); and **internal rhyme**, in which a word within a line rhymes with another word in that line or rhymes with a word of similar placement in the following line. There is also a type of rhyme called **slant rhyme**, in which the sounds nearly rhyme but do not form a "true rhyme" (land/lend).

Knowing what types of rhyme we have available to us, let's just talk briefly about what rhyme does and why it's used at all. Rhyme can do a few things for a poet and her poems. First, rhyme can help a poet measure lengths of verse, either line by line or in larger chunks of language. It can do this by setting up recurrent points of rest in the language. Second, rhyme can help set a rhythm to the language we are using. And third, rhyme can help words become glued together in their sound and meaning so the poem gains a quality that is both pleasing to the ear and intellectually or emotionally stimulating. At its best, rhyme does not beat us over the head—in fact, we may read right past it or it may help us to read, guiding us musically through the poem, taking us up and setting us down in all the appropriate places. At its worst, rhyme can make a poem seem like a wrecking yard of greeting-card verse, and it can create a sense of predictability in lines and stanzas that makes us want to abandon the poem for something more fresh and alive—something that spurs our imagination.

Now that we have a bit of knowledge about the types of rhyme and why rhyme is used, let's browse the lot a little and see what we like. Remember in this discussion that these are only types of rhyme. It's how and when they are used that either make the rhyme effective or not. One poet we're nearly all familiar with, who used a great deal of rhyme, is Robert Frost. His poems are Cadillacs. Frost used end-rhyme frequently and was great at it. Emily Dickinson used a great amount of rhyme, and her poems move so acutely through the rhyme (internal and end-rhyme) they're like fine-tuned sports cars. Of course, these are poets from the earlier part of the century. Consider

James Wright's poem "Two Horses Playing in an Orchard." This poem is somewhat like a Frost poem. He is a mid- to late-century poet who rarely wrote a poem with this much controlled rhyme and meter and it is a beautifully moving poem. We need not model these writers, but by examining their work, we can learn from them.

Now let's take a look at a poem by a past student. I use this example because this student, Amity, walked onto the poetry lot saying, "I hate rhyme, and I never use it." Well, from the first time she brought something in to workshop, what we all noticed was that her poems had rhyme in them. And, what's more, she didn't even know it. In one sense, that was good. Obviously, the down side was that she wasn't paying close attention to the sound when she went back to her poems. But what was good was that the rhyme was natural— it was coming out, and she didn't even notice. She wasn't imposing. That's important, because during the writing of a poem, as Denise Levertov tells us, various parts of ourselves are working together and are heightened. Ear and eye, intellect and passion interrelate very subtly. And so, for the precision of language that must take place during writing, it is not a matter of one element supervising the others, but of intuitive interaction among all the elements involved. This is advice from a master. And it's good advice because what she's telling us is to use rhyme naturally and not let it overtake the poem— don't let it drive the poem. It's only one component. In the way that all the components of a car need to be working together to have the car drive smoothly, so do the components of a poem. Amity's poem follows:

March Day Kaleidoscope

> Sunlight scalds neon yellow
> scuffing feet up city streets.
> Hawaiian flower in your hair,
> and in the minds of kids wishing for paradise.
> I sit and absorb colors
> of the day and tie-dyed shirts.
> Hues of the universe
> mesh into marble and granite.
> Hawaiian flowers paint the planet.

AMITY SKELTON

There are some things here we worked with for revision—such as images, and lines. But we're not going to go into that now. I want you to overlook the dents on the front of this car. Let's look at the rhyme. Notice the rhyme in just the first four lines of Amity's poem. While there is no end-rhyme until the end of lines three and four, notice how much internal rhyme we have (*sun/scuff*,

scuff/up, feet/street, neon/street, light/Hawaiian, Hawaiian/minds, kids/wish). For someone who asserted so adamantly in class that she "hated" rhyme, that amount of rhyme is remarkable. What is even better about it—and the reason I think Amity didn't even notice—is that the words that rhyme are not exact masculine and feminine rhymes. In other words, not all the vowel syllables rhyme, nor do all the consonants sound the same. So we get all the benefits of rhyme without it imposing itself on the poem or getting in our way—it's transparent to us. So the poem goes on like this until the last two lines where we can feel the intentional nature of that end-rhyme (*granite/planet*).

So something to notice about Amity's poem and the one we're about to look at is the amount of internal rhyme. It seems to me that, when most young writers think of rhyme, they immediately think of end-rhyme, "old" poems, and greeting cards. Ah, but now you see it doesn't have to be that way at all. You can rhyme a great deal within the lines and get great mileage in your poems from doing so. This is the kind of technique that allows you to couple a technical use of poetic elements with an intuitive use of language and that plays upon the intellect and emotion of the readers without their consciously knowing it until they go back and look for rhyme.

All right, now here we are at the next example I want to show you. But this time, I want you to walk around it, take a look, kick the tires if you want—it's sturdy. Admire the paint job and some of the subtle exterior detail. Sit in it if you want. This is a nice compact one that gets good mileage.

At the corner of 38th and Division, my car stops

The meadowlark has returned again.
I watch a pair sing of winters spent
in warmer climates.
Watch as they play out their ballet
of clouds.
They fly past me.
My feet are cast in lead.
My arms bear no feathers.
My eyes sort out the twisting metal
made by man's hands,
see that I am not owned.

BEN RICKARD

I'm not going to say too much about this poem. But let's quickly look at a rhyme we haven't yet pointed out: the slant rhyme. Notice that in the first four lines, Ben ends the lines with words that almost rhyme (*again/spent/ballet*). Hence, we have a sense that there's a connectedness to the place through the birds and what they are doing. He does a nice job of subtly weaving those rhymes together with images and a sense of how the birds are moving. This one runs pretty well.

Let's talk for a moment about the end-rhyme that creates a greeting-card-type poem. I had a student ask me once (and not because he wrote this type of poetry—rather, because he was a retired social worker who loved to ask good and interesting questions), "What's wrong with writing greeting-card verse and using all that hokey rhyme? I mean, if that's what they're trying to do, why not?" Ahh. Tom had me. "O.K.," I said, "You're right. What's the big deal—if that's what they're trying to do, then great." But then I added, "Tom, I'm trying to teach people to write literary poems that deal with the complexity of the human experience. They can write greeting cards to make money later." In the end, what I was really trying to tell Tom was that greeting card-type verse is fine if that's all you're after—that's not too hard to write. But when you're approaching poetry from a literary standpoint and weaving together elements of the craft to create a finely-tuned poem that moves us deeply, it's important that you not rely on one element, like rhyme, to make your language move. One other thing that happens in standard greeting-card verse is that strict repetitive meter is employed—usually iambic pentameter—and the poetry becomes driven largely by one element that is being imposed on the poem rather than a smooth blending of many elements, all of which might seem entirely natural to the poem.

So let's talk a bit about meter: what it is, how it occurs, what types there are, and what it does. First, **meter** is the arrangement of measured rhythm in poetry (*measured* is a key word here; you might think of how music is measured). This measurement is based on where the stressed and unstressed syllables are in words. On one hand, that makes it easy because the stressed syllables and the unstressed syllables in words don't change—they are what they are. But meter becomes a bit more complicated as we put a number of words together. Meter is measured in what are called **feet**. A **foot** is one measurement of stressed and unstressed syllables. Types of meter are based on these measurements.

Types of Feet in Poetic Meter

iamb	ă é
trochee	é ă
anapest	ă ă é
dactyl	é ă ă
spondee	é é

The above are examples of the types of feet in poetry. When we place these in lines and have a number of feet working together, we get a type of recurring meter (you may know the term *iambic pentameter*, for instance). Within these types of feet, we have what we refer to as rising and falling meter. **Rising meter** occurs when we go from unstressed syllables to stressed syllables. Therefore, the iamb and the anapest are rising meters. **Falling meter** is just the opposite—it occurs when we go from stressed to unstressed. The trochee and the dactyl are feet with falling meter.

When there is one foot in a single line of poetry it is called *monometer*; when there are two feet it is called *dimeter*; when there are three feet it is called *trimeter*; four feet: *tetrameter*; five feet: *pentameter*; six feet: *hexameter*; seven feet: *heptameter*; eight feet: *octameter*. These are the types of meter that we have, but it is rare to find poetry with more than six feet in a line. To illustrate, let's look at examples of two types of meter. The first is iambic (a rising meter) trimeter (three feet to a line) from Theodore Roethke's "My Papa's Waltz." This is a relatively common meter.

> The whiskey on your breath
> Could make a small boy dizzy;

Something to note with this poem is that Mr. Roethke must have chosen this meter because it mimicked the beat of the waltz. Hence, the meter seems very natural in the poem and rises out of the poem—it is not imposed on the poem. Mr. Roethke couldn't have written this poem any other way.

To illustrate a falling meter, here is a line of trochaic tetrameter, meaning the line has a stressed/unstressed foot (the trochee) and it recurs four times (tetrameter).

> Fighting / was her / huge ob / session;
> she threw / pitchers / at her / husband.

Notice that the last foot of the first line breaks in the middle of a word. This is a reasonable thing to do when constructing meter and will provide you some latitude in your word choice and line structure.

This may all seem very technical, and to go back to our car metaphor, this is like the strokes of cylinders. In poetry, where we want a strict meter, and especially formal poetry, where we pay close attention to recurring metrical patterns, the beats in each foot of each line are like the spark plugs firing inside the engine. With a well-tuned line, the poem runs smoothly. We get recurrent points of rest in the poem, natural rhythms occur, a pattern to the poem very well may unfold, and we begin to get a coupling of ideas with the sonic quality of the poem. Hence, the experience of the language will be much more than simply sighted and read; rather, it will be an aural, oral, and bodily experience. As a writer, when we feel the poem missing, we need to tune-up the lines and make sure the meter is in place. And we can remember that a poet might sometimes break the recurring meter for effect.

In the end, meter provides us with a sense of rhythm. At the least, say in nursery rhymes, meter provides for us a sense of beat and music and bodily pleasure. If we use it to mirror what is happening in images, we can recreate the natural rhythms that are taking place—such as a horse galloping or people dancing. As we saw earlier, the meter in Theodore Roethke's poem, "My Papa's Waltz," mimics the waltz; it even mimics the father missing a step. At its best, skillfully used, as in Roethke's poem, meter is woven into the subtleties of the language. It is used according to the natural cadences of speech and the meanings of words. And so this is tied up in *how* a poem means something and feels. The rhythm and meter of lines creates connections; and while moving the poem, we too are moved emotionally and psychically, under our conscious surface.

Now that we've browsed the lot, looked at a number of things, sat in a few models, and done some comparison shopping, sit back and think about which works best for you—what's going to get you through the long haul. Test drive a few models and figure out what you like. Choose what fits comfortably and what you can integrate into your poems without imposing too much on your craft. Be aware of your natural impulses and the rhythm of your language.

METER AND RHYME

James Hoggard

Although an organized use of rhyme and meter can enhance the elegance of a poetic passage, their major function is something other than decorative. Meters have particular effects, while the several types of rhyme organize passages by means of repeated, or echoic, sounds. Rhyme and meter both have their vocabularies, and it's important for poets to learn those terms so they can take advantage of the concepts behind them. Problems in poems often occur when rhythms or sounds are inappropriate to the experience being conveyed. Having access to terms of measure and rhyme, a poet can diagnose problematic passages more surely than one can without the terminology. Concepts of language, after all, are major tools a writer needs.

A. Meter

There are five kinds of metrical feet commonly used in English, but before we define them, we should recognize that the custom of dividing sounds into two levels of stress—accented and unaccented—is more convention than hard reality. We commonly use four different levels of stress in ordinary conversation, but conventional marking identifies only two. This means, of course, that when we talk about meter, we are not dealing with metronomic purity, and for the sake of poetic pleasure that's fortunate. Jingles suggest triviality, not deeply moving speech.

The major patterns of metrical feet include the *iamb* (unaccented syllable followed by an accented syllable, or ˘ ¯, as it's often written), the *trochee* (¯ ˘), the *spondee* (¯ ¯), the *dactyl* (¯ ˘ ˘), and the *anapest* (˘ ˘ ¯). One should also be aware of the *amphibrach* (˘ ¯ ˘) and *monometer* (¯). Except for possibly the *spondee*, the odd appearance of one of the feet is not likely to be notable; but when used in a sustained way, the metrical patterns have particular effects.

The dominant rhythm of spoken English is *iambic*. That does not mean, of course, that in our conversations we speak in perfectly turned iambs, but it does mean that a sustained use of the iambic rhythm gives a conversational effect. A good example would be these opening lines of one of Shakespeare's sonnets:

> That time of year thou mayst in me behold
> When yellow leaves, or none, or few, do hang
> Upon those boughs which shake against the cold

If one reads the passage out loud in a normal voice, one hears how conversational it sounds; and it should sound conversational because its rhythm is perfectly iambic.

The *trochaic* rhythm is much more rapid than the iambic one. Because of the quick, falling rhythm (¯ ˘ / ¯ ˘ / ¯ ˘), a series of trochees might call to mind someone moving the feet rapidly in front of each other to keep from falling. Lines three, four, and five of Robert Browning's "Meeting at Night" illustrate vividly the quickness of predominantly trochaic lines:

> And the startled little waves that leap
> In fiery ringlets from their sleep
> As I gain the cove with pushing prow

One also notes that Browning sustains the trochaic pattern from line to line by enjambing the first line above so the rhythm continues without a pause into the next line, with *leap* being the first syllable of a trochee that is completed by *In* at the beginning of the next line, then followed by three trochees. The line closes with the monometrical *sleep*. The anapest and three iambs of the next line create a rhythm that is slower than the previous two lines that are dominated by trochees.

Although lengthy passages aren't ordinarily written in **spondees**, the spondaic rhythm does have a dramatic effect by slowing down the pace of a passage. The first two lines of the same poem by Browning illustrate this:

> The gray sea and the long black land
> And the yellow half-moon large and low

One might say that the first line begins with an iamb followed by a trochee then an iamb and finally a spondee, but that's not the way we hear it. We hear *gray sea* as a unit of sound just as we hear *long black land* as a unit. When we read the line, we realize that its relative slowness is created by the **spondaic** patterns in it. The second line begins rapidly with two trochees then is slowed down notably by the sudden appearance of three accented syllables together: *half-moon large*.

The next two metrical feet, the **dactyl** ($\bar{\ }\ \breve{\ }\ \breve{\ }$) and the **anapest** ($\breve{\ }\ \breve{\ }\ \bar{\ }$) create swinging rhythms C *tum da da* | *tum da da* then *da da tum* | *da da tum*. It's easy to forget the rhythm that identifies each term, but there's a (literally) handy mnemonic device that helps us remember which one is which. The word **dactyl** comes from the Greek word *dactylos*, meaning *finger*. If one looks at one's index finger outward from palm to fingertip, one sees a long joint followed by two shorter ones, or $\bar{\ }\ \breve{\ }\ \breve{\ }$, and the **anapest** is just the opposite. In fact, the Greeks themselves used the same mnemonic device. *Dactyl* comes from the word for *finger*, and *anapest* comes from the word that means *reversed*—here, in effect, the opposite of dactyl.

The terms ordinarily used for the number of metrical feet per line also came to us from the Greeks. Sonnets are said to be written in iambic pentameter, which means five feet per line and most of the feet are iambic. **Penta** means *five* and **meter** means *measure*. Other terms to note include **hexameter** (six feet), **tetrameter** (four feet), **trimeter** (three feet), **dimeter** (two feet), and **monometer** (one foot). Another term one sometimes sees for **dimeter** is *dipody*, or in its adjectival form *dipodic* (coming from *di* meaning *two* and *podos* meaning *foot*). One should keep in mind the relative effects of these measures—the longer the line, the lengthier, the more sustained the flow from line to line; the shorter the line, the quicker the flow.

B. Rhyme

In an essay titled "The Figure a Poem Makes," Robert Frost called poems "momentary stays against confusion." By that he meant that a work of art can have an order that is not present, or at least not apparent, in nature. The poet, then, is a maker, a shaper, or even an inventor of experiences; and rhyme is a common indicator of an order that has been either created or discovered in the portion of the world described or evoked. Rhyme has also been used as a device to help make a work memorable, both for the audience and for the person reciting or singing the piece.

In terms of placement and exactness of sound, there are several types of rhyme. *External* (or *end*) *rhyme* refers to the repetitions of sounds at the ends of lines, whereas **internal rhyme** refers to sounds that are repeated within lines. Although external rhymes are usually thought of as regular in their patterns of repetition (lines one and three rhyme, say, or lines two and four rhyme), internal rhymes are usually employed irregularly in a passage. In both cases, the sounds that are repeated, or used echoically, include both the closing vowels and consonants, as in *yellow, bellow; loon, rune; walk, talk*. If only one of the closing elements (a consonant but not a vowel, or a vowel but not a consonant) is repeated, one has *approximate* *rhyme*; other terms one might see that mean the same thing are *slant rhyme, half-rhyme,* and *pararhyme.* Since rhyme, whether full or half, involves echoic effects in words, the sonic repetition needs to be close enough to its mate for us to notice the similarities of sound. That's especially true for internal rhyme. If, for instance, the sounds that get repeated internally are several lines apart, one is not likely to note the repetition.

Examples of both full rhyme and approximate end-rhyme are found in John Crowe Ransom's "Bells for John Whiteside's Daughter." The stanza that begins the poem sets the pattern for all but the middle stanza, with lines one and three closing with *approximate rhyme* and two and four closing with *full rhyme*:

> There was such speed in her little body
> And such lightness in her footfall,
> It is no wonder her brown study
> Astonishes us all.

Body and *study* give us half-rhymes, whereas *fall* and *all* rhyme exactly. Because this pattern is repeated throughout the poem, we find that a sense of tension in the speaker is expressed sonically; the poem alternates between fullness of order and incompleteness of order. This tension is also amplified in the speaker's phrasing: *her brown study | Astonishes us; we are sternly stopped; we are vexed.* Sounds, we begin to learn, can affect the mood of a passage just as rhythms can. In the middle stanza of Ransom's poem, the rhyming pattern changes. Instead of the alternation between approximate rhyme in lines one and three and exact rhyme in two and four, found in the other stanzas, here both sets of lines rhyme exactly to indicate the Edenlike harmony of the child's world:

> The lazy geese, like a snow cloud
> Dripping their snow on the green grass,
> Tricking and stopping, sleepy and proud,
> Who cried in goose, Alas

When rhyming lines follow one another without intervening non-rhyming lines, the jingle-like repetition can create a perkily light mood, as we see in the wittily suggestive opening lines of "Sweet Lemon Iced Tea" by the undergraduate poet Nekesha Meals:

> do you like what you see
> when you look at me
> this tall slender glass of sweet lemon iced tea

The enjambment between lines two and three softens the rhyme and prevents the effect of monotonous repetition that one often hears when end-stop lines rhyme.

Several other sonic devices that are related to rhyme need to be noted. These refer to the types of sounds, vowels, or consonants, that are repeated and to their positions in words. The three sonic devices noted here are **alliteration, assonance,** and **consonance**. It's also important to keep in mind that these sonic devices refer to sounds that are repeated, but not necessarily to letters.

Alliteration refers to the repetition of initial consonant sounds in words either within a line or close enough to each other to be registered by the listener. An example would be:

> In the deep-**b**lue **b**ay, **b**road sails
> **b**ellied in the wind

or:

> The **b**ig waves **b**eat the hulls
> of the **b**oats, all of them **b**lue

Assonance refers to the repetition of vowel sounds in a passage, with no distinction being made to placement, as in these two lines with their long *i*-sounds:

> but the other n**i**ght just after dusk d**i**ed
> **I** heard the first bullfrogs explaining spring

The other *i*'s are not included because the qualities of sound they evoke are different from the long *i*-sounds noted. Another example of assonance is also present in the first line, with the short *u*-sounds in *but, just,* and *dusk*. One might also note the internal rhyme in the last two syllables of line two: "explain**ing** spr**ing**."

The third sonic device noted here is *consonance,* the repetition of internal consonant sounds, or consonant sounds appearing at places other than the beginnings of words, as we hear in the *d*-sounds in this passage from a poem titled "Springsound":

> They soun**d**e**d** as if they won**d**ere**d** which kin
> woul**d** not anonymous escape the clay
> but stay beneath a sun**d**ried roof baked har**d**.

The *d* in *baked* in line three is not included because here the *d* is pronounced like a *t*. One also notices that assonance is prominent in the same passage, in the long *a*-sounds of the two *they*'s in line one which are echoed in *escape* and *clay* in line two, and *stay* and *baked* in line three. In effect, these sonic devices are musical in their effects as they organize phrases with clusters of sound.

Two other sonic devices that are especially important to know are *liquids* and sibilants. When used repeatedly, they give a soft, gracefully flowing, lyrical effect to phrases. Because they create particular effects, because they refer to particular sounds, and because their positions in words are not an issue, these two are considered separately from alliteration, assonance, and consonance. The liquids are the *l*'s and *r*'s, and the sibilants are the hissing sounds: *s*'s, *sh*'s, and aspirated *f*'s. Again, we're referring to sounds, not necessarily letters. The words *rough* and *tough*, for example, close with the *f*-sound, though the letter *f* does not occur in either word. On the other hand, the word *of* has the letter *f* in it, but no *f*-sound. A word like *nation*, for instance, contains a sibilant because the *ti* in the middle of the word is pronounced *sh*. Two other sounds ought to be mentioned as possible sibilants, though some readers do not include them in the group. They are the voiceless interdental fricative *th* (as in *pith* but not *the*) and the *z*-sounds (as in *blows*, *noses*, and *cries*). Two passages quoted below illustrate the smooth, whisperily graceful flow that occurs when numerous clusters of liquids and sibilants work together. The first includes the closing lines of "The Yachts" by William Carlos Williams:

> they cry out, failing, failing! their cries rising
> in waves still as the skillful yachts pass over.

The second example is the first stanza of Browning's "Meeting at Night," a poem referred to earlier in a different context. As we did above without distinguishing one from the other, we put the liquids and sibilants in boldface to emphasize their prominence in the stanza.

> The gray sea and the long black land
> And the yellow half-moon large and low
> And the startled little waves that leap
> In fiery ringlets from their sleep
> As I gain the cove with pushing prow   5
> And quench its speed i' the slushy sand.

Thinking in terms of sound and measure, one begins to realize the points of intimate involvement linking form and subject. In some cases, and they're often glorious when one discovers them, a sizable passage or even at times an entire poem may create or recreate simultaneously both the sensory and thematic dimensions of an experience; in fact, they might do that so intensely that the poem itself does not simply describe the experience but evokes the presence of the experience itself. When that happens, the passage—sometimes even the entire poem—becomes onomatopoetic, and the work truly sings.

NOTES FOR SELECTED READINGS

Note the use of rhyme and meter in Elizabeth Barrett Browning's poem "Sonnet 14" while comparing it to the rhyme and rhythmic (but not strictly metered) lines of Phyllis Wheatley's poem "On Being Brought from Africa to America."

Exercises

1. If you're a poet who doesn't care much for rhyme, write a rhyming poem. Or take a poem you wrote recently and comb through it to see how much rhyme there already is in it. Then revise it to add more rhyme. If you're a poet who likes to write rhymed poetry, then write a poem that has no end-rhyme. This may be hard. It may feel as though you are working against yourself, but trust that you are still getting your rhyme in; it's probably happening more naturally.

2. The poet Robert Hass says "There's a sense in which poetry is not so much the writing of words as much as it is the movement of breath itself. To write it you must pay attention to the breathing of poetry, to *all* speech as breath, to the relationship of our thoughts and emotions and the actual way they fill our bodies. This is the emotional, physical centering of the activity of poetry." Take this quote and apply it to either a new poem you are writing or a poem you've already written. Notice how it might affect the rhythm or meter based on how the breath—your breath—is connected to the experience in the poem.

3. Look in the newspaper and choose three short articles. For each, write a stanza or two about it or from it. In each stanza, employ a different rhythmic or metrical pattern and a different rhyme scheme. For example, make each stanza 3, 4, or 6 lines. Then create a rhythmic pattern out of meter or syllabics and create a recurrent pattern of rhyme throughout the stanzas.

6

VOICE AND HOW WE CREATE IT IN POEMS

Having talked about diction and tone a bit in the previous chapter on sound, this is a natural place to begin talking about **voice** in a poem. Voice is the expressive force and tone of the words spoken by the author and the **persona** in the poem. And, the persona is the person who is the speaker of the poem. When we read a story, we often know, very definitively, who is talking at any given time. Of course, we meet the narrator immediately, and we come to know the narrator's voice quickly and well. But in a poem, sometimes the identification of the character to whom we are actually listening can be a bit more ambiguous. This is not a bad thing; remember, ambiguity is part of poetry. But we also need to remember, as we write poems, that it is important to create a very solid voice. This way the poem will avoid confusion.

So what makes voice and how do we control it? Voice in a poem rises from diction and syntax—put simply, the way we use language and the way we combine our words. The other thing that causes a voice to take shape is setting—the place from which the persona is speaking. Why setting? Setting is more than simply where and when a poem or story takes place. Rather, the setting is the physical and cultural context for the way the

An author, that is to say, is a fashioner of words, stamps them with her own personality, and wears the raiment she has made, in her own way.

Marianne Moore

world is viewed by the persona, the writer, and ultimately the reader. So as we create a poem, we may begin by thinking of a very distinct persona (speaker) and we know that there is a distinct set of circumstances that has formed what he will say and how he will say it. Take, for example, Gary Snyder's poem "Axe Handles." This poem begins with a father speaking about teaching his young son how to throw a hatchet into a stump. During the poem, the father realizes that, as a parent, he is not only a teacher. He is, and has been, a student of life. Throughout the poem the voice maintains a sense of consistency because of where the poem takes place (a rural setting, clearly the home of the father and son, and a place where he can teach his son to throw a hatchet) and the way in which the father perceives and expresses the experience. His connecting to his son in the natural world, in taking the time to help shape an experience for him with natural elements, causes the persona and the persona's voice to reach a level of clarity. The poem ends with the realization that generations shape each other and the realization comes in very clear and accessible language.

For another example, let's look at what a student from a workshop put together. Kevin lived and had grown up in a farming and logging community. Notice how he uses the setting of the poem to spark the action and ultimately the sentiment of the experience—the missed connection between father and son, the want for love and togetherness, and the inability to escape the fact that they are tied by blood and generations. But what happens here is that while all of these things in the poem are tied to the setting and the actions there, it's Kevin's fresh use of language—his ability to keep this experience from sounding trite, saccharine, or even forcedly angry at key moments—that keeps it original and controls the language throughout the poem.

By Barbed-Wire Fences

We stood silent and waiting
for a calf to cross
through a gate; its mother
waited. And in the truck, traveling
to town you were silent,   5
I kept talking, kept wanting
to find you. Unknowingly and
unwantingly those moments
lost themselves, soured
like milk into years, and a gate   10
between them I'm sure, no longer
reachable by foot.

In consistent light I thought was love,
through our barn, you and I,
but you turn away   15
the hay swirling glow—your back shining.
You look like memories;
my grandfather, your father, your
Irish hair dark as sorrow
shadows furrowed deep.   20
So that is why: your hands,
those hands of scars and strength,
those sawmill and logging town hands,
would slap my mother and choke her.
Those hands I longed to admire   25
to hate, a love like hard water.
How when we were rabbit hunting I wanted,
and turned the gun towards you.
Now, when you come home from work,
I am old enough. We walk silent to the barn   30
and I watch you load hay into the truck.
How I want to reach you;
slip my hands past your canvas
coat and hold you in the barn light as
night folds its dark clench over us. And winter,   35
winter we can bear because the numbness
is familiar. We will stand silent and knowing
that rain will be soon—it comes uneasy.
It arrives—sweet.
Together, in the only light we know,   40
the barn braces us against the cold east wind,
and I am no longer scared.

KEVIN SULLIVAN

In this poem, Kevin uses phrases such as *soured like milk into years, you look like memories,* and *hay swirling glow* to achieve some sense of freshness and originality in his language. But notice that they are directly tied to the setting and action of the poem. So what we have is the voice of the poet and persona directly tied to what happens and how it happens in the poem. This poem is actually long enough that toward the end we come to anticipate how Kevin might turn a phrase.

So once we've created a persona and a voice, we have to remember to control it in a way that makes it sound natural. How do we do this? First, we write from experiences that we know. We hear this all the time—our writing instructors have always said this. One of the reasons for writing what we know is that we need a voice that is authentic. When we hear a voice speak a poem or tell a story, we as readers should not have to concentrate on the words. Louis Simpson said, "The words of poems should become transparent." But this will only happen if the language use and the setting and the perception of the character(s) all fit together naturally. As writers, we need to know the difference between the reaction of the mother who has just gone through labor and then holds her baby and the reaction of the obstetrician who has helped deliver the child. This only comes from real experience. And the sense of knowing this real experience will be delivered in our own unique and fresh voice.

THE WRITER'S VOICE

The writer's voice? Surely there is such a thing. It has been tracked like elusive, hunted lions and finally bagged after an exhaustive search with experienced guides. Maybe. We've all heard people talk about "when they came into their voice" and "I think I'm really developing a voice." But what does that all mean? Does it mean we should be able to sit down with passages in front of us and identify, without title or name, poets and their poems? Possibly. But let's not forget that the early work of a poet may sound different from the middle and then the late work of a poet. The reason for this is that language use changes over time. On one hand, as individuals we have adopted very distinct ways of using language. But because our views of the world change as we age, grow, mature, and develop, our language use also changes slightly. My best advice is this: don't try to sound any given way, just write things the way you might tell things to someone. Take to heart William Stafford's old maxim of *use the language you know*. Maximize the gains and minimize the losses and you'll be all right.

   This technique of writing the way we might tell someone something and using the language that we know brings us back to that good old technical term: *diction*, or word choice. I often find that students have an idea of their own language use that goes something like this: There's the language you speak and the language you write. In the language you speak, there are all sorts of types—slang you speak with friends, a more standard polite language reserved for work or school or more conservative public occasions, and language with family. In the written language, there is a formal type of writing for essays and research papers (this has short sentences, big words, sometimes many quotes, and never seems individually identifying) and a more informal type of writing for letters to friends or family, shopping lists, notes left on the kitchen table, and e-mail. I say, bring all of these closer together. Why have such a broad spectrum of language use? To me, it seems daunting to keep it all straight and pull out the appropriate one at the appropriate time. I say, elevate the level with which you speak to family and friends, abandon the myth of short sentences and big words in academic papers (that just breeds bad writing) and begin to create a way to express your views about the world—a way that is largely the same whether you're writing or speaking. This way, you have one language you know well and are familiar with. Hence, when you write, you will not be searching a bed of language you don't know well or using a language based on the big-word myth.

Does this mean that if you do this you'll develop a voice and someone might be able to identify your poems without name or title? Well maybe, but not necessarily. It's not that important that someone be able to identify your poems anyway. Some poets argue that if identification can take place the writer has stagnated and become stale. So it means that the voice you create as a writer comes from the way you express the world and fashion language. Voice is in the way we construct sentences and put word combinations together. It lies in original language use and it's as simple as the way two friends might choose to describe the same scene differently. When we create an image in a poem, we choose certain words because of who we are and where we're from. This combination helps create the force of our language.

The poet William Butler Yeats said that a poet's words have to be wedded to the natural figures of his or her native landscape. This is a concept that is not too difficult to understand on one level. Consider regions and their accents and their expressions—the way someone from Texas may say something versus the way someone from Columbus, Ohio would. Certainly, the way in which we form expressions and phrases and our word choices are based on where we're from, what we've heard, and how we've heard language used. And because this helps create our perspective on the world, it also helps shape our voice in writing. It becomes the foundation for the way we express ourselves.

VOICE: WHAT YOU SAY AND HOW READERS HEAR IT

Kevin Stein

No aspect of poetry writing is more fundamental to the art—and yet more thorny to define—than *voice*. Critics give us a slew of technical terms meant to delineate subtle shades of difference in how poets use and readers respond to, voice. Poets, on the other hand, speak of it in hushed tones tending to beatify the mysterious process of "finding your voice." In truth, most poets own little idea of how they came to find the voice their readers recognize immediately as those poets' own, as distinctly James Wright's, or Anne Sexton's, or Frank O'Hara's. The usual bromides—read widely, write daily, risk daringly—seem just that: meaningless patter meant to keep the learner in the proverbial dark. Still, the good news, and the bad, is that finding one's voice really is a long trip in an ill-tuned Yugo, a journey that asks poets to read, write, revise, and to think about writing and think about thinking about writing.

What is voice? Well, I'll avoid hairsplitting technical terms in favor of simplicity: Voice is the way you, the poet, speak a poem. Of course, such a seemingly simple thing as how you speak a poem involves a gaggle of choices and decisions, some of them conscious and some of them not. Most folks will agree that voice involves two basic components: (1) *subject matter*, that is, what you choose to talk about in the poem, thus, what matters to you and just as importantly, how and why it's come to matter, and (2) *tone*, how you feel about the specific subject of the poem and your audience, as well as how you feel about yourself and the world in general. Big stuff, to be sure.

One helpful way to consider such an unwieldy subject is to appreciate the beautiful duality of the term *voice*. When we think of voice, we most often fall upon the literal sense of the word—the actual physical and auditory sense of spoken voice and language. Still, poets concern themselves equally, if not more, with the metaphorical sense of voice: what poets talk about in a poem, the language they use, their attitude toward the world and their place in it. When you've read enough poets, you'll find yourself able to identify a poem you've never heard simply by paying attention to these issues of subject matter and tone: "Oh," you'll say, "there's Dickinson again contemplating death in her short, tight line," or "There's another Sharon Olds poem openly grieving her father's death with strangely lush, almost sensual language." You'll *hear* a poem the way you *see* an unfamiliar painting, one so obviously cubist it must be Picasso's. In fact, most of you already do this with popular music. You know halfway to the chorus the song's by Mellencamp or Marley or Madonna. At first the sound of the voice may clue you, but after a while you notice the consistency of subject or attitude, the kinds of things the singer chooses to sing about and his or her feelings about those things. Maybe something similar has already happened to you. Say you've shown friends a new poem, and they've remarked, "Oh, that's just like you to write about your trip to Europe by gushing about Italian waiters and the erotics of foreign toiletry." If so, you've begun to develop and to exhibit a personalized sense of subject matter and tone.

Now, keep in mind this voice your poem presents needn't always be your personal voice, laden with your own opinions and concerns. It need only seem believably human and real, like that of a real person speaking about matters that concern him or her. You can always concoct a persona or mask and thus speak the poem as if you were Winston Churchill, Nelson Mandela, or your own mother. Why not, for that matter, violate the very rule I've set down above, and speak the poem as someone or something not human but surprisingly close to it—perhaps Mr. Ed, the talking horse of television sitcom fame?

Above all else, a poem's voice establishes a relationship among speaker, poem, and reader. Readers respond to speakers—and thus to poems—that convey an urgency in the way they talk. Readers want to believe speakers have something meaningful to say to them, and they respond most passionately to speakers who do so using memorable language, image, emotion, and thinking. More than anything else, a poem's voice—its subject and tone—determines how readers feel about the speaker and in turn how they feel about the poem. This accounts for advice such as Aristotle gives writers in his *Rhetoric*. There, Aristotle urges prospective writers to make readers care about them as humans, to display aspects of *ethos* and *character* in their work that will encourage readers to admire them as persons and thus to be more likely persuaded by their arguments. The poet W. B. Yeats, however, distrusts this notion of rhetoric applied to a poem. He suggests that while rhetoric is an argument with another person, true poetry is an argument with the self.

How then to make a poem's voice cause readers to feel they are witnessing, and perhaps partaking in themselves, a passionate argument with the self? How to make a voice so authentic readers believe the speaker bristles with humanity, the electric mix of flaws, foibles, and desires we recognize as human? How do you make readers succumb to an experience very much like falling in love with a voice on the telephone? You know, the person never seen or touched who exudes such vibrant energy readers easily imagine eyes, lips, hair, the curve of waist and thigh, laughter supple and intelligent.

One way to learn to do so is by trying on other poets' voices, as poet Theodore Roethke suggests in "How to Write Like Somebody Else." Roethke believes poets come to find their own peculiar voice by trying to learn to speak a poem in the manner of great poets. Read widely, the story goes, and finding a poet you like, try to mimic that poet's subjects, language, and form. One month W. H. Auden, the next Gwendolyn Brooks or John Donne. Try to discover what it is that makes that poet so unique, so distinguishable from others. None of these voices, of course, will fit you like your favorite pair of jeans. Your voice, like those jeans, is something unique fashioned by wearing it over time. With effort and faith, you'll gradually abandon or subsume those other voices as you shape your own.

Not everyone, however, agrees it's literally possible to "find" your voice. Philip Levine, for instance, thinks young poets spend altogether too much time worrying about this quest. "I never tell younger poets to find their own voice because I don't believe that's how voice comes to us. Once a poet discovers what his material is, his voice will come to him. The best thing is to practice good writing until you've got something to say so urgent it's got to be said. . . . I don't think anyone ever found his own voice; it found him." Find first what you *must* talk about, Levine argues, and your voice will come along in the bargain.

What makes the matter of voice so frustrating is the simple fact that it can't be taught. Your teacher might be able to give you exercises to sharpen your use of metaphor or image, for example, but no teacher I know can lead you to your voice by dint of classroom assignment. Voice isn't a technique, a trick, or even a skill. It's nothing less than the way you feel about yourself and your world, all that music plucked through the strings you choose to speak those feelings and ideas. Voice is individual and unique, a fingerprint in language. Voice speaks the world through your lips, and hearing it, readers understand it is yours and yours alone.

Here's a poem by a student of mine, Scott James. As you read it, look for spots where the poem springs alive, where a quirky and original voice is heard. Look for the human in the human words:

Exhale

I've got volumes of myself
stored back in my silences,
devoured by pyromoments
of misguided release.
I like the warm feeling   5
when I smile with my whole face,
skin that compresses into my eyes,
but the whole white picket grin
stands before a crude house,
and the distances that cower   10
are scars on skin.
I like stars behind clouds
that appear for blinks
then fade to aftertaste.
They say truth comes   15
through drunkenness,
our inhibitions demolished,
but I'm always sorry for something
when the sun returns.
I like clean socks.   20
They just feel good,
cotton and all, soft
and unaware

of the mouth they carry
or the mind it hides.   25
I guess I lie on greenish grass
six feet away
from "the other side."
My mouth
a six-pack away from honesty.   30

SCOTT JAMES

The poem moves lithely through a series of revelations disguised as friend-to-friend chatter, reader sitting on the grass sharing the moment with the contemplative speaker. The speaker begins to talk about his shyness punctuated by "pyromoments" of things spoken that shouldn't have been said. What follows, though, is a litany of some things the speaker likes in this world he also pointedly distrusts: how his sweet "white picket" fence smile hides a house of crude scars, for instance. Then the speaker, probably drinking a beer and smoking a cigarette (see the title, "Exhale"), swerves toward the apparent subject—how when one is drunk such false fronts always collapse into the rubble of day-after apologies.

That's enough to make an interesting poem, but note how the speaker allows his mind to follow its own path. The wonderful line about liking "clean socks" comes seemingly out of nowhere, and its surprise sweetens the pie. Sure, we've all thought something similar while pulling on our socks in the morning, and thus we laugh and agree but ask, "What does this have to do with lying?" Then the socks become associated with the speaker's mouth and mind, and their apparent purity is besmirched. Can nothing in this world be trusted? Is nothing innocent really what it appears to be? Not even clean socks? The poem's subject matter becomes expansive, far reaching, and troubling—this, suddenly, is no simple poem about the intersection of shyness and drunkenness. When the poem concludes with a nod toward the grave, we readers get the notion the speaker believes there's nothing trustworthy in this flawed world. Take a breath, Dear Reader, and "exhale" at the news.

NOTES FOR SELECTED READINGS

Compare the difference between Albert Garcia's poem "Waking," Beckian Fritz Goldberg's poem "The Passing House," and David Bottoms' poem "Sermon of the Fallen" in order to see the difference between three distinct voices. You might pay particular attention to their word choices and syntax in order to create a voice in the poem.

Exercises

1. Often, after reading a poem we particularly enjoy, we say to ourselves, "I wish I had written that poem." When we hear ourselves say this, then we need to write the poem. What's happening is that we're recognizing our idealized voice. So, capture it. For example, if you read James Wright's "Lying in a Hammock . . ." and thought, "That's the poem I want to write," then you need to sit down and write it. Doing this will help you exercise your poetic skills in the voice you'd most like to have.

2. Create a character who speaks very differently than yourself. Maybe he or she is from a different region than you are and has an accent. Maybe they just use very different words. Maybe they're older. Write down five questions for this person and interview them. Then use that person to tell one of your poems.

3. Write a new poem or take one you've already written. Go through the poem placing marks next to all the images in the poem. Then, note which images are central to how you (the poet) feel about the world. Identify which images are your fingerprints on the poem.

7

POINT OF VIEW
IN POEMS

One of our responsibilities as poets—writers of any sort—is to avoid beating up on people with language. They get that enough in the day-to-day world. We need to be honest in the way we come at things. That doesn't mean we can't alter our experiences or tell half-truths—as long as they represent our real experience we're all right. What I'm talking about is tricking the readers, deceiving them, making them believe something they shouldn't. Raymond Carver used to say, "At the first sign of a trick, I'm running for cover." So it's up to us to capture our experiences and relay the intellectual and emotional power behind them so that the readers feel they have experienced the world in a real and honest way. But how? By creating a speaker who can convey experience powerfully.

Now we've already talked about the speaker, the persona, who is the one who takes on the point of view in a poem. The **point of view** is the stance taken by the persona, the attitude, and the view of the world he imparts to the reader. Along with this stance and attitude comes the **tone**—the emotional sense behind the voice of the persona. Without a clear and defined point of view in a poem we can lead the reader—and sometimes ourselves as writers—right into a murky swamp

And you've got to hear voices, from wherever they come. Sometimes I guess my own voice is coming in different kinds of ways, and I have to trust that there is something there.

Sekou Sundiata

of problems. The readers may not understand who the speaker is. They may not understand why the persona happens to be the one narrating the experience; this confusion usually comes from a problem in the relationship between persona and place or experience. This persona needs to fit into the context of the poem so that it seems real. Remember, no tricks. Let's take a situation. A white man and a Native-American woman walk into a restaurant in, say, any rural area near where you live. They are hungry and want to have breakfast. They wait at the chrome-framed sign that says "Please Wait to Be Seated." No one comes to seat them. There are only two tables in the place being served. The rest are empty. Finally, the man says to the host, "Can we just go ahead and sit down?" The host glares a little and then comes up next to the white man and says—"We don't serve your type here." Thoughts race. What exactly does he mean? *Her* type or *our* type? O.K., he's a racist. Let's beat the hell out of him. What do we say? The couple leaves. As they do, the waitress gives them a sympathetic and pleading look like "I'm so sorry; he's a horrible man."

   All right, there's our situation. Now we want to write a poem about it. First we have to decide how the story should be told. Should it be first person (I/me), second person (using "you" and addressing some other being seemingly reading the poem), or third person (he/she). Of course it could be third person limited, in which our narrator knows only limited details about what's happened or it could be omniscient, in which the persona/narrator knows all—maybe even knows that this man did the same thing only half an hour earlier. So let's say we decide on first person. Now, we have one more consideration, and this is an important one: Who should be the persona—the man, the Native-American woman, or the waitress? Examining this question will show us how the persona, the experience, and the context of place and time all help to build the evocative power of a poem. And remember, we have a different poem for each person in this situation. For years, the waitress has seen this man act this way. The white man is stunned and hasn't experienced either the man or the depth of racism and oppression the women have, especially the Native-American woman. But he's empathic and in a relationship with her. The Native-American woman, on the other hand, has seen it before, can't stand it, wants to collar the white man, but has enough control from having endured it before to walk right out the door. All of these points of view bring up very different emotional and intellectual stances in the poem.

   What comes of all this? We need to remember that our persona is the spokesperson for the psychological reality that plays out in the poem. And in this psychological reality, the kernel of the poem is delivered. This is the way the truth of the poem is handled—it needs to be handled well. Needless to say, in this example, there is a different truth for each possible persona. As the poet we need to decide what truth it is we want to tell, what truth it is we know best, and what truth we can best show the reader. Outside of showing and telling the experiences, we need to remember that choosing the right point of view for the right experience lends itself to fresh insights and some surprise for the reader—provided we adhere to the Carver maxim and don't surprise the reader with tricks. For instance, we all probably expect the poem to be told from either the man or the woman's point of view. The least expected point of view is the waitress's. But maybe that's the freshest poem. Provided we can evoke the depth of experience we want from her, then we have a fresh approach.

I had a student who wanted to write a whole series of poems about the Korean war. Well, he decided he'd write them from different points of view, mostly from the points of view of different soldiers he had encountered or read about. But then came a twist. He started writing poems from the mother's point of view back in Nebraska, and the point of view of the sister of one of the soldiers who lived in Winnemucca, Nevada. And it turned out that these were the most riveting poems. We had a sense of expectation—and it was achieved—in the poems from the soldiers. But the poems from the family members were unexpected and a little closer to many readers' realities because of their domestic quality. And there came a change in tone. And the change in tone and expressiveness in the stance of the persona became something we all attached to in the workshop.

When we decide who tells our poem, when we listen to the voices coming through to us, our inner voices, and those of our characters, we need to pay close attention to them. We need to choose the voice that can express our moments in ways that are natural and honest—the voice that recreates the world so that what was once private to us becomes a shared and sensational moment for the reader. We need to pull the reader down the throats of our speakers and into their hearts.

POINT OF VIEW IN POETRY

James Hoggard

Understanding point of view is as important for writers and readers of poetry as it is for those concerned with prose fiction. In fact, the first thing a writer or reader of a poem should probably do is ask three simple questions: Who is the speaker of the piece? What physical or psychological situation is the speaker in when making the statement? Is there a notable connection between the situation the speaker is in and the subject he or she is talking about? If we begin with these questions, we can avoid some serious misreadings that come about when one mistakes the speaker for the poet; we can also see more clearly than we would otherwise the attitude and circumstances that guide the narration. A prominent example to illustrate this idea is Robert Browning's dramatic monologue "My Last Duchess," whose murderous, self-centered speaker represents the opposite of what Browning considered heroic and good. If we begin the poem assuming that the speaker is Browning himself, we seriously misread what the poet is doing. Poets, we should remind ourselves, have been storytellers at least as often as they have been direct singers of sentiment and opinion. Because of that, they are as inclined as short-story writers, novelists, and playwrights to use voices other than their own; and the range of voices available to all of us is as broad as the sweep of our imaginations.

In lyric poetry, that form of speech that most prominently filters the world through self—or *a* self—the first-person point of view is most common. The narrator refers to him- or herself as "I." Whether the speaker represents the poet or someone else, the narration's point of view is guided (and limited) by the speaker's perception. An interesting example of the first-person point of view is seen in Renée Klein's poem "Before Bed." An undergraduate student when she wrote the piece, the poet here is using the convention of direct quotation. In this work a child speaks to his (or her) parent, more than likely the mother, before going to sleep:

> Does broccoli float in a glass of milk?
> Is a tree a house for leaves?
> How many stars in Infinity?
> I love you five hundred and three.
> Can I go down the bathtub drain?   5
> Does Jesus make the crickets sing?
> What do cats dream when they're asleep?
> I love you five hundred and three.

The child says the entire poem and the poet says nothing directly. Certainly at times the child's speech resembles chattering as much as serious questioning, but that is appropriate because the poet here is conveying the personality of the narrator, in this case a child who, while delightfully expressing his love for the parent, cleverly uses delaying tactics to keep the parent around.

In poetry as well as in fiction, the second-person point of view is rare, most likely because it creates an odd effect in the narration. That also makes it intriguing. For example, instead of having the narrator say:

> Running against the wind again
> I keep thinking about you
> and can't stop wondering why
> you quit coming by

the poet would have the narrator say:

> Running against the wind again
> you keep thinking about her
> and can't stop wondering why
> she quit coming by.

In an interestingly illusory way, the reader becomes the narrator, and the effect this point of view has, when sustained, can be eerie. A curious tension is stirred in the reader. Perhaps the best-known work that uses the effect extensively is Carlos Fuentes' novella *Aura*. Being told that *you* are doing this and *you* are doing that, the reader of the work quickly feels disjointed, but that's appropriate and even useful because the reader has the same disconcertingly narrow range of understanding that the main character has. During a conversation I had with Señor Fuentes several years ago, I asked him why he had turned to the second-person point of view, and he said, "Poets have been using it a long time. I thought I'd try it in fiction."

The third-person point of view can take one of two forms: the limited or the objective. In the third-person *objective* point of view, the writer records surfaces without going into the mind of a character or narrator. Connotations of detail and phrase can, of course, suggest internal attitudes, but in this mode the writer maintains a distant stance, as we see in another poem by Renée Klein:

Mariya's Geese

Krym, Ukraine

> Mariya Gerasimenko herds her geese,
> guiding them to market
> with her simple branch broom.
> The goslings toddle with their heads down,
> searching for grain and bugs,   5
> while the large geese blare in protest
> and Mariya urges them on,
> *"Tega, tega, tega."*

RENÉE KLEIN

Keeping us at a distance from the character's internal concerns, the poet gives us a vivid image that suggests an ancient way of life; and even though the poem closes with a term from a language that is most likely foreign to the reader, the ending simultaneously emphasizes our closeness to the observed event and our cultural detachment from it.

The third-person *limited* point of view, however, allows a more direct presentation of internal concerns, as we see in another poem by Ms. Klein, "Behind the Screen Door," in which, while presenting the experience primarily from the outside, the poet's use of vocabulary— "She notes" (l. 4), "a merry cacophony" (l. 8), and "She . . . sleeps for tomorrow" (ll. 13–14) among others—takes us into the character's mind.

Her ancient hands rest
on the splintering divider
of the balding screen door.
She notes that the nests in the tree
have emptied and are tattered.   5
The trunk is adorned with cicada shells.
The crickets used to sing for her,
a merry cacophony of strings.
Then autumn arrived
and left her alone.   10
Sunrise
Sunset
She hangs up her cardigan
and sleeps for tomorrow.

RENÉE KLEIN

The omniscient point of view, which allows a narration to reveal internal responses of the various characters in a scene, is rarely used for several reasons. For more than a century, psychology has reminded us that we are all limited in our ranges of perception; none of us has direct access to the thoughts and feelings of others unless they reveal them to us. So a work told from an omniscient point of view might not be believable to readers or listeners. The omniscient point of view also tends to scatter a work's focus. If a narrative slips into the internal responses of various characters, the story's point of concern may blur and thus diminish a reader's involvement with the work. A version of the omniscient point of view, however, can be used effectively in relatively long works, or others made up of numerous sections. In novels or long poems, for instance, a writer might tell different sections from different points of view, as T.S. Eliot does in "The Waste Land." Usually, though, one would not mix different points of view within a single section.

The speaker of a piece, then, is the reader's immediate guide through an experience, that personal voice that brings portions of the world before us. At the same time that we see those images and hear ideas associated with them, we need to remember that we are not seeing the world directly; we're seeing it through the filter of a character. It's important, then, to recognize the situation from which the narrator is speaking. In Dylan Thomas's great poem "Fern Hill," for example, the narrator is describing the magic of the farm where he spent time as a child, but the incantatory quality of the language he uses, as well as the conceptual organization of his phrases, indicates that he is speaking years after the fact; the images and situations he recalls are not seen directly when they occur but through memory. Thomas even lets us know that the act of writing itself is the method by which the narrator is recalling the past. We see this most directly in the last stanza, which begins:

> Nothing I cared, in the lamb-white days, that time would take me
> Up to the swallow-thronged loft by the shadow of my hand,
> In the moon that is always rising

During the act of writing, as his phrases indicate, he notices the shadow under his hand, that shadow being a metonymic emblem of the act of writing itself. An idea like that is important because it reveals a context for the statements made by the narrator, and that context itself often reveals the terms of a drama. Keeping all of these matters in mind—speaker, dramatic situation, point of view—we become increasingly alert to the layers of a presentation, and we see the poem itself as a story whose narrative stance is both motivated and modified by the point of view from which the poem is told or said. Becoming more alert to that, we become more sensitive as well to the truth noted by the late Nobel laureate Octavio Paz in his book *The Bow and the Lyre:* "Every word implies two persons: the one who speaks and the one who hears" [35].

NOTES FOR SELECTED READINGS

Note how the persona in Lorna Dee Cervantes' poem, "Poem for the Young White Man . . ." is really the only person who can tell this poem. This exemplifies our position of a poem sometimes calling for only one "right" person to tell the poem.

Exercises

1. Create a situation or take a past situation you were in. Analyze all the different possibilities for speakers in a poem. Who ought to tell the poem? Then write the poem from that point of view. Then rewrite the same poem from a different point of view and notice how significantly changed the poem is.
2. Write a lyric poem in the first person point of view. Once the poem is finished go back to the poem and try to use the "I" only one time in the poem.
3. Find a news article or local event and write a poem about a person in the event from the third person point of view.

CHAPTER

8

FIXED FORMS: CREATING OUR POETIC WORLD

Form in poetry is something that can be very difficult to work with. But at the same time, it is one of those things that, once engaged in, can bring a great amount of satisfaction and knowledge. It seems to me that the thing I hear most about form from students is that trying to write in a fixed form of poetry—say a sonnet or a villanelle—does nothing but inhibit their creativity. Generally I agree. But I agree not because I think form itself inhibits creativity, but because many people try formal writing at a time when they aren't yet comfortable with it. They try to adapt their work to the form rather than adapt the form to their work.

Take the process of cooking. I cook and I love it. It's important to me to eat well and because I can't afford to hire a cadre of chefs, I need to know how to cook well. But I'm an entrée and sauce guy and always have been. I've spent time learning how to clarify butter for sauces to accompany quail breast or chicken. So when a friend asked me to bring a pie to party, I shuddered nervously and said I'd be happy to. After ruining one crust and then throwing another whole pecan pie across my kitchen—I know that sometimes it would give writers great pleasure to be able to heave the weight of a poem across a

> *I am more and more fascinated by the idea of form as creation or fiction of a universe, as a way of "knowing" the real universe. Form as a mode of participation in the real. It is not only in order to participate in the universe but also to participate in the self.*
>
> Robert Duncan

71

room—I finally half succeeded. Funny, but that was five years ago and it is only now that I have really learned how to make pie. But it didn't just come five years later; I've been making pies all these years. I've had the occasional masterpiece of a pie, I've burned some, I've ruined some. But now I can make a pie. I learned by following form and learning the necessary fundamentals of pastry baking and desserts. Now, I can get to creating in the kitchen.

Take, for instance, someone like the French poet Rimbaud, who seems not at all a formalist. But in breaking conventions, he circled round and round to fixed forms of poems. Take Picasso and his painting. Most people think of Picasso as a very abstract artist who did not necessarily adhere to fixed forms or formal elements of painting. But I marveled at his sketch books—especially his early sketch books—in one of the rooms of the Picasso museum in Barcelona, Spain. He had books and books of sketches that were almost classical in nature. Finely detailed portraits. Landscapes with the most minute and real details. Why? Because by understanding those fundamental rules that formed over the course of history, both artists were able to smash them later in their lives.

Understanding poetic forms can be a part of the creative process; and it is an engaging intellectual exercise which involves some memory. So it is important to approach fixed forms in poetry with an open mind and an ability to laugh while also taking them seriously. You're going to need to be able to look at some of the poems you create and laugh at them. But don't throw them away, as they give a yardstick of improvement and may, in fact, have something quite worthwhile in them. What will come of working through fixed forms of poetry is the ability to see practically and creatively how some elements we've already spoken of come together in a very structured way. Most importantly, we will see that form is something that requires all of our poetic attentiveness.

Start with something that seems easy. I'd suggest a **limerick** or a **haiku**. While I say they're easy, I mean only in relation to such other forms as the **sonnet** or **sestina**. We can move up to these. The haiku, for instance, was and still is a highly-refined and conscious art form. It attempts to express much but suggest even more in the fewest possible words. Hence, the haiku uses seventeen syllables in three lines of five, seven, and five syllables respectively. So begin with this. Write a number of them. Spend an hour a day for three days doing them in the morning and see how many you come up with. Some of the Japanese masters wrote thousands of them. While writing the haiku, you'll see something else happen, something that was part of their practice. As you form these three lines, often with three images, maybe linked explicitly, but often implicitly because of the need to suggest so much, you will find yourself becoming more alert to the world around you. This notation of what's around us centers us—and this was part of their practice. So you can see that, as our quote at the beginning of the chapter suggests, engaging in form is participating in the self and the universe.

Now that you've tried your hand at some form by working with haiku, you might try something a bit more difficult—such as the **sonnet**, sestina or villanelle. What is important to remember is that while we may work these forms with the understanding that they are from hundreds of years ago, we need to remember that our language has changed. Because it has changed, we need to try to avoid becoming archaic in our diction and syntax. Rather, try to use the language you know. Use the regular poetic language that you would use if you were working in free verse. What comes of this poetry is the type of contemporary twentieth-century formalism that has been exemplified by such poets as Mark Jarman and Stephen Dobyns in their sonnets.

While we have three major forms of the sonnet, you may like one more than the other. In her essay that follows, Lynn Hoggard discusses the structure of these three and how each develops in its form and content. Try them all and see how you do. Maybe you find your niche in the Petrarchan sonnet. But after you've tried writing all three, maybe you find that you blend the Petrarchan and Shakespearean sonnets. When writing initial drafts in these forms, try to remember two things: first, give yourself some breathing room constructing meter and second, keep slant rhyme in mind. These two things will help you get through a draft without getting hung up on the end of a line not rhyming exactly with the previous line. You can come back and work with the rhyme and meter. And I think it is important to avoid letting rhyme push you around. Elements need to work together—we need sound quality, rhythmic quality (meter), image quality, and rhyme. That's tough, but prioritize which of these is most important and then choose your words. What the sonnet can show us wonderfully is how textured a poem can be if we skillfully blend such things as rhyme, meter, a stanzaic pattern, and the qualities of image and other elements. And that is being truly creative.

If you decide to have a go at the villanelle, remember that this is a very strict form too. People like Elizabeth Bishop, Theodore Roethke, and Dylan Thomas have used it so well in our recent memory that it seems all else pales in comparison. At its best the villanelle can set up chant-like qualities that can be haunting and remarkably musical. But at its worst, as I have experienced many times, it can be monotonous and remarkably boring. As Ms. Hoggard points out, the trick is to have the key lines grow in their force and "then give a final, concluding punch." I would add, too, that it seems necessary to come up with interesting and creative lines as well. Without them the poem may fall flat and seem not to carry the weight we'd like. But it can be very hard to master this form in its traditional sense and capture the sense of language that is so incantatory. What Elizabeth Bishop (in her poem "One Art") and Julia Alvarez (in her poem "Woman's Work") show us is that this poetry can become highly stylized and very interesting when we use our natural, contemporary language and patterns of speech with (or against, as the case may be) this very traditional and tightly-woven form.

In many ways, the same goes for the sestina. Give the sestina a try. It may turn out to be a brain-twisting exercise for you, but it will no doubt help you appreciate the artistry behind coupling form and content. The structure of a sestina is technically difficult—a complicated play of words. The sestina is a poem comprised of six stanzas that each have six lines, and the poem finishes with a three-line stanza called an *envoy*. Hence, there are always thirty-nine lines in a sestina. The last words of the first six lines of the poem are repeated as the end words of the following five stanzas, and all the words must be included in the envoy. It is a traditional Italian form that was used as a form for love poetry in the thirteenth century. So if you wish to be somewhat true to form, here's your chance to write a love poem. What seems most taxing about the sestina is making our word choices work in each stanza. Hence, diction is at the center of this form. And we not only need the words to fit, but we hope that the words fall into the other stanzas and lines in a very natural and meaningful way.

While you may feel a bit beat up after working on some formal poems, don't despair. With all of this practicing of form, you hopefully will come out on the other side having learned some things about the tradition of poetics and how elements and structure can enhance your work, not hinder it. We would not have beautiful houses or plates of food without builders and chefs who know the form and function of all their elements. And whether we believe in the Big Bang and evolution or some higher deity and creationism, we can all marvel at the order in the universe and the remarkable order in our bodies; and we also marvel at the universe's ability to create and adapt. While we function within forms as poets, we must not allow our language to be owned by the form; rather, we create and adapt. The use of form should not be imposed on our poems. Rather, form should be chosen as an accompaniment to our content and used to illuminate what it is we have to express—the discovery of our world and of ourselves.

FORM IN POETRY

Lynn Hoggard

Why not let the poem flow however it chooses from the poet's imagination? Why box it into an artificial structure that can hinder its freedom and movement? The answer to these and similar questions regarding poetic form carries us inevitably to the nature of human creativity. We know that our universe has form and structure at every level—from the cosmic to the subatomic. As *homo sapiens* we are ourselves a form, distinct from bees, bears, and bulldozers, who tend to follow particular patterns of design and behavior. Our nature consistently pushes us to understand the forms around and within us; our acts of creation, like small imitations of our world, also have formal boundaries.

So form is important to us. But why have we loaded certain types of poems with such exceptional burdens, such as the breathtakingly complicated *sestina?* Can there be any reason for such complex structures other than sheer pyrotechnical display?

The answer, quite simply, is yes. The vast body of lovely, noble poems created in amazing complexity tells us that not only does form seem not to hinder the poet, it seems, at least some of the time, to inspire poetry to greater heights. The Italian Renaissance poet Petrarch, for example, wrote 366 poems to and about his beloved Laura, most of them in a sonnet form that came to bear his name.

If poetic expression differs from prose in that it tends to be more condensed and highly charged, then this expression, within a congenial form, can become even more intense and perhaps truer to the form-conscious nature of human experience. For the poet (as well as for the appreciative reader), the successful marriage of poetic impulse to form reaches an artistic pinnacle that shows how imagination and craft can join self (poetic impulse) to world (the forms we live in). The very best poems may not always be the most formally complex, but they are poems in which form and content most consistently sustain and enhance each other.

The limerick, for example—one of the simplest and most playful of poetic forms (an impression created by its anapestic [˘ ˘ ´] beat that jogs between dimeter and trimeter feet)—works best with a simple, jaunty subject matter that sometimes ends with a smart-alecky kick:

> There was a young man from Laredo
> who ate nothing else but potato;
> he swallowed one down
> then remarked with a frown:
> "I prefer my potato *alfredo!*"   5

Poetic scansion shows the five-line rhyme scheme to be *aabba;* lines one, two, and five (that is, all the *a*'s) are, with some variation, basically anapestic trimeter, and lines three and four (the *b*'s), dimeter. The ensemble rocks along with the insouciance appropriate to humor and satire but alien to serious or searching reflection. Most importantly, however, content and form are joined.

Whereas the lighthearted limerick is closely allied to Irish popular culture, the haiku, another technically simple form, comes from Japan and is often spiritual and reflective (requiring 17 syllables divided into three-, five-, and seven-syllable lines; the haiku in English translation sometimes varies this pattern). In fact, at its deepest levels, the haiku harks back to Zen Buddhism and the work of a seventeenth- and eighteenth-century monk named Bashō. Haiku has no jaunty meters or rhymes. Usually, it has an image of nature (a crow, for example, settling on a branch) followed by the superposition of another image (an autumn nightfall), leading us to see one image in terms of the other. This delicate, surprising, and understated perception of oneness in nature happens because the haiku form shapes and sustains the images:

> On a withered branch
> a crow alights, then settles:
> now, autumn nightfall.

English and American poetry have tended to prefer the iambic (˘ ´) stress or foot in a five-stress (pentameter) line, although the iambic tetrameter (four-stress) line is also popular, perhaps because these two meters approximate more closely than others the rhythms of ordinary English speech. The four-line stanza (or quatrain) has also become the most common division of a poem into segments; rhyming variations on the quatrain abound, but the most common are *aabb, abab, abba, xaya,* and *axay* (in which *x* and *y* indicate nonrhyming lines).

Among the more complex forms of poetry that incorporate the quatrain, the most well-known is the sonnet—a term from the Italian *sonetto* meaning a little sound or song. In English, the classic sonnet form is fourteen rhyming iambic pentameter lines. Variations in rhyme pattern divide the sonnet into three major types—the Petrarchan (or Italian), the Spenserian, and the Shakespearean—with each type suggesting its own formal structure. A brief look shows how each works.

The Petrarchan sonnet comprises an *octave* (or eight-line sequence) usually rhyming *abbaabba* and a *sestet* (six-line sequence) usually rhyming *cdccdc* or *cdcdcd*. As the form indicates, the rhyme divides between the *octave* and *sestet*, suggesting a division in thought as well. That division, in fact, is what Petrarch emphasized in the example cited below, in which the persona in the *octave* expresses sublime and undying love for Laura (a love that continued even after her death), then, in the *sestet*, falls back to earth to assess a less-than-sublime reality:

> Those eyes I raved about in ardent rhyme,
> the arms, the hands, the feet, the loving face
> that split my soul in two, and made me pass
> my life apart from all the common throng,
> the tumbled mane of uncut gold that shone,   5
> that angel smile whose flash made me surmise
> the very earth had turned to Paradise,
> have come to dust: no life, no sense. Undone.
> And I live on, in sorrow and self-scorn
> here where the light I steered by gleams no more   10
> for my dismasted ship, wracked by the storm.
> Let there be no more love songs! The dear spring

of my accustomed art has been drained dry,
my lyre itself dissolved in so much weeping.

WESTERN LITERATURE IN A WORLD CONTEXT, VOL. I, #292
(trans. by Patricia Clark Smith)

This two-part structure, then, dramatizes a dialogue between oppo-
sites. In the Romance languages (including French, Italian, and Spanish),
where rhymes are plentiful, the four-rhyme Petrarchan sonnet is less difficult than it is in English, which is a relatively rhyme-poor language. The
Spenserian and Shakespearean sonnets, therefore, enlarged the English
rhyming possibilities while also modifying the way the poem develops.
The Spenserian (named for Edmund Spenser, the sixteenth-century poet
who wrote "The Faerie Queen" in honor of England's Elizabeth I) has
three loosely-interlocking quatrains (rhyming *abab, bcbc, cdcd*) followed
by a rhyming couplet (*ee*). If content parallels form, we can assume a
series of three loosely-connected thoughts followed by a terse summa-
tion, perhaps delivered with flair and wit.

The Shakespearean sonnet relaxed the sonnet form even more by
breaking the linking rhyme among stanzas (*abab, cdcd, efef*); one could
therefore choose whether to interrelate the stanzaic ideas while still keeping, of course, the airy panache of the concluding couplet.

> Let me not to the marriage of true minds
> Admit impediments. Love is not love
> Which alters when it alteration finds,
> Or bends with the remover to remove:
> Oh, no! It is an ever-fixéd mark,   5
> That looks on tempests and is never shaken;
> It is the star to every wandering bark,
> Whose worth's unknown, although his height be taken.
> Love's not Time's fool, though rosy lips and cheeks
> Within his bending sickle's compass come;   10
> Love alters not with his brief hours and weeks,
> But bears it out even to the edge of doom.
> If this be error and upon me proved,
> I never writ, nor no man ever loved.

SHAKESPEAREAN SONNET #116, NAP

Even more daunting than the sonnet are the French *villanelle* and the
Italian *sestina*, used nevertheless with success in English by some of the
world's most renowned poets (including Dylan Thomas, T. S. Eliot, and
W. H. Auden). The villanelle contains five three-line units (call *tercets*)
rhyming *aba*, followed by a quatrain (*abaa*); however, instead of simply

rhyming end-words, the villanelle repeats the entire line, as indicated by the following schema (whose numbers indicate lines): *a(1)ba(2), aba(1), aba(2), aba(1), aba(2), aba(1)a(2)*. Notice that line one of the poem is also the last line of the second and fourth tercets and that line three is the last line of the third and fifth. Lines one and three also form the last two lines of the poem. The trick, obviously, is to have these lines grow in the course of the poem to mean slightly different things each time they recur, then give a final, concluding punch. Dylan Thomas's poem at his father's death is perhaps the best-known villanelle in English:

Do Not Go Gentle into That Good Night

Do not go gentle into that good night,
Old age should burn and rave at close of day;
Rage, rage against the dying of the light.
Though wise men at their end know dark is right,
Because their words had forked no lightning they   5
Do not go gentle into that good night.
Good men, the last wave by, crying how bright
Their frail deeds might have danced in a green bay,
Rage, rage against the dying of the light.
Wild men who caught and sang the sun in flight,   10
And learn, too late, they grieved it on its way,
Do not go gentle into that good night.
Grave men, near death, who see with blinding sight
Blind eyes could blaze like meteors and be gay,
Rage, rage against the dying of the light.   15
And you, my father, there on the sad height,
Curse, bless, me now with your fierce tears, I pray.
Do not go gentle into that good night.
Rage, rage against the dying of the light.

NEW DIRECTIONS PAPERBACKS

The *sestina*, the most complex of the many forms used by medieval troubadours, contains six stanzas of six lines each followed by a conclusion or *envoy* of three lines. Each stanza includes the same six end-words, but in a constantly shifting yet fixed pattern (for example, the schema of end-words might look like this: 1. *abcdef*, 2. *faebdc*, 3. *cfdabe*, 4. *ecbfad*, 5. *deacfb*, 6. *bdfeca*, and as envoy, *eca* or *ace*, possibly with the *bdf* rhymes recurring internally in the envoy).

Much less complex is the folk ballad, which is a short narrative song usually in quatrains (*xaya*) in which iambic tetrameter lines (one and three) alternate with iambic trimeter (two and four). Ballad meter, also called common meter, is used in hymns as well as folk ballads:

> The wind doth blow today, my love,
> And a few small drops of rain;
> I never had but one true-love,
> In cold grave she was lain.
> . . . .

"The Unquiet Grave," NAP

Finally, we come to free verse. What relationship exists between the set forms discussed above and the seemingly unstructured poetry often written in America today? Doesn't this contemporary style actually involve the absence of form and a rebellion against the patterns of the past? The poems themselves yield interesting answers. Yes, there does seem to be a desire to "free" poetry from rigid obedience to set forms, but this move to freedom does not, in its better moments, abandon form. Rather than being set previously and externally, free verse is more individualized, more impromptu, and more organically part of its context. Abandoning strict patterns of rhyme and rhythm, free verse searches (as did many forms of ancient poetry) for line divisions based on rhythmic phrases, breath units, or syntactical possibilities and for assonance, alliteration, and internal or approximate rhyme rather than end-rhyme. In free verse, words, rich with relationships to one another and full of connotative aftershocks are extraordinarily charged with formal responsibilities. Throwing off external restraints, free verse grows its own form from within:

> Let the snake wait under
> his weed
> and the writing
> be of words, slow and quick, sharp
> to strike, quiet to wait,   5
> sleepless.
> . . . .

William Carlos Williams, "A Sort of a Song," NAP

NOTES FOR SELECTED READINGS

Note Kevin Stein's use of multiple sonnets in a sequence in his poem "An American Tale of Sex and Death." Compared to Sor Juana Ines de la Cruz and Elizabeth Barrett Browning you can see a contemporary use of the sonnet from compared to more traditional uses of the sonnet.

Exercises

1. Spend some time devising two lines that are related to each other in concept. Also, make the lines imagistic and rhythmic. Then use these lines to write a villanelle.
2. Using a current love in your life, a friend, a romantic partner, or a child in your family as your subject matter, write a sonnet about them and the love present because of them.
3. Write a three-, four-, or six-line stanza and don't concern yourself with it as a poem. Then create a metrical pattern in the stanza. You can also infuse it with rhyme if that helps to find the meter.

CHAPTER

9

PUTTING IT ALL TOGETHER: THE WHOLE POEM

When I was a third-year college student I spent a year studying abroad in London. To this day it remains one of the most pivotal and important experiences in my life. I gained a sense of independence, learned how to adapt in new places and cultures, broadened my view of the world, and created friendships with people from around the globe. I learned, from seasoned experts, the value of traveling and how to do it well. And now when I travel I like to experience the whole of a place as much as I can. I like to eat as much as I can of many different kinds of food. I like to drink the local wines. I enjoy hearing music from different regions, seeing folk dances, talking to people, and sitting to watch people in a plaza. Shopping can also be great fun. I try not to miss the museums and places of religious worship and I soak in the architecture. If I can, I fish in the area. I know this sounds ideal, maybe even a bit extreme. And it takes more than a few days. But when I leave, I feel I've had a chance to see the whole of a place, and that's important to me. A bad day of fishing on a chalk stream in England can be counteracted by the charm of nice people and a few good pubs. Or reverse this last statement. A few bad pubs and rude people can be counteracted by good fishing. So, the beauty of traveling comes from having the whole of a place represented.

A carpenter, a builder knows what Ponderosa pine can do, what Douglas fir can do, what Incense cedar can do and builds accordingly. You can build some very elegant houses without knowing that, but some of them aren't going to work, ultimately.

Gary Snyder

It isn't much different when it comes to writing poetry. We've already talked about many parts of the poem as separate entities. But as we write a poem these parts come together to form a whole. They work with and against each other. They brace each other the way beams on a house hold up the roof and they give us room to move around inside. For instance a poem, perhaps fifteen lines long, narrative in style, and portraying just a few images while trying to make a point, may seem to almost work. But ultimately it's like a house that has only been framed. We know from the street that it's a house. We can even walk through and see where the kitchen goes, where we'd sleep if we moved in, even where the toilets go. But, it's not finished. Add some sound quality with careful diction, some rhyme (maybe internal, maybe end-rhyme), a close attention to the rhythm of lines, a bit of metaphor and/or simile in the images, and soon the house becomes walled in and filled with character that speaks to us. Add the poem's core experience (the triggering and real experiences maybe) and now we have a place where we can live— now we (the reader and the writer) have a home. This is what a poem ought to be. And in all of this metaphor about the house, let us not forget Hemingway's advice that the elements are not mere decoration and adornment but the structural and the architectural integrity of our writing.

When putting together a poem, it's important to remember that the poem doesn't just piece itself together. Nor does it just come all at once as a package. As Naomi Shihab Nye states in one of her poems, *You can't order a poem like you order a taco.* Maybe not, but you can build a poem like you build a taco. And that takes work. It takes moving through the initial process of homing in on that triggering subject, then following that into the poem, letting the poem turn you in different directions, and coming out the other side with a draft of something to work with. Along the way, count on it, we've included some things like rhyme and line breaks that have added some resonance or depth or artistic quality to the poem. But then again, we've missed some too. So, that's when we head back to work on other parts. But the only way we can do this effectively is to know where and when and how the pieces fit. Take the following lines, for example, in a poem about a boy growing up and living on an almond orchard.

> I climbed them and knocked
> the skirts of blossoms to the ground,
> the sweet smell of trees.
> If I got caught, my dad lashed us
> like an old school teacher.   5

Well, there are some good things here. But this was a first draft and in our workshop we all told the student to go back and work on it some more because this was one of his better outings. So he and I talked over the poem and I told him to revise for his images, sound quality (maybe some internal rhyme), and line breaks. As you can see, he was well on his way. The poem started when he came to class one day saying "I think there is a poem in the almond orchard I grew up on." Of course, there's a book of poems hiding in the orchard. Here's what he came back with.

> I climbed them and
> skirts of blossoms danced
> to the ground around the tree,
> the scent of young girls made of smiles.
> To be caught, a dry switch sharp as fire   5
> lashed my leg, quick as the wing of a bird.

We were impressed with the revision because he changed some things significantly, added new elements (note the internal rhyme and the end-rhyme), and revised his images to include similes. And the piecing together that really showed some thought was taking the father out and only implying that he was the one to lash the boy. While this was a case in point about the quality of revision, it also illustrated how taking the time to add the elements together could help strengthen the whole of something. In this case, he derived more resonance from the lines and more power from the images. After getting his subject down, he took the time to go back and work in the rhyme. He told us in class that he wanted to include as many parts of poetics as possible, so he made a list and checked them off as he went. That may sound like a funny approach, and in class we all had a good laugh with him. But let's face it, it worked.

What he did was what the fiction writer Ron Carlson calls "taking inventory." While Mr. Carlson talks about taking inventory in the first paragraph of a story to see what's there, what will come up again, what won't, what might, and what's there that's unexpected, we can do the same with a poem. While writing poems, it's important to take stock of what you have included and what you haven't. In the preceding example, the writer knew the orchard images were coming. He knew his father was coming although he didn't intend him to come out so mean. But the girls? Where did they come from? For our writer, that was an unexpected twist that he liked—we all liked it. So he took stock of it. That specific image of girls didn't work itself into any greater image or thread in the poem but it did come out later as another poem. But then an inventory happened on another level, which was what really caused the writing to gain steam. He asked what poetic elements he had included and what he hadn't—and this led to building more and more inside the poem. Asking ourselves what we've included is important. Listening to where the poem wants to go and facing that is important too. If we do both of these things we'll wind up building a poem in which the reader can live and experience the world.

NUTS & BOLTS ADVICE

What follows is some advice that I've picked up while writing. It's all been passed on to me by other people, and I wish it had been given to me a long while back. But then, that's not how we get advice. Some of it has come as rules or maxims I apply to my own writing and some has come in the form of quotes, but all of it is intended to be helpful in building poems.

- You can't write a good poem without having a subject to write about.
- Don't try to achieve greatness—you'll be disappointed. Often, as Marianne Moore points out, "a result which is sensational is implemented by what to the craftsman was private and unsensational."
- A poem should have the appearance of having meant something to you when you wrote it.
- William Archer said, "We have literature when we impart distinctiveness to ordinary talk and make it still seem ordinary."
- Let's face it, love and poetry are linked. When we fall in love, we write poems. But as we make mistakes in our relationships, so do we foul up poems. We can write bad poems about good relationships and good poems about bad relationships. And we can fix both.
- Write your dreams down; they tell us a lot.
- Don't throw things away because you'll never know when you might need them. A line that seems bad today may seem useful tomorrow.
- Read your poems aloud—to roommates, to your parents, to siblings, to your kids. Read them to anyone who will listen, and you too should listen. If something is wrong with the poem, you'll hear it.
- Don't be afraid to change the *truth* in order to help a poem. You own the poem.
- Listen to your parents and grandparents; they have stories to tell and they're our links to the past.
- Write about the tragedy in your life and make it ours.
- Each time you feel yourself getting better and reaching a new level of competence, find a few elements of poetry you haven't used or tried before and use them as much as you can, even if you use them badly.
- I had a teacher who said "Never use more than one abstract in the first sentence (not line, *sentence*) of a poem." Be concrete.
- Why avoid rhyme? That would be like a trumpet player avoiding slurs or sixteenth notes or holding notes. Rhyme helps create music and rhythm in the lines as well as other things.
- Write regularly and be receptive to what comes. Know that some days you'll be good and others you won't. But if you do this, you won't have to wait for impulses or subjects to come—they will be there waiting for you to open the door. And even on days when it seems as if you haven't written a poem, you will have written possibilities.

These nuts and bolts are intended to be helpful pieces of advice for the building of poems. When we sit down to write, there is much to put together and much we need to be attentive to. Write, and rewrite; write, and rewrite: that's the building process. Within that process, be creative and put together an approach that works for you. Take note of your voice and how you begin to sound in poems. Notice what kind of stamp you put on your poems— maybe you use internal rhyme regularly. Maybe your favorite thing is metaphor or alliteration or ambiguity. No matter; these are the components, the materials which build that house we spoke of earlier, which frame it, wall it in, give us room to move inside, and give it character. In the long and short of it, build us into your life, mortar us into your experience, and paint us into your flesh so we see your world as ours.

LORCA'S *DUENDE*, THE ART OF ZINGERS IN POETRY WORKSHOPS, OR HOW TO TEACH STUDENTS TO ENERGIZE THEIR POEMS

Virgil Suarez

Federico Garcia Lorca, while writing *Poet in New York*, listening to jazz and blues in New York's night scene, and while studying English at Columbia University, theorized about what he termed *"Duende."* In Spanish, *duende* has several translations, and the particular one I remember from my childhood is that of the *duende* being a gentle guide, a sort of gypsy of the countryside, not entirely bad or evil, simply a force to be recognized and nurtured. It is a certain charm, recognition of darkness and light, a deep feeling, whether melancholia or joy that comes to the poet, the artist, anyone who believes in craft. When you work on a poem from invention, through revision, to its final form, the *duende* will be there. For *Star Wars* fans, the *duende* is like The Force the wise Yoda reveals to Young Luke Skywalker.

Lorca means for *"duende"* to be a positive force, not only in the *cante jondo* music he so loved, but in poetry. Having grown dissatisfied with early Romantic theories of *cante jondo* as a form of popular folksongs as "impersonal, vague, unconscious creation," he set out to define clearly what he meant by *"duende."* In his lecture on deep song, he states that "the difference between a good *cantaor* and a bad *cantaor* is that the first has *duende*, and the second never, ever achieves it."

Without *duende*, the poet is left empty-handed, his or her poems will be flat, uneven; in many cases not even a strict form can help. Nothing will without it. Young poets in poetry workshops always mention that moment of pure inspiration when only then can they sit down to write. With *duende*, the moment is always there if you learn to summon *duende* through hard work and know-how. Craft comes to the poet through practice, through developing skills. The beauty of writing poetry is always that deep sense of discovery, the twist along the way that can surprise us, awaken in us a tremendous sense of awe. As a young poet myself, I had very good teachers who recognized early on not so much the talent, but my ability to be open for the *duende's* influence. Through the act of writing every day, you learn to stay in touch with the *duende*. By writing ideas, brainstorming for possibilities, contemplating the world around you, paying very close attention to the small details, through layering, through the dynamics of word choice, sentence (line) structure, grammar, you cause the *duende* to arrive. The trick of everyday writing is to stay close with your *duende*.

If you think of "*duende*" as the equivalent to what we call "mojo," then you are closer to understanding the force that makes poetry cry out with distinctive energy, and what I would call zinger.

A simple formula to remember as a student of poetry is *duende* = (unknown + known) = zinger. Zinger is a word for word energy, word combinations that will make your lines so distinctive and clear, nobody could ever mistake them for someone else's. I think here of three poets who come quickly to mind: Charles Simic, Charles Wright, and Billy Collins. If you look at each of these poets' poetry, word by word, line by line, stanza by stanza, impact for impact, you will see that their poetry breathes newness, originality of thought, pure zinger! I also have two good poet friends whom I consider masters of the zinger: Juan Felipe Herrera and Ray Gonzalez. You couldn't, having picked up a poem by either of these two poets, mistake their work. Every word is chosen carefully, combined with others that are fresh, thought-provoking, that constantly move the poem and the reader to a new level of meaning and observation about things that matter in the world.

Later in the same essay, Lorca approaches a more formal definition of *duende*: "The *duende* is a momentary burst of inspiration, the blush of all that is truly alive, all that the performer is creating at a certain moment. The *duende* resembles what Goethe called the 'demoniacal.' It manifests itself principally among musicians and poets of the spoken word, rather than among painters and architects, for it needs the trembling of the moment and then a long silence."

We are to believe, based on this definition, that the poet is possessed by both possibilities: the trembling of moment and then a long silence. I teach my students that they can train themselves to "know" how to recognize those moments when ideas will grip them, hold them, and that if they don't learn to summon the "*duende*," learn to trust it almost as a sixth sense, then they can never write poetry that matters, that lasts. I'm intrigued, I confess to them, by the process of writing poetry, the mystery of the act itself, if you will, when suddenly an idea for a poem strikes you, and you better act, sit down and write, sit down and listen carefully. I've always written from having paid close attention to those voices that suddenly speak in my mind.

The *duende* is a helpful guide. When the right mood or inspiration doesn't arrive, the *duende* can see the poet through. Once the student has learned how to tap into this source for ideas, for what is known or not known, then the poetry will come easier. The job of writing poetry is never easy or to be taken lightly. It is work, like any other, and in order to achieve a mastery, one needs all the help one can get.

The *duende* can be coaxed through intense meditation upon the act of writing, the act of creation or invention, through revision, mostly during these long stages of revision, and during the completing stages of a poem. I know a lot of good poets who have learned to call their *duendes* forth through their rich, distinct voices. They have been able to unify content, poetic voice, and technique into one, which whether or not they recognize it as such, I would call *duende*. Among contemporary singers, *duende* is easy to recognize. Billie Holliday had it. So did Patsy Cline. So did Janis Joplin. So does Aretha Franklin. Frank Sinatra had it. Tony Bennett has it. It is always easier to recognize *duende* in performance. The poet works behind the scenes. In the lonely light of a room. In silence and solitude. All the poet can do is create the poem, then let it stand on its own. If it has *duende*, it travels far. If it doesn't, it dies instantly.

One more aspect of the *duende* is its insistence on perfection, follow-through of technique, its stubborn need to craft a better poem. It might take you a long time to finish a poem, but if it is possessed by *duende*, the payoff is tremendous. In my conversations with my good friend, colleague, and fellow poet David Kirby, who writes very long narrative poems, I've learned that his *duende* is with him at all times. I have been with David Kirby when he's reached into his pocket to bring forth a little scrap of paper and a pen to write something down. I've learned to recognize the flashes of ideas in his eyes, and he acts on them quickly. He is also one of the most voracious readers I know. David Kirby reads everything, from biographies to travel guides, magazines, newspapers, lots of contemporary poetry, essays on craft, interviews, and all the literary journals he can get his hands on. The poet learns not only through writing, but through intense reading and contemplation.

At the beginning of every semester, I tell my students in the poetry workshop to keep a living, breathing (I'll explain more in a moment) journal, to observe life in the world as though they were social scientists. I encourage them to read magazines like *National Geographic, Time, Double Take, Orion,* and many other wonderful magazines that mix photography with articles and essays about other people, other cultures. About nature. I encourage them to collect How-To books, field guides, dictionaries like *The Facts on File Visual Dictionary,* which I received as a gift from my roommate when I was in college. He had a form of dyslexia that prevented him from remembering simple names for objects, and I fell in love with his copy because in it you can find practically everything. For example, when you look up rifle, which I had to do recently while working on a poem, it names the parts, the all-too-important parts that make up the whole of the rifle—*hammer, firing pin, breech, firing chamber, trigger, lever, stock, butt*, et cetera. I urge my students to keep their junk mail catalogues, which list gadgets, things that clutter our daily lives, but which might make interesting ideas for poems.

The more the students read, the better. I encourage them to start their own poetry collection of works by other poets, a neat shelf by their worktable or computer, to begin with those poets they like, admire, whose own poetry inspires, reveals, enlightens. In my case, I keep Pablo Neruda, Stephen Mallarmé, Mary Oliver, Pat Mora, Leroy V. Quintana, and many others quickly at hand. When I sit down to write a poem and I get stuck, I reach over and page through someone else's poems. You take a little in, and a little goes a long way. It's good to know how other poets craft their poems. I read interviews like those found in so many literary journals and magazines. Both *Poets & Writers* and *The AWP Chronicle* are excellent sources.

By keeping a journal, the student keeps track of thoughts, ideas; you can cut and paste things into it from newspapers and magazines. What I believe most students like about keeping a journal is the individual feel it brings to the act of writing, taking notes, remembering interesting moments. So much of my poetry comes from things I've written down in my journal: seeds for ideas, titles, even particular lines that come to me in the middle of the night or, more often than not, while I am driving.

If the *duende* is the method by which we allow ourselves to be open to and keep track of good ideas, then my idea of capturing the zinger is the daily tool. When we begin to workshop poems in the classroom, I tell my students to circle all the most striking words, images, lines in their classmates' poems. This is a good way of isolating the specific from the general bulkiness of a poem.

For example, last semester one of my students wrote this poem:

Spirit Warrior of Wisconsin

The story goes that Kenny just vanished in the woods
north of Menomonee Falls, WI, when he was fourteen,
that spirits of old Menomonee Indians crept from the furrows
of tree-shadows, their graves, to claim him, retribution
for a village with McDonald's, Wal-Mart, and Denny's   5
overrunning their ancient land. After two weeks,
the police stopped searching and it became local legend,

every missing softball at the park or MIA kitty was Kenny's
fault, now a junior Indian spirit warrior, indoctrinated
into a culture long-dead, his body tucked under mossy   10
logs and rotting like fruit left out too long in the sun, never
to be found again. When I was twenty-three, I saw Kenny
in Tampa, on a Carnival cruise ship heading to the Bahamas
on a three day turn-around. He dealt blackjack at the neon
glitz casino and served pina coladas during the midnight   15
variety show. The last night, he brought me a free whiskey
sour and asked how his parents were, and could I tell them
that he was okay, that he was just young and foolish
and didn't mean to hurt anyone? I said yes, but never breathed
a word to anyone. Some legends are meant to live, and I wanted   20
Kenny's soul awake on the mouths of children to come,
generations of kids who would fear the dark, the deep quarry
shadows, always wondering if Indian spirits stalked them,
war spears feathered and ready, longing again for bloodwork.

RYAN VAN CLEAVE

Obviously this is a poem from a more advanced student, but one that
can get the workshop thinking in terms of zingers, those interesting
words and lines that can be mined for energy and originality. A poem like
this is always a good place to start, a poem that tells a story, not that they
are the easiest, but they get a narrative started. It gives the poet (and
reader) the sense that it has a beginning, middle, and end.

The analogy I use to introduce the idea of revision with a poem like
this is the story of how I went out and bought a Sears lawn tractor, and
how when asked by the salesperson what diameter blade I wanted I said
the smallest, which baffled the salesperson because they are used to getting the right answer, which is bigger, and wider. The less time on the
tractor to cut two acres, the better. With me, it is the other way. I opted for
a smaller blade diameter because I enjoy mowing my lawn. I cut it every
other Saturday. It's the rhythm of the cutting, the back and forth, the circling around each tree on my property, much like what happens when
I write, then revise, my poems.

The student of poetry needs to realize that simply sitting down to
write a first draft is not enough. As good as each word may be, as inven-
tive as the idea, as energized as each line may sound, feel, a first draft is
only a beginning. Like my riding a lawn tractor and cutting grass, the
student needs to learn to ride through his or her poem time and time
again. Slowly. Paying close attention to every word on every line.

I call this layering, this act of the back and forth. When I look at my
lines or the lines of my students' poems, I like to isolate them. I often cut
a rectangular window out of another piece of paper, wide enough for a

single line to peek through, and I move the window down as I read. I isolate the lines, read them one at a time, pointing out what my expectations as a reader and writer are for the previous and subsequent lines. It's a good method to help imagine what is likely to come before and after each line. I did this with the student poem I've chosen to discuss here.

"Spirit Warrior of Wisconsin" is a very strong beginning. I like the idea immediately that the poet is going to tell us a story, that there are very specific details, names of places, popular culture infused early on. There are also interesting word combinations like "furrows of tree-shadows," "blackjack at the neon glitz casino," and "awake in the mouths of children,". . . . And the poem turns unexpectedly for the better when the voice in the poem tells us that "I saw Kenny in Tampa, on a Carnival cruise ship heading to the Bahamas." This is a most welcome twist, one that I use to remind everyone in the class of the possibility of *duende*. One problem remains though. A problem with fact. Yes, poets are also responsible for verisimilitude and accuracy of fact. Carnival cruises don't leave for the Bahamas from Tampa. It's closer from Miami. I was able to bring this out simply because of personal experience. It sounds nit-picky but we want the poem to work at all the levels here. It is only when everything sounds and is right, that we breathe life into the poem. But the twist in the poem is extremely effective. This is precisely the kind of twist that knowing and trusting our individual *duende* can be illuminated in our poems.

There are times in the poem when the language gets a little tired, overused, like "fruit left out too long in the sun," "some legends are meant to live," and "local legend." They bring a chatty quality to the poem that's not necessary. I think the poem works best at the level of surprise and discovery. Things happen because they are possible in the world of this poem, and in our world as well. The fact that Kenny disappears, never to be heard from again, is an interesting challenge to pull off, not only in the poem, but in real life. It is an interesting question. Can someone simply disappear one day and never be heard of or from again? Sure, it happens in America every day. When it happens in this poem, it awakens a sense of interest in us: the possibility that, like in real life, someone can walk away. Then the poem takes a leap into new territory. You could argue that the voice is as surprised as the reader by this "setup" of finding Kenny dealing blackjack on a cruise ship. Even the brief exchange between the persona of the poem and Kenny is an interesting turn because, why not? Kenny should come back; he should speak. That he asks the persona to tell his parents that he, Kenny, is okay, is good. The part about being young and foolish is not needed in the poem. I urged the student to cut that out.

Another important point is the connection between what happens to Kenny and the persona's recognition that "Some legends are meant to live, and I wanted Kenny's soul awake in the mouths of children to come. . . ." This is what the poem is about, but it is written in an extremely flat and too-straightforward a fashion. The zinger needs to be discovered, a way by which the last three or four lines of the poem can be reenergized. Ending lines need to be as interesting as the beginning lines that beckon or hook the reader. I like "deep quarry shadows" and "war spears feathered and ready." These are interesting images, or image constructions, but the poem doesn't end correctly. "Longing again for bloodwork" doesn't leap at us the way a strong zinger line ending should.

I almost wish the poem ended with a strong realization about the connection between the persona's desire for the universal and Kenny's sudden departure. This is what happens to people alive in the world—people who on a daily basis walk away because of a job in another state, because they go off to college, because they get married, because of madness, because of a crime—people can disappear. Vanish. This is a powerful idea for the poem. This can be a strong connection. Death makes us aware of what happens to people, though the debate still rages in terms of whether they go to a place called heaven or simply return as fertilizer to the earth. Regardless, the poem should end with a flash of recognition for these things.

The *duende* doesn't come fast, or cheap. The student must learn through daily discipline and work to coax it to come and stay. Many contemporary American poets are witness to the power of the *duende* in their poetry. Great readers know of the *duende* in poetry they like because they can recognize it on every line, every page. It's what brings them to the poetry of so many wonderful poets like Adrienne Rich, Sonia Sanchez, Alberto Ríos, Quincy Troupe, and countless others.

May the *duende* be with you, too.

NOTES FOR SELECTED READINGS

Note how the various levels of Bruce Weigl's poem "Song of Napalm" come together, mostly in the form of images and memories, to form a resonant closing to the poem.

Exercises

1. In a poem you've written, take inventory of the concrete objects in stanza one. Then ask a question of them and the poem: Do they come back later in the poem and do they hold any importance or resonance to the poem? If not, why? If so, are they pulling the emotional or intellectual energy of the poem through them?

2. Choose two narrative lines that will go in the same poem, perhaps one about your grandmother's death and one about ice skating

with her as a child. Then write a poem using both narrative lines and make them converge by the end of the poem.

3. Take a poem you've already written and analyze its movement. Does it have a high level and a low level—what Billy Collins terms the Alpha and Omega? Does it surprise us and turn somewhere unexpectedly? Does it drive on like a team of dogs? Does it pull back?

CHAPTER

10

REVISION

I grew up fishing with my grandfather. When I was very young and we fished together I couldn't bait a hook, tie a leader, or put on a lure without him checking my work. And it's only now that I really recall how much he did check my work. This didn't bother me; I learned from it. He was an artist with a tackle box, and I considered him a master. He could rig lines, tie knots, bait hooks, weight lines, release fish, and clean fish with amazing grace and patience and elegance. He was better than anyone I knew. So when he checked my work, I watched and either got his approval or got a lesson in doing it better and then did it again. This was revision at its finest. And it was my earliest lesson at how to go about revising.

Since then I've learned a thing or two about revision in my life. Specifically, I learned how to revise my writing. Moreover, I realize that there's not a process we engage in that we don't revise. We are constantly revising. When we cook, we give the sauce a taste to see what it's missing before we serve our guests. When we mow the lawn, we go back and get the long spot in the middle that we missed on the first pass. When we raise children, we go back and assess how effective we were in praising or scolding. When we go

Those of us who find life bewildering and who don't know what things mean, but love the sound of words enough to fight through draft after draft of a poem, can go on writing—try to stop us.

Richard Hugo

out on a date, the next day we always say, "My God, did I sound like a total idiot when I asked her why she . . . ?" So there's no reason to avoid revision when we write.

The reasons we invent for avoiding revision when we write, however, are many. As writers we ought to love revision—it's our chance to make things better, to tighten our hold on something, to take out bad lines, or to add something delicate or something powerful. And yet for many, revision is the scourge of the writing process. It's the moment in creating a poem that we like least, that we sometimes don't engage in. And then when we do, it's minimal. I see people regularly in our workshops who hand in "revised" poems with only one or two words changed. At the most, maybe a line is broken slightly differently than in the first draft. That line change is a step in the right direction, but one- or two-word changes don't really constitute revision. Why do we avoid it with such vigor? Maybe because we have spent so much time creating the poem that we think we are finished with it. Or maybe we feel we would impose too much on what was "creative." Maybe we're simply overwhelmed by or uncomfortable with revision—we don't know exactly what to revise or how to go about it.

Before we talk about how to go about revision, it's important to briefly address the previous reason for avoiding revision. If you feel that you will take out the creative purity of a poem by revising it, just remember that you become creative when you revise. And that makes revision part of the creative process. Consider the fishing metaphor. When my grandfather was fishing and he wasn't catching fish, he'd change things. Maybe he'd change the bait or the lure. But maybe he'd just reel the lure a little faster or slower, maybe give it a little jig up and down occasionally. Sometimes he'd change the depth where he was fishing. But many of these little revisions to his presentation produced fish, and, of course, that was the exciting and fun result we were looking for. If, for instance, you're someone who is overwhelmed by the thought of revision, don't worry—taking it slowly will produce results. I often hear from beginning writers, "I can't even think of where to begin. It took so much to write the poem, I can't imagine how to find what to fix. I just wrote it—you're the poet; now help me." These are exceptionally valid and powerful feelings that can certainly inhibit the revision process. But, even the least experienced writer of poetry can go back and measure her work, check the reactions of her classmates, and see if she's hooking fish. If not, let's jig that lure a little. And so we learn to revise.

HOW SHOULD I BEGIN REVISING?

"What should I revise?" can be a daunting question sometimes. In fact, many beginning writers feel that they put so much into the initial draft that there's nothing left to put into subsequent drafts—that they've used all their knowledge and creative talent the first time around. But, going about revision by asking more manageable questions will push us into the process of revision. Approaching revision by asking questions is a helpful way to proceed because it gives us concrete points to focus on while we revise. What's more, we can take revision in a somewhat systematic way without getting overwhelmed by everything at once.

Ah, but where to begin? Consider the core of the poem. Ask yourself what the seed was. What was at the heart of the poem? What was I really trying to say? Then maybe look at the poem and make a list of what you see in it. Are the feelings or thoughts from the seed of the poem there? If so, note how they appear in the poem and when you think they are the strongest. These are creative points and places we will need to focus on and come back to. Some we will want to come back to as anchor points, as moorings if you will, to keep us from floating too far from the heart of the poem. Others we will want to work on so they become stronger and more centrally connected or rooted in the heart of the poem. Once we've done some of this conceptually creative revision we can begin asking some technical questions about our creative elements and tools.

We can proceed much the same way as we did with the creative concepts— by asking questions. Is there alliteration, assonance, internal rhyme, or slant rhyme? Are there strong images? Are there metaphors and similes? After creating this list you can figure out a bit about what you have, and you can ask yourself what's missing. Once you know what you have, go through those things and check them for their quality, their relationship to the seed of what you wanted to say in the first place. Then you can begin to work with what is not there. I remember that when I first began to write poems, the one thing that was regularly missing from my poems was similes. Once I noticed this missing link, I made a conscious effort to include them. But often this didn't happen until I revised. And maybe I had a great image of, say, a lemon tree, but when I added the metaphoric side of it, "the lemon tree stood like . . ." that's when the image took on some power.

After having done this type of revision and thinking both on and off the page, I've always found the beginning a logical place to go to revise. For many reasons that happen during the initial writing and first few drafts, there's a momentum, an opening into the poem, that gets building near the start. So, I find myself asking whether I'm making things move in the early part of a poem. Are the lines sparking energy? Do I have some image that the reader can hold onto? How central will it be to the poem? Ultimately, a few questions like these get me tapped back into the root energy of the poem, the creative movement that was happening early on, so that I feel reconnected in a vital way but I'm also looking at the poem in a very fresh way. And then as I near the middle of the poem I can begin to see if it's turning the way it ought to, if the lines are carrying a rhythm and trajectory that is necessary, and if the words I've chosen will allow me to create some emotional resonance at the end. Of course, toward the end of a poem, I'm looking for how I've gone about closing things off, so that while I've concluded the poem I have not concluded the experience.

Let's look at an example of some revision. In the following poem, our author sets up a number of images in the first stanza. We can see by the second stanza that the poem might focus on the sister, the husband/accountant, or maybe the uncle. Then the persona comes in and is taking photos and there is a very self-conscious sense of the persona's relationship to her sister. And, by the end of the poem all of these things converge in some rather moving lines with a focus on the father being central. But there's just something missing. Here's a draft of stanzas one, two, and three.

Walking the Aisle

Walking beside Uncle, my sister's white satin gown
Lit up the dim church

She was marrying the accountant
A wedding, long months in the making

Behind the camera I clicked the shutter away   5
And from where I stood, they were two figurines.
I focused the lens and caught sight of her accountant

Something was familiar in the way his shoulders slanted
Our father's sternness,
All with the resolve of a lumberjack.   10

Amy Wong

The following is the revision of the poem. Amy has gone through a few drafts by the time we get this following draft, but it came by tinkering here and then tinkering there. One of the important things to notice in her revision is how much more amplitude she gets out of crafting new, fresh images. There are a number of places in the initial draft where the language is simply flat and does not move anywhere very significant. And, of course, what also happened in changing images was that the dominoes began dropping in relation to how the focus of the poem changed. The evocative elements of the poem came naturally when Amy found the power behind the images. The uncle becomes central instead of the accountant. The sister is very prominent, but in a very subtle denounced way. And the use of "I" for the point of view drops from three times to one. That may seem like a small change but essentially it shifts the psychic focus of the poem from the persona to the connection between all the family members.

Walking the Aisle

My sister was a lantern in her white satin gown.
Radiating the way I always knew she would
For the clicking camera shutters.

Beside her was our uncle, scuffling without his cane.
An arthritic leg he fittingly called his lame oar.   5
To be certain,
Our uncle would one day soon
Find himself at the mercy of a wheelchair.
And though we did look, there was no one left to give my sister away.

AMY WONG

The revision we've just looked at is something that has caused us to change our entire reaction to the poem. By the time it's over we've changed our connections within the poem from first to second version pretty significantly. Amy has achieved the goal by focusing on the core of the poem without superfluous interruption. She's also created language that works on us at a very figurative level. This should be a goal of most revision we make: to change the poem in a way that shifts our understanding of those lines and situations we revise. Consider those times when we say to ourselves "if only I had . . ." or "if I could do it over again . . ." Well, consider revision our chance to do it over again and we can do it the way we feel it might have been best done the first or second time. Unlike a real-life situation, with a poem we can go back and do it over as many times as we please—that dirty word: *drafting*.

Let me suggest a process that can be helpful in revising by drafting. Rather than spending a long time going through a poem and stopping in each line or every couple of lines and asking what can be done here, set up a revision situation that will be successful. Set down for yourself what you will look for and revise for as you go through the poem. Say to yourself, "I will go through this draft and look now only at images. Then I'll come back and comb through the poem for sound quality, specifically, internal rhyme in my lines." If you proceed this way, it's likely you'll avoid that overwhelming feeling that can cause us all to abandon revision for the thirty other things we'd rather do.

Let's look at a poem that was revised significantly—in fact, so significantly that it looked like a different poem. But on close inspection we can see that, in fact, Jenelle has kept the core of the poem alive in both drafts. The situation here is that Jenelle has revised the poem so significantly that now she has to work through the revision process on the new draft. But she's hung tightly to the core. The poet Richard Hugo states that a poem has two subjects, the **triggering subject**, which causes the poem to come up in the first place, and the **real** or **generated subject**, which is what the poem comes to say. He also states that, in fact, we may not even consciously know what the real subject is but just have some instinctive feeling about it. This idea of two subjects becomes clear in Jenelle's poem and her revision.

a long time ago

the hand shakes as it reaches out
to touch his pale lips
the mouth reaches down
to plant a goodbye kiss
gone is the lover   5
with golden hair
and bright blue eyes
why are angels always
blue eyes and fair hair?
I was an angel once   10
far away
but that was a long time ago
now I have black hair
and I suppose
I'm not an angel anymore.   15

JENELLE EAGER

This is definitely a first draft. She has started to do some things here that have merit and potential. There's some play with language, we have some ambiguity happening, and there are certainly contrasting images creating some tension. Note that there are two subjects here. As the readers we can see what's going on. Jenelle may not have seen the "real" subject rising but she maintains it in the second draft.

Search for Pride

I was not made
in the image of God.
My ancestors did not live
in the Garden of Eden.
They tell me it's   5
Adam and Eve
not Adam and Steve,
not "Brother Adam" and

"Sister Eve" from the hood,
or Eve, the slant-eyed   10
yellow-bellied gook.
Golden hair and
bright blue eyes
the epitome of "good"
the poster-child for "princess."   15
No, I was made in the image
of my mother
my father and
my ancestors,
who were made in   20
the image of beauty.

JENELLE EAGER

Such revision is dramatic. But note what she's done. The sense of the poem is actually made stronger by her having collected ideas and placed them in stanzas—this allows for her tone to be a bit more provocative. And stanza two—entirely new to the poem—allows Jenelle to connect the speaker of the poem to a broader set of lives and members of society who she also feels are outcast and who are being moved against. Jenelle was also tapping into her roots of growing up Asian American; tapping ethnicity, history, and the tensions of finding all that in America. While there is much good here, now Jenelle is ready to go back and revise this draft again, this virtually new and different poem. But, in calling it "different" let's also note that she has remained attached to the triggering subject and actually heightened the real subject by using it in the title, by creating stanzas and circling back to the first stanza at the end of the poem. Our writer here has hung tightly to another Richard Hugo maxim of revision: "When rewriting, write the entire poem again. If something has gone wrong deep in the poem, you may have taken a wrong turn earlier." We can see, based on Hugo's advice and our writer's example, that this type of revision can pay off with a little sweat and hard work.

But once we engage in this type of rewriting it's necessary to be able to gain momentum, to shift things, to change things as we see fit. While we need to write from our own experiences, we need to be able to think about them in a frame of reality/fiction that allows us the elbow room to create. Memory is an important element here and we all remember things slightly differently. A student wrote the following lines about his grandmother's death despite his not having been there when it happened.

She lay on the ground
the beating stopped
her face gray as the cement
on Christmas day.

and later my brother   5
threw her fruit basket out the window
screaming down the 405

He came to class and said "I want to change them." "Why?" I asked. I was thinking, *why in the hell would he want to change these lines?* And he said "because my mother flipped when she read this. I wasn't there and she said this isn't the way it happened." And I was thinking, *to hell with his mother,* but I told him, "Look, you may not have been there, but it's part of your experience and how you remember and want to express how your grandmother died. Tell it the way you want." My point was not to create an irreconcilable rift in his family, but rather to get him to keep his sense of how something had happened. This was his poem. I later found that in fact his brother didn't throw the basket out of the car window—he tossed it in the garbage at home. But the student thought that was a more poignant and compelling detail. He was right. What I found compelling too, as a teacher and a writer, was that he had the nerve and sense enough to change a detail from how it did happen to how he thought we'd want it to happen so we'd feel more in the experience. Now, that's getting to the core of revision. Because he saw that in the end, the reader wasn't going to say "Nice writing," no, the reader was going to say "Wow, *I* feel that deeply."

When revising poems, remember that no matter how you go about it, whether you've adapted rules or mantras from this chapter or made your own, the importance of allowing yourself to create and recreate is paramount to success. And remember in revision, too, that nothing is permanent—if you don't like it, go back and change it. Try new things, reshape the experience, change the memory, and take us deeply into the heart of the matter.

MOONSHEEN AND PORCHLIGHT: REVISION AS ILLUMINATION

Gary Thompson

A very good poem might matter to the poet who wrote it for much of a lifetime. The poem brings pleasure and insight each time the poet reads it, especially when reading it aloud. Not surprisingly, that same good poem will very often provide pleasure and insight to others. Galway Kinnell has probably read or recited "The Bear" a thousand times in the thirty-some years since he wrote it, yet each time I hear him read the poem, I notice the great joy he takes in saying it aloud, and how that plea-sure has shifted from one section to another over the years. Needless to say, "The Bear" is a very good poem and it has provided both pleasure and insight through these decades. But in the midst of writing a new poem—in struggle or frenzy, pain or joy—how do we poets make the decisions that might turn this emerging poem into a good poem, and hence a poem that matters to us, and perhaps to others, for a lifetime?

For most poets I know well enough to be privy to their working methods, initial revising is a basic part of writing that first draft. My first drafts, for example, always have words erased, or lines scratched out, stanzas eliminated or moved, titles changed, linebreaks shifted. These decisions or hunches are an integral part of the discovery, and they come within the rush and flow and excitement of a first-glimpsed poem. Most poets have experienced some version of this simultaneous writing/ revising, although it is true that some prefer to jot down a very rough, yet whole, draft before making even small changes. It is also true that it becomes more difficult, and probably less thrilling, to make productive revisions after a few hours, or days, or weeks, or months have passed since the initial excitement of creation. However, these later revisions, made under the full light of conscious scrutiny, are often the most important ones we can make because they help us illuminate the deepest and often the most difficult parts of our poems. Simply, we can come to see our poems, and perhaps ourselves, better. Revision, then, is a way for the poet to learn what is important. Like all worthwhile knowledge, revision is an art we must teach ourselves, but we can learn this art more quickly if we are honestly open to the comments and observations of other poets, readers, and editors. We must make ourselves vulnerable.

There are many ways to think about poetry, many models and metaphors that attempt to explain how poems actually affect the reader or how poems are written. There are so many models, of course, because poems are, at best, mysteries. It's unlikely that any one explanation will satisfy a poet or reader for any length of time, let alone a lifetime. Our understandings change, broaden with each poem we read or write; therefore, our personal model (and we all have one, consciously or not) of poetry subtly shifts and evolves over time, and obviously then, our sense of what makes a good poem will change too. So it is remarkable when a poem of ours continues to provide pleasure and insight after any length of time at all. Most fail this test, but when one succeeds, it succeeds mysteriously. In a talk about revision given at the Foothill Writers Conference, George Keithley suggests why the very good poem continues to resonate: "Remember that the mystery which moves us in a poem is not the meaning of the poem, but how the poem achieves that meaning. Its existence is the essential meaning of the poem."

> "Writing is seen as a splurge of emotion rather than a combination of inspiration and craft."
>
> MATT BARNARD

This observation, cited from *The London Times*, suggests two ways (from a myriad of ways) of looking at the process of writing poems, and each contains its truth. Also, and perhaps more significantly, each implies a completely different approach to revising poems, and again, each has its validity. If we look on writing as a "splurge of emotion," then how do we revise the words, phrases, lines that were created by this emotional outpouring? Certainly it would be helpful to listen to what others have to say about our draft, but do we really want to change anything, since to change the poem in a different, perhaps cooler and less expressive, mood would diminish the splurge effect that we so value? The poem is what it is: words caught in the moment of emotional excess. The way to revise, it appears, is simply to write the next poem, hoping that each poem teaches us something that will be useful in the next. Eventually, the poet hopes to find a burst of words that produces the very good poem. In this, it resembles learning to surf where the novice, after perhaps a few words of wisdom from a teacher and a couple of lessons on the beach, paddles out and tries to catch waves. Each teetering ride teaches something, but the wave can't be caught again. It's the next wave, the next poem, which is important. Eventually, given luck, that great wave and the skills required to ride it will come together at the same time, and that ride will be remembered and celebrated for years.

However, if we look on writing as a combination of inspiration and craft, then we have ways to set about revising the first draft of a poem. Certainly, this model brings the craft of poetry, the various skills a poet learns and uses, to the forefront and more likely into our consciousness. The poet might find it useful to analyze the sounds and rhythms of the poem, for example, and ask questions about the findings. Linebreaks, images, and all issues of craft could be isolated, scrutinized, and nudged toward perfection. After all this precise work, however, will we have written our very good poem? Not necessarily. We've all read poems that are soundly crafted; yet they have no life, no magic, no surprise, no mystery. This is where inspiration plays its important role in our model. *Inspire*: the word has many meanings and contexts, and several apply to the writing and revising of poems—to fill, to arouse, to impel, to animate, to give rise to, to infuse by breathing, to inhale. In other words, the poem begins to breathe, to be filled with life. At some point, the very good poem mysteriously takes on a life of its own, and this is both because of, and in spite of, the poet's craft. It's important to remember that this inspired moment can occur at almost any stage of the creative process. It might happen just as the poet is penning the first word, or at any stage of that initial draft, or later when the poet is concentrating on issues of craft, or during the later stages of revising. Eventually, something *must* inspire the poem or it will remain simply a construction of words. So the first stage in later revision for me, whether looking at a poem of mine or a student's, is to ask: What is inspired in these lines? Where does the poem come to life?

Let's turn to a specific example of the revision process. This poem is by Karen Seipert, a bright, talented, and serious student in my recent summer workshop. I think this poem may be especially instructive because it was discussed in an earlier workshop taught by another instructor, and Karen kept the various drafts, worksheets, and notes about her observations. So the poet had been thinking about this poem for some time before she brought it to my class, and we can follow her thinking pretty clearly as she revises over a number of months and with various sources of feedback. The first draft was written on a computer, so she doesn't have a record of the earliest revisions made during the initial writing. She does remember that the changes were minimal. Draft one:

Jealousy

The sill creaks
while the window
groans upwards.
Faded paint,
the peeling culprit,   5
telltales pained ascent.
My cousin Jeffrey,
halfway in
mostway out
escapes   10
onto the roof.
Moonsheen
on his Chevy
illuminates the plan.
I tiptoe   15
across cold wood
a willing conspirator—
but the Chevy's rolling
lights extinguished
down the gravel   20
drive towards emancipation.

KAREN SEIPERT

What's inspired here? For me, it's the first view of cousin Jeffrey being "halfway in / mostway out" of the window. That "mostway" certainly catches a visual image of the teenager sneaking out the second-story window. It also mimics the slangy quality of teenage talk, as well as implying the fact of his age, since he is mostly grown and mostly gone. The second inspired moment in the poem is the description of light on the Chevy. "Moonsheen" is a fascinating coinage here. It suggests the romance of sneaking off into the night world, as well as the illicit quality of the action (perhaps by its proximity in sound to moonshine). Finally, the third inspired moment in the poem is the image of the Chevy's "rolling / lights extinguished / down the gravel / drive . . ." This clear image of the car also suggests the way some teenagers speed off, blindly and dangerously, into the world. So there's much to admire here, even in this very early draft.

What might the poet consider in her next version of the poem? Certainly, there are some craft issues, such as linebreaks (why does the next-to-last line break differently from all the rest?) and why does the strategy change from detailed punctuation to almost no punctuation? Also, most of the poem is so concrete and visual that three phrases stand out as being quite different, quite abstract: "telltales pained ascent," "a willing conspirator," and "towards emancipation." The question might be put this way: Can the simple, playful, almost-childlike language of this poem carry the extra weight of these abstractions? All of them? And finally, why is the poem titled "Jealousy"? Jealousy connotes a certain bitterness and anguish, but who is jealous of whom or what? These are some of the questions Karen might mull over before revising her poem, and it appears that most of these questions were brought up during that first workshop, because her next draft responds in part to these issues.

Draft two, revised a month or so later, is called "Envy," a title that better prepares the reader for the wistful and yearning tone of the speaker, without forcing us to ask questions that lead outside the emotional territory of the poem. Other notable changes: the window is now an *aged* window; the paint now telltales *painful rising*; and the Chevy's *already* rolling—a small but brilliant change that reinforces the unfolding action in the present tense and adds to the drama. She also changes the inconsistent linebreak, and attacks the punctuation issue by placing periods after each short phrase, a strategy that seems at odds with the relatively smooth flow of the speaker's thoughts and words. Karen's notes about the class discussion of this draft indicate that she is still uncomfortable with the "telltales" line and the overall punctuation scheme; she also recognizes that "Faded paint. / the peeling culprit" simply explains that the window is old, which has already been stated by adding "aged." A student in the workshop has evidently questioned whether "moonsheen" might be too romantic, and Karen notes this observation with two poignant question marks.

Draft three is the end-of-the-semester version to be turned in to her instructor for comments. Three significant changes occur in this draft. First, Karen begins to solve the problem of inconsistent and ineffective punctuation by eliminating all punctuation (except parentheses that enclose lines 3–6) and allowing the natural linebreaks to control pacing and meaning. In conjunction with this strategy, she also eliminates all capitalization (except for proper nouns and the first person pronoun), and this emphasizes the lines as lines, rather than as parts of a sentence. In her notes, she surmises that writing in lower case is more "dreamlike," and I suppose it is. The third significant change is not so productive, at least in my opinion. Apparently swayed by her fellow student's argument, she replaces the splendid "moonsheen" with the ordinary "porchlight," perhaps feeling that the first draws too much attention to itself for this little poem. Adroitly, her instructor responds: "I somewhat prefer 'moonsheen' because it adds to the furtiveness and romantic excitement/ longing that the young girl must feel." This advice is sensitive and clear, and it helps steer the poet back towards the strengths of her poem.

Draft four, the draft submitted to our summer workshop, reflects the many small decisions the poet has made over the months since that first draft called "Jealousy."

Envy

the sill creaks
while the window
groans upward
(faded paint
the peeling culprit   5
telltales pained ascent)
my cousin Jeffrey
halfway in
mostway out
escapes   10
onto the roof
moonsheen
on his Chevy
illuminates the plan
I tiptoe   15
across cold wood
a willing conspirator
but the Chevy's already rolling
lights extinguished
down the gravel drive   20
towards emancipation

KAREN SEIPERT

The discussion that followed Karen's reading the poem aloud (a practice that helps the class, as well as the poet, hear each poem's distinctive music) was lively and productive, and I think it allowed her to think about the poem in ways that hadn't come up in her previous workshop. Our discussion, as I recall, began with praise for the clear, fresh, unpretentious imagery that conveys so much about the people and the situation. We also took delight in the music, especially the sounds and rhythms of the second stanza. One student even traced the sound patterns in that stanza, and then explained why he liked them and what they contributed to the poem. It could be implied, I suppose, that the music in the first stanza isn't quite as interesting or as integral, and that may be something the poet wants to attend to, should she decide to write yet another draft. The third major area of our discussion focused on diction, the word choices the poet makes as the poem unfolds, and this conversation opened up our primary suggestions for revision.

1) "Emancipation" is an odd word choice in the last line. It is quite abstract, and if it is meant to convey a general sense of freedom, then that is already implied in the previous lines. We know cousin Jeffrey is stealing away from the authority and rules of the house. If emancipation is meant to be a legal term (as in cousin Jeffrey driving off to attain his legal civil rights), then there is much that is unexplained in the poem. Also, the young speaker is envious of the older cousin's freedom, though she isn't particularly angry about his betrayal at not taking her with her. Would she be likely to think about legalities at this point? Most agreed with the suggestion, as I recall, to omit the last line which allows the final powerful image to speak for itself.

2) There also was a good deal of discussion about the sixth line: "telltales pained ascent," and rightfully so. Her notes indicate that both poet and reader have been uncomfortable with this line since that first draft. Let's look at it more closely. "Telltales" seems like an interesting coinage, changing the noun/adjective to a verb form. It hints at the fact that the speaker didn't tattle, although the old house tried to, albeit unsuccessfully. "Pained" is playful, a pun on windowpane. This explains why the poet has chosen one form or another of the word in various drafts. However, clever as it is, the resultant personification of the window blurs the image and we tend to lose sight of the main point of this stanza, which is cousin Jeffrey's escape. The class offered a number of suggestions, but the more I consider this line, the more I've come to believe that the solution is not so easily confined to that single phrase. The first six lines describe the window and sill, and there are three qualities that must be made clear for the reader to fully appreciate the rest of the poem. First, the window and sill must be old because the house symbolizes the adult world of authority that the cousins wish to escape.

Second, the window must open or rise so that we are catching the cousins as their scheme unfolds; in effect we share their secret and become conspirators. Third, the window must make some sort of noise, a groan or creak, to indicate that this escape scheme could be discovered and thwarted. My suggestion to Karen, after these days of following her poem from draft to draft, is to rethink the opening and rewrite the lines. In so doing, she will likely rewrite these lines with the same insight, zest, and inspiration that already define the best of "Envy."

This shouldn't have to be said, but experience tells me it does: any suggestion for revision—whether offered by a friend, classmate, teacher, or editor—is just that, a suggestion. The poem is the poet's to tinker with as she sees fit. The poet is not just learning to use the tools of her craft, she is also developing and refining a sensibility, her own way of shaping and understanding the world. When she studies her poem, when she turns the tensor lamp up high, the poet may illuminate a self she has only glimpsed in the past, and this vision could be the essential insight she needs to write new poems. That is why revision is an art.

Exercises

1. Take a poem you wrote a while back. If you're new at poetry, even just a month ago will do. Read through the poem aloud. Then read through the poem for analysis and make some lists. Note what elements it contains. Note what you like about the poem and why. Note what you think the poem is really saying—and along with this note the triggering subject and the real subject.
2. Take a poem you've written and revise the poem one element at a time. Go through it just for imagery, then just for tone, just for rhyme, etc. Make a number of passes at the poem. You will have a number of drafts by the end of this process, but ultimately a draft that ought to look significantly revised.
3. Take a poem you've written, one that you like but that you also know—in your gut or heart—that it needs revision to be the poem you want. Create for yourself the personality of the poem. Now, interview the poem as if it was a celebrity on a poetry talk show. Ask it questions like, "you've created some nice images in stanza two, but why the sudden shift from images in line four—what were you after there?" Then answer the questions as if you are the poem. Use your answers to revise.

CHAPTER
11

THE POETRY WORKSHOP

The cornerstone of a workshop's success is participation. That sounds simple enough, but it's really not as easy as it seems. First, not everyone is comfortable speaking up in a group setting. Add to this that it's even more nerve-racking to talk about something (in this case, poems) that may cause us to feel a bit like a novice. So it's no surprise that the first day of workshopping poems can be utterly silent. When I teach a poetry class we don't workshop a poem until the third—sometimes the fourth—week of class. This is for a good reason. We go over elements and writing strategies, do exercises, get comfortable with the process of producing work. But still, that first day of workshopping is a doozy. Inevitably I have students who come up and say, "I didn't know what to say, how to comment—this is so much better than anything I could write." If I'm lucky, they show up at my office door before class asking for help, but they still say the same thing to me.

   And this is a reasonable thing to say. But I like to draw the analogy that there are plenty of coaches out there who coach athletes who are better players than they are. Take Michael Jordan for example. People say he's the best basketball player ever. Does that mean he shouldn't have a coach? Of course not, and Mr. Jordan (humble as he is

. . . a poetry workshop/an epicenter of originality, companionship, / pain and openness . . .

Jimmy Santiago Buca

about his talent) would probably be the first to tell us that he appreciates what his coach can do for him. Once we've settled into the coaching role, the peer, the colleague—all the terms that calm the nerves—we can start talking about workshopping. The first thing I always tell students who are uncomfortable commenting on someone else's work is, "Start with something positive. Then you can get to the not-so-good."

I have a theory about emerging as a writer that can be summed up in one word: *accident*. There are times when we do very good work and it happens by accident. There are also times when we do very bad work and that, too, can happen by accident. But, I'm more inclined to think that bad work happens by a lack of intellectual or creative effort. So the way in which this affects the workshop is that when something good happens, maybe an image in the poem everyone is taken by, the writer needs to know why it is good. They may not have even thought that the image was a main concern. But by accident it becomes a pulse in the poem. And they need to know why it's good so they can see how they created it and then they can do it again in another poem. This is one of the main goals of the workshop—to learn to figure out how and why we've done things and then repeat them or stay far away from them. Figuring this out in others' poems helps us find it in our own. A second goal in the workshop process is to learn to be able to go through one's own work with the clarity with which we view others' work.

I usually set up a few simple rules in my workshops:

1. No meaningless answers (e.g., I really like this poem, that's a great image, it's nice).
2. Don't get personal (Boy, Randy, that poem is really horrible. The whole subject is stupid—why are you even in here writing poems?). I know, you're thinking that nobody would ever say this, but I've seen some rude people in creative writing sessions who think they have a license to say whatever is on their minds. Stick to the work at hand and to the text in that work.
3. Find positive things to say and give reasons why the work you're noting is good.
4. Be gentle with negatives and again give reasons. Help by showing someone how they might fix it. If something isn't quite right but you don't know why, you can bring it up and defer to someone else for technique on fixing.
5. The writer who has her work on the table for review doesn't get to talk unless we need an answer to a question regarding why she did something. The author ought to be taking notes.
6. For your own sanity, don't idolize anyone else in the class because you think they write better than you'll ever write. We all do good work and we all do bad work.

I know, it may sound pretty rigid, but these rules simply provide the highway we drive on all through the class. And it gives a framework within which we function, a road map of sorts, so we're all headed in the same direction. When someone brings in a poem to be workshopped, she needs to bring the poem to us on Tuesday if we're going to look at it as a class on a Thursday. We all take it home, and on Thursday everyone is to bring back the poem with handwritten remarks on it and a paragraph or more of typed comments, all of which gets returned to the writer. The hope then is that there is plenty of solid feedback for the writer to go out and work on revising his poem. Then she can bring it back to us if she wants, or simply turn in at least two drafts of it in a portfolio at the end of the quarter. In the end, we hope that all the writers get solid feedback. And while providing solid feedback, the classmates learn more about creating constructive feedback for their own work and can hone their editing skills. Finally, it's applying all the technical and elemental sides of poetics to the practical side of creative writing.

12

WORKSHOPPING A FREE VERSE POEM

WORKSHOPPING A POEM

Let's take a look at one of the poems that came in and was discussed in a beginning poetry session. Jake hadn't been writing poetry long, but had always had an interest in reading both novels and poetry. He is from a rural community and went to high school in Estacada, Oregon—a traditional logging town. But he is far from being traditional, has traveled widely, has a passion for learning Spanish, and is a relatively avid conservationist. So here's a poem he brought in at the start of the quarter.

For the New People

There is a dead dog buried in the ground.
Actually, there are three dead dogs
down a ways from the house,
by the creek. Other places have more.
It's the road you live on.   5
Claims about a dog per summer,
At least it used to, when
twenty or thirty log trucks
barreled by in one day.

Your dogs will be fine.   10
Besides, don't you raise
really smart dogs?
Not too many cats have died here.
They live much longer than dogs. But
you won't believe the birds. It is beautiful,   15
the view from three windows six feet by
six feet. But you won't believe how many birds
try to fly right through.
Sipping whatever you drink will
sometimes be made less pleasant   20
when a hollow thud jerks your eyebrows.
You do love them, animals, and
often times a bird can be nursed back
to fine shape. Still,
You have purchased   25
an extraordinarily large space of land,
with so many birds
and such a generous amount of air
in which birds gain tremendous speed.

JACKOB CURTIS

Now that we've read the poem, in order to comfortably form a solid
response to the piece we can ask some questions and think about the techniques and elements of writing poetry we already know. This poem lends
itself to asking a multitude of questions from the basic to the complex. But
let's focus on a few that will allow you entry into Jake's poem and almost any
poem you come across.

1. Is the language accessible and why? In other words, do you understand what he's saying?
2. Are there images in the poem? If so, how well has he used imagery?
   Why do you think the images work or don't work in Jake's poem?
3. Where does line structure help the dynamics of the poem and where
   is the poem hurt by its line structure?
4. What types of sound elements does Jake employ in the poem and
   how do they function—what do they do for the poem?
5. Is there a triggering subject and is there a real subject and how do
   these work in the poem?

Answering these questions will give us a handle on what kind of comments
we might want to give Jake. What's more, these questions get at elements

that ought to be present in most poems. But specifically they get at the heart of what elements ought to be working in the poem Jake brought to the workshop.

Now that you've had a chance to think about what kind of conclusions you'd draw about the poem, let's look at the poem with margin comments, talk about why the comments were made, and then see what Jake decides to do with the poem in the long run.

Great title and good subject matter

For the New People

Nice use of the element of surprise.

There is a dead dog buried in the ground.
Actually, there are three dead dogs
down a ways from the house,
by the creek. Other places have more.
It's the road you live on.   5
Claims about a dog per summer,

Good momentum

At least it used to, when
twenty or thirty log trucks
barreled by in one day.
Your dogs will be fine.   10
Besides, don't you raise
really smart dogs?

Where is this going?
This is almost cliché
and has some troubling
line structure. Consider what it
is you really want to say and do
here. Then consider how the
lines might work.
A great shift into
the "real" subject.

Not too many cats have died here.
They live much longer than dogs. But
you won't believe the birds. It is beautiful,   15
the view from three windows six feet by
six feet. But you won't believe how many birds
try to fly right through.
Sipping whatever you drink will
sometimes be made less pleasant   20
when a hollow thud jerks your eyebrows.
You do love them, animals, and
often times a bird can be nursed back
to fine shape. Still,

This ending has resonance
because you've used original
concepts and images
to represent them

You have purchased   25
an extraordinarily large space of land,
with so many birds
and such a generous amount of air
in which birds gain tremendous speed.

JACKOB CURTIS

Jake,

Well, there are some fine things in this poem. It's obviously an early draft, but you're doing some good work and following some varied and deep currents in the poem. What's more, you follow some good basic tenets about writing. Jake, you're writing about what you know and using a language that is natural and accessible for the readers. After stating these foundation points, we can head into the poem and look at what there is that you've done well and what it is you could revise, take out, or reshape in some way.

So, let's start with some of the good you have going in the poem. First, there's a great title working here and it is because it is not a title that gives away the poem or predisposes us to view it one way or another. If anything, it's relatively obscure until we read the poem. Then we realize it is tied to both the triggering subject and the real subject, and that in fact the poem is not about birds and dogs at all, but about the new people moving into rural areas and ostensibly folks from the suburbs. Then you move into the poem with a wonderful beginning. Not only does the first line work well but the first stanza does a fine job setting the tone of the poem, establishing both the voice of the poet and the voice of the persona. Largely this is accomplished through the use of short and emphatic statements. What's more, they're statements that surprise us—dead dogs? We might ask—and at the same time intrigue us, pulling us into the poem. Here you're following the old rule of beginning in the middle of things, after things have happened. In these emphatic statements you do well for yourself and the poem by establishing some very concrete imagery and a sense of where the poem is and what is in the poem. You are not pelting us with a spray of abstracts.

In the second stanza you continue with this very strong sense of the images and action in the poem. And the action and tension mount with log trucks. As well, the tone is heightened a bit by using the direct "you" of the second-person point of view—as well as a question pointed at them—to address these "new people" and the way they perceive the intelligence of their dogs. So, the momentum of the poem is moving ahead, and some dynamics begin with the rhythmic quality of the lines and the sound quality of your word choices. Notice that there are some rough spots in the line breaks and grammatical structure in stanza one, but in stanza two you're really moving along with some tight lines that are broken at similar lengths. I say "tight" because of your use of elements of sound (the "*s*" in line 1, the rhymes when / twenty and log / dog, the alliteration in "barreled by") as well as a line structure that moves quickly. And, it almost feels like the lines are barreling by like the log trucks.

Now, in stanza three there is some good imagery but this is a problematic stanza for its syntax, its line structure, and subject matter. Jake, where are you going with the cats? It seems this is an interruption to the poem that potentially throws us off the track. I'll address this just a bit later.

Now, in stanza four, notice the consistency in voice and the persona's tone. You have remained consistent in point of view, and opened this stanza with a wonderfully fresh image of the "new people" sipping their drinks. And then, not entirely surprising, but somewhat, you have the birds mentioned above slamming into the "wonderful" plate glass windows, which is a fine twist to throw at us in the poem. Here is where you have left the triggering subject behind—the dogs—and gone on to the real subject, that of people moving to the country and living their entire lives (from their animals to their houses) in a way that isn't suited to rural living, and maybe it's not suited for anyone. What's more, Jake, you continue your very fine use of sound quality throughout the stanza.

And moving into the final stanza, we're right on target with the real subject and things are still fresh and interesting for us. Here are the birds being purchased with the land, a sensible image since birds live in trees, but then another slight twist. Who thinks of buying air? And you have made some wonderful word choices, images, and line breaks in *and such a generous amount of air | in which birds gain tremendous speed*. There is a very subtle and implicit quality to what the persona is trying to tell us and since it is done with images, rather than abstracts, the power is not lost on us at the end.

So largely we have a reasonably strong poem here. It's a poem that is really ready to be worked on hard in the revision process and turned into an even better poem. While there are many things here which work well, there are some rough spots to the poem too. For instance, let's look at some of the grammatical structures (syntax, punctuation, etc.) as well as line breaks. In two stanzas in particular you have trouble around these and it harms the dynamics of the language that might occur if they were smoothed out.

In stanza one, the first line and sentence is great. But then we move on to another longer sentence where you employ some enjambment. This works fine. But starting a new sentence in line four (*Other places . . .*) and then stopping and then starting again creates a jerky motion in the language. In lines five and six, seemingly these two thoughts are related and would normally go together, but you've separated them and have actually tied line six in stanza one to line one in stanza two. That seems grammatically odd and it seems to affect the rhythm of the language as well as the meaning. I'll be interested to see later what revision takes place.

In stanza three, we get into the bit about the cats. Here is where the turn to the real subject begins, but cats are superfluous to the real subject. It's almost as if the cats were just a way to get to the birds. And let's look again at what has happened with line structure.

Not too many cats have died here.
They live much longer than dogs. But
you won't believe the birds. It is beautiful,
the view from three windows six feet by
six feet. But you won't believe how many birds   5
try to fly right through.

As the line breaks occur, I wonder why you've broken the sentences into lines the way you have—leaving "But" at the end of line two, starting line five with "six feet," the last two words of the sentence. And the syntax of the sentence *It is beautiful* . . . is a bit odd. Why start with a pronoun reference using "It"? Why not start with the words "the view"? After all, this is more concrete and tighter given word economy. Well, this is an awkward stanza, and given the cat and bird relationship, almost too "cute" for the poem.

Jake, there's some real fine work here. I look forward to seeing the revision.

Jeff

Jake got quite a lot of great feedback from the class when he brought this poem in. People genuinely liked it, felt they could relate to it, and thought it embodied enough poetic elements to make very natural language seem poetic. When we asked Jake how much of this was conscious, he said only part was—the rest just fell in. That's fine, because at some level he was thinking about it and it made it onto the page. In fact, one of the biggest compliments to Jake the day he brought this in was that one young woman in the class said, "You know, what's great about this is that you just say it, but it really is a poem." And isn't that the goal?

Revised Version

For the New People

There is a dead dog buried in the ground.
Actually, there are three dead dogs
down a ways from the house,
by the creek; other places have more.
It's the road you live on—   5
claims about a dog per summer.
At least it used to, when
twenty or thirty log trucks
barreled by in one day.
Your dogs will be fine.   10
Besides, don't you raise

smart dogs?
The view is beautiful,
from three windows
six feet by six feet.   15
But you won't believe the birds, how many
try to fly right through.
Sipping whatever you drink will
sometimes suffer interruption
when a hollow thud jerks your eyes.   20
You do love them, and
often times a bird can be nursed back
to fine shape. Still,
You have purchased
an extraordinarily large space of land,   25
with so many birds
and such a generous amount of air
in which birds gain tremendous speed.

JAKOB CURTIS

Jake,
Good work here in the revision. You have done some things, largely with
the language at the sentence and line level, which help tighten the poem.
Your only large-scale revision, which was a necessary one, was getting
rid of the cat lines in stanza three. That also meant that the revision to the
dominant image of that stanza had to be somewhat significant. So stanza
three becomes relatively big, but that's an important stanza because this
is where the poem makes its run into the real subject.

    If we take the poem stanza by stanza, some of the subtle changes
smooth the poem's nuances of sound. And while some of the changes
may not seem altogether large, the changing of nuances between the
drafts makes all the difference. Remember Jake, in crafting poetry, sometimes a subtle change in where a word falls, or how a line ends, or how
enjambment is used may stir the reader in just the right direction. You've
done well cleaning up your grammatical structure in lines four, five, and
six of stanza one. Adding a semicolon, which seems to work rather well
for those two thoughts, was a good idea. But more, you've connected the
last two lines of the stanza and kept them from running into stanza two.
So you've solved a line problem, a stanza problem, and a meaning problem all at the same time. Good work.

    Almost entirely you've left stanza two alone with the exception of
deleting "really" which is one of those vague words which did nothing
for the line or images. This is fine as that stanza was doing well already.
So in stanza three, I'm glad to see you've made some significant revision,

and it's here where the poem turns. And rather than trying to grab the wheel and jerk the poem in the right direction, you subtly let us move with the language and take us to the real subject through setting. Following the comments from the workshop on this stanza—which indicated there were unrelated subject matter and awkward lines and an inconsistent voice—was a fine idea for revision. I think you hit the mark. Hence, you've revised to a shorter line free of grammatical or syntactical problems. As well, you set up the lines to heighten the effect of the internal rhyme as well as the alliteration. What's more is that this stanza now cleanly takes us into the final two stanzas.

Fine work revising, Jake. And a good job noting what ought to have been left from your previous draft.

Jeff

Ultimately, Jake came away from this poem feeling as though he had done something pretty well. That's good, and I would hope he'd feel that way. And he felt as though working through this poem with the feedback he received in the workshop gave him a better idea of how to implement elements of poetics at a conscious level during revision. As for the things that just showed up during the first draft, Jake's comment was that he'd just let the chips fall. But I attribute the chips falling to Jake's thinking very consciously at some point about all the elements (rhyme, alliteration, imagery) that showed up in the poem. Outside of Jake, many in the class felt that they got even closer to their work by workshopping his poem. Part of this was because many related to it because it was local in its setting—they knew where it was set. But really, the setting and tension in the poem could happen anywhere, which is good because that is part of what allows for any audience to read it. It seems the class found the poem an example of using real, ordinary, accessible language to get at the heart of something.

13

WORKSHOPPING A FIXED FORM POEM

Writing a fixed form poem can be tough. But most of us, no matter the torturous nature of it, could sit down and at least do it as an exercise. It may not come out very well, but we've tried. On the other hand, it might just come out fine, and then we try again. Maybe we begin to write great quantities of fixed form poetry. Whatever the outcome, writing it is different from workshopping it. So, even if we've given it a try—and most of us have—it can still be disconcerting when a classmate, colleague, or friend walks into our workshop or writing group and says, "Hey, I brought my sonnets for you to look at today." Inside we groan and think, why? Oh, but come on, is it really that bad to have to workshop fixed form poems? I don't think so, and I'd venture to say that after a workshop session, at worst, most people are a little enthused about what fixed forms can accomplish and at best, someone runs right out and tries it. But somewhere in the middle—the average response—is that we come away having learned something about form and writing. And that's both rewarding and enlightening.

But why this groaning reaction? Because deep down, as contemporary writers, most of us resist form for one reason or another. But to be able to workshop it we need to know something about it.

All of the questions that students have and the discomfort of workshopping someone else's poem is only heightened with a fixed form poem. When we spend the time to learn a bit about the form, and we give some knowledge-able, grounded feedback, we also become better poets. Whether we write one or not isn't the issue. The issue is that we've given some fine advice and we've learned a little something about the tradition in which we're working.

WORKSHOPPING A VILLANELLE

Many students today would say that a villanelle is a difficult form to work with. In a recent workshop, I suggested that a student should try turning one of her poems she brought to class into a villanelle. When I made the sugges-tion, Matt, a student from my intro to creative writing class the previous semester, groaned and said "good luck." Matt knew the difficulty because he'd tried it. He had actually tried it to a reasonable effect, but still felt it was a difficult form. Part of that runs in him because he did only one instead of ten—maybe. Or the frustration runs in him because the villanelle he wrote never seemed natural enough within the rules of the poem. When writing a villanelle, though, it's not an exceptionally difficult form—the success of the poem lies within the repeating lines and creating those lines in a way that allows them some flexibility. In other words, while creating a line that repeats (a bit like the chorus of a song) we also want to create a line that can change slightly as we repeat it; however, it needs to keep the essence of its meaning. And, of course, these lines must also embody the core concept, or emotional force, of the poem. There lies the most difficult thing about the villanelle.

Now, one thing we've already discussed in regards to form is that form should never be imposed on a poem. The form should provide a sense of structure and boundary—essentially it should provide us a way to say what we want to say. So, that means we need to consider what kind of poem might have a repetitive line, what kind of content might call for an almost chant-like quality, and what kind of content calls for a poem that repeats a stanzaic structure with repetitive rhythm and rhyme. So, let's take a look again at the structure of a villanelle.

A villanelle runs as follows: It consists of nineteen lines divided into six stanzas. There are five tercets (three line stanzas) and a final quatrain (a four line stanza). The rhyme scheme of the stanzas is *aba* for each of the tercets and *abaa* for the concluding quatrain. Further, the lines repeat in the following order: line 1 appears in the poem as lines 6, 12, and 18; and line 3 appears in the poem as lines 9, 15, and 19. It's this repetition that can cause the villanelle to take on almost chant-like qualities. And though the form does not require a line length of recurring metrical pattern, most poets attempt to at least build some sense of rhythm throughout the line with approximate syllable structure. The form is strict and rigorous. Because of its rhyme and line repetition, it has a very songlike quality. Well, that's reasonably complicated, and is slightly more complicated when we think about how the words ending the lines will also complement the repetitive lines. This can be a sticking point for any type of form because we might get hung up on what words to use at the end of lines or on the line repetition that the villanelle requires. And well we should think about this, because some of these words will be repeated over and over and will ultimately produce a given effect of sound and meaning within the poem. One way to go about this is to think about your subject and poem, make a list of words you see as key to the subject of the poem, and think about how they might work as key words in the repetitive lines and as end words. Then begin crafting the lines that you will use as those repetitive, chanting lines. Another way to proceed is to begin drafting the poem, and at the end of the first stanza decide how your line breaks should fall. This will allow you to set up a pattern of a rhythmic line and also to establish what sounds may come. I'm also a believer, when I write in forms, that one should just write and go back later and tinker with creating the end rhymes and other effects. Either way it is not easy.

So, when it's finished and we read it, what should happen? Well, one thing that should take place for us in the experience is that the music of the poem should be unbound from the language and should really drive the poem. And the recurrent lines should produce an effect that is, at the least, a chant, and possibly at best quite haunting. We should also be pushed forward by the way all the lines work around the repetitive lines. In other words, the "normal" or "standard" lines of the poem should be offering us images, turns in the poem, tensions, and some intelligence regarding what we should know from the poem. All of these are the conventions that we pay attention to in a free verse poem, but as we do these things within the form they begin to take on a new power as they spark against the rules or rhyme and of rhythm pulling us through the poem and into the repetitive lines that we have to come to at the various points. And so our narrative lines or images are broken by the chant that comes in and it's almost as if there is a voice behind the voice already speaking in the poem. It is difficult. But the beauty of the form is that it actually makes things happen in the poem without the writer controlling them—in essence the poem fools us and controls us—if we get out of its way and let it. So, let's take a look at the following villanelle brought to an introductory workshop, and then look at its various revisions.

Perseverance

Wage war against the tide
whose salty mist blurs thy sight
Until endless waves subside

And though the sailor's stride
Falls heavy on the deck at night
The ship still rages against the tide

The depths below may not confide
The endnote of the tireless fight
Until the sea grows calm and the waves subside

In the dusk the gulls ride
The cliffs in open flight
whose face stands against the tide

Ho Ho the tuna far below do hide
From the net that flies like a kite
In the endless waves that don't subside

Though the storm bursts quite contride
Even if the shore is far from sight
Wage war against the tide
Until the endless waves subside.

JENNIFER VAN DYKE

When looking at this poem and creating some responses to it that might be helpful to the writer, we can ask ourselves some questions based on the previous discussion of the villanelle.

1. Does it follow the form? Map out the lines and take a look.
2. This one breaks a little you'll notice—slightly—but it still breaks. So what effect on the poem does breaking from the tradition have? Does it matter? Do you like the way the lines and words fall? Why?
3. Has the author created lines that repeat, that seem to move the poem forward, that provide the chanting, haunting, melodious effect they should? Has the author used rhyme in an effective manner (think in relation to sound and meaning together) and does she use it to its potential?
4. Does the language seem natural? Has the poet adhered not only to form but also the standard elements of poetics (imagery, line breaks, point of view, voice, etc.) that help to make a poem "good"?

Perseverance

Wage war against the tide   >   Though close to Thomas, it will
whose salty mist blurs <u>thy</u> sight   serve you well
Until endless waves subside   archaic diction

And though the sailor's stride   3 empty words in a row
Falls heavy on the deck at night
The ship still rages against the tide   >   good shift of line

The depths below may not confide   This stanza is getting there,
The endnote of the tireless fight   but could we build the image?
Until the sea grows calm and the waves subside

In the dusk the gulls ride
The cliffs in open flight   nice
whose face stands against the tide

Ho Ho the tuna far below do hide   >   watch syntax. Ho Ho?
From the net that flies like a kite
In the endless waves that don't subside

Though the storm bursts quite contride   not a word
Even if the shore is far from sight
Wage war against the tide
Until the endless waves subside.

JENNIFER VAN DYKE

Jennifer,
This is good work for your first time out with the villanelle. I'm glad you
chose to write in a form because it really does show some discipline
and what putting the form to use can do for the poem. You have created
some good phrasing and taken small liberties with altering it to get the
sense of incantation and chanting you want—and let me tell you, it
works. There's a real beautiful sound to the poem and a real haunting
quality.

Now, as for the poem, let's talk briefly about imagery. Though the
poem has a nice sense of being on the boat, I think there's room to build
a sense of the images in the poem so that we really see it precisely
and concretely. One spot in particular is lines 16 & 17 where we have a
feeling about the storm rather than what it is. It's simply a spot to consider how the power of that would change if you changed it to an image.
Also, in stanza three you use the abstracts of confide and tireless.
Remember that a concrete image that carries the abstracts under the language—off the page—always does more for us than a straight abstract. I love the images of the net flying out like a kite and the face of the
cliffs—nice.

I like your sound in the poem—the assonance, consonance, and
rhythm. It's just wonderful. And the use of the form—coupled with your

agile use of the repetitive lines—really creates a chant-like quality. It's lovely, Jennifer. And you get mileage from your lines by changing them slightly in the process of reusing them. I find this a very good technique when writing a villanelle. Now, one thing to look at for revision though is your sense of language being a bit archaic. It's as if this is really a kind of "mariners" song. And it may well be, but that comes off a bit like it's the 19th century. Your use of "thy" and "Ho Ho" are a bit dated and unreal. Go hang out with a tuna boat operator and crew and I'm guessing you won't hear "Ho Ho" once. So, try to make the language natural and real and contemporary—language we expect. And, because we understand the abstract from the title, do we really need it? Unless it's the name of the boat, I don't think so—maybe give us something concrete, like a place, or a title about the crew.

It's nice work, Jennifer. Let's see a revision in two weeks.

Jeff

January off the Oregon Coast   >

Nice title change

Wage war against the tide
whose salty mist blurs the sight
Until the endless waves subside

Echoes of the sailor's stride   >
Falls heavy on the deck at night
While the ship rages against the tide

Good revision—you might look at
"Echoes" again

Six months at sea; God and compass to guide
Pen and paper used to write
Messages waiting for waves to subside

I like this revision. It has built an
image and a sentiment in the poem

In the dusk the gulls ride
The cliffs in open flight
whose face stands against the tide

The tuna far below do hide   >
From the net that flies like a kite   >
In the endless waves that won't subside

Come back to this line
good simile

Though the storm bursts revive   >
And scurry threatens to bite   >
Wage war against the tide
Until the endless waves subside.

We're getting there with this one
confusing line

JENNIFER VAN DYKE

Jennifer,

Well, nice revision. You have left some things alone and let them work for now and then altered some other portions of the poem quite significantly. And in doing so you've managed to keep intact the rhythm and other sonic qualities of the poem. Let's talk about the changes you've made, how they're working, and then a few more things to consider for one more revision.

First, I like your diction choices and how you've focused on word choice. And, I hope you saw—as you expressed the other day in the workshop—how focusing on single words or small groups of words and changing them can cause the domino to drop and cause other changes in the poem very naturally. First, your title change is wonderful. Your change in stanza two to the word "Echoes" is a good change. But I have a small problem with the logic of the image, because I'm going to say that out on a deck of a fishing boat in the water you don't hear any echoes. It would be one thing if it was somehow connected to a ghost-like quality of those who have gone before, but it isn't, so the image for me needs more thumping type of pounding of feet—not echoing. Now, stanza three is a good change—well done. This works well because by giving the focus to the boat workers and the specific things like paper and pen and God and the compass, there's a whole sense of fear and longing and loneliness and dependence evoked. That's what I was talking about in the first set of comments about how concretes can bring up much for us that is off the page.

Now, as for things that still might be worked on: This line about the tuna hiding. You might see if there is something more natural for the image. I like that you use tuna, but hiding is applying a human assumption to something we haven't even yet seen. It implies omniscience on the part of the persona, and if you do that we at least need to see the tuna before we get the omniscient view of them. And finally, you've changed this second line in stanza six—but what does it mean? What is that "scurry threatens to bite"? There's my poetic side that just gets caught up in it and like to play with figuring it out, but my reader side says, what are you talking about and please don't confuse me now.

You've done some real nice work, Jennifer—let's see one more revision. It's lovely. Keep working with the form. The most important thing to remember when using forms is that you should never impose the form on the poem. Rather the form should rise out of the subject matter naturally. In poetics we call this organic form and it allows the poem to keep a natural sense of language and meaning while employing the form to do work for the poem.

Nice work.

Jeff

January, Just from Tillamook off the Oregon Coast

Wage war against the tide
whose salty mist blurs the sight
Until the endless waves subside

The heaving feet of the sailor's stride
Falls wet on the deck at night
While the ship rages against the tide

Six months at sea; God and compass to guide
Pen and paper used to write
Messages waiting for waves to subside

In the dusk the gulls ride
The cliffs in open flight
whose face stands against the tide

The tuna, deep, in darker currents ride
From the net that flies open like a kite
In the endless waves that won't subside

When the storm bursts revive
With stiff backs to a shore that's far from sight
Wage war against the tide
Until the endless waves subside.

JENNIFER VAN DYKE

Ultimately, this is the change that Jennifer brought back. We'll notice that she tinkered with the title just a bit more and took it one level further in specifics. What I particularly liked about that change was that she invoked a sense of leaving port and that she couples this with the revision she makes in the last stanza with the line "with stiff backs to a shore that's far from sight." And she gets a real sense from that line and the title of working, of leaving home behind, and of being far from land. And we can also see that she paid attention to detail once again—as well as how one shift brings on another— by revising the word "echoes" to "The heaving feet," which provides a sense of work and brings on "wet" in the next line—which gives a detail about the boat.

In the end, I'd consider Jennifer's first time trying a villanelle a successful one, despite some tight language moments and taking her inspiration from Dylan Thomas. That's fine to me, that she's read in the tradition and found something to guide her. She's ultimately made a nice coupling of a form to contemporary language, to capturing a sense of hard work on a fishing boat, not just some romantic mariner's song that is filled with abstractions. And she's let the form do work for her by providing a sense of rhythm, sound, and song-like movement around the tradition of work. So, in the end, she hasn't traded her creativity over to the form for a mere adornment of language.

POEMS FOR FURTHER READING

On Reading Poetry

It's a funny thing to ask writers who they've read recently. Often, we get the expected answer that's something like, "well I've just been reading James Dickey's collected poems." But, there are strange answers that range from things like poets telling you they've only read novels lately to a recent student of mine telling me he read only his own work. I believe it was T.S. Eliot who once said that as writers, when we're young, we read everything; when we're middle aged, we read only our friends who are writers; and when we're old, we read only ourselves. Well, maybe by the time we're as old and accomplished as Stanley Kunitz we've earned the right to read only our own work, though I suspect he reads others' work voraciously. But when we're young writers (meaning young in our writing careers) we ought to be reading everything we can get our hands on. When we read, and we read broadly, it opens our view to the world; it opens our poetic sensibility to a range of styles; and it opens our creative prospects to myriad possibilities. Essentially, if we read closely and we're sharp, reading is the best thing a writer can do.

A friend of mine who works in politics recently said to me, "You know, I just want to sit back and enjoy the poem." And, of course, my response is to do so. But as writers we must read a poem the way a carpenter strolls through a house. He may just be at a friend's house or out enjoying a home tour. But, he knows that the person who did the framing used certain materials. He can see whether a stairway has certain integrity in key spots. He knows the tools a finish worker might have used piecing together walnut wainscoting. As writers, we come to gain this same skill by coupling our processes of writing and reading. For instance, when we build a poem and work and rework our images, we find the precise words that cause the image to become compelling. And, if we're paying very close attention, or maybe we have much experience, we know exactly why the words work—it's not simply a happy accident. Then as we talk through other poems, we begin to see that, in fact, Bruce Weigl's careful attention to the detail in the first image in "Song of Napalm" is actually what makes the middle and final images so compelling—because we never forget what the rainy view across the field looks like. And then we decide, "Ahh, that's what I need to do in one of my poems."

So as writers, we come at things from a structuralist standpoint. It is no wonder that the Russian formalists (as literary theorists) developed a literary theory of interpretation around structure—it is no wonder because they were writers themselves. Poets come to understand why and how a poem works because we understand the value of a rhyme scheme, syllabically measured lines, metaphor (in all its various forms), syntax, line breaks, and all the other poetic elements. And if we don't know all these things, or if we don't feel comfortable with them, well, then we come to be comfortable with them in our own work by reading, and reading, and reading the work of others so that we see those things being used in ways that cause us to understand their value. We understand these things in relation to the heart, how they make a poem feel. We finally say, after reading a poem such as Leon Stokesbury's "Unsent Message to My Brother in His Pain," that we understand how similes can cause emotion to roll forth like thunder. I know that writers want to read poems like my friend, Maria—I want to read them like that all the time— just sit back and read. But we must always take a pass (or four) at a poem with structure and work in mind. If we are to glean from the masters, if we are to understand that we indeed are working within a long, world-wide tradition of art, then we have the responsibility of paying attention to ourselves and those voices of our community and culture that we represent in our work. And we must pay attention to *how* we represent experience.

When we've read a poem, we might ask some basic structural questions of it so that we can begin to make sense of the poem:

1. Who is the persona of the poem—who is speaking/telling the poem?
2. What is the point of view of the poem?
3. Are there key images in the poem? How has the author used metaphors, similes, or symbolism to advance the poem in any way?
4. What sonic qualities are in the poem? How has the poet used rhyme (any of the types of rhyme), rhythm, meter, or alliteration to create some effect in the poem?
5. How do line breaks and stanza breaks affect the poem?
6. What do we come to learn about the persona of the poem and/or the experience they have just shared in the poem? What poetic elements help us learn this?

Obviously, as we read poems, we are hard at work answering some of these questions. The poetic elements might begin to work on us unconsciously as we lie on the couch reading. We might come to the end of a poem and have an immediate conclusion about it. We might come out of it and be sent straight back to the start. But as we look over it, line by line,

we need to remember that we have the masters whispering in our ears,
saying "Try this, try this, come, you'll see."

The Eagle [1851]

ALFRED, LORD TENNYSON   (1809–1892)

He clasps the crag with crooked hands;
Close to the sun in lonely lands,
Ringed with the azure world, he stands.
The wrinkled sea beneath him crawls:
He watches from his mountain walls,   5
And like a thunderbolt he falls.

Because I Could Not Stop for Death

EMILY DICKINSON (1830–1886)

Because I could not stop for Death—
He kindly stopped for me—
The Carriage held but just Ourselves—
And Immortality.

We slowly drove—He knew no haste
And I had put away
My labor and my leisure too,
For His Civility—

We passed the School, where children strove
At Recess—in the Ring—
We passed the Fields of Grazing Grain—
We passed the Setting Sun—

Or rather—He passed Us—
The Dews drew quivering and chill—
For only Gossamer, my Gown—
My Tippet—only Tulle—

We passed before a House that seemed
A Swelling of the Ground—
The Roof was scarcely visible—
The Cornice—in the Ground—

Since then—'tis Centuries—and yet
Feels shorter than the Day
I first surmised the Horses' Heads
Were toward Eternity.

I Think I Could Turn and Live With Animals

WALT WHITMAN (1819–1892)

I think I could turn and live with animals they are so placid and
self-contained;
I stand and look at them long and long.
They do not sweat and whine about their condition;
They do not lie awake in the dark and weep for their sins;
They do not make me sick discussing their duty to God;
Not one is dissatisfied—not one is demented with the mania of
owning things;
Not one kneels to another, nor to his kind that lived thousands of
years ago;
Not one is respectable or industrious over the whole earth.

On Being Brought from Africa to America

PHILLIS WHEATLEY (1754–1784)

'Twas mercy brought me from my *Pagan* land,
Taught my benighted soul to understand
That there's a God, that there's a *Saviour* too:
Once I redemption neither sought nor knew.
Some view our sable race with scornful eye,
"Their colour is a diabolic die."
Remember, *Christians, Negroes*, black as *Cain*,
May be refin'd, and join th' angelic train.

She's Free!

FRANCES E. W. HARPER (1825–1911)

How say that by law me may torture and chase
A woman whose crime is the hue of her face?—

With her step on the ice, and her arm on her child,
The danger was fearful, the pathway was wild. . . .
But she's free! yes, free from the land where the slave,
From the hand of oppression, must rest in the grave;
Where bondage and blood, where scourges and chains,
Have placed on our banner indelible stains. . . .

The bloodhounds have miss'd the scent of her way,
The hunter is rifled and foiled of his prey,
The cursing of men and clanking of chains
Make sounds of strange discord on Liberty's plains. . . .
Oh! poverty, danger and death she can brave,
For the child of her love is no longer a slave.

Killers

CARL SANDBURG (1878–1967)

I am singing to you
Soft as a man with a dead child speaks;
Hard as a man in handcuffs,
Held where he cannot move:

Under the sun
Are sixteen million men,
Chosen for shining teeth,
Sharp eyes, hard legs,
And a running of young warm blood in their wrists.

And a red juice runs on the green grass;
And a red juice soaks the dark soil.
And the sixteen million are killing . . . and killing and killing.

I never forget them day or night:
They beat on my head for memory of them;
They pound on my heart and I cry back to them,
To their homes and women, dreams and games.

I wake in the night and smell the trenches,
And hear the low stir of sleepers in lines—
Sixteen million sleepers and pickets in the dark:
Some of them long sleepers for always,
Some of them rumbling to sleep to-morrow for always,

Fixed in the drag of the world's heartbreak,
Eating and drinking, toiling . . . on the long job of killing.
Sixteen million men.

Sonnet: 14 "If thou must love me. . ."

ELIZABETH BARRETT BROWNING (1806–1861)

If thou must love me, let it be for naught
Except for love's sake only. Do not say
"I love her for her smile—her look—her way
Of speaking gently,—for a trick of thought
That falls in well with mine, and certes brought
A sense of pleasant ease on such a day"—
For these things in themselves, Beloved, may
Be changed, or change for thee,—and love so wrought,
May be unwrought so. Neither love me for
Thine own dear pity's wiping my cheeks dry,—
A creature might forget to weep, who bore
Thy comfort long, and lose thy love thereby!
But love me for love's sake, that evermore
Thou mayst love on, through love's eternity.

In Which She Satisfies a Fear with the Rhetoric of Tears

SOR JUANA INES DE LA CRUZ (1648–1695)
TRANS. BY WILLIS BARNSTONE

This afternoon, my love, speaking to you
since I could see that in your face and walk
I failed in coming close to you with talk,
I wanted you to see my heart. Love, who
supported me in what I longed to do,
conquered what is impossible to gain.
Amid my tears that we poured out in pain,
my heart became distilled and broken through.
Enough my love. Don't be so stiff. Don't let
these maddening jealousies and arrogance
haunt you or let your quiet be upset
by foolish shadows: false signs of a man's
presence; and as you see my heart which met
your touch—now it is liquid in your hands.

The Movies

FLORENCE KIPER FRANK (1885–1976)

She knows a cheap release
From worry and from pain
The cowboys spur their horses
Over the unending plain.

The tenement rooms are small;
Their walls press on the brain.
Oh, the dip of the galloping horses
On the limitless, wind-swept plain!

A Winter Ride

AMY LOWELL (1874–1925)

Who shall declare the joy of the running!
    Who shall tell of the pleasures of flight!
Springing and spurning the tufts of wild heather,
    Sweeping, wide-winged, through the blue dome of light.
Everything moral has moments immortal,
    Swift and God-gifted, immeasurably bright.

So with the stretch of the white road before me,
    Shining snow crystals rainbowed by the sun,
Fields that are white, stained with long, cool, blue shadows,
    Strong with the strength of my horse as we run.
Joy in the touch of the wind and the sunlight!
    Joy! With the vigorous earth I am one.

The Fathers

GARY THOMPSON (B. 1947)

They bake bread
late into the night,
needing kitchen smells, the lights
to overtake dread.

They look around
the empty room

with empty eyes, but doom
is not a sound

their ears will hear.
Sadness, yes, and loss
of some vague self across
a recipe of years

that came to this—
the fathers baking bread
into the night, the kneaded
dreams, the hiss

of steam, their children gone
into the night, and done.

An American Tale of Sex and Death

KEVIN STEIN (B. 1954)

Before I'd felt the promised kiss of either —
pink tongue of one, feathered breath of the other —
I knew their kinship among lords of life
and fealty I'd pay from pocket and heart,
or both. Stoic Catholic teacher-priests
had ceded the subject to shocked locker
room gossip, so imagine my wonder,
child of the fat book, when I blundered on
Romeo & Juliet in the library
Carnegie's steel monopoly gifted
my Hoosier town. Oh how the bard's language
spilled like sunlight through the oft zitted dome
shrouding my green teenage brain, a verbal
hubbub above the flesh and brash sword play.

                    *   *   *

Our play at home featured yardstick-duels,
my sister trilling, "Avaunt, errant knave"
until I thwacked her knuckles and she cried.
Sent to my room, I bled Mercutio's
last gasp into red carpet, perfecting
the raised head's fall. By luck, Zefferelli's
classic movie remake graced the downtown
Paramount's sagging screen. It cost a week's
lunch money, glad fasting, so friends and I

might treat a sweet trio of girls beneath
the balcony's stiff lip. I'd love to say
our hand-holding, like any gateway drug,
led to higher pleasures, but mine was greased
with popcorn slurb and hers was wet with sweat.

            *   *   *

Don't sweat the truth: It wasn't my heart's first
nor last diffident failure, and this time
I looked up when Olivia Hussey's
olive chest splashed on screen, each breast maybe
four feet across and deeply cleaved. Though I'd
seen others flashed in sticky magazines
flooring the burned-out basement where bad boys
sniffed glue, and though since I've held love's ample
gifts, none was as monstrously glorious
as these Shakespeare conjured in serif type.
Who was Capulet and who Montague
I don't remember, nor the actor's name
Who played Romeo in stitched elastic
tights, that too prissy narcissistic fool.

            *   *   *

We three fools of brushed velour mourned those breasts
amidst the climax's sad collapse. Moping
and hushed, we walked our brick streets home, the girls
safely station-wagoned off by mommy.
That not one of us boys had touched any
sweatered breast meant not a lick. Confusion
fueled our hormonal musings, April '68,
a few ticks late for the Summer of Love
we'd read about soundly after the fact.
A crowd frothed around the YMCA,
someone with a yellow bullhorn lathered
the night faces that dipped and rose like waves
of inland seas. When we turned on Lincoln,
the bullhorn's feedback asked, *Hey, what's the time?*

            *   *   *

The time's answer: One fist smashed my glasses,
another my white cheek. Each swing brought its
own brass knuckled reply: "Time for Dr. King,"
"Time for Rosa," "My time, motherfucker" —
each quick punch a blunt, punctuated grunt.
I rope-a-doped as would Ali in his
Thrilla in Manilla, till each had done
with me what he would. The yellow bullhorn

bellowed, *What's the time?* The brothers answered,
Black Power, Black Power, until I knew
what it was to have none. In dewy grass,
beneath a sappy maple, I looked in
their eyes and they in mine. All right, we looked
but didn't — this, the day Martin got his.

*   *   *

His was death, though I'd like to say I learned
a fleshed lesson — one you carry folded
in the pocket your wallet's in, something
to mull in traffic, awaiting the doc,
or popping corn for the rented movie
the kids can't watch. You're waiting to hear it
white America, so you can smirk your
absolution. And yes, you're waiting too.
black America, so you can shake your head
I don't get it. When the twenty finished
with me, they chanted down Lincoln's rubble.
One man, eyeing my near-sighted fumble
and plea, picked up my too thick black-rimmed specs
and placed them gently on my swollen face.

*   *   *

"Face it, you at the wrong place at the wrong
time, brother," He said, *brother*. Through cracked lens,
we might've been — his face pieced together
as Picasso knew before the first war,
before the second, before Jeanie Peek,
tended my lumps, she pregnant by a black
guy her parents wouldn't let her marry.
Her radio spun the web we're trapped in,
as Zombies sang "it's the time of the season
for loving." My friend Clayton, black as his name,
kicked the gang leader's butt. For me, he said.
I looked in his eyes, he in mine. America?
Sure: Clayton's in prison, I write sonnets.
The truth? Look it in the eye or you're blind.

The Passing House

BECKIAN FRITZ GOLDBERG (B. 1954)

The way cat fur comes in cool from the night. The way you pour on your hand
the white flour kept in the fridge. If coolness could be powder. If our atoms were

infinite beings. And now the smallest things are so important, especially when your heart is broken as it is by the white. Imagine if the downy moon rose tonight and, while the husbands slept, you finally got to think. And that thinking, of course, involved a lifetime and the three seconds of your skin thrilling against the damp swimsuit. Chilled rose petals at the florist's shop. You felt them between your fingers. Your skin was luck. It proved whatever dies in true love can be found living elsewhere, in woven cotton or in a sudden pocket of November chill or in the hum of a mysterious machine at night. And not by the way of compensation only but as a little thunder far away is comforting when you listen from your bed. Or as the aroma of hickory smoke can be years ago in the morning in Thebes, Montana coming from a passing house.

At a Wedding in Mexico City

LISA CHAVEZ (B. 1961)

We watch the bride and groom at the altar,
their faces bright as torches
that fire-eaters swallow on the streets
of this sprawling city. First marriage—
our friends' faces glow with all
that they don't yet know.

This is the city of sacrifices, a city
honed sharp as an obsidian blade.
A city where smog devours mountains,
where police and taxi-drivers
make people disappear, where children
beg and sleep on the street.
This is the city of our ancestors—mine,
the bride's—a city where rituals were writ
in blood, in flesh flayed from bone.
There is no innocence here.

And yet there is—in our friends' faces,
blazed with joy. Oh what
could we tell them, you and I, if our mouths
weren't seared into smiles, silent
and grim? How love tarnishes
like the silver on the altar cross? How
it can be extinguished, dramatically
as the fire-eaters' flame?

Or how, as with us, it can simply gutter,
go out, til nothing remains
but a bundle of burnt rags? We could

tell them the truth, you and I: we hurt
each other. We betray
those we love. Everyday we enter
into a city of sacrifices,
and what can we offer but our own hearts
wrenched bleeding, beating
into the harsh light of day.

Nureyev's Feet

For Arlyn Garcia-Perez

SCOTT HIGHTOWER (B. 1952)

My friend's loops have always served up treasures;
Rarely a trawler of her own Sargasso Sea.
While wrenching bandaids, she mumbles
Something about preventing callouses.
Something she had learned. . . . I lean in a little;
And, sure enough, there it is: the center
Of her story, a marrow, glistening and succulent,
Nureyev's feet.
                    It seems she, front center
Had a great view of them at a performance
Of "The King and I." Unexpectedly,
She could see for herself how the great
Artist had pressed them for everything.

Found Map of Spain

GAYLORD BREWER (1965)

This Spain is distant
from the dusted, glowing orchards
of Valencia, the workers'
shacks in crumbled Alicante,
Barcelona's guitarists and Modernisme,
the plumed marble of Madrid.

Farther still, an age
and a history removed at least,
from the Muslim temples
of Granada, the silent shuttered alleys
of Córdoba, Sevilla's bulls
glistening with sweat and death,
the scrub desert of Almería,
the raw-knuckled bars
of Cádiz, its oily docks
squinted toward a failed new world.

No, this Spain is a stone house
chiseled to a mountain, a table
of six eating late in a room
of candles and photos and soft chairs,
a room warmed by a stove
They sit secure from ice storm
such as none remembers
in June or any time.
All around, summer gardens destroyed;
gales kick at slate roofs,
bulbs blink, a wall quietly weeps.
They are grateful, though,
alive and blessed, and know it
and speak it. Sausages in an iron pot
sweet with honey and curry;
onions roasted whole, black skin
sticky on fingers; bread;
a copa of wine. Marcel, the farmer
up the road, 81 who lives
alone, later reports by telephone
that he was perhaps a little
frightened but is alright. Tomorrow
the mayor of this village
and the next will examine flattened
fields and declare disaster.
Now hail the diameter of pearls
hammers shivering doors,
assaults panes fogged by curiosity.
A string of lights flickers.
glasses raised again, finger punching
an exclamation into cloth,
a woman rising, eyes bright,
to improvise that goat's horny ceremony.

As if this small country
within a country, this Spain,
of cats and valleys and the old language,
recognizes itself still
in the remote cartography of its heart,
and the surety of its blood.

Anniversary

TERESA LEO (B. 1966)

I said I wouldn't, the date that started on the back stairs, birdfeeder empty
because November meant silence or bodies stiff from the freeze,
the blue-black mouths that choked back breath in the wind.

I don't need to go there, the juke joint, the pool cue
and speech impediment, your reckless car, a lent heart
joyriding the cornfields, and me, bright lights,

small-town girl with a decent shot from the top of the key,
all rural routes and vegetable stands, a duck pond in winter
with a vacant, imperceptible longing, spring rain.

We drove the cow country, bags of peat moss we stole
wedged in the trunk, two 8-balls, felons, delirious
from the bereft/theft rhyme of *desire* and *seizure* under our skin.

Now that you've called to remind me, to hear it break
in your voice like a bank shot, the three years blow open again,
jumping betties, booby traps, and it's 6am with the engine on,

windowfog, your hand on my finger pressed against the glass,
our secret chirography: *cellardoor.* You ask how I am. I'm dazed,
damaged, living too long under a stark coal miners' sky.

I block the shuck and jive, the *take me, shake me* of Solomon Burke,
the concrete and talk, torso, tangle of birds on electric wires,
one always opposite the rest before it suicides and takes off.

But I say *good* and you say *great*, then we disconnect, two fugitives,
and disappear again into the cruel complicity of self-imposed exile,
knowing that no matter what safehouse, what asylum of state lines
and time zones, there is no witness protection for the lost.

Waking

ALBERT GARCIA (B. 1964)

He woke in the dark to feel
her changed. Her hip, the same
he'd let his fingers graze
each morning before sunrise,
felt cool, odd. Her hair—
what was it?—almost
like a doll's, not real.
He touched her shoulder, that round knob,
then reached for the nightstand lamp.
Her mouth, lips parted
nearly in a word, as if to say,
I'll be up, I'll get breakfast,
as she'd done for forty years,
lay still, open. Under their lids
her eyes had receded. He felt
his own stubbled jaw,
then her cheek, her neck
under the flannel, traced
with his eyes her body's length,
the small mounds it made
in the quilt, then turned off
the lamp—carefully
placed his arm across her chest—
choosing to stay in bed
to wait for whatever would come
with morning's cold light.

Unsent Message to My Brother in His Pain

LEON STOKESBURY (B. 1945)

Please do not die now. Listen.
Yesterday, storm clouds rolled
out of the west like thick muscles.
Lightning bloomed. Such a sideshow
of colors. You should have seen it.
A woman watched with me, then we slept.
Then, when I woke first, I saw

in her face that rest is possible.
The sky, it suddenly seems
important to tell you, the sky
was pink as a shell. Listen
to me. People orbit the moon now.
They must look like flies around
Fatty Arbuckle's head, that new
and that strange. My fellow American,
I bought a French cookbook. In it
are hundreds and hundreds of recipes.
If you come to see me, I shit you not,
we will cook with wine. Listen
to me. Listen to me, my brother,
please don't go. Take a later flight,
a later train. Another look around.

Sermon of the Fallen

DAVID BOTTOMS (B. 1949)

From an east window
a screen of light sliced across the walnut box.
I sat and watched the grain rise dark,
and listened to him tell
how muscles wither under the skin,
and the skin dries and flakes away from the bone
like gray bark flaking from the trunk of a fallen pine,
how the forest trembles once as the tree falls
and somewhere a bird whimpers from a ridge,
then nothing,
and what needles are left yellow-green
and clinging to limbs
shimmer a few times in the train, then lose
all color and drop away,
and the gray pine shines through the bark like bone,
cracks and sours, softens with larva,
collapses in shadow, belches gas
from its grainy soup, dries
in sun to a black forest dust, then seeps
with rain through the pine-needle floor.
So, he said, you had come to fall.
Even as a boy, I could feel the trembling in us all.

Those Riches

ROBERT WRIGLEY (B. 1951)

The week after your father left
you still carried his note in your wallet,
and on the night before the bank
said they'd come for the car,
we were on our way to St. Louis,
our last dime in the gas tank, and you
every way you could find
abusing that sad family sedan,
pounding the dash for the radio it lacked,
shifting without the clutch
and wringing from its feeble six
every stinking, oil-ridden mile per hour.
Down the long hill past the Catholic cemetery,
under the dead viaduct
and into the bottom lands we rolled.
You spoke of jobs you might have soon
at this or that plant or refinery,
smoked my cigarettes, thought
you'd save up for a car and a tattoo.
Through the banks of smog,
the swampland haze, great flames rose
above the foundries and steel mills,
and there was nothing in school
so bright. It was Saturday night,
and you would never go back, not ever.

We found our way to Gaslight Square
and drove slowly down its streets.
You refused to acknowledge the sidewalk crowds,
the soul and blues, the smack jazz
seething from the nightclubs.
At the last bright reaches we were stalled
by traffic, and a whore in hot pants
called from a Laundromat doorway. Sugar,
she sang, and came outward. She walked
to your window, leaned her breasts on your arm,
grinned, and you turned and spat in her face.

What you could not accomplish that night
a handful of outraged, high-heeled prostitutes could.

They kicked at our fenders, spit
with amazing accuracy through our windows.
And with what you claimed to have seen and known
as a blackjack, one leering redhead
bashed in the windshield, turning all
its clear expanse to a sagging honeycomb
of safety glass, before the traffic opened
and we were on our way half blind
into the diesel-scented city night.

Could that have been what we were after,
that joy, those riches
reeling from destruction?
Ten blocks farther on we stopped
and forced the whole window out, down
onto the dash and floor and front seat,
then drove home with the summer highway
wind in our faces, laughing
sitting in a gravel of glass
that flashed under streetlights,
in the full of the moon, like a carload of diamonds.

Funeral

HARRY HUMES (B. 1935)

Drunk, an older brother
burst into our living room,
pushed aside the preacher,
cursed, waved his arms,
lurched against the coffin,
and knocked it over.
My Uncle Nate's body
in good suit and black shoes
rolled onto the floor,
rocked once and settled.
I held my breath,
forced back laughter,
while the undertaker's white hands
eased my uncle back into place,
straightening flowers,
patting down clothes and hair.

My mother raised her eyes
to heaven and moaned,
as the screaming brother
was dragged through the kitchen,
down twenty-five porch steps
into our backyard,
slapped, kicked, warned,
and thrown into the alley.
When I went out hours later,
he was still there,
coat sleeve torn off,
somehow sadder than the coffin,
waving me close
with his dirty, crushed hair,
weeping, mumbling through bloody lips
something like love.

Song of Napalm

BRUCE WEIGL (B. 1949)

For My Wife

After the storm, after the rain stopped pounding,
We stood in the doorway watching horses
Walk off lazily across the pasture's hill.
We stared through the black screen,
Our vision altered by the distance
So I thought I saw a mist
Kicked up around their hooves when they faded
Like cut-out horses
Away from us.
The grass was never more blue in that light, more
Scarlet; beyond the pasture
Trees scraped their voices in the wind, branches
Criss-crossed the sky like barbed-wire
But you said they were only branches.

Okay. The storm stopped pounding.
I am trying to say this straight: for once
I was sane enough to pause and breathe
Outside my wild plans and after the hard rain

I turned my back on the old curses. I believed
They swung finally away from me . . .

But still the branches are wire
And thunder is the pounding mortar,
Still I close my eyes and see the girl
Running from her village, napalm
Stuck to her dress like jelly,
Her hands reaching for the no one
Who waits in waves of heat before her.

So I can keep on living,
So I can stay here beside you,
I try to imagine she runs down the road and wings
Beat inside her until she rises
Above the stinking jungle and her pain
Eases, and your pain, and mine.

But the lie swings back again.
The lie works only as long as it takes to speak
And the girl runs only so far
As the napalm allows
Until her burning tendons and crackling
Muscles draw her up
Into that final position
Burning bodies so perfectly assume. Nothing
Can change that; she is burned behind my eyes
And not your good love and not the rain-swept air
And not the jungle green
Pasture unfolding before us can deny it.

Fish

TOM CRAWFORD (B. 1939)

Outside it's Korea and snowing.
White flakes float in under the eaves
and slide sideways into my window.
Inside I'm talking to this big Asian ink brush
about a fish I'd like us to draw.
I've loaded it with the blackest ink
and now I'm holding it, poised

over a clean sheet of 3-foot-long white paper.
I'm keeping my voice down
though I'm pretty excited
and the snow falling outside doesn't help,
but here's what I say, "You know
already from the way I'm holding you
that I'm not an artist."
All right, that's out in the open.
It can't hurt, I figure, to own up
to what the brush knows anyway.
"I'm asking for just one terrible black fish," I say
and inch the brush closer to the white paper.
I know it's cheap of me
to imagine the brush could actually be tempted.
Outside snow's beginning to pile up
on the metal railing, the patio.
The bare branches of the maple below my apartment
look like tall zebras. Very beautiful.
In the distance the buildings of Kwangju
grow even bigger, darker, in the falling snow.
"This fish, I only want to look at it!" I implore.
"If not the whole fish, then at least some part of it.
Draw me an eye for god-sakes!"
I hate it when my voice gives me away
like some old man who's discovered
he's on the wrong bus.
In my hand is a long length of yellow bamboo with a
shock of horse hair black with ink.
Made in Korea, it says,
and not the Romantic Period. I let that go.
There will always be the detractors.
Outside it's growing dark, Presbyterian
as the red, neon crosses begin to come on
across the city.
I put my tongue on the glass window
to feel the cold,
to feel what snow feels.
If I could leave my body right now
where would I go more amazing than this—
this black fish for company,
alive down there somewhere in the paper
and me, up here,
happy, alone in the snow.

Poem for the Young White Man Who Asked Me How I, an Intelligent Well-Read Person, Could Believe in the War between Races

LORNA DEE CERVANTES

In my land there are no distinctions.
The barbed wire politics of oppression
have been torn down long ago. The only reminder
of past battles, lost or won, is a slight
rutting of the fertile fields.

In my land
people write poems about love,
full of nothing but contented childlike syllables.
Everyone reads Russian short stories and weeps.
There are no boundaries.
There is no hunger, no
complicated famine or greed.

I am not a revolutionary.
I don't even like political poems.
Do you think I can believe in a war between races?
I can deny it. I can forget about it
when I'm safe,
living on my own continent of harmony
and home, but I am not
there.

I believe in revolution
because everywhere the crosses are burning,
sharp-shooting goose-steppers round every corner,
there are snipers in the schools. . .
(I know you don't believe this.
You think this is nothing
but faddish exaggeration. But they
are not shooting at you.)

I'm marked by the color of my skin.
The bullets are discrete and designed to kill slowly.
They are aiming at my children.
These are facts.

Let me show you my wounds: my stumbling mind, my
"excuse me" tongue, and this
nagging preoccupation
with the feeling of not being good enough.

These bullets bury deeper than logic.
Racism is not intellectual.
I can not reason these scars away.

Outside my door
there is a real enemy
who hates me.
I am a poet
who yearns to dance on rooftops,
to whisper delicate lines about joy
and the blessings of human understanding.
I try. I go to my land, my tower of words and
bolt the door, but the typewriter doesn't fade out
the sounds of blasting and muffled outrage.
My own days bring me slaps on the face.
Every day I am deluged with reminders
that this is not
my land

and this is my land.

I do not believe in the war between races

but in this country
there is a war.

PART TWO

Fiction

CHAPTER

14

SURROUNDED BY STORIES: WHERE OUR STORIES COME FROM

It seems that if someone wanted to be a writer but could not think of anything to write about, he would have the proverbial cart before the horse. Why would you want to write if you didn't have something you wanted to write about? Why speak if there is nothing to say?

With that said, it is apparent that you, the reader, are interested in the creative arts, and specifically in the craft of writing fiction. Each of us has a unique world view and it is through our stories that our view will be given the light of day. But where do our stories come from? The short answer to this is that the stories come from our own lives and from the lives of others. Remember this: *We are surrounded by stories.* Anyone suffering from the psychosomatic syndrome known as "Writer's Block" might do well to repeat this over and over again as a mantra to unleash the mind: *We are surrounded by stories. We are surrounded by stories. We are surrounded by stories.*

Certainly, the more experiences we have, the more stories we have to tell. It seems to me that one of the more beneficial things you could do for yourself as both a person and a writer is to travel as widely as you can afford. The reason for that is twofold. First, by traveling away from home, you

> *I write about my personal experiences whether I've had them or not.*
>
> Ron Carlson

will see home with new eyes, and in that sense you will be seeing your home for the first time. If you have never left your hometown of Portland, Oregon, for example, what do you have to compare it with? But if you have been to Prescott, Arizona, then you will see Portland with new eyes and you may recall detail that you would not have brought to your level of conscious thought (and to your writing) unless you had gone somewhere else. I believe the only way you can truly see your surroundings is to leave them in your wake.

The second benefit for the writer who travels is the more obvious of the two: travel is almost always adventure—unless you dilute the experience by staying in five-star hotels—and from adventure comes stories. Whether you drive from Seattle to Boise or take a train from Shanghai to Beijing, you will see places and people worthy of writing about. The key, of course, is to keep your eyes open. When I have finished a writing project, especially a long project, I like to go somewhere I have never been before. It invigorates me, and from these new settings new stories always come. The destination need not be exotic, however; it could be a part of the city where I live but have never been. It could be just around the corner.

In 1987, my wife and I took a ship from Kobe, Japan, to Shanghai, China. It was a small ship, more of a ferry than a cruise ship, really, and nothing terribly exciting occurred on the two-day voyage. In 1994, something reminded me of that trip of seven years before, and I thought that a small ship cutting west through the East China Sea to Shanghai would make a compelling setting for a story, and I wrote "Slow Boat to China." Travel to new places offers new settings which can always provoke me to use them as foundations for stories to stand upon.

But even if we never left our hometowns, there would be enough stories to write for the rest of our lives. I believe eavesdropping to be not only one of the most enjoyable and beguiling of pastimes, but also to be one of the most fertile activities from which to harvest new stories (I do not advocate a literal interpretation of the word, however, for you could slip and fall). People may say that eavesdropping is rude and to them I say that we do not walk through town with our eyes closed, nor should we plug up our ears with cotton balls when there are good things to be heard. I overheard (*overheard* sounds so much more polite than eavesdrop, yet it also implies listening from an elevation) an absolutely fabulous anecdote the other day, but alas, I will not divulge it here for I am still writing a story born of that juicy tidbit (note that it is unwise to tell your stories before you have written them, for it diminishes your ability to make them fresh on the page).

One of the assignments I give my students is to go to a public place, say a restaurant, and eavesdrop on a conversation between two people. The students are to write down what is said as best they can. The assignment is actually a dialogue exercise explained later in this book, but it also allows the students the chance to realize the wealth of stories that eavesdropping affords.

Of course, there are also the stories we hear from friends and family, and they, too, can be seeds from which stories and even novels may germinate. A word of warning, though: if the story was about an event that occurred to someone you are familiar with, you might do well to avoid showing him or her your version for it will necessarily be different from what actually happened. This is because the story must *carry on the page*. In other words, it must be able to stand alone with an arc of its own and thus, it is almost always necessary to change what actually happened to what will work on the page.

An example of this type of story-genesis is Raymond Carver's "Why Don't You Dance?" Carver was sitting around with friends and fellow writers one evening when one of them told of how he had passed a driveway where all of the house's furnishings—bed, sofa, table, chairs, record player, lamps et cetera—were neatly arranged in the driveway as if someone lived *there*, outside. Then he asked the group which one of them was going to take this setting and write a story. Carver spoke up and the rest, as they say, is history.

Assuming that you never leave your house, and that you have no family, friends or acquaintances to draw from—and this all seems very postmodern and rather unlikely—then you may use the newspaper as a source of your stories (Robert Olen Butler wrote an entire collection of short stories, *Tabloid Dreams*, each story idea having been taken from a tabloid headline). Newspapers are full of intriguing stories. Taking the idea for a story from a newspaper article, by the way, is not plagiarism because you are simply basing a story on another account of something that happened to someone somewhere, and you are then making your own story from that kernel event. You may use the plot of the newspaper account and create new characters and maybe even a new setting.

When telling a visitor how he came up with stories, Anton Chekhov implied that the genesis of many of his ideas came from simple objects. He picked up the first thing he saw on a table, an ashtray, and told the visitor that he would have a story called "The Ashtray" by the next day.

The point to all this is to remind the writer that there are always stories, that we will never run out; one must merely keep one's eyes and ears opened. And if there were a finite number of stories we could tell, that would not matter in the least because in reality, we just keep retelling the same old stories anyway. "Romeo and Juliet" has been told hundreds and hundreds of times since Shakespeare's time; it is just that we put the star-crossed lovers in different settings in different times. That, and we change the names to protect the innocent.

One of a writer's greatest assets is his imagination. The English word "imagination" is derived from the Latin *imaginari*, meaning to form an image in one's mind and to create a picture for oneself. Thus, we create that picture in our mind and develop it into a story on the page, a story that will allow the reader another vicarious voyage wherein another shred, no matter how slight, of the human condition may be viewed. Yes, we do make up stories.

It is certainly useful to keep a writer's journal. Our memories are not infallible, and though we think we will remember an idea or a phrase, more often than not that idea—no matter how profound—gets lost. I keep a journal of not only story ideas but also of phrases and descriptions and characters' names. In short, I write down whatever I find interesting. When I have finished a story and am ready to move on to a new project, I look through the journal and inevitably, a story idea will come from its tattered pages.

You will find your stories. You will never suffer from Writer's Block. It does not exist. There will be more stories than you will ever have time to tell. Just keep your eyes and ears open. And remember: *We are surrounded by stories. We are surrounded by stories. We are surrounded by stories.*

THE SECOND STORY: HOW A PROMISING SINGLE EPISODE MIGHT FIND ITS FULLEST USE IN OUR FICTION

Ron Carlson

So many of my students' early stories are single moments, episodes, which are presented in the first person. The narrator, many times, appears to bear a strong similarity to the student. An example would be the "spring break in Mexico" story. In life spring break offers young people bonafide adventure, and if you go to college in Arizona many times these adventures are found south of the border. Three guys will pack up and head down to Rocky Point (*Puerto Penasco*), the town nearest Phoenix on the Gulf of California. There'll be camping and drinking and members of the opposite sex who are also camping and drinking, and all of this on spring break. A friendship will be tested by a decision made late the second night (never the first night) and the story will close on the ride home as the world and his best friend look different to the narrator. I'm being glib here, and such stories (the five or six I see every year) are never bad. There's always good humor in them and the imagery is mostly convincing, and because they are never quite bad, overtly shallow, or melodramatic, I've tried to wrestle with how the writer might get the next thing out of such a story.

In some way, such stories full of sand, sun, and Mickey and Doris far from home are stories we're just going to have to write. We went to the beach on our own for the first time and sat under the stars with people we'd just met, and we held our own in the conversations which were sophomoric and profound, and we made a mistake or narrowly avoided one, and we should write it down. I'm convinced that how we feel about the material, our emotional commitment to the material, is more important than the drama innate in the material; and by material here, I simply mean the data from the event we're using as basis for the story.

Do we write from our own experiences? Absolutely. But fiction, as all the big books have it, is different from recorded event. How? Somehow the teller changes, or we let the written record evolve from actual events in a process we call fiction writing. It evolves because we let go of the actual episode while we are writing it, the way you let go of the handlebars of a bicycle, and you follow as much as lead as you go forward. Your weight and velocity and angle suggest real good possibilities on how not to fall, and you listen to them. Writing a true story is often not about where you were going, but about how you didn't fall.

But the topic here is the single story, the episode which while pretty good, still could go farther. The craft exercise illustrated by the attached story could fall under the heading **narrative distance**. Narrative distance is how far the narrator is (in time and sometimes in place) from the story she is telling. When I recount my trip to Rocky Point it will be at the removal of twenty-five years, and there will be signpost transitions in the text to indicate that, such as: "In 1974 in a blue Volkswagen Bug Elaine and I crossed the border into Mexico . . ." Or: "Twenty-five years ago in a car my wife brought to our marriage, we drove south on the continent until we struck the first blue water bay . . ." et cetera, et cetera. Sometimes the distance is years and sometimes it is months or weeks, or most often it is an implied "recent past." The effect of distance like this is to shift the emphasis slightly from the episode to the effect of the episode and thereby, sometimes, get two stories where there might have been one.

I'm oversimplifying this, but for our purposes, that's fine. I'm speaking, I think, to the writer who has a hot episode and is not sure that it is enough of a resource to make a story out of, but wants to worry it north and south for a while just to see.

For that writer, I would suggest this jewelry metaphor: hold your gem and consider how it might be best displayed.

The more glittering your idea/event/episode, the more important it is to hold fire before starting. We see these one-note stories which are absolutely "on topic," stories which want to have a point, make a statement. This is limited fiction. Limited by being overtly neat, pat, smug.

My example is a student story that tantalized and ultimately stunned me, and I include the story of that story here.

My student, Bob Nelson, presented a story to me in consultation about a strange investment seminar. One evening a man, the narrator, goes to an elementary school to attend a generic mutual funds seminar. He's come into a little money and is thinking of learning how to invest. While he is waiting for the seminar to start, there is an act of violence. A man attending a parent-teacher conference in a nearby room pulls a gun, threatens several people and then, in front of the group, the distraught man kills himself. Our narrator leaves in a confused, bemused, philosophical state. The end.

Of course stories which end with the narrator in a bemused, confused, philosophical state are quite common, and in apprentice writers these stories usually end with what I call soundtrack; that is, natural symbols from the real world. Such as: *I left the building and began searching the dark parking lot for my old Camaro under the cold stars.* Or: *The wind was strange now and urged me toward my car, my footsteps slapping the dry pavement.* These endings aren't bad. (A stark epiphany and full understanding of what had happened and how nothing would ever be the same would be a bad ending.) But, again, how can the moment be more, make a bigger splash, get some on us?

Nelson chose to wait to find another situation to couple his episode with. Lessons from literature show us that the broader and more overt/violent/extreme/melodramatic/magical the event, the better it is served by narrative distance. There is the story of a man who gets his face slapped, and then the story of somebody telling a story about a man getting his face slapped. In which is the slap louder? In which is the slap more resonant? (True answer: it depends. Suggested answer: the latter.)

You can check this out with the Slap Exercise. Write a first person account of slapping or being slapped (one slap please!) in one page. Then write a second short story also in one page in which one person tells another a story of a slap or being slapped.

Bob Nelson waited and found his frame story after writing two other stories. He gave the seminar story to a character named Harley Sjostrand and had it emerge in an interview conducted by his new narrator, a young man looking back on the day he went out to see Harley in the village of Two Rivers. There is another story, of course, the story of the lost sister, and its shadow falls across Harley's seminar story to create a powerful and believable moment.

The story breaks down this way. The first twenty-five percent is the frame, the set up. The narrator tells us of a day years ago when he drove back to his home village to see Harley Sjorstrand. The connection between Harley and the narrator's sister Annie is established.

The main body of the story (more than sixty percent) is given to Harley and his telling of the seminar episode. This was Bob Nelson's original gem.

The return to the frame story composes fifteen percent of the story and goes on to earn a new surprise (beyond the bemused, confused, philosophical moment) when the narrator addresses what that day and those stories made him decide about his life. The catalogue of inventory in Harley's old truck from page one returns, having collected meaning from the interview.

It is a simple and affecting story, built (it would seem) in layers, each having an echo for us. What I like best is that the lost sister is an aching gap in the narrator, but he never tells us that or asks for sympathy. It swims under the body of Harley's story, threatening us the entire time.

MUTUAL FUNDS

Robert Nelson

It was raining when I left the dorm. I ran across the parking lot and tossed my dirty laundry into the car. On my way out of town, I stopped at Sears to buy a cheap tape recorder for the interview. The drive from Grand Forks to Two Rivers took an hour and a quarter; somewhere along the way, the rain turned to drizzle.

Harley Sjostrand's pickup was parked at the curb in front of Folke's Bar. I pulled in behind it. The tailgate was dented, the bumper flecked with rust. The license plate hung from a mess of twisted wire. Scattered about in the back were a dozen or so doubled-over Grain Belt Beer cans, a flat tire, a logging chain, hubcaps, a coil of rope, a rusty jack and a rain-soaked cardboard box. The windows of the pickup were rolled down, and since I had it in my mind to be a journalist, I looked inside. The truck stank of stale beer and cigarette smoke. The ashtray was piled high with butts. Others were scattered on the floor.

It was 1976. I was a sophomore at the University of North Dakota, and was taking a class called Special Articles Writing. It was this class, or an assignment for it, that brought me home to Two Rivers for the weekend. The assignment was to write an article about a character who seemed out of place. Out of place could mean anything, the instructor said, because place could mean anything. Place could be physical, temporal, spiritual. There was even a place exclusively defined within each one of us, the instructor said. After the class that day, I called Harley Sjostrand long distance and asked him for an interview. He asked me what I was after. I explained about the class. I explained about being out of one's place. "This isn't about your sister, then," Harley said. That subject, I told him, was ancient history; we wouldn't talk about Annie. "Off limits," Harley said. After I hung up I called my folks to say I'd be home for the weekend. "Bring your dirty laundry," my mother said.

I went inside the bar. Harley was shooting pool. Art Sorenson, an old man who had once been a farmer, stood behind the bar; he had a cup of coffee and a newspaper. Other than that, the place was empty. I ordered a pitcher of beer. When the old man brought it, along with a tall glass, I moved to a booth and sat down. Except for the occasional crack of the cue ball, the place was quiet. And then Harley said, "I been shooting stick since nine," and he slammed the eight ball in harder than it needed to go, but it stayed. He laid the cue stick on the table, grabbed his half empty glass off the bar, and walked over.

Harley was a tall, slender man, with a dinky round beer-belly that hung over his belt. His forearms were muscular, and still tan from a season of farming. He wasn't a farmer in the true sense of the word—Harley didn't own land nor did he rent it—but he was a hired man for a family that farmed on the Minnesota side of the Red River, not far from the old house Harley and my sister, Annie, had lived in.

I pulled the new tape recorder from my backpack.

"What you should do," Harley said, "if you really want to learn something, is ask me about my pool playing."

"This isn't a comedy piece I'm writing," I said, opening my "Reporter's Notebook."

Harley pushed his hat back. "A smart ass. Just like your sister." Harley's eyes were deep-set and blue and narrowly-placed. They could be piercing. He reached for the pitcher and filled his glass with beer.

I knew a couple of things about Harley already. He had left Minneapolis seven years earlier, and then, 360 miles later, he had picked up a hitchhiker standing on the outskirts of Two Rivers. That hitchhiker was my sister, Annie. She was unmarried and pregnant and had just moved home from college in the middle of the fall semester. It didn't last at home. She quarreled with my father and mother. Then finally there was a big blow out and Annie left. When Harley picked her up, she took him to the old farm house my father had just bought along with some land. Harley didn't just drop Annie off, he moved in with her instead.

"There's only one thing you need to know about pool," Harley said. "And that is that it's not a sport. It's a social event. You could go a long way in life just knowing that much."

I jotted down "pool, not a sport, a social event." I also noted that Harley was playing alone. What are the rules when you play pool by yourself? I wondered. Can you win? What's to keep you from losing?

"How old are you?" I asked, checking the level on the tape recorder.

"Thirty-four."

"And where are you from?"

"Minneapolis. Born and raised."

I wanted to tell him that you raised crops, that children, you reared; it was something I'd learned in my reporting class. But instead I asked him how a city boy like him ended up in a place like Two Rivers.

"Two Rivers is every boy's dream, isn't it?" he said.

Harley reached into the pocket of his t-shirt and pulled out a pouch of tobacco, a packet of cigarette papers and a matchbook. He snapped a paper from the packet and formed it into a trough. He laid a line of tobacco along the trough, smoothed it, twisted, then licked the glue. "My old man was dying," Harley said, looking at his handiwork. "And I was getting money, right? And all along he'd been saying, 'Mutual funds, boy, put the cash into mutual funds.' Hell, I didn't know squat about mutual funds. That kind of thing don't interest me. But then I saw this ad for a class in the newspaper so I signed up. Hell, I even went." Harley yanked a match loose and struck it. He lit the cigarette and exhaled a cloud of smoke.

"They had the class in this old school building off of Lake Street. Do you know the Cities?"

I said I didn't.

"Doesn't matter," Harley said, "the building's tore down now anyway."

I took a drink of beer. Harley spat a fleck of tobacco from the tip of his tongue.

"So what happened was the class started late and I sat there in the lobby waiting and there's this Indian—not an American Indian, an Indian from India Indian—sitting behind a desk in the lobby. He was all dressed up in a suit and he had on a vest and a tie and so naturally I figured he was the teacher, but I was hoping he wasn't 'cause India Indians are so hard to understand. You ever been around an India Indian?"

I said no.

"Most people around here haven't," Harley said. "Anyway, other people started showing up and when they did the guy behind the desk kept telling them the classroom wasn't ready yet and so please sit down and have a smoke. When the guy finally stood up and said something else, I was on my third cigarette and lost out in some daydream. So, when I finally did hear him talking, quick-like, the way they do, it was too late. But everyone else stood up and started down this hallway so I figured I better keep up for a change, I mean that was the whole idea of the class, to show a little gumption, do something with my money, with my life. I walked past the Indian. He gave me one of those looks. But that kind of thing don't bother me. If you know me at all, you know that much."

Outside the window of the bar, Harley's burnt-orange pickup stood in the rain. I wondered what kind of thing did bother Harley. He drank the last of his beer and poured himself another.

"We ended up standing around in this classroom full of kids' desks. You know, those little pink desks—or maybe blue—with fake wood tops and chairs that turn halfway around. Some of the desks were pushed to the side so a foldout type table, a lunchroom table, could be set up in the middle of the room. I remember there were clowns hanging all over the walls. Paper clowns, with strings scotch-taped to their palms and balloons tied to the string ends. The whole place smelled like paste.

"There was a little kid sitting in one of the desks. Otherwise, the place was empty. Except for us standing there. The kid's chin was on his hand and his wrist was bent like it was double-jointed and he had his head propped up against the wall. His little legs were stretched out. He didn't look at us but his foot kept tapping on the desk leg in front of him. The guy in the suit came in and said to find a seat at the table and sit down.

"I sat across from a blond. I scoped her out first, then I sat across from her. Then the Indian started heehawing around about this and that and then he said, 'Please refrain from smoking in the classroom.' He might have been looking at me when he said that but like I said, that kind of thing don't bother me. It turned out he wasn't the teacher anyway, so it didn't matter at all.

"I hadn't noticed it before but there was a closed door to a small room or office or something off to one side. I thought I heard talking coming from in there is why I noticed it.

"I turned back to the table and counted heads. There were eight of us. One guy was about sixty-five. He said, 'Are we all gonna learn to make money?' Then he smiled and looked around at us. He thought we needed perking up, I guess, 'cause we'd been hanging around so long. But I don't care much for perky or for getting perked up. Your sister was always trying to perk me up. 'Harley,' she'd say, 'perk up.' But she was the one in need of perking up."

"Help's what she needed," I said. I remembered the day she left, the day Harley must have picked her up. We were in the kitchen and my father told my mother to let her go, she'd be back. She'd be all right, my mother said. She just needed time. Time to think.

Harley took a swallow from his beer and set the glass down inside the ring of water it had made, then left behind. "So the old guy— Mr. Perky—he says, 'This is the class on mutual funds isn't it?' and about then I hear a noise coming from that small room. The noise was talking. I don't know if the guy just started talking in there or if he just started talking loud or what, but he said, 'Don't you talk to me about facing facts,' Then it was quiet, and then, 'I can't believe she's telling me to face facts.' Then it's quiet again. Then the door opened a crack and I heard the man snort, like maybe he couldn't believe what was happening. Then the door opened wider and he walked out.

"I can picture this guy even now. He was the kind that's short, but dresses tall. He had on a long tweed coat and he was wearing platform shoes. You know about platform shoes? There ain't no good reason for platform shoes 'cept to make yourself look taller than you are. If he was surprised to see us, he didn't let on.

"He started walking behind my side of the table and he's walking real slow and he says, real quiet this time, almost whispering, he says, 'Christ, she talks to me about facing facts.' Then he says, 'That's funny,' or 'That's not funny,' something like that, but real quiet, like maybe he's alone somewhere trying to figure it out, trying to talk himself into understanding it. But then I turned on the bench to get a better look and when I did the heel of my boot scraped along the floor and it made a sound something like a fart and then someone at the table laughed. It was a short, stupid laugh. I looked up. The man behind me looked pissed so I turned back to the table. Then he said, 'You got a problem?'"

Harley stopped his story and smiled at me and shook his head and laughed and said, "I looked at those clowns hanging on the wall and I smelled that paste and I said to myself, well here's ol' Harley in the wrong place again. And the guy said, and this is where it gets good I suppose, he said, 'I asked you, you got a problem?'

"I looked at that blond sitting across from me. Earlier, when the old guy was spouting off about it being a mutual funds class or not, I'd raised my eyebrows and the blond had smiled at me. It wasn't often I got smiled at. I was looking at her for another one. But she wasn't looking at me. She was watching the guy. Then her eyes swung to the right so I looked too and there was this woman standing in the doorway of that little room and from behind her, from inside, somebody was saying to let him go, but the one in the doorway? she's not worried about the man. She's worried about the kid.

"I heard movement back there then, rustling and scraping, and the guy said, 'A dying man don't care,' and I see the woman in the doorway's eyes get big and she ducks back and there's this roar and wood chips fly off the door frame, I mean the thing just explodes. I turn around and the guy's already yanked the kid out of the desk and he's jerking him around by his shirt and buttons are flying all over the place. He twists him around until he gets him facing us then points the gun at the side of his head, the side of the kid's head. Then the man looks at me because I'm standing now. Then he looks back toward the little room, then back at me because now I'm moving; I've decided to do something.

"'If you got to shoot somebody,' I tell him, 'shoot yourself.'

"'Maybe I'll just shoot you.'

"I figure it's not my time, so soon after the old man going, and if it is . . . well so what, I'm not heading anywhere special. And then the guy says, 'A dying man don't care.' And I said, 'What's this dying man don't care shit?'

"'You tell me,' he said, and he sticks the gun in my face.

"I laughed. I mean it. I laughed right out loud.

"'You think this is funny?' the guy says. 'What's funny about this?'

"I told him I didn't know.

"'Laugh at this, then, funny man,' he says, and he puts the gun to his head and pulls the trigger."

Harley sat back hard in the booth and looked at me. His eyes were wide and dark but the whites were tangled in red.

"So what happened," I said.

"So he blew his brains out is what happened."

I looked away from Harley. Rain, rolling down the large front window of the bar, warped the orange pickup outside.

"Your windows," I said.

"Windows?"

"Your pickup. The windows are down. It's raining."

"It blew apart," Harley said. "The guy's head jerked and then it blew apart. Then he fell. The kid fell too. Then the woman ran out and grabbed him."

Harley slid out of the booth. He looked down at me sitting there. "The next day there was a story about it in the paper. The guy had cancer and his wife had left him. They were meeting with the kid's teacher."

Harley filled his beer glass. "The newspaper called but I had nothing to say. I've never told anyone about it, except Annie, until now. I guess that makes you quite the reporter.

"I took the money I was going to invest in a mutual fund and bought that pickup out there in the rain. A couple days later, I threw my junk in the back and left town. I was on my way west when I saw your sister hitching. And that's how I came to Two Rivers."

Harley set the pitcher down. He walked to the bar and sat on a stool. I switched off my tape recorder, closed my notebook, pushed it all into my backpack.

"And what about my sister," I said. "What did you say to her that night?"

"I never said anything to Annie," Harley said. His back was to me. "I wasn't even there when she did it."

"You were living with her."

"But I wasn't there that night."

Harley swivelled around on the stool and faced me. "Look, your sister was carrying a load of shit before I came along. It got to be more than she could handle. It gets that way sometimes. Someday you'll see."

Harley turned back to the bar. His fingers slid around his glass. He didn't lift it, he only held on. "I want to see that article when it's finished," he said.

I shouldered my backpack and walked outside. The rain had stopped. Water was dripping from the awning over the doorway. The air smelled like melted snow, a springtime smell, though it was late fall. Across the street, two grain elevators stood like giant gray markers against the clouds breaking up in the west. I stepped off the curb into the space between the car my parents had bought me and Harley Sjostrand's pickup. In the box of the beat up truck was a flat tire, rope, a chain, two hubcaps, a jack, and several empty beer cans. In the corner behind the passenger's window lay a rain-soaked cardboard box.

I didn't stop at my parents' that weekend. I didn't rush back to the dorm to write an article for my journalism class. I wrote a story about my sister, instead. I've written other stories. But that first one, the one about Annie, that one started with the junk lying in the back of Harley Sjostrand's pickup.

Exercise

1. Start a writing journal today. Make at least one entry in it each day. Anything and everything goes into this journal, whether it be a story idea, a title, a name, a phrase, a description of a place, etc. The purpose of this regimen is to force you to write down your ideas (ones you think you will remember, but may not) for future use.

C H A P T E R
15

POINT OF VIEW

One of the first decisions a writer must make in starting a new story is what point of view to use, and one of the most natural acts of an emerging writer is to start a new story with what is one of the most deceivingly complex points of view. I am alluding to the **first person point of view**, of course. In a beginning creative writing course, my students are not allowed to write their first story in the first person. The reason is that I want the students to separate themselves from the story itself, and I believe that is more easily done in the **third person limited, third person multiple**, or **third person omniscient**.

While employing the first person as the point of view of a story is the most natural of acts, it is often the most difficult, because the writer must become the character of the story. Inherent in that task is a whole list of demands, not the least of which is that in order to adopt the character's psyche, the writer must shed his or her own identity, and that is no easy trick. Let's say the writer is an eighteen-year-old male from the suburbs outside of Portland, Oregon. He has chosen to write his first story about a rancher in Eastern Oregon who has shot and killed his neighbor because of a dispute involving the neighbor's cows which have been grazing on his land. So far, so good.

The choice of a point of view is the initial act of a culture.

Jose Ortega y Gasset

Now, when he starts writing the story in the first person, he must become that rancher, of course, and to become the rancher he must think like the rancher, talk like the rancher, walk like the rancher, et cetera. He can no longer be an eighteen-year-old college student from the suburbs of Portland.

It goes without saying that in the third person limited he must also understand the rancher, but it will be easier for this writer to narrate in the third person; if he chooses first person, all of the exposition he writes as well as the rancher's dialogue must be written in the persona of the rancher.

With these introductory remarks having been made, let us take a look at the various third person points of view before discussing the use of the first person.

THIRD PERSON LIMITED

Third person limited is just that: it is the third person limited to *one* of the character's points of view (pov), often that of the main character, though not always. In a third person story with the characters Bill, Ed, Sally and Louise, we refer to the characters as he, she and they, of course. But in third person limited, we must decide which character will be our lens through which the story will be seen; in other words, to which character we will limit the point of view from which the story is being told.

If we decide that we will limit the pov to Bill's, we can only narrate when Bill is present. Thus, we might write the following: *They sat in Louise's living room playing four-handed cribbage. Bill got up from the sofa and went into the kitchen for more beer.* Using these two sentences as an example, the reader will see that if the pov is limited to Bill, we cannot describe what the other three characters are doing when Bill is absent from the scene. We cannot write *Sally asked Ed to pass the nuts* because Bill, the lens through whom the story is being told in third person limited, is not present to be our witness. However, given the same scenario, we could write *Bill opened the refrigerator and though the cans of Budweiser were in plain view on the top shelf, he opened the vegetable drawer and rummaged through the sacks of fruits and vegetables until he found what he knew he would find: two bottles of Heineken safely hidden beneath the broccoli and lettuce.*

THIRD PERSON MULTIPLE

The third person multiple pov allows us to have more than one character serve as the lens through which we view the story. Using the example above, if we had chosen Louise to be another lens through which to view the story, then we could have her ask Ed to pass the nuts while Bill is in the kitchen

searching for the imported beer. But the writer has to make a conscious decision as to why he would want to use third person multiple, for while this
point of view is often employed in longer works such as the novel, third person multiple can be jarring to readers in a short work as they bounce back and
forth between characters.

Sometimes a student writer will have unconsciously chosen third person
limited for his story, and halfway through the draft, I will find a scene in
which the character whom the writer has chosen to be the lens is not present—
a scene wherein we are viewing the action through the eyes of another character. This is what is known as a **shift in point of view** (of course, there are
more egregious shifts such as from third person to first or second). A shift in
pov can tumble the reader right out of the hammock where she was quietly
reading, leaving her somewhat dazed and confused.

Because of the sheer scope of a novel, we will often need scenes without
our protagonist and thus, we will need to use a third person multiple point
of view. That does not mean, however, that we must utilize the third person
omniscient point of view.

THIRD PERSON OMNISCIENT

A third person omniscient narrator is not only third person multiple; such a
narrator also knows what even the characters do not know, and hence is all-
knowing. Stephen Crane's third person omniscient narrator in "The Open
Boat" tells the reader that, although the characters in the life raft are in search
of a life-saving station, "It is fair to say here that there was not a life-saving
station within twenty miles in either direction." Although such narrators
were often the norm in eighteenth- and nineteenth-century fiction, use of this
kind of narrator is much rarer today (Brian Moore's novel *The Magician's Wife*
is a contemporary example of this point of view). Henry Fielding's eighteenth-
century novel *Tom Jones* is a good example of the third person omniscient
personal wherein the author often editorializes and may even address the
reader in **metadiscourse**. Fielding often digressed in the novel with this point
of view: "Reader, I think proper, before we proceed any farther together, to
acquaint thee that I intend to digress . . ." In this pov, where the author
announces his presence, the reader is asked to believe the author to be, in a
sense, one of the characters in his own book. Today's readers sometimes find
this intrusive and even incredible. Still, it is possible to use an impersonal
omniscient pov wherein the narrator knows all but does not intervene in the
text with casual asides to the reader wherein the reader is awakened from
what John Gardner referred to as the fictional dream. Gardner wrote that
good fiction "does its work by creating a dream in the reader's mind . . . that

if the effect of the dream is to be powerful, the dream must probably be vivid and continuous." With that in mind, then, using metadiscourse by addressing the reader risks awakening her from that dream.

FIRST PERSON

We are all well acquainted with the first person pov because we employ it every day. As I mentioned earlier, however, the first person is deceivingly complex, for when we write *I* in the voice of a serial killer, we must remember that *he* is not *me* and we must sustain that separation from page one to the end of the story. In other words, we must not slip into our own natural voice. Once we fail to maintain that separation between our own voice and the one we have created, the reader becomes confused and may ascribe a possible mental disorder to either the character or the author.

If you were to write ten different short stories, each in the first person, each narrator would be inherently different and so would be his voice (see Chapter 20). The first person is not one point of view; it is several, and in any given story you, the writer, have a choice of whom you could have narrate. You could choose to narrate the story through the voice of the protagonist, he who is central to the action, and thus be privy to the narrator's thoughts as he is engulfed in the action of the story, or you could narrate that same story through the voice of another character in the story, say a detached observer. Employing the latter point of view would allow the reader to make judgments along with the observer who narrates the story.

Another possibility with the first person is to have more than one narrator. Because of the length of a short story, this is often more manageable in a novel wherein the reader will have more time to make the transition between one narrator and another. William Faulkner uses this pov in his tour de force *As I Lay Dying*, a novel in which he employs fifteen different narrators to tell the darkly comic story of a funeral journey. I call this technique "reality disjuncture" and find it a compelling pov; we get a clearer picture of reality by having more than one person describe the same event, because each person has a different background from which to view that same event—in other words, your reality is different from my reality.

Whether you choose a first person pov through the eyes of the protagonist, a detached observer, or through several narrators, you must decide upon your **narrative distance** (see Ron Carlson's essay "The Second Story" in Chapter 14), that period of time between when the event occurred and the narration of its occurrence. If you have an adult narrator telling a story of something that occurred when he was a child, he will necessarily tell it in a different way as an adult than if he were a child narrator telling the story shortly after the event occurred with no narrative distance. The establishment of the narrative distance gives the reader a clearer picture of the narrator, and it helps the reader ascertain the reliability of the narrator.

SECOND PERSON

The second person voice of *you* is given little attention in these pages for it seems a bit artificial, but Jay McInerney makes good use of it in his novel *Bright Lights, Big City*, a story of a drugged-up and totally disenfranchised young man in a lost society where alienation reigns supreme. McInerney sustains the pov from the first sentence of the novel—"You are not the type of guy who would be at a place like this at this time of the morning"—until the last sentence some 182 pages later: "You will have to learn everything all over again." Although the second person often distances the reader from the work, it is successfully used in this novel because of the subject matter. The second person is another possibility for the writer to consider.

A NOTE ON VERB TENSE

One might note how verb tense affects the pace of the story. Most of our stories are written in the simple past tense. This is, in part, because of narrative distance—because our narrators are looking back—but telling a story in the past tense also speeds up the action and increases the pace of the story.

Bobbie Ann Mason's story "Shiloh" is told in the third person limited point of view employing the present tense. Notice how using the present tense slows down the pace of the story: *Leroy Moffitt's wife, Norma Jean, is working on her pectorals. She lifts three-pound dumbbells to warm up, then progresses to a twenty-pound barbell. Standing with her legs apart, she reminds Leroy of Wonder Woman.*

Notice what happens if we rewrite the paragraph using the past tense: *Leroy Moffitt's wife, Norma Jean, was working on her pectorals. She lifted three-pound dumbbells to warm up, then progressed to a twenty-pound barbell. Standing with her legs apart, she reminded Leroy of Wonder Woman.*

Using the past tense the action is already completed, but using the present tense the reader is waiting for the action to be completed and thus, time moves more slowly. You can see that the action is slower in the first paragraph, which uses the present tense, and Mason consciously chose this tense because everything in their lives has slowed down: Leroy, a truck driver, has been injured, and he now stays at home getting stoned. Only slowly is Norma Jean realizing that their marriage is falling apart.

Much of the reward in writing is that you are in control. You have hundreds of choices to make in any given story, and two of them are verb tense and pov. There will be times when you will write a story and after a few drafts you will realize that the pov is not working. This happened to a student of mine who wrote a twenty-page story in the first person. It was a haunting story of a disenfranchised and angst-filled man who was totally alienated from the world to the point at which he would drive to restaurants and ask to take his meals in his car.

The problem with the story was that in the first person voice, the narrator was too close to his own problems and it seemed as if he was explaining them to the reader. Thus, I asked Jacob to try writing the story in the third person limited and he took on the arduous task of doing so. The new draft, with that one step of removal from the character, was greatly improved: his alienation now seemed to be real.

Remember that when you begin a story using a pov, you can always change it. In fact, that is one of the exercises I ask of my students.

TOUCHING THE ELEPHANT

Melissa Pritchard

> Some Indians kept an elephant in a dark room. Because it was impossible to see the elephant, those that wanted to know something about this exotic beast had to feel it with their hands. The first person went into the darkness and felt the elephant's trunk and announced, "This creature is like a waterpipe." The next person felt the elephant's ear and asserted, "No. It's like a giant fan." A third person felt the elephant's leg and declared, "That's not true. This animal resembles a pillar." A fourth person felt the elephant's back and concluded, "Not at all. It's like a throne." Different points of view produce different opinions. If someone had brought in a candle, they would have all felt like fools.
>
> SUFI TEACHING STORY

Years ago, as a young, impressionable writer, I came across a statement in a book on the craft of writing fiction declaring point of view the most crucial choice the writer could make at the outset of her story. Choosing the wrong vantage point would doom a story to immediate failure. This gloomy bit of news, offering no explanation, no reason for why this was so, terrified me. The opinion of the unremembered author, printed in a now-forgotten text, was laid down without evidence or guideline. Years later, my beginner's terror has been replaced by hard-won conviction. Now, I offer my own explanation, my own reasons for believing point of view a pivotal, imperative point of authorial decision.

In the Sufi teaching tale offered above, each person believes she can describe what an elephant is. The person touching the leg metaphorically describes the leg, the person touching the ear describes the ear, and so on. The body of the elephant as a whole escapes each of the four individuals standing at four different vantage points. That is the point of the teaching—each person in the tale, and by extension, each one of us, is limited to her own experience, her own vantage point and perception. Were a candle or a lamp to be lit, each person would then see her own position, its humility, humor and constraint. In light of this wider view, this larger world, this vaster creature before her, she might then understand the foolishness of her own firmly fixed opinion. And hopefully, to simultaneously glimpse the wider view while confined to a single vantage point, suggests the path and essence of human wisdom.

The fiction writer, while understanding the restriction of her form, can still consciously select her point of view in relationship to the wider view, the deeper meaning offered by her theme, the ethical question she has poised at the heart of her story. The most powerful vantage point will suggest or infer the greater whole, cast light on the body of the elephant in its dark room. If my character stands here, she will see—and describe—mainly this; standing there, she will see—and describe—mainly that; each vantage point, each perspective revealing the nature of reality a little differently. Reality reflects perception. Today, my own conviction about the importance of point of view in fiction aligns with the opinion of the unremembered author of years ago. Point of view is crucial to the success or failure of a story, and the vantage point the writer must locate at the outset of her story is the one that best illuminates her story's deeper meaning and by inextricable relation, uncovers the truths residing in her own heart.

Most often, when point of view is discussed as an element of craft in fiction, the technical aspect of person, first person ("I"), second ("you"), or third ("he" or "she"), is inevitably and necessarily raised. The gifts and challenges of each are discussed—the effects of intimacy and authority rendered by first person versus the troubling danger of monotony and claustrophobic style; the unusual effect of second person, its way of putting emotional distance between character and her truth; and, the "workhorse" capacities of third person, its less glamorous but dependably sturdy and occasionally profound range and effect. Such discussions of technical effects of person are useful and certainly important. During in-class writing exercises, my undergraduate students are as impressed by the immediate authority of the "I" voice as they are eventually challenged by its boundaries. They enjoy experimenting with the unique slant offered by second person, and are gradually won over by the opportunities for character exploration offered by third person. Writing exercises assigned both in and outside of class can be striking ways for students to practice and observe the effects of person on point of view.

But point of view also involves who tells the story and from what vantage point in time and space and memory. Many of my students, both graduate and undergraduate, frequently begin by choosing the safest or most obvious character to tell the story, the character they feel they know best, can identify with most closely. Should a story about a father who is having a schizophrenic episode and his young daughter, driving west across the desert, be told from the point of view of the unravelling father, the innocent daughter, or the stranger they happen to meet at a critical juncture in the story, thus leaving the stranger to recount the tale to us? A recent graduate student of mine struggled with this choice in her story, eventually choosing the point of view of the eight-year-old daughter who loves her father deeply and is only beginning to understand that while he may be quirky and adventurous, more so than most adults she knows, he also shows increasingly poor judgment, putting her well-being in jeopardy, changing from a father she trusts to protect her, to a man who, under the spell of his own growing delusions, puts her in danger from which she must somehow extricate herself. Had this student told the story from the point of view of the father, it would have become his story, his journey, with the reader emotionally invested in the father's tragic descent into mental illness. Had a stranger come along, becoming involved with a crisis in the lives of the father and daughter, we would have been introduced to the stranger's perspective, and as an additional layer, the stranger's own life experience, which then interprets the characters' actions.

A story can have only one heart. Whose story is it? Which character owns the story most deeply? You can ask these questions of your story, of your characters, at the outset. I often instruct my students to visualize a great circle around the still fluid body of their imagined story, place the characters around the circumference of the circle, then move from character to character, listening to each one recount events from his or her point of view. Give each character the candle to hold up to the body of the elephant, and then see which casts the most rich, complex illumination, the darkest, most mysterious shadows. This act of imaginative listening can prove remarkably accurate in unveiling the character who most truly "owns" the story, the character you will get the most emotional voltage out of, the most complex thematic and ethical currents.

Courage and patience are the unheralded virtues of the fiction writer. Often, without realizing it, a writer will choose the most conservative path into a story both in terms of its action and its characters, thereby limiting the story's power and arc of achievement. To be willing to sit patiently and to hear the story, internally, from each character's vantage point, sensing the emotional range in each voice, the glimpse of something greater offered beyond the character's narrow perspective, is one of the most useful "invisible" exercises I know to practice before setting the first sentence down on the page. Be willing to be inclusive of the most overlooked or least expected of your characters, for the humblest or least impressive figure may be the truest teller of the tale. Be open to surprise, to possibility, to the understanding that like your characters, you are placed in life, confined by experience and perception and thus limited. Be willing to expand perception, multiply experience. The author's magic is to find that perspective, that point of view that casts the widest light into the darkness, that takes us on the farthest journey from the spot on which we necessarily stand. In one recent student story, the author began with the viewpoint closest to her own, that of a young woman in college taking a summer job cleaning rooms at a swank resort in Phoenix and telling of her eccentric, disturbing friendship with another worker, an older man recently arrived from Eastern Europe. The story was extremely well written in terms of language, style and setting—her fellow students were impressed by the author's level of intelligence and sophistication. But something was "off." The story, while stylistically impressive, lacked power. In the best kind of collaborative classroom discussion, someone suggested the real heart of the story might lie with the older man from Eastern Europe, that his air of emotional desperation, suggested by the author, had gone unexplored in the story. Perhaps the story was his, not the young college girl's. The author took these suggestions to heart, and when she brought in her next draft for critique, the class was astonished, moved, elated. She had given the story to the Eastern European, a middle-aged man whose wife, as it turned out, was terminally ill, a man half-mad from the war-time brutalizations he had endured. By simply changing points of view, vantage point, shifting the story from events and emotions belonging to the smart, witty but fairly inexperienced college girl to this complex, suffering man, the story took on an emotional power and ethical depth that was nothing short of stunning. Simply by shifting points of view, the student's story (the elephant in the room), remained the same, but the light, held up by a different character this time, shone brilliantly and cast the longest, most profound shadow. Here, then, is the undeniable and crucial power of point of view in fiction, its capacity to illuminate the wider world while uncovering and laying bare, the wilderness in the human heart.

NOTES FOR SUGGESTED READINGS

Note the use of the first person child pov in Toni Cade Bambara's "The Lesson."

Note how Bobbie Ann Mason slows down time by using the present verb tense in "Shiloh."

Exercises

1. Take a short story you are currently working on and rewrite it in another pov. For example, if it is in third person limited, you might try rewriting it in third person limited in another character's pov. Or, try writing it in first person.

2. In the first person, write a paragraph describing your first kiss. Then describe that same kiss through the pov of the recipient (again, first person). Then describe the same kiss through the third person limited pov of either of the two characters. Note the changes in the way the kiss is described.
3. Employing the present tense, write a short scene in the first person through the eyes of a young girl or young boy being pursued through a deserted city park at dusk by a crazed man with a knife. Then rewrite the scene in the first person through the eyes of the man with the knife. Finally, rewrite the scene in the third person omniscient point of view. In all three scenes, note how slowly time passes. Also, note the different diction in all three scenes.

CHAPTER
16

PLOT

In the evening, after a long day at school or at work, we gather at the dinner table with our families where we ask each other about our days. In asking "How was your day?" or "What's new?" what we are really asking is *What was the plot of your day?* In other words, what happened?

Plot is simply the set of events of a story and they can be relayed in any number of ways (note that plot is not necessarily the chain of events because for this phrase seems to indicate chronology and plots do not have to be organized in chronological order although they often are).

If, though, we say that plot is the set of events of a story, that plot is quite simply the things that happen in a story, it seems obvious that what is important is *to whom* these things happen and/or *who* makes them happen, and that brings up another element of fiction, that of **character**. In other words, it is rather awkward to discuss plot in a separate section from character, especially given that in literary fiction character is almost always greater or equal to plot.

With that said, we will go on to discuss plot in terms of story structure before discussing the writer's search for plots.

As stated earlier in this discussion, the organization of a story may be chronological or it may

There has to be a tension, a sense that something is imminent, that certain things are in relentless motion, or else, most often, there simply won't be a story.

Raymond Carver

be one interspersed with **flashbacks** and **flashforwards** (see William Faulkner's story "A Rose for Emily"). Regardless, a story's structure—its **arc**—is an inherent part of plot, and it can be broken down into four basic components: the conflict; the escalation, or rise in complication; the climax, or the turning point; and the denouement and conclusion (one often thinks of these four components as the three even more basic components of beginning, middle, and end, with the middle consisting of both the rise in complication and the climax). It might be illustrated as follows:

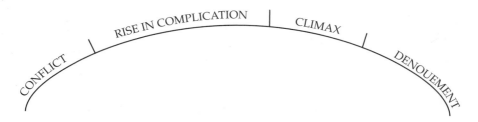

The above illustration outlines the arc of the plot. This plot, the set of events in the story, will go through the four components and we will call this the outer story. For example, **conflict**: John wants to take a trip to Las Vegas, but his wife Heide does not. **Escalation of conflict**: John decides to take the trip alone and he buys a ticket. **Climax**: Friday night Heide finds the airline ticket and hotel reservation for that weekend in his jacket, and she confronts him at dinner. John grabs the ticket from her, grabs his bag, and heads out the door. **Denouement**: Heide is on a plane to Las Vegas.

Now, with the above scenario, you could end the story any way you want: it could be a happy reunion or a bitter end. All we have done here is chart out the outer story. The key, of course, is the inner story, that subtextual arc lying beneath the outer story, Hemingway's seven-eighths of the iceberg that lies beneath the surface, and the key to the inner story is the characters. The following illustration outlines our outer story and a possible inner story.

You notice that we started this story of John and Heide with immediate conflict; in other words, we started *in medias res* or in the middle of things. All too often, a writer feels that his reader needs to know everything in a character's history before we even introduce conflict. This is, of course, a mistake and will create a huge problem of **pacing** wherein the editor will quickly put the story down because there are too many good stories to be read to spend time with those that bore us to death with long-winded exposition. A writer will, however, write his way into a story: A writer may sit down and start typing without a clear direction which is O.K. because writing is, in large part, a process of discovery. When working this way, the writer may discover the beginning of his story on page seven. What the writer needs to do, of course, is throw the first six pages away. There is nothing wrong with that. His time was not wasted; what

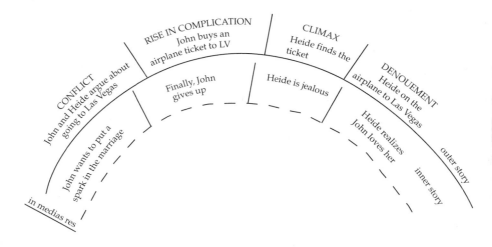

he did was work his way to the beginning of the story. (Writers who refuse to work their way to the beginning of the story and who, instead, sit and wait for the beginning to magically arrive, are those who often complain of writer's block. Again, there is no such thing as writer's block unless you refuse to write.)

The writer needs to know the character's history, of course, but he does not need to regale the reader with all of it. It is true that the more the writer knows about his characters, the more clearly defined they will be on paper, even though he does not include all he knows about them in the story. In other words, it is important for the writer to know his characters' backstory if the reader is to have some idea of their futurestory after the story ends.

From the illustration on page 177, we can see that a story certainly has a **backstory** that may, if necessary, be alluded to indirectly or directly through flashback, and the story has a **futurestory** that the reader should be able to at least partly discern. In between these two "stories" is the story on the page, one that you will have, after several drafts, plotted out either chronologically or otherwise.

If you are employing a chronological plot, then you are going to have a series of events in order of occurrence from page one to the last page of the story. After reading the story, the reader will be able to recount your outer story by stating what happened first, second, third, et cetera. As you, the writer, are working your way through these plot events, you will have to decide which of the events should be handled through **exposition** and which should be handled through **scene**.

This sounds like an obvious and easy task, but it is not necessarily so. First, remember the admonition to writers that has become a cliché: *Show, don't tell.* While this is often good advice, it is not always true. Exposition is telling and scene is showing, and there are times when the reader needs to be told some information or the story may not make sense.

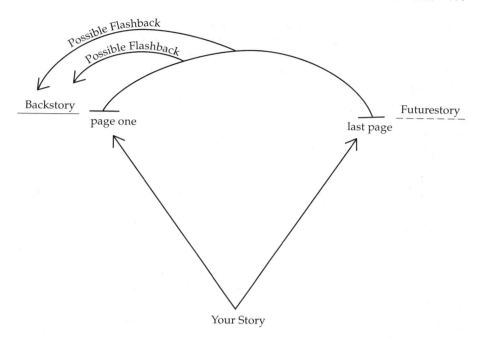

In the plot we created at the beginning of this chapter, we have four plot events: John and Heide argue about Las Vegas; John buys an airline ticket to Las Vegas; Heide finds John's ticket in his coat pocket and confronts him and John leaves; and in the fourth and final plot event of this story, Heide is on an airplane to Las Vegas.

Of the four events, which should be done in scene and which in exposition, and what are your criteria for making that decision? The first element would make a vibrant scene, of course, for we would watch the husband and wife argue about a trip to Las Vegas and in this *live action* scene, the tension would rise and grab our attention as the conflict escalates. Also, we would learn a great deal about each character (and about the state of their marriage) in this scene by the way they act toward one another.

The second plot event—John's purchase of an airline ticket—might be better handled in exposition, however, for although it is integral to the story that he do so, we would learn very little by watching him at the ticket office or on the phone.

The third event of this plot—Heide discovering the ticket—might also be best handled in scene because the reader would learn much about her and how she felt by watching her as she discovers the ticket; the same goes for the fourth event when she is alone on an airplane to Las Vegas: watching her on a plane and what she is doing—reading (reading what? *Mademoiselle* or a How-To-Play-Blackjack book?), looking out the window, conversing with a fellow passenger, drinking Scotch—the reader will be with her and experience some of what she is experiencing and will therein gain the empathy for the character, the empathy that is so important in fiction.

In conclusion, then, we could say that the preceding story could be plotted chronologically as scene, exposition, scene, and scene.

Exposition is also used to form narrative bridges between scenes so that, in this example of four plot events, wherein the second event is handled through exposition, we may indeed have more exposition in the story. For example, there could be exposition serving as a transition between the last two scenes, wherein she has discovered the ticket and she is last seen on the airplane: there could be a paragraph or two of exposition describing her packing for the trip (what she is putting in that suitcase might be very important: a black negligee and a cotton nightgown pack different emotional weights).

How we plot a story depends on a great number of variables, many of which are discussed in the other elements-of-fiction chapters in this book. The POV I employ will greatly affect the plot structure (if, for example, I chose to use third person limited through the character John, I would not be able to describe Heide on an airplane to Las Vegas, so while she may be on that plane, it would not be one of the plot events of the story).

The next question we should address is where our plots come from. The answer to that is quite simple. They come from all around us. We've all had compelling experiences from which to draw, but even if we were to completely run out of our own experiences to write about, there are the experiences of others to draw from. Pick up the newspaper any given day and you will be sure to find a compelling plot.

I tell my creative writing students that, among other things, I will teach them to steal. What I mean by that is that I will teach them to find plots, whether they be from the newspaper, from the lives of friends, from the lives of coworkers, or from other stories they've read.

Who among us does not eavesdrop? Many of my own plots come from others as I am an inveterate practitioner of the art of eavesdropping. My plots also come from my own experience and sometimes they are composites of that experience and ideas I've taken from stories I've read and stories I've heard. The point is, no writer should ever have to suffer from a shortage of plots, because although there may be a limited number of plots in the world, what writers do is recast those plots with new characters. How many stories of unrequited love have we read? How many stories of star-crossed lovers? David Guterson's fine novel *Snow Falling on Cedars* is in one sense a retelling of Shakespeare's *Romeo and Juliet*.

John Gardner said that there were really only two possible plots: either a stranger comes to town, or someone leaves town. We can literally disagree with Gardner, of course, but implied in his statement is that there is a finite number of plots. What matters most is who the characters are in those plots, as it is the characters who people the plot who help us to understand the human condition.

FAIRY TALES ALWAYS COME TRUE: PLOT AND IMAGINATION

H. Lee Barnes

Is something or someone menacing your character? If nothing is, you probably don't have a plot. To some student writers the most challenging element of a short story is the plot, moving the action to a resolution that is satisfying. The reasons are several: the writer's concern with character development, the limited space of short fiction, the sense that plot is more artifice and less art than other elements, and even the desire by the writer to be "subtle." On the other hand, too much focus on plot or too obvious a plot or a surprising ending come off heavy-handed. Yet a story must have a plot. The plot simply fulfills the understanding the reader has that something is going to happen. The writer accomplishes her end by asking the right questions about what could happen and eliminating bad choices; the reader reads the story without questioning the choices made by the writer. It's a communion—two people sharing one imagination.

To move forward a story must present complications or obstacles for the protagonist, and reach a climax followed by a resolution, at which point the character or the character's life is somehow altered by the event. Note that I don't state that the character *must* be altered. A man's life changes if he's sent to prison or divorced or abandoned, but he may never change. The notion that characters must experience an epiphany leads some writers to focus on this aspect at the expense of plot, and consequently, story. A story may be so subtle that it is difficult to find. Writers should remember that a reader wishes for more than language and artfulness from a story. Sometimes the protagonist should just ride off into the sunset or catch a plane to Mali. A story does not need a complicated plot to be complex; in fact, a story's complexity comes through a layering of elements.

Long before Poe thought to compose his theories on short fiction, short prose existed in forms such as Viking romances and fairy tales. These early stories were structured around external conflict and obvious themes, usually good versus evil. They generally contained cultural parables and were intended to entertain and enlighten. I mention these tales because, like short stories, they are sustained by complication linked to resolution. Contemporary stories differ; the plot is layered. Conflict exists at two primary levels: external and internal. In addition, some conflicts are peripheral and some tangential. Think of plot as a chain towing a heavily-weighted object and being jerked back and forth. How much stress can the chain take? Only as much as its weakest link. What will it strike if it snaps? The tension in a story is built around the link that is under the most stress. If the writer finds the weak link in the character's life at the moment the story begins, the plot will almost write itself.

A character pushed by circumstances in two or more directions is compelling. Dramatic irony results when the reader sees a character's dilemma, but the character does not. The audience is compelled by Hamlet's circumstances because he avoids the inevitable decision he must make, and when he makes it, it's too late. A character's indecisiveness is the core to many stories. For the character the central issue becomes what course of action to take. As an example, we can use a woman who is in an abusive situation, a stock theme in the creative writing classroom. Many students treat this complication in an all-too-obvious manner. They fail to be persuasive. The woman is beaten and wants to forgive and makes excuses. He is a monster. The writer wants the victim to overcome, wants her to be strong. It is a decent impulse on the part of the writer but does not make for a very compelling story line. The question the writer should be asking centers on why the woman has remained in an abusive relationship. What behavior of her own has she failed to see? We know the woman must leave, but we must also deal with her reasons for not leaving. We must be exposed to her fuller humanity, including *her* weaknesses, to admire her strengths.

Another approach the writer may want to consider is to write the abuser's story. Try to see what the abuser experiences. An exercise that may help a writer to better understand conflict is to begin with the same character(s) and a central conflict and write drafts of the story with three different scenarios. One or all may or may not work, but the insight gained is worth the effort. It is important to remember that writing is an act of imagination, which translated for the purpose of plot means, imagine what happens if . . . .

Raymond Carver wrote "The Bath," a rather short story of a husband and wife whose son is hit by a car on the boy's birthday. The central complication is that the son goes into a coma. The parents keep vigil beside him. The peripheral complication occurs because the mother has ordered a birthday cake from a rather dour baker who menaces her with hang-up phone calls. The mother leaves her husband at the hospital and goes home for a bath. The story ends with the phone ringing and the mother picking the receiver up. The ending is open. It may be bad news or good news from the hospital, or it may be the baker. It stands on its own as a story, very Carveresque in terms of economy of language and action. But Carver saw another story in "The Bath." The second seems to begin with the question: What if the child dies? And the final question to resolve the story is: What if the parents confront the baker who continues to call? The answer here is that the baker feels deep remorse. He has forgotten the human contract, but rediscovers it by giving food and comfort to the grieving parents and sharing in their grief. I recommend reading and studying the way Carver develops this single complication into two stories.

To illustrate how a story has many potential paths, let us take the example of a girl, age fifteen, who's dating, against her parent's wishes, a boy of eighteen. The obvious external conflict is parental control over her freedom, and the internal conflict is the girl's desire to break free of these restraints. We can also add to the equation the intensity of young love and its inherent passion. This is the stuff of *Romeo and Juliet*—nothing new to literature. For the writer, the central complication is only the springboard. The writer dictates the circumstances. For our purposes, we will add that the girl is a Jamaican immigrant and the boy is a white, middle-class kid who has a drug problem. Is this getting to be too much for a short story? Is it novel-size material? This depends on the writer's ability to reign the story in and decide what complications best feed the plot. What the story needs is a critical moment. If the reader understands the central conflicts, the moment of crisis, the finite period of time that the characters exist on the page will spring to life for her. If the writer allows the story to get out of hand, it will become soppy and trite. The potential dies. Here are some possible scenarios: the boy is driving her to an abortion clinic where protestors walk the sidewalks; the girl is sitting in a crack house with the boy; the boy is pressuring her to have sex. Any one of these scenarios has potential to develop the conflict to a crisis. Each choice could result in a solid story or a limp story. But whatever choice the writer makes eliminates other possibilities.

A story is usually better discovered than predicted. More often than not, a character will tell me what he or she should do next. A writer is dealing with human frailty and human strength and everything in between. Thinking of a character as an individual helps. Is she or he willing to quit a job and walk away on a principle? Or is the character too weak or too rigid to quit? Will the character experience a profound change? Will she have an epiphany? The tactic to use is simply to follow a scenario and continue to ask, what if? Think, "What menaces my character?"

Emerging writers must be aware that a resolution is not a solution and guard against forcing fraudulent complications and circumstances into a story. Too often a writer wants to plot a puzzle because she has a clever ending in mind. This does not allow for spontaneity (events in life and on the page often result from impulse or spontaneity). By working toward a fixed end that reeks of solution, the writer is not solving the problem of the character but forcing pieces into a puzzle. The writer solves only the puzzle of the story itself.

When I get a student story that lacks imagination, that reads like an essay, invariably the student says, "That's how it is." Writing from life is a fine inclination, but a hindrance to the imagination. Ron Carlson wrote "Zanduce at Second," a story about a baseball player who kills fans in the bleachers with his powerful foul balls. A story such as Carlson's is metered by possibility, not reality. He asks the seemingly impossible, simply stretches the borders when he asks the "what if" questions. "What if Zanduce hit a ball so hard it killed a fan? What would he think next time he came to the plate?" Stories spring from such imaginings.

A creature that hinders novice writers (and may present a problem to established writers as well) is the adult mind and its sophisticated world view. It understands ambiguity and desires to weave subtlety and layering into a story so that it reflects concrete human experience. There it is looming over the shoulder, whispering, "That's not possible. That doesn't reflect experience." The inner voice wants the story to be "true" to life or something called "reality." Shut the voice off; it's censoring you.

How would Gabriel Garcia-Marquez ever have written "A Very Old Man with Enormous Wings" had he confined his imagination to concrete human experience? He begs the question: How might people react if confronted with a miracle? In essence, what Marquez wrote is a fairy tale, albeit an ironic one that probes human faith. The first complication is Pelayo's sick child; the second is the mysterious presence of an old man with wings. Of course the story takes ironic twists and turns after that as the skeptics seek Christ-like miracles from the old man, who is indifferent to them. What Marquez's gifted imagination does is blend the borders of the real with the fantastic, basic human nature with the enchanted, which is what fairy tales have always done.

A fairy tale contains elements of magic and usually relies on conflict that pits innocence against evil. Often evil comes in a disguise. I'm convinced that many contemporary stories are, whether consciously or not, rooted in the fairy tale. One would be Joyce Carol Oates's highly anthologized "Where Are You Going, Where Have You Been?" Could any contemporary character be more evil than Arnold Friend? He certainly comes disguised, and one could reasonably argue that his knowledge of Connie and her friends is magic. Oates possesses a multitude of tools and tricks herself, and weaving plot is one of them. The tension in the story is wonderfully developed, and one of the reasons is that Connie, through her innocence and vanity, contributes to the drama. The reader sees what Connie cannot until it is too late. Probably no contemporary writer understands the enduring power of fairy tales better than Oates.

As an assignment, I ask students to write a fairy tale. For a variety of reasons, some respond well to the assignment, a few do not, but it's a useful exercise that results in some pretty imaginative writing. The fairy tale naturally provides a structure that feeds off complication and moves toward resolution if the writer only begins with "Once upon a time" and asks the obvious questions who, where, what, and then discovers how and why. I maintain that a writer who can write a fairy tale, can weave a plot. If a writer understands that plot is not a separate but an integral element of the whole story, that it exists because the characters exist and the setting exists, she can ask the necessary questions. A student, in writing a fairy tale, must separate herself from the anchor of "realism" and enter into the world of imagination.

In the student story provided for this chapter, Trinae L. M. Rivas begins with the classical opening line of *Once upon a time,* provides the where, Neider Valley, the who, Sara, and the what, a girl who was terribly lonely. Trinae immediately introduces magic into the story in the form of five fairies who arrive to solve Sara's problem, but Sara, of course, is not satisfied. Trinea's story is a fairy tale, but is the story, as structured around the first complication, much different from a contemporary story? What if Sara lived in Los Angeles with her mother and was lonely? What if a man came along who promised to end her loneliness? What if there was a catch? Take note of how skillfully Trinea handles Sara's request to become a fairy. Trinae's fairly tale doesn't end up "happily ever after," but then, for that matter, neither do many contemporary stories.

WISHES COME TRUE

Trinae L. M. Rivas

Once upon a time in a small far away place called Neider Valley lived a girl name Sara. She was a lonely girl, for no other people were allowed in the valley, and her parents worked two jobs so they could drive a Mercedes S.U.V. and vacation in Hawaii. Sara had but one person to talk to, a tutor named Calphurnia who spoke only in Latin and laughed at her own jokes before she got to the punch line. Sara was so lonely that for her birthday she wished for friends. A single tear rolled down her cheek as she blew out the candles on the cake that she herself had made. That night in bed she chuckled to herself as she thought about the wish. How silly for a girl to wish for friends where there are only three adults and no people.

In the morning Sara awakened to whispers and giggling. She opened her eyes to find five fairies fluttering about her head. They introduced themselves as Rose, Hyacinth, Daisy, Daffodil, and Lily.

Sara was excited. She jumped out of bed and nearly fell over her own feet. "This is so incredible!"

"Well, you wished, now we're here," they chimed in unison. They were obligated by Fairy Law to uphold the most sincere birthday wishes.

"O.K., so are you my friends forever?" Sara asked.

"Most certainly," they all said at once, their voices sounding like bells.

Sara danced around the room. Her new friends waved their wands, and the room danced around Sara. She seemed about to burst with happiness. She was smiling so widely that she was sure the back of her head was wrinkled from being pushed together.

Time went on. Sara played with her friends. At first they seemed the same, but Sara came to know each by the hum of her wings. And they were individual in other ways. Rose and Daisy were average fairies. They had wands and used their magic in moderation. Lily and Daffodil were sisters; that is why Daffodil wanted to be called Dilly. Dilly and Lily were regenerated from the same larvae, much like worms are, but it was not fairylike to talk about pre-wing days. Hyacinth was a very proper fairy. She considered herself a higher class fairy because she was cocooned way up in a tree where the air was fresh, rather than under rocks like the others.

Sara was very happy. Her friends fussed over her and played any game she chose to play, but she did not quite fit in with them. After all, they could fly and use magic. So being merely human, Sara wanted more. She decided she wanted to become a fairy, but never dreamed it might truly be possible. Then one day she was sitting in a patch of grass while her fairy friends were weaving marigolds into her hair. Marigolds were Sara's favorite flower even if they did not smell so good.

Sara sighed. The fairies flew around her to see why Sara was depressed.

"What's wrong, Sara. Aren't you happy?" Daisy asked.

"I am, but . . . Oh, I wish I could be a fairy," Sara huffed out.

"It's not all it's cracked up to be," Rose said.

"Don't be silly, Rose. You can fly. Anything you don't have you can conjure with your magic. The whole world is at your command. What could be better?"

"Being a little girl," Rose said, trying to discourage Sara from really wanting fairyhood.

The fairies hovered over her to see if she was serious. They didn't understand why Sara would want to be a fairy except for Hyacinth, who knew exactly what Sara was going through.

"I just want to be one of you," Sara stated firmly.

Once a long time ago Hyacinth was a girl named Helen who, too, had wished for friends and had been transformed into a fairy. She knew the way back to the human state, but at the moment it seemed a cruel knowledge. After all, she did like Sara, truly, but there comes a time in a convert fairy's life when she just wants to die. Hyacinth had reached that point. She fluttered forward. "It can be done. Are you absolutely sure?"

"Hyacinth!" Daisy snapped.

"Ah-ha! You've never been human, any of you, so don't interrupt," Hyacinth said. "Sara, are you sure?"

"I am," Sara said.

Waving her wand, Hyacinth chanted, "I am the fairy; Sara's the girl. I'll forfeit my wand to switch our worlds."

In an instant Sara was wrapped so tightly she could hardly breathe. "What happened?" she asked.

Dilly said, "You're not Sara any longer. Hyacinth is Sara and you are Marigold, the pre-wing fairy."

"One thousand years before you emerge from your cocoon," the fairies chimed. "We'll stop in on you now and then."

"But I thought you were my friends."

"We will always be your fairy-weather friends," they said, giggling.

"If I'd only been satisfied with myself and my life before," Sara lamented. She hoped that Hyacinth understood Latin.

The End

Trinae says, "I wrote this piece to try to reaffirm to people that sometimes the life we are presently living, though it may seem bleak, may be far better than what we think." Many students set out to write a story incorporating this type of theme, and their stories fail because theme dominates the tale. Trinae's story, while thematically inspired, is driven by the plot, yet at the same time, she uses all the elements of fiction, blending them carefully so that the theme, which is stated by Sara at the end, is well earned. Plot cannot be isolated from the other elements, just as a fairy tale cannot be totally isolated from realism; a reader understands a piece of fantasy only as it relates to some type of reality.

Except for the magic and the fairies, the rest of Trinae's story is firmly rooted in a sense of the real. Neider Valley could easily be Mill Valley or Lost Desert Valley, anyplace where a young girl is separated from playmates by circumstance. We understand that this is as much a place of the mind as it is a physical setting. Sara is an ordinary girl in most senses. We assume this because she does nothing extraordinary and the narrative voice reinforces this impression. I think it is important to note that Trinae keeps descriptions to a minimum. She keeps what is absolutely essential to the tale, using language that services the fictional form. The reader is never aware of the language. It could be the Brothers Grimm who wrote the piece.

What makes this story work is the unpretentious introduction of the extraordinary. Once Trinae decided to insert fairies to solve Sara's loneliness, the story began to write itself. The result was a fully-plotted story written in less than 850 words, a story that moves from external complication to solution, to internal complication, to final complication, to resolution. Sara goes from solitude to companionship, to dissatisfaction, to transformation, to regret. She is menaced first by loneliness, then her inability to accept herself, and forever by her impulsive choice.

Could Trinae have plotted a similar story reflecting realism? Undoubtedly. Let's make Sara's ambition to become a model instead of a fairy. Introduce an unscrupulous agent, the fast life of a fashion model, the need to stay thin, the competition to stay on top, and the ubiquitous presence of drugs and see what happens. Plots need not be complicated to appeal to a reader, but a character must confront complications. The secret to a successful story is that there is no secret. It's about creating engaging characters, finding a voice appropriate to telling the story, using the elements of fiction, and keeping the question "What if?" going until you know it's time to type "The End." And then you rewrite until it's right.

NOTES FOR SUGGESTED READINGS

Note how Mary Robison creates a plot with an arc in her very short "Yours."

Exercises

1. Browse through a newspaper looking at headlines. When you come across one that is compelling, read the article. Then, write down the plot points in chronological order. For example, in a long article about a woman and her son whose car broke down in a snowstorm when they were out looking for a Christmas tree, you might outline the plot as follows:

   > First: car breaks down.
   > Second: woman bundles up infant and sets out on foot.
   > Third: she gets lost in the storm and digs a snow cave.
   > Fourth: rescue workers find them the next day.
   > Fifth: both the woman and her son have toes amputated in the hospital.

   While this is a true story I came across in the newspaper, it is not very compelling because I have only given you the five plot points. You can make it compelling, however, when you take the time to develop the character of the woman.

2. Take a story you have written and outline the plot points as you did with the newspaper article in exercise one. Ask yourself if you have established the conflict early in the story and if you have a rise in tension before some kind of resolution. Then ask yourself if any of the plot points can be eliminated or rearranged by using a flashback or flashforward.

3. Using a highlighter, highlight the scenes in one of your stories. Then spread the story out on a dining room table or tape it, page by page, to the wall and look at the ratio of unhighlighted text to highlighted text. If you have many more blocks of white text, you may be using too much exposition and too few scenes.

CHAPTER

17

CHARACTER

Think back to the most memorable story you've ever read and chances are you remember it because of some unforgettable character. As mentioned in the previous chapter, character is almost always greater or equal to **plot**, for it is *who made it happen* or *to whom it happened* that draws the reader's empathy. Plot, after all, that set of events, is a thing; character is a person. One cannot have empathy for a thing, but when we watch someone struggle, we struggle with him.

Aristotle wrote, *Man is his desire*. We can translate that as *people are their desires*. Think about this. What this means is that we can be defined by what it is we want. Everyone wants something. Even the most humble of gurus wants something, be it serenity or be it enlightenment, it doesn't matter; what matters is the fact that we all want something.

Who we really are can be most clearly illustrated when we cannot get what we want—that defines our character. As a writer, you give a character a desire—such as John, who wants to go to Las Vegas—and then you place an obstacle before him—John's wife does not want to go to Las Vegas—and see how John acts or reacts. This will help us understand John and it will help us understand a little more about what it means to be human.

> *Sow a thought, and you reap an act; Sow an act, and you reap a habit; Sow a habit, and you reap a character; Sow a character, and you reap a destiny.*
>
> Anonymous

Etymologically, the word character indicates uniqueness in that the word comes from the Greek *kharakter* which means *engraved mark*; hence, one particular stamp marked one thing as different from another and this difference could be referred to as its "character." With that in mind, we see the need for our characters to be realized as different from one another on the page, as they are in life. Think of five friends or acquaintances and it will only take a minute for you to outline some severe differences among them. The difference may lie in what it is they want or it may lie in their individual mental attitudes. Readers expect the characters in the stories they read to be different from each other in these respects as well.

In a letter to his wife Alice in 1878, William James wrote, "I have often thought that the best way to define a man's character would be to seek out the particular mental or moral attitude in which, when it came upon him, he felt himself most deeply and intensely active and alive. At such moments there is a voice inside which speaks and says: 'This is the real me!'"

Creating a developed character with James' mental and moral attitudes is quite likely the most difficult aspect of writing fiction. Devising a plot—a path the character can follow—is relatively simple. In order to establish a character's moral or mental attitude, it is often useful to elucidate that character's inner turmoil. In other words, what is at odds with his mental attitude? With his moral attitude? When the character is torn apart by contradiction—by what he thinks and by what choice of action lies before him—we grow to understand his human dilemma, and in that, we are given a broader perspective of what it means to be human. Ralph Waldo Emerson said, "The key to every man is his thought." When he acts in conflict with his own thoughts, he becomes more human.

And act he must. The word *drama* is derived from "doing" and hence, you had better have your character do something—act—or there will be no drama. Any action is inherently a choice (one could, for example, refuse to act at all), and we learn about our characters by what choices they make, right or wrong, and how they react to having made their choices.

There are as many types of characters as there are people in the world, but it may be useful to think of characters in E. M. Forster's terms as either *round* or *flat*, the former being a developing three-dimensional character and the latter being a static and undeveloped character of two dimensions. A story's **protagonist**—she who is central to the action—must almost always be a round character while peripheral characters may often be flat. The criterion for deciding which characters should be round and which flat is relatively simple: if the character is central to the action, if he or she is one of the main actors, then that character should be round. If the character is peripheral, if he or she is not central to the action, then he or she often may be sketched as flat.

In Bobbie Ann Mason's short story "Shiloh," the protagonist is Norma Jean. She is growing both physically and mentally in the story and is portrayed as round—one who is developing. Her husband, Leroy, is the

antagonist (someone who provides a contest with the protagonist) and he remains static and is essentially a flat character (although he desires change when it is too late, at the end of the story, as Norma Jean is leaving him).

Norma Jean's mother, Mabel, another character in the story, is a flat character and her lack of development suffices for she is a **foil** (a flat character who, by contrast, is used to enhance another character) against whom Norma Jean is contrasted.

A good exercise when reading a story is to ask yourself whose story it is you are reading: in other words, which character(s) is facing some conflict and choice. As a writer, you know whose story it is and thus, you know which character must be defined as round.

Developing a character as round can be done in many ways. Before one begins the writing, it is often useful to develop a character chart outlining the character's life. Start with the obvious vital statistics such as name, sex, age, and family and move on to education and occupation before addressing moral attitude, religion, politics, and desires. Once you have created such a chart that can be referred to during the writing process (it is especially nice to have such a chart during the process of writing a novel for it is easy to forget whether a character named Billy Freeman is left- or right-handed when you are on page 456 of the manuscript and Billy is at the ball park where he reaches out with his left hand and catches a hard foul that was about to strike a beautiful young woman sitting in the row before him), you might conduct an interview with the character, again recording it for future reference during the actual writing of the story or novel. For example, you might ask Billy what major league team he supported as a child and continues to support today, and if he tells you the Chicago Cubs, well, it is somewhat revealing of his character.

Obviously, you would never include the pages of information you have recorded about a character in this way, but your knowing the information—even though you never mention Billy's not having inhaled in the story—will make the character more developed in the story simply because you, the creator, know the character so well. Because you know so much about the character, you will be defining him subtextually as well as textually on the page.

But how do we characterize textually? Often, the best way to reveal character is to do so scenically. We learn about people through the way they act, and this is also true of characters in a story or a novel. When observing what the character does and how she does it, the reader will learn a great deal about her.

Another way we develop character is through **dialogue**. What the character says and how she says it reveals a great deal about her.

It does take considerable space to develop a round character through scenes and through the use of dialogue, however, and sometimes the writer needs to add additional information about a character. We can do this through **exposition** or summary. The adage *show don't tell* is often good advice, but it is clearly a faulty imperative in that most stories (and certainly most novels) have narrative bridges of exposition between scenes.

Depending on the plot you have devised, the setting you have drawn, and the character(s) you have created, your characters may react to the world in one of four ways. They may see this society and its values and assimilate by adopting those values as their own; they may accommodate in that they do not like those values but will adopt them anyway if only to get along; they may rebel against those values in any number of ways; or, they may take flight from that society and, as did Huck Finn, head out to the new territories. Unfortunately, there are few new territories to head out to any longer.

As the writer, you do not consciously need to think of the four options, but after having finished a draft of a story, you might be very suspicious of a character who does none of the four, because it may be that the character is unaware of that world you have so painstakingly created.

I tell my creative writing students that one thing they will learn in my course is how to steal. In relation to character, I mean taking traits from people we know or know of, and using them in the creation of a character of our own. Sometimes a character becomes a composite or synthesis of actual people we do know, and we change their names to protect the innocent. (Speaking of names: avoid giving characters names that sound alike. When searching for a name, you might try the telephone book or the obituaries in your newspaper.)

Finally, remember that these round characters of ours are three-dimensional as are we, and that if you have a "good" man, be sure to give him a flaw, just as you would give a "bad" man a good trait. This is contradiction however slight, and that is how the most interesting of people live: in a state of tension.

Remember what Heraclitus said: "A man's character is his fate." The futurestory of those men and women you create on the page will be determined by how deeply you have created them.

A CHARACTER'S SKIN

Tracy Daugherty

If I encounter the following character in a story, what do I know about her?

> The house fell silent, as it had every morning after Josie had gone, but today, as she watched her mother's gold Mercedes wink like a brooch rounding the corner, Jude was aware of the coffee aroma rising from Josie's still-warm demitasse on the countertop, and it seemed as if she had been vaporized: here one moment, gone the next. Maybe she hadn't been there at all. Maybe she would not come back. Jude twisted a magazine in her hands. A too-thick emptiness seeped into the kitchen, and she startled when the coffeemaker exhaled a gurgle of steam. The loaf of bread under a tea towel on the counter

seemed like a sleeping animal. The Swiss cuckoo clock above the doorway might explode any moment with chaotic birds. It was time to get out—not just out of the kitchen. Out. Away. Somewhere.

Immediately, I know that Jude is anxious, twisting a magazine, jumping at the coffeemaker's sounds, fearing a clatter of chaotic birds from the clock, seeing the loaf of bread as vaguely threatening like an animal she doesn't want to disturb. The strength of this writing lies in its attention to detail: the "still-warm demitasse on the countertop," the tea towel covering the bread. I see Jude clearly in a setting, a well-heeled domestic setting, in relation to her mother, and furthermore I have some idea of Jude's feelings about her mom. Jude watches her mother's car "wink like a brooch" (expensive? delicate? stately?—all are implied, and not about the car, which, after all, is a Mercedes and needs no further comment, but about the mom). Jude feels her mother's absence more strongly than her presence—"Maybe she hadn't been there at all"—a loss powerfully conveyed by the cup. The writer, Lisa Raleigh, has effectively used third person limited point of view to filter details through Jude, giving us not only the setting, but a sense of how the setting affects Jude.

Still, as strong as the writing is, I find myself aware of the writer *manipulating* details, calling attention, ever so slightly, to herself, and away from her character. The key to this, I believe, lies in my earlier statement: the details are *filtered through* Jude. This is exactly what young writers are taught to do with third person limited point of view—the reader perches on the character's shoulder, sees what she sees—and Ms. Raleigh does it well here, but something else is required, I think, for us to fully *experience* a fictional character. Rather than noting objects as they're distilled through Jude, we want to feel we're observing the world *as if we were wearing Jude's skin*. This is a subtle distinction, achieved by an exacting balance of rhythms, of distance and intimacy in the language.

First, what do I mean by "manipulating details"? We're told that the "coffee aroma from Josie's still-warm demitasse" made Jude feel as if her mother "had been vaporized." How do we get from the coffee cup to Josie's annihilation? As I read the sentence I connect the linguistic dots, perhaps subconsciously the first time through: the words "aroma" and "vaporized" echo one another, sensually. *Aroma* reminds me of steam, particularly if it's rising from a hot cup of coffee, and steam leads me to the *vapor* in "vaporized." From there, it's easy to imagine Josie disappearing the way coffee steam rises and vanishes into the air. The image, though it's only implied, is subtle, potent, and logical, and as "Jude was aware" of all this, it reveals a great deal about her character. It feels niggling of me to say, then, that this very admirable sentence nevertheless strikes me as *writerly*. For all its effectiveness, it finally reveals the author's presence more than her character's. The connect-the-dots game tends to leave us thinking, "What a clever imagination!" not "What a troubled young woman!"

Put another way: I can readily see, here, a writer working out the subtleties of imagery; I have more difficulty imagining Jude in her mother's empty kitchen, working out *aroma-steam-vapor-vaporization*. After all, the whole point of the sentence is that Jude feels bereft in this house, numbed, unable to think clearly, "as if [her mother] had been vaporized . . . [and] would not come back."

If I'm going to *experience* Jude, I need to be aware, not of details sketching unspoken connections, but of Jude's utter emotional devastation.

As the paragraph unfolds, a "too-thick emptiness" seeps into the kitchen. Here, the writer is strangely removed from her own character, not nestled inside Jude's skin, where the emptiness *really* simmers, ready to boil over and swamp the kitchen, but outside Jude, outside the kitchen, even, reentering it, imaginatively, only as the emptiness seeps in—from where, we never learn. I suspect Ms. Raleigh was still thinking about the cup—half-empty, "still warm," at any rate—rather than her character's emotional state, making another rational association instead of crawling inside the mess of Jude's heart.

The scene ends with another neat connection: watching the clock, Jude thinks it's "time to get out." But again, the neatness here is cerebral, not emotional. *Clock* means *time*. I follow the sentence's logic, but I've failed to feel the crushing despair driving Jude from her home.

It's not an *explanation* the reader longs for at this point, but an *experience*, a sense of living in the moment with Jude. *As* Jude.

I began by saying I know, from the scene's generous details, that Jude is anxious. But by the paragraph's last line, that's still all I know. The coffee's smell, the coffeemaker's gurgle, the lurking bread, the ticking clock, all point in the same direction: Jude is an anxious daughter.

Young writers are taught that every detail should count, and should illuminate a story's themes to its readers. Good advice, and Ms. Raleigh has taken it to heart here. But the problem is, illuminating a story's themes often *competes* with creating believable characters. People are multi-textured, never just one thing or another. For the sake of clarity and economy, Jude's anxiety may be the most important thing to know about her, but if that's *all* we know, she's not going to feel fully alive to us.

Ms. Raleigh, a student of mine in a graduate fiction writing workshop, was aware, after her first draft about Jude, that she hadn't gotten completely "under the character's skin." She wanted to "push deeper." Oddly, for all the intimacy implied by such talk, it was greater distance from the character that finally enabled Ms. Raleigh to enspirit Jude—or more accurately, greater flexibility, movement, a delicate dance of distance and intimacy.

Just as the various parts of a person's skin may be soft *and* hard—muscled from dancing, say—rough and smooth, familiar and surprising, public and private, the language a writer uses to inhabit a character's skin must be varied, rippling, unexpected. Not random; skin, after all, is whole, of a piece, a secure container—in that sense, *focused*. But startling.

In her second draft, Ms. Raleigh composed another scene with Jude and Josie in the kitchen. Here, Jude is somewhat younger than she was in the first paragraph. Again, what do we know?

> Jude's mother was fixing her own breakfast plate. Her hair was clamped in rows of hot curlers, giving her a vaguely robotic appearance—but this did not detract in the least from her elemental grace. Standing at the stove, her back to Jude, she scraped eggs onto her plate with a light-wristed turn of the spatula; she might have had a book balanced on her head. Perfect posture, proportions, effortless gesture. If anything, the spiky curlers made everything else about her more feminine by comparison. She wore her special bathrobe—fuzzy, plush, trimmed with satin collar and piping. Though it was pink, a much paler shade than the Berry Belinda table, Jude felt a soft, fluttering contentment in the presence of this robe, the way it flowed as her mother moved; she knew how it would feel to be hugged by those sleeves and she wanted to rise as if taking her plate to the sink, drifting over to her mother. But her mother would notice the pooled yellow yolk on her plate and remind her how many vitamins and minerals it had, what a waste of nourishment it would be.

To begin with, I suspect it's harder to say what we "know" from this paragraph, as compared to the first one, because—on the surface, at least—the details (beautifully observed) aren't all pointing the same way. Furthermore, the linguistic texture here is thicker, less logical, more sensual, moving from abstract formal phrases—"elemental grace"—that we wouldn't normally link with a little girl's perceptions, to specific details—"the Berry Belinda table"—firmly anchored in childhood. (I'll address, in a moment, what might seem to be inconsistent diction.) Still, I think we come away from this scene with a much fuller experience of Jude than we did the first time around.

We're not being told what Jude feels, nor are Jude's emotions described from the outside in, like the "too-thick emptiness" seeping *into* the kitchen the first time around. Here, we're working from the inside out—everything begins in Jude. There's a subtle, but enormous, difference between *filtering* details through a character, and actually *seeing* through a character's eyes. In the first case, we're told that "Jude was aware" of the objects in the room—in effect, we're invited to watch Jude watching. Then we get the details, the coffee aroma, the bread, the clock. Finally, we see how Jude responds to them. She twists, she startles, she imagines chaos.

In this second draft, we're automatically placed inside Jude's skin, watching her mother fix breakfast, just as Jude is watching her. We're not *directed* to see what Jude sees; we see it ourselves, experiencing first-hand Josie's every "effortless gesture." At the same time, the narrative voice is flexible enough to describe what Jude herself is probably not mature enough to articulate—her mother's "elemental grace." Certainly, a little girl wouldn't think those words, but she could be aware of the physicality behind them. The perception is followed by a fragmented sentence, "Perfect posture, proportions, effortless gesture," like a sudden memory of lessons Jude has likely heard from her mother. By solidly grounding each observation inside Jude, Ms. Raleigh allows herself a free range of expression, from Jude's conscious thoughts at the moment, to impressions she's only dimly aware of, which will come back to haunt her later, as an adult, when she remembers that morning in the kitchen.

We know Jude longs for connection with her mother, a longing conveyed in strong tactile detail. The "fuzzy, plush" bathrobe "flowed as her mother moved"—this is how a little girl learns "elemental grace," and it fills her with "fluttering contentment." Note, again, the voice's flexibility. The reader accepts the word "contentment"—a rather distant concept for a child, perhaps—because it is "fluttering," physical, tickling, and anxious, precisely the way Jude's skin would react at that instant.

In the first draft, Jude is left alone in the kitchen, absorbing her mother's actual absence. In the second scene, we endure Josie's loss, along with Jude, even as Josie is still fixing breakfast. Jude wishes to drift over to her mother, to be hugged by "those sleeves," but "her mother would notice the pooled yellow yolk on her plate and remind her . . . what a waste of nourishment it would be." These last lines begin with Jude's desire and end in Josie's scolding voice *as it's lodged inside Jude,* thwarting her desire. The mother is both here and not here, present but unavailable to Jude. No explanation is necessary. We have just experienced why Jude feels her mother's absence so keenly.

The language pays careful attention to rhythm as well as detail, moving far beyond mere logical connections. The long, sensory sentences in the paragraph's center, with their soft sounds (*f,s,sh*) give way, at the end, to the harsh, almost pounding insistence of one-syllable words, one after the other—"yolk on her plate," "what a waste . . . it would be." We slip from the rich, "fluttery" textures of Jude's need for contact to the slap-slap of Josie's refusal. Literally, we're stopped short as we're reading. In this way, we share Jude's devastation. We inhabit her skin.

Language, after all, is the only skin a fictional character has.

In this second draft, Ms. Raleigh reached the heart of character. Usually, young writers are taught to build character through detail, to let a character's actions and observations reveal her emotions, her personality. But as we've seen from these examples, detail alone is not enough.

Sifting detail, like sand, through a character's mind is not enough. The language must act as the character's skin, *registering awareness* of detail through its rhythms. What do we know? We know what we feel. And feeling begins with the skin.

NOTES FOR SUGGESTED READINGS

Note how Ron Carlson brings the narrator to life by contrasting him with his family and by showing him performing his duties at his job at a motel in "The Ordinary Son."

Exercises

1. First name each of the following characters (don't be too exotic or too mundane). Then give each character a trait opposite his presumed nature. In other words, characters who are inherently bad usually have some redeeming qualities just as those inherently good characters have some flaws.
   Example: An embezzler. Name: Roland Banks. Quality: A volunteer in the Big Brother program

   > A priest
   > A fire fighter
   > An emergency room physician
   > A PTA president
   > A Peace Corps volunteer
   > A drug dealer
   > A bank robber
   > A poacher
   > A corrupt politician
   > A mafia assassin

2. Now do the same with one of your own characters.
3. With a tape recorder, interview a character from one of your stories. As a newspaper reporter, prepare a list of questions to ask your character. As you will also be giving the answers, this will require you to wear two hats.

CHAPTER

18

SETTING

All too often, beginning writers pay too little attention to setting, the very foundation on which the character stands. Yet when we travel, it is the setting that is most often the focus of our attention. We don't backpack through the Himalayas with our eyes closed; rather, we walk through new worlds in awe, with all of our sensory organs barraged by new stimuli. We are sentient beings and our senses are even more aware when entering new territory.

The poetry of earth is never dead.

John Keats

The same goes for the reader—when he enters a short story or a novel for the first time, it is a new world for him, never before explored, and his senses are on alert for new sights, new scents, new sounds, new tastes, and yes, for something new to touch. The reader is as wary of a story without a setting as a traveler is wary of a place totally devoid of sensory appeal. If there is such a place, I have never been there.

Think back to the last time you traveled to a place where you had never before ventured. The place itself does not matter; it might be Mexico, Cameroon, France, Oregon, or California. Close your eyes and recall your arrival in this new world. What was it that first struck you about the place? Was it the sweet aroma of plantains roasting over a charcoal fire? Was it the sight of young girls in green and orange *saris* walking barefoot through the market with pans of water precariously balanced on their heads? Was it the whinny of a horse as you walked by a Paris slaughterhouse? Was it hiking in Oregon's Coast Range through a spring rain storm, your soaking shirt wrapping you like some new and heavy skin? Was it pulling off the highway into the dust of a California roadside fruit stand, parched and tired from the long drive, taking a heavy strawberry as big as a thumb, and biting into an explosion of sweet, red juice?

All of these appeals to our senses are touches of setting. Setting can certainly be defined as place—again, Mexico, Cameroon, France, Oregon, or California—but what is truly place? It is necessarily a combination of space and time for, quite simply, place changes as time passes. A short story set in Kansas City in 2000 would, quite obviously, have a different setting than would that same story set in that same city in 1910, because half of our equation of *place + time = setting* is now different. (It should be noted that, while the mantra "write about what you know" is good advice, it does not mean that the writer cannot learn more; if you want to write about Kansas City in the year of 1910, learn about that place and time by doing some research in the library.)

Setting, then, is necessarily a combination of space and time, and time has as much to do with the second, the minute, the hour, the day, the week, the month, and the year as it does with the character who inhabits your setting and what this character's particular **mood** is.

Example: *The place: Bangui, the capital of the Central African Empire. The Time: September, 1979.* I have established setting by indicating the place and the time. Or so it seems. But who is to people this setting? By asking this question, I have inextricably linked **character** and setting (and POV, as well, for through whose eyes are we viewing this setting?).

Bangui is a beautiful city situated between rising hills and the wide expanse of the Ubangui River. Having lived there for some time as a Peace Corps Volunteer, there is much I could describe. As often suggested in advice on descriptive writing in textbooks, I could appeal to all of the reader's five senses, and I could focus on a dominant impression, the humidity, for example. But what criterion do I use for choosing which aspect of a setting to describe? The answer is often, but not always, *mood*.

What first comes to mind is the mood of the character. Certainly, if a story is told in third person limited through the eyes of a young, naive Peace Corps Volunteer, a devout Catholic from Boston who is depressed at the poverty he has encountered in Africa, we might describe a section of Bangui's Centre Ville, where the New Palace Bar is situated across the street from several mango trees, like this:

As Johnson walked up Avenue Boganda from the Peace Corps office, he stopped to watch two small boys throw rocks up into one of the green mango trees that lined the avenue.

The boys' bellies were distended from a lack of protein, and they were dressed only in tat-
tered shorts. One boy had a goiter the size of a grapefruit growing from the back of his
neck. Johnson tried to spy out a mango in the dense tangle of green leaves and branches,
but he couldn't see a single one. He turned and walked on past the crowded veranda of the
New Palace Bar.

The reader sees that Johnson is focused on the boys and their hunger—
that is the setting Johnson observes. Yet in that same setting is the veranda of
the New Palace Bar which Johnson ignores. Another character, we'll call him
Smitty, is also walking up Avenue Boganda from the Peace Corps office.
Smitty is from Arizona and is finishing his second year as a volunteer and
will be going home in three weeks. He is excited about returning to the States:

Smitty walked up Avenue Boganda past the African boys who were throwing rocks into
the thick foliage of a mango tree. He climbed the stairs to the veranda of the New Palace
Bar. It was not yet noon, but the veranda was crowded with government functionaires
and French expatriates drinking beer in the morning sun. It was the first of the month
and the functionaires had been paid; the French, they were always there. There was
laughter and shouting. Pops, the Cameroonian waiter who waddled his great bulk from
table to table, waved to Smitty as he cleared a table for him. Smitty shook his hand and
kissed both of his cheeks before ordering a beer and a Croque Madame. As he waited for
his beer, he watched two boys throwing rocks at a mango tree across the avenue.

From the two examples, we can see that what we describe may greatly
depend on the point of view employed by the writer; that what we describe
may, indeed, depend on the mood of the character from whose lens we are
watching events unfold.

However, when we use the word mood in relation to setting, we often are
more concerned with the **theme** of the story. Granted, a writer very rarely
goes into a story knowing its theme. In fact, a writer very rarely enters a story
knowing its plot; one must remember that in first drafts, the writing of a story
is very often a process of discovery for the writer. However, after several
drafts, the writer will have discovered what she wants the story to mean and
she may then go on to write subsequent drafts in which she hopes to use the
setting to help reflect that very meaning.

If one were writing a story focusing on the disparity of wealth in the
Central African Empire, one might juxtapose the descriptions of the French
expatriates drinking on the veranda with the two boys trying to knock down
a meal from a mango tree. This visual image would, undoubtedly, help
inform the reader of the writer's concern without ever having used any overt
exposition—informing the reader, then, by showing, not telling.

Any aspect of setting can greatly influence the mood of a story, and James
Joyce makes great use of light in his story "Araby." The narrator, a young
schoolboy in Ireland, has fallen in love with a neighbor's sister. She tells him

of a bazaar she would like to attend but cannot. He decides he will go to Araby where he will buy her a gift that will represent his affection for her. As he moves through the story, it grows progressively darker until, at the end of the story, the lights of the bazaar go out and it is completely dark. The story ends: "Gazing up into the darkness I saw myself as a creature driven and derided by vanity; and my eyes burned with anguish and anger."

What Joyce has done is to use the darkness to represent the boy's realization that his naive hope for reciprocal love was no more than a pipe dream and that having moved from this youthful naiveté, he has entered the darker realm of the adult (there is also the sense that the boy has lost his religious faith as well; the description of the bazaar is similar to that of a church and again, in the end, the lights go out).

Setting, of course, does not have to represent theme; it is just one of the many possibilities that setting possesses. Another possibility is one of choice. In Ernest Hemingway's story "Hills Like White Elephants," the setting plays as important a role as the two characters. The setting is a railway station in Spain wherein a man and a woman are discussing whether she should have an abortion. Actually, the man is manipulating the woman, trying to force her to make the choice to have what he calls "an awfully simple operation."

In this very short story, Hemingway describes the setting very clearly. There is a train station set between two lines of rails. On one side of the station, where the couple is sitting, the hills are big and barren; these are the hills the woman describes as being like "white elephants." On the other side of the station, there is a river, there are fields of grain, and there are mountains and trees. Obviously, the woman has a choice to make: near the end of the story, she gets up and walks along the platform, turns her back to the barren hills, and looks to the verdant fields beyond the river on the other side of the station. Hemingway has used setting to represent the choice the woman has before her: two sides of the station, two sets of tracks.

Sometimes a beginning writer will be so concerned with character or plot he will forget to create a credible setting. In early drafts that may be O.K., but eventually the setting will have to be painted in, because the reader needs to be grounded in a believable world. The setting does not have to represent the mood of the character, nor does it necessarily have to represent the mood of the story; those are just possibilities. What it must do, however, is represent a credible world wherein the character can make choices. And if the story is science fiction or fantasy, it is even more important for that setting to be credible, because if the writer wants the reader to believe that humans on earth can be vaporized in a millisecond only to reappear on Mars in human form one second later, then that writer had better have a detailed, concrete description of the machine that does it, or the reader will call foul.

As the writer Ron Carlson says, "Solve your problems in the physical world." To the writer, that physical world is the setting.

TAKE *PLACE*

Valerie Miner

I don't know whether I am first a writer or a traveler, but I got interested in exploring and storytelling at the same time. In the kitchen, I listened to my mother's memories of her native Edinburgh: walks up Calton Hill, windowshopping along Princes Street, errands to the corner shop to buy chipped fruit and *The News of the World* for her father. In our back garden, I sat on the lawn while my seaman father tied up his beefsteak tomatoes, drank iced tea, and described brilliant fabrics he had seen in Argentina and the strange, tasty seaweed he had eaten in Japan. During the many months he was gone at sea, I awaited his return, eager for more stories and especially eager for the new doll he would bring dressed in a local fashion. Those dolls from Korea and Japan and Holland and Jamaica and the Dominican Republic now sit together on my bookcase. Just as I always knew each one had a distinct personality, I knew this personality was related to her place of origin.

Before I write a short story or teach a fiction class, I remind myself that "Place" is a verb as well as a noun. We're not talking painting or postcard description here. We're dealing with dialect, music, the angle of the sun, moisture in the air, historical kerfuffles, whispers of the spirits. Setting is action and being and states of being.

Grade school geography classes made me even more curious about people in their settings. Vividly, I remember photos of the Acropolis, vowing I would go to Greece when I grew up (and, indeed, I recently made my fifth trip to that country, this time to do research for a collaborative theatre piece.) Tungsten and soybeans—natural and agricultural resources of China—were still on my mind in the 1980s as I was escorted around literary salons in Beijing, Shanghai, and Guangzhou by members of the Chinese Writers' Association. Surely the precise, colorful maps I constructed of Morocco in the fifth grade later persuaded me to travel in 1975 on those rickety local buses from Tetuan through the Riff Mountains and down to the Sahara, where I met blue men of the desert carrying white sacks on camels. Although I didn't visit any of these places with the intention of writing about them, short stories eventually emerged from each experience.

Such traveling made coming "home" that much more fascinating because I now knew other places (settings) to which I compared familiar food and voices and climate. Home became something smaller and larger and far more complicated than the place I left. And I was never able to think about home again without seeing it on a map—in context— home wasn't the center of the world any more, but it was finally *in* the world.

One of my favorite stories about "home" is "Presents," written by Julie Gard, a graduate student at the University of Minnesota. In fourteen compact pages, Gard reveals significant shifts in perception and action between Michael and Karen, a middle-aged couple living in a roomy suburban Philadelphia house. As her story opens, they are preparing for the visit of a twenty-five-year-old daughter and saying goodbye to a Japanese family who have been staying with them for a month as part of a cultural exchange program. Karen's appreciation of their home is external. "After twenty years she still can't get over it, how beautiful their home is surrounded by maple and oak. She'll often touch the stone and stand back to admire the deep green of the shutters, almost black . . . . The way the roads curve, the Welsh names of the streets, how everything is tucked behind azalea and rhododendron and hard to find. And the trees, the way they tower over the houses."

Meanwhile, Michael's sensibilities are all inside and right now they are focused on a beautiful old bookcase he is refinishing as a birthday present for his returning daughter. "Michael likes to work in the basement. It smells like sawdust down there, and turpentine. Often there is paint or shellac in the creases of his palms."

Unlike Gard, some students omit setting from their stories. Perhaps too much daily life is spent in our heads. Our idiosyncratic characters, forced to muck their ways through our tepid grey matter, emerge in consequent colorlessness. Technology validates the cerebral over the sensual. On the Information Highway, an e-mail from Sri Lanka looks like an e-mail from Ohio. And even when we leave town, it's easy to confuse one airport with another. If we're going to succeed as writers, we want to step away from the computer, escape the airport—well beyond the car rental satellite—onto the small streets where we witness climate, culture, geography, history, people mowing lawns, telling jokes, having fights, fixing dinner. We want to listen to their accents and diction and vocabulary. We want to smell what's simmering on the stove.

"Karen starts passing around the food: sushi, lasagna, French bread, green salad, a bowl of dumplings that Miki made fresh. Michael breathes in tomato and soy sauce . . . ."

Julie Gard's ability to write so precisely about her Philadelphia suburbs comes, in part, from the distance she has experienced living long periods in Russia and attending colleges in Iowa and Minnesota. In "Presents," Michael and Karen can compare home to places they've visited. Meanwhile, the Japanese family allow them to see their home in yet a different light.

Setting influences character. Sometimes setting is character. The pleasure Michael and Karen take from their home mirrors their family love, and their risk in opening the house to international visitors is the best expression of their generosity and curiosity.

When I read Gard's carefully observed story, I wonder how some of her peers simply "forget" setting. Perhaps it's because so much of our celebrated literary fiction is character-driven. An almost pathological focus on the isolated individual's quest, combined with the "action-driven" nature of film culture encourages storytellers to overemphasize character and plot at the expense of setting. But whether we're talking about powerful scenes of home birth or gruesome portraits of mass murder—the setting of these scenes is important; all dramas take *place*. Setting is inextricable from character and plot (even if that setting is a fantasy or a mystery to the reader). The best writers allow themselves to be surprised by complications of place, derailments, astral projections.

Here are some common omissions my students and I have noticed: (1) Three pages of dialogue in which the speakers don't seem to move any body part except, possibly, their lips (Are they in the kitchen? the bedroom? the old tree house built when they were children?). (2) The long, grim narrative that gives us no city name, no history, no hint about the age or ethnic mix of local citizenry. (3) Elaborate lyrical passages in which every flower in the garden is sensually sniffed by a disembodied nose.

After we laugh good-humoredly at such encounters, I ask students to consider the *sources* of setting. We discuss: (1) Direct and careful observation (a form of reportage). (2) Memory (from yesterday, from childhood, from someone else's yesterday). (3) Imagination (the creation of a new planet or an underwater world). (4) Cultural mythology (Judeo-Christian scriptures, the oral history of Plains Indians). (5) Gossip (the legend of ancient Mr. Simplegreen who never left the house on the corner for fifty years; the rumor about the cheerleader and the basketball star murdered in lovers' lane a quarter-century ago). Once the list of sources begins, it expands, and students get excited about the wealth of their artistic inventories. We talk about how "writing the familiar" is the trickiest task because we assume too much, don't look closely enough, and thus the first-draft setting is often too implicit. Then we begin to do basic archaeology about the most familiar places—finding maps, photos, news articles, oral histories, of places students believed had *automatically* come alive in their first attempts. Suddenly setting is neither a supernatural gift nor impossible drudgery, but an aesthetic opportunity that opens our stories (and ourselves) to deeper sensual pleasure and emotional power.

Narrative place attends to time. We all live in history. To convey the spirit of a town in 1999, we need to know the skyline of ten years ago, eighty years ago. What was the village/town/city like when there were more trees and fewer people? How do the oldtimers relate to the incomers? Western Civilization has erected the aesthetic of the scaffold—on Fifth Avenue, at Notre Dame, the Sydney Opera House—which allows us to imagine the future through the protective brace of the present. Yet there's nothing to keep us from looking beneath the scaffold, around the scaffold, into our imaginations.

Today, here, now is perhaps the hardest to describe because we don't look at our costumes, hear our own music. But the dailiness of today can be just as provocative as the Czar's elaborate parties at the Summer Palace in the last century. On a sweltering August afternoon, we want to know that our hero is wearing army boots, a long, sheer red dress and tatooed arms. How many rings does her boyfriend wear in his nose? Does the antagonist dye his hair black or is that the natural color? Why does his mother insist on wearing those faded hippie skirts from twenty years ago? Perhaps these don't seem like historical costumes now, but think about describing them as a sharp-eyed feature journalist. If journalism is "literature in a hurry," perhaps literature is journalism with breathing space.

In "Presents," "Michael remembers when Jeannie and Rachel dressed up in Wonder Woman outfits, using their pajamas and bits of old Halloween costumes . . . his daughters decked out in red and blue, big Ws taped to their chests, Rachel in red snowboots and Jeannie in red magic-markered ballet slippers."

The historical moment of our fiction includes season and time of day. Each term, my students and I begin with a short short story in which I make only two requests—that all writers *subtly* convey the season and time of day in their narratives. Always, always, half the class forgets one or both assignments and we have an album of stories that take place at no particular time of day in no particular season!

Gard uses narrative time effectively when she shows that Michael is so excited about his daughter's return that he can't sleep, and he gets up in the middle of the hot summer night to finish the bookcase he is making for her. "The stairs to the first floor creak in the dark; his bare feet sink into the basement stairs, thick with old carpet. The mildew smells stronger at night. The dehumidifier has gone off again; he kicks it and the buzz starts up . . . . He starts from the top, pushing the rag into the twists and crevices in the wood. He works his way down the flat sides and cleans off a tar stain near the bottom. Soon his bookcase stands wet and dark in the pool of light, and he stands next to it. Around them, the room is all shadows."

The next assignment of the term is to take the same story and change just one element—either the time of day (dawn to noon or early evening) or the season (spring to fall). Usually people are astonished by the difference this makes in their characters' possibilities and behaviors. We discuss how a writerly attention to absence (such as the silence of traffic in a scene that has shifted from midday to midnight) as well as observation of such often overlooked details as temperature, the texture of grass, the intensity of the sun, the color of the sky, makes our characters feel different and act in new ways.

In Gard's story, we find that Michael's attitude toward the bookcase is very different during the midday buzz than it is in the quiet hours of the morning. It becomes a companion and eventually a sedative.

Setting, as Gard demonstrates, is inside as well as outside—the inside of a house, apartment, jail, makeshift cardboard box claimed by a homeless person. The interiors can be as dramatic as the features of the external world.

Some writers fret that their places will be too common or too exotic for readers. Several years ago, a graduate student asked me whether she should abandon her collection of New York stories because New York had been *done* before. "What can I add to Paley, Doctorow, Mailer?" None of these authors, to my knowledge, had written from the perspective of a young WASP woman from the Midwest camping out in Manhattan for a couple of years in the 1990s. Her New York would be a completely different location, perhaps an infinitely more fascinating city than their New Yorks, because of her foreignness, much in the way that nonnative speakers of English (Eva Hoffman, Joseph Conrad) often compose our most musical prose, for they are not frozen by conventional idiom.

Speech is a primary element of setting. Dialect and vocabulary hint at where our characters have been, where they think they're going. So do the rhythms of conversations, from the fast-paced, ever-interrupting chats one experiences in Greenwich Village to the slower, more collaborative exchanges one hears in the Big Horn Moutains. Randall Kenan's exemplary story, "Tell Me, Tell Me," opens with a middle-of-the-night telephone conversation between two women. From their vocabulary, we realize they are old white southerners ("grandboy . . . pickaninny"). We gather something about their social status when one of them suggests that the other has had a bad dream, "Probably those oysters you ate at the club. You had oysters that other night too. Remember? Oysters just don't agree with you. They didn't agree with my mama either." Although the story proceeds for many pages in a more conventional mix of dialogue, summary, and action, these first four pages of conversation are the key to our understanding of Bella and Ida's places in Tims Creek, North Carolina, in American social history.

Even when characters disguise their native dialect, readers' appreciation for place is enlarged. What's happening when the North Dakotan living in London pretends to be Canadian or even English? What do we intuit about a character's shame or ambition or dexterity when we hear him speak in an artificial accent?

When Miki Yamanaka speaks, we learn that she is comfortable in English if not completely fluent. Her speech is careful, unpretentious, communicative. "Miki is still working at the counter. She lays out strips of something green and wet, seaweed, he thinks, white rice, a pile of cut-up vegetables. 'I make sushi for tonight,' she says. 'Your wife make lasagna to go with it.'"

Ultimately, one wants to create, construct, divine a setting that is not only credible, but memorable, so palpable that we can't remember whether an image comes from a story or from our own lived experience. Gard ends her story memorably, in keeping with setting and character, as Michael stands on the front step of his cherished family home waving, "He wants to wave until Jeannie comes, until his goodbye to the Yamanakas is a greeting for his younger daughter. He wants to skip church and stand on the front step out in the sun, just stand there and wave all day."

It makes me want to wave back.

How do we discover or name or claim our own artistic home and how does this influence our practice writing in terms of setting? My Scottish mother and seaman father taught me that the difference between being a wanderer and a traveler is the gift of finding a particular home. My California cabin allows me to write about Norway, Kenya, India as much as it nudges me to evoke the American West. Setting comes from experience in a place, a retreat from that place, and a return to that place. While I'd never write about a location I didn't know, I find it's very helpful to get far away from the setting, at least for the first draft of the book. The physical separation allows memory to work creatively and ensures that the narrative swells from imaginative depth rather than from a more reflexive impulse to record or report.

Knowing my artistic home has not been confining. Quite the opposite, it has freed me to roam, sometimes forced me to travel that artistic distance to where I can no longer hear the quiet sound of the tall grasses dancing. But no matter where I am, I know that the Pacific Ocean creates the currents I imagine *against* and *with*. Have you found your artistic home? What are the currents that carry you onto the page?

NOTES FOR SELECTED READINGS

Note the symbolic function of the setting in John Steinbeck's "The Chrysanthemums," especially as described in the first paragraph.

Note how Raymond Carver uses light to mark the passage of time in "What We Talk About When We Talk About Love."

Note the symbolic setting throughout Bobbie Ann Mason's "Shiloh."

Exercises

1. Print a draft of a story. With a highlighter, highlight all references to setting in the draft. Now go back and estimate the percentage

of all references to setting as they address our five senses. You might come out with something like this:

1% tactile
3% taste
5% olfactory
30% sound
61% sight

There is, of course, no correct ratio in defining a setting, but if your story is set in Fairbanks, Alaska, in January and after having done this exercise you see that only 1% of your setting falls in the tactile category, you had better go back and add some appeals to that sense. After all, Alaska can be cold in January. After having done this exercise, if you see several pages with no highlighted material, be very suspicious.

2. What is described in a particular setting often depends upon the point of view of the story. Describe a real park you have visited, first in the first person pov through the eyes of a young man or young woman in love, and then through the eyes of an old widow or widower. After you have finished, note the differences in setting even though it was the same park. You can do the same exercise using third person limited.

3. A. After doing minimal research in the library, describe a man in the third person limited pov as he walks along a Bismarck, North Dakota street in January of 1923.

   B. Again, after doing research in the library, describe a woman in the third person limited pov as she lies on a Key West, Florida, beach in August of 1968.

   The purpose of this exercise is twofold: it is designed to help the writer realize that while "Write what you know" is good advice, through research you can "know" anything; and, it is designed to show how a setting can affect a character.

19

DIALOGUE

The act of speaking is an act so natural to us that it would seem that writing dialogue would come just as naturally, but unfortunately it does not. It is not that writing dialogue is particularly difficult. Rather, the difficulty lies in choosing *when* and *how* to use dialogue to enhance your story by enriching your scenes.

Direct dialogue occurs when two or more people are speaking in a scene (see the chapter on *plot* for the distinction between *scene* and *exposition*) as opposed to **indirect dialogue** which is reported speech. Certainly, if what the characters say is important in developing the plot or in characterization, the conversation should be handled directly as follows:

> *"Las Vegas will be fun. Hell, you've never even been there," John said.*
>
> *"And I don't want to go for the first time," Heide said.*

If, however, we chose to handle this dialogue indirectly, it would appear as follows:

> *John told Heide that it would be fun to go to Las Vegas, but she said she did not want to go.*

Speech is a mirror of the soul: as a man speaks, so is he.

Publilius Syrus

The difference between the two is obvious; in the former, we have a scene, and in the latter we have exposition. In the interest of pacing, there will be times when you will mix the two, because there will be instances in which the reader needs to know some information that may slow the story down and would thus be better handled indirectly:

> "Las Vegas will be fun. Hell, you've never even been there," John said.
>
> "And I don't want to go for the first time," Heide said. She went on to remind her husband of how her own father had lost everything the family owned, including the house, when she was nine years old. She told him again of how her mother had divorced him and how her father had committed suicide. Then she began to cry.
>
> "It's okay," he said as he took her in his arms. "Relax now. It's okay."

From this example, one can see how we can use both direct and indirect dialogue to advance the story and thereby keep up its pace. Notice too that the only tag verb used in the example is the verb *said*. It is a perfectly good verb that reports the action of speech without drawing attention to itself; the attention should be on the dialogue itself and not on the verb that reports it. *Said* is almost always the right verb for dialogue. Reading a passage like the following sours the stomach:

> "Las Vegas will be fun. Hell, you've never even been there," John stated.
> "And I don't want to go for the first time," Heide exclaimed.
> "Oh, come on. Let's just go this one time," he pleaded.
> "I said no once and I meant it," she pronounced.
> "Well, the hell with you then," he barked.
> Ad nauseam.

One should also avoid the use of adverbs to describe the way someone says something. What the writer is then doing is telling and not showing. To wit: "And I don't want to go there for the first time," she said cleverly. One can see that the adverb is meant to clarify the way she made the statement, but if the statement has been made the way the adverb says it was made—cleverly— then it would be redundant to employ the adverb. If the statement was not clever, but we wanted the reader to think it was, using the adverb is the lazy way out. Far better to take your time and think of something clever in the first place.

It is also important to realize that rarely do we have a conversation about one limited topic without talking about something else at the same time. In other words, if you are talking about your day at work while sitting at the dinner table with your spouse, you will probably also talk about the food.

> "Las Vegas will be fun. Hell, you've never even been there," John said.
> "And I don't want to go for the first time," Heide said. "Pass the butter, will you?"

Sometimes writers will forget that our characters do not drop everything to have a conversation. In other words, they are physically active as they talk. It is important to embody the dialogue of your characters. They should not be physically frozen as they speak. Again and again I tell my students to avoid naked dialogue.

> *"Las Vegas will be fun. Hell, you've never even been there," John said as he poured wine first in his wife's glass and then in his own.*
>
> *"And I don't want to go for the first time," Heide said. "Pass the butter, will you?"*
>
> *She took the butter from John without looking at him. As she buttered her bread, she went on to remind her husband of how her own father had lost everything the family owned, including the house, when she was nine years old. She told him again of how her mother had divorced him and how her father had committed suicide. Then she began to cry.*

There will be times when you have set your story in Mexico, France, or some other foreign locale, and you want your reader to believe that the characters are speaking Spanish or French or some other language, yet you do not want to write the entire dialogue in that language for fear of confusing your reader and/or because you do not know the language. Usually, incorporating a foreign word from time to time will remind the reader of the language the characters are speaking. Hemingway was a master at doing this.

It should be noted that we do not speak on point as people do who are being interviewed. Dialogue should not be done in a question and answer form, because that is not how we speak and neither should our characters.

Finally, a word on quotation marks. Some writers, such as Cormac McCarthy, do not use quotation marks to delineate the dialogue of their characters. You can get away with this only if you write very good dialogue as does McCarthy. One would think that a reader might have trouble differentiating the dialogue from the exposition, but in McCarthy's work, this is simply not the case. A good exercise for all aspiring writers is to write a scene with two or more characters conversing, and not use quotations marks (you must include some exposition in the scene, of course). Note how this forces you to make the dialogue different in style, tone and voice from the exposition of the narrator, thus rendering the quotation marks obsolete.

ON DIALOGUE

Diana Abu-Jaber

Dialogue can be just as slick and slippery as everyday conversation, but what sets it apart from conversation is that dialogue is *shaped* and that it exists to *advance* and *deepen* the story. Great dialogue writers know that dialogue is a kind of sleight-of-hand: you create the illusion of eavesdropping on completely natural speech. What's not said is often as important as what is said, and when you combine the words and the silences with body language—gestures, tics, poses—then you have a fully-realized form of dialogue.

Well-written dialogue is one form of *action*, and action is what keeps readers close and involved in reading. Writing is, after all, a fairly abstract form of art: words on a page signaling the world beyond. While straight narrative is descriptive and informative, dialogue allows characters to speak directly for themselves. Suddenly things pick up; we break free from blocks of looking and thinking and shift into faster slices of listening. Run your eye down the page and you'll notice that passages of dialogue have more "eye-appeal." They signal a break from the hard work of concentration into a more performative and entertaining area. There's a sense of spontaneity and unpredictable freeplay about well-written dialogue that mimics the spark of real-life conversations. But, of course, that's all an illusion.

A writer has to exert close control over her characters' dialogue; it's easy to fall into the "Talkative trap" where dialogue lapses into the patterns of everyday blather, or worse, chitchat, small-talk, or speechifying.

So when Gary, a student in my fiction workshop, wrote the following lines in a story:

> "Have you heard bout, oh, ah, hey hi, you know bout the guy, what'sisname. Yeah. Wait. But I mean like have you?" Gary said.
> "Yeah? What? What guy?" Walter said. "Who? Him? Old Jones?"
> "Well, yuh, who else? I mean, who else would I even be wasting my time talking about, okay?"

he was erring on the side of realism. By faithfully recording the nuances of patterns of everyday talk, it might seem as if he'd created a wonderfully authentic piece of writing. But remember that (1) recording is not the same as writing, and (2) real-life can be confining to a story. In so-called real-life, we have more patience with conversation because we're all in the same boat: thinking on our feet. Have you ever seen courtroom transcripts? They're full of umm's and uh's and you-know's and assorted other stammers and stutters. We have much less patience with that sort of flotsam in literature because we want to read a story, not a transcript. And, unless for some postmodern reason your story is about the fragmentation of conversation—or something equally dull—it will not be advanced by that sort of detail.

Bear in mind that Dialogue should only SEEM spontaneous. Meanwhile, you should cut out all the filler. Sculpt it, bend it, mold it to reflect what's happening. Write it spontaneously, but go back and shape it up later. That's the secret beauty of *revision*: nothing is unfixable.

So the writer above tightened the little exchange to:

"Have you heard about—what's his name—that new pharmacist?"
"What guy?" Walter said. "You mean Old Jones?"

And the sequence was brisk and readable, with just a soupçon of realistic hesitation and misdirection. It receded back into the momentum of the story, which is exactly where it belonged, because it wasn't that important an exchange. A story is an organic entity—all its parts need to fit together. Readers should only really "see" the important moments, and that goes double for dialogue.

Hence, dialogue has to do a couple of jobs at once. It should never simply exist for filling in "local color."

My student Charmane wrote a long monologue for one of her characters, a bored corporate executive who spends a lot of time in one scene talking about a yellow coat she sees in a store window:

"I'd love to get that coat. This time of year a woman needs a good coat, that's what I say, and that's what I'll always say. A good coat made out of yellow cotton and wool. A winter-into-spring deal. Just you wait. A good yellow coat like that, just waiting for me to come and get it. It's sayin' hello-dolly, come and get me!"

The problem, as I pointed out to Charmane, was that her story was not about coats. If anything, allowing a character to go on about a particular distraction or digression can become a bit of a **red herring**. Readers will resent feeling that they've been misled, that some sort of big clue or broad hint has been thrown out that really doesn't lead to anything more in the story.

But Charmane claimed that this passage lent a kind of depth to the character. The monologue was deliberately pitched to show the incongruity between the executive's personal history of growing up in poverty and her current station in the fast lane. Problem is, that's not enough. Even though this segment gave us some insights into the woman's character, it gave very little into the nature of the story. Remember, you can—and should—always make dialogue do double-duty. To paraphrase Heide Fonda, make it work for you. Not only should the monologue tell us about the character, it should give us important information about what's happening to her in the story. The monologue about the yellow coat would be fine if the yellow coat somehow figured into the overall scheme of things—or possibly if the character had a tradition of going off on tangents in order to avoid the main topic. Otherwise: make your dialogue MATTER.

Bear in mind that when I say dialogue should matter, that doesn't mean that the characters should be narrating, explaining, or describing the actual events of the story. Assuming that you're not Edgar Allen Poe and plan to have an obsessive-compulsive type sit down and reel off the creepy family history, and assuming that you're not writing a soap opera where characters need to catch each other up constantly ("So you're saying that Jeremaia is not, in fact, Scurval's second cousin once removed . . . that Norbert never really loved Tessie Mae or their father . . . and that you are the actual heir to the throne of Micronesia . . . ") it's safe to assume that successful dialogue usually directs through indirection. As in this section of dialogue from my student Deborah Reed's short story:

"My lawyer said no way. He's one of the best you know. He said it was clear as the day is long that we could win so we took them on and boy did he know his stuff. You should have seen him in that courtroom!"

"Why? What did he say?"
"Oh I don't understand all that legal mumbo jumbo. All I know is he's a charmer and that was something the judge and jury just couldn't deny either."
"So what exactly did you sue for?" I ask her.
"Well, damages of course. You know how my back is. I'll be damned if I was going to let them slave drivers kill me. They had no idea who they were dealing with. I'm considered disabled now, you know?"

And so on. This is a mother and a daughter who *seem* to be saying one thing to each other on the surface, but manage to be saying many other things hidden beneath the literal meanings. The mother is slightly crazy and very manipulative and the daughter has been trying for years to escape her mother's emotional invasions. At first glance the conversation might appear to be civil, rational—if a bit intense—and friendly. But in the context of the story, their exchange gives us both *character information*—the mother is nuts and the daughter is fleeing—and *story information*—the mother is a scam artist and the daughter may get dragged into her mother's web again.

Ultimately, if you want to write great dialogue you have to learn how to *listen*. Deborah's dialogue captures the little bits of slang, *mumbo jumbo*, just the right amount of cursing for this mother, and the right sorts of silences and pauses for the daughter. Read authors who have a great "ear" for dialogue, like Raymond Carver, J. D. Salinger, and Louise Erdrich, and notice the way their dialogue is not only informative and textured, it's also shapely and interesting. If you learn to zero in on the key phrases, the hesitations, the parries and jokes, suggestions and intimations, and to express what needs to be stated as well as what needs to be unspoken, your dialogue will be eloquent indeed.

NOTES FOR SELECTED READING

Note how Melissa Pritchard uses dialogue to differentiate the three characters in "Sweet Feed."

Exercises

1. The "dead horse" exercise: Write a scene in the third person limited pov where two characters are charged with the task of removing a dead horse from a field before morning (it is the neighbor's horse and he has asked them to remove it before his daughter wakes up on Christmas morning to see her favorite horse dead in a field). They can remove it any way they find possible. As they work, they will be talking about the huge task at hand, but they will also be talking about their own lives. The objective: to realize that whenever we have a conversation, we usually talk about more than one thing at a time. Also, we are usually doing something as we talk, and thus our dialogue is embodied.
2. Go to a public place such as a restaurant and get near enough to two people in conversation to enable you to transcribe what they are saying. (Don't be too obvious, because you could offend someone.) Do not describe what they are doing; just transcribe the dialogue. After fifteen or twenty minutes, you'll have several pages of notes. Type them up verbatim. Then type the conversation again, this time embodying the dialogue any way you choose. Now, note the difference between the two sets of pages. The objective: To avoid naked dialogue. We move when we talk.
3. Tape record a scene from a story you are currently working on. Listen to it carefully and determine whether the idioms are appropriate for the place and time; whether there are some long speeches that need to be broken up with interjections from the other characters; and, whether some of the direct dialogue could be better handled indirectly in the interests of improved pacing.

CHAPTER

20

STYLE, TONE, AND VOICE

I have never really heard a good definition of *voice*, but I have seen *voice* and *tone* and *style* so stewed together that one is hardly distinguishable from another so that when one speaks of voice he really means style and when another speaks of style he really means tone. Thus, let me attempt to clarify the three here: If a writer's style is the way he uses language—her rhetorical strategy, such as variance of sentence length and word choice and punctuation—and if a writer's tone is his use of irony, understatement, and hyperbole and the like—when we put the two together we come up with the equation *style + tone = voice.* Thus, your individual voice comprises both your style and your tone.

Many books on creative writing forgo a discussion of voice. It may be that they do so because voice is something that is honed from years of writing, not something that you pick up and utilize as you might an omniscient point of view after reading a chapter about the various points of view. But voice is as important as the other elements of fiction, because it is the voice that carries the reader through the story. Unless you are a disciple of Evelyn Wood and you burn through the pages to get to the end of the book, it is the voice of the writer that you hear as if she were sitting on

Great writers leave their mark by the originality of their style, stamping it with an imprint that imposes a new face on the coins of language.

Jean-Joseph Goux

your shoulder and whispering in your ear. When I am reading fiction, I often stop and read a particularly good paragraph two, maybe three, times. If the book is good, if the voice is compelling, I am the slowest of slow readers. This past winter, I read Jim Harrison's novel *The Road Home* as slowly as one possibly could because the understated voice was so enchanting that to no longer hear it would be, well, disenchanting. I am unsure of how many times I have gone back and reread passages such as this one that opens the novel:

> It is easy to forget that in the main we die only seven times more slowly than our dogs. The simplicity of this law of proportion came to me early in life, growing up as I did so remotely that dogs were my closest childhood friends. I've always been a slow talker, though if my vocal cords had been otherwise constructed I may have done well at a growl or bark or howl at scented but unseen dangers beyond the light we think surrounds us, but more often enshrouds us. My mother was an Oglala Sioux (they call themselves Lakota), my father was an orphan from the east, grayish white like March snow, under which you don't count on spring, intermittently mad as he was over a life largely spent on helping the Natives accommodate themselves to their conquerors. After his release from the Civil War (sic!) until December of 1890 he burned up body and soul in these efforts, fixing on botany as the tool of liberation and this in an area, the Great Plains, that is ill disposed to the cultivation of fruit-bearing trees, or berry-bearing bushes of an Eastern nature. The fact that he failed utterly in his life's mission only increases my reverence for him, though he was much easier to live with dead than alive, so powerful were the spates of irrationality that came upon him in the last twenty years of his life.

Harrison sustains this voice, never wavering, for some 446 pages.

A writer develops his style through years and years of practice, and while that style may be relatively constant, the demands of different stories may require different voices. Imagine that your writing career spans fifty years and that in those fifty years you write 500 short stories. Undoubtedly, you will have employed different points of view, but if you did write every story in the first person, you would have many different voices unless each story were narrated by the same character. If you write a story in the first person voice of an unemployed mill worker on the Oregon coast, that voice will necessarily differ from the first person narrator who is a lexicographer at a New York publishing house.

The very language you employ will also contribute to the voice of the story and using the idioms of your setting will help create a credible world and credible characters. Reading a group of stories by creative writing students from the South, Flannery O'Connor lamented that the stories lacked Southern flavor despite being set in the South. In her lecture "Writing Short Stories," she emphasized how important the use of local idioms is in creating a credible setting: "An idiom characterizes a society, and when you ignore the idiom, you are very likely ignoring the whole social fabric that could make a meaningful character. You can't cut characters off from their society and say much about them as individuals." In speaking of the students' individual stories, she pointed out that while all the stories were set in the South, "there was no distinctive sense of Southern life in them" because of their lack of employing Southern idioms, and though "a few place names were dropped, Savannah or Atlanta or Jacksonville . . . these could just as easily have been changed to Pittsburgh or Passaic without calling for any other alteration in the story. The characters spoke as if they had never heard any kind of language except what came out of a television set."

The proper voice adds credibility to a story and whether that voice is given life through a first or third person narrator, the use of the idioms of the setting and of the characters who people it will give the story that credibility.

It takes years to be comfortable in writing with different tones, and years to develop your own style, but it is a mistake to think that you have but one voice and through it your characters will always speak. Your voice—the voice you use in an individual story—will vary from story to story and experimenting with different voices allows you to learn as much from writing the story as the reader learns in reading it. And that, after all, is one of the reasons we write: to better understand the world we live in.

VOICE IN FICTION

Amy Sage Webb

A proper discussion of voice is difficult because the definition of voice, as it pertains to writing fiction, is difficult to create. We speak of authors having a distinctive "voice," by which we mean their tone and their original use of language. This is, of course, a function of narration, but voice is not the same thing as narration. The writer's notion of voice would seem to indicate that an author's voice or style would be recognizable whether the piece were in first or third person narration. In novels such as *The Sound and the Fury* and *Absalom, Absalom!* for example, William Faulkner uses different character points of view and narrative technique, but the combination of all of these is what would be viewed as Faulkner's voice. Similarly, though, Toni Morrison might write from the point of view of a male character in *Song of Solomon* and through a woman's point of view in *Beloved*, both novels are marked by what we might call Morrison's distinctive authorial "voice."

For our purposes as writers, then, what is voice, and how do we get it? How do we recognize and develop the voices we have? Should we ever change them to sound like something else? David Huddle writes in *The Writing Habit* that one of the things we have to face as writers is the fact that our best voices may not be something worthy of great literature. This is in some respects true, for we all come to the art of writing with different degrees of learning and exposure, as well as different life experiences and perspectives, all of which color the way we tell a story. The telling of the story, for its own sake, is a redemptive act in that it puts into words the images and stories most crucial in our lives. For this reason, Nobel Prize-winning author Nadine Gordimer calls the writer's act her "essential gesture" as a social being. The writer's craft is her contribution to the world as she finds it. All of this seems to suggest that we are stuck with the voice we have, and that it is this voice which will inform the writing we create and which will be our contribution to the world of letters.

What if, however, voice were more supple than that? What if, rather than viewing voice as something innate, a gift from the muse and our lives' experiences, we viewed voice as something we could create at will? That if, as David Huddle points out, our best voice is not the best voice for the story at hand, we could change it? I find it more empowering to view voice as something we can create to suit a given piece or context, and I believe my students profit from this view. Rather than attempting to create their own style of writing before they have mastered the art of a good story, the students try to create voices which will enhance the stories they wish to tell. Through this process, of course, we usually discover that one particular voice seems more natural to us right now. Other writing seems forced. In this way, we discover what may be our true or natural "voice," but are not necessarily limited by it. We can also see that our true voice is likely to change and develop as we do, and that the later voice in which we write is not necessarily better than the first voice that felt natural to us; it is simply different.

Voice or language will not suffice to create good prose if a story lacks other fundamentals such as plotting, dialogue, or scene. When a story reads well and contains the fundamentals it needs, however, voice or original language can create magic, such that the piece shines where before it only read well. A student in my writing courses over the past few years, Lynnae Lewellen, finds that she has many different stories to tell, from many different perspectives. Some are nonfiction, some are highly fictional, even romanticized. Other stories are designed to feature vivid characters and situations. For each type of story, Lynnae faces the same dilemmas of plot, characterization, description, setting, dialogue, and scene. Each piece needs to strive for the shape and grace of story. She can use her voice, however, in different ways to highlight different aspects of these stories and create different moods.

Lynnae brings to her writing a sharp sense of humor and a strong regional dialect, peppered with colloquialisms of the Great Plains. Her life experiences have lent her a keen eye for character and plot, and a good ear for dialogue. Thus, Lynnae's natural writing "voice," we might say, is something closest to the voices of the point-of-view characters in

"Save the Last Dance for Me" and "Jubilee." In "Save the Last Dance for Me," she writes from the point of view of a rural Kansas man in his seventies who is none too happy about celebrating his birthday with his wife and his newly-single best friend, H. J. Hawkins. Lynnae has lived in and around Kansas her entire life, listening to the language of people around her such that she can reproduce it fairly effortlessly. In this excerpt, the language is appropriate to the point-of-view character and his perceptions. He is both a jealous young lover, and a typically meticulous crank of an old man:

> He'd given the SOB one dance with her and already he was regretting it. Dave Boseman had been dancing with his wife, Carlene, most of the evening until he'd begun to feel they were neglecting Hawk. Now Hawk was doing one of those dip things with Carlene. Her back was bent over Hawk's left arm and when her head gave in to gravity, her throat showed pearly white under the dance floor lights. They had been married for fifteen years and Dave still felt cold-cocked every time she tipped her chin up for him and exposed that so-soft little pulse spot for his searching lips . . . . Dave thought birthday cake stunk, just like the booze. In fact, birthday celebrations were not his thing at all . . . . Carlene had brought the cake and Hawk had ordered the champagne. Dave thought champagne was a sissy drink. He'd get some nuts with that beer. Now nuts you could bite . . . .

In "Jubilee," Lynnae writes from the point of view of a Kansas girl whose domineering mother insists on packaging her in a too-tight dress for a school dance. The voice here is closest to the typical speaking voice Lynnae would use in conversation, with terms indicative of her (and the story's) generation such as "brassiere" instead of "bra" and "nylons" instead of "panty hose." The truncated sentences call attention to Carrie's halting, uncomfortable emotions. The mother's dialogue also demonstrates the kind of language Lynnae herself might use, but is carefully crafted to be emblematic of the mother's ability to see every external factor but not the girl, her daughter, in front of her.

> Carrie had breasts. Not normal breasts like the other girls in school. Carrie's breasts made her feel different. Made her feel humiliated when she received her first bras, in front of the family, in a Christmas package, a year earlier than her classmates but still much later than she should have received them. Her grandmother tried to soothe her. "You're lucky to have breasts like Jayne Mansfield, dear," she had said with a reassuring pat on the shoulder. Carrie knew she would never have to resort to stuffing her brassiere with nylons the way her mother did. But at fourteen, Carrie felt only that her breasts were like baggage, only there was no trip, and they were always in the way. Like right now.
> Carrie studied her red-taffetaed reflection which seemed to fill the round mirror over her mother's dressing table. Her peripheral vision caught her

mother's long, slender fingers picking over the top layer of a sewing basket, probing for a seam ripper . . . . "I swear, Carrie, I do not know where you got such a matronly figure," she said. "Size ten dresses are just not made for thirty-six inch busts! I wonder if Dr. Daniels would prescribe some of those new diet pills?"

When Lynnae wanted to write a magical realism piece called "Dreamboat," she found that her naturally factual, conversational voice did not lend to the story the necessary aura of mystery it needed. Once she had plotted the story and designed the scenes she needed, Lynnae began reading some Gothic horror stories to get a sense of the language used by authors such as Angela Carter and Edgar Allen Poe. She read some magical realism pieces by authors such as Gabriel Garcia Marquez. Then, armed with her greater reading background, she wrote "Dreamboat" in a voice all her own, but steeped in the traditions of the type of story she wished to create. This first paragraph of the story demonstrates the Gothic formality of diction and the distinctive, dreamy language appropriate for this narrator and such a time-period piece.

> His was a devotion I did not suspect until he began disappearing from time to time a few weeks before our wedding. He was not gone long, usually just a day. This apparent secretive leaving left me devastated when he did not tell me where he had been and what he had been doing. Did not our love mean that we were now spiritually joined into one entity, moving in perfect unison in our universe, finishing each other's sentences, knowing each other's thoughts and desires?

Another one of Lynnae's great interests is nonfiction. Possessing as she does a rich family history of tales and characters, Lynnae wishes to preserve her family stories for future generations, as well as pass along some of her original perspective on those stories. The story of her great aunt Leila (Lee) is one of Lynnae's favorites, and in it Lynnae wished to pass along not simply the daring exploits of Lee, who was an aviatrix and successful single woman during the 1940s, but also her own admiration of Lee. Because she never met Lee when Lee was young, Lynnae could not rely on the voice of her own memory to describe her in her somewhat swaggering, younger days. In order to make Leila shine on the page, Lynnae needed to apply some of her fiction-writing techniques to the factual data that had been passed along to her so that she would seem to be observing Aunt Lee even though she was not there. Her natural voice is applied to information others have told her to make the third-person-omniscient narrative position more informal, a narration not of the story, but closer to it in voice. She has also interspersed the piece with dialogue from Aunt Lee and terms Aunt Lee would have used. Thus, the voice of the piece is observational and a bit detached, but filled with the essence and language of Lee herself.

> Fairly tall, raw-boned and lean, she could look down on my grandma, her little sister. If Grandma had not been such a little banty hen, Aunt Lee probably would have bullied her. As it was, when they would get into an argument, Aunt Lee would just roll her eyes, purse her lips, and toss her head back as she turned and walked away muttering, "I don't give a rat's ass what she says." Grandma usually got the last word, but it was a pretty limp thing by the time it had bounced off Aunt Lee's back . . . . She often wore halter tops and shorts with her midriff showing. She walked with her shoulders rolled toward herself, waist tucked in and hips thrust forward, probably from years of trying to appear less tall. There was a kind of saunter to her gait that told you she wasn't in much of a hurry for anything. She smoked a lot and often pulled her cigarette pack out of the front of her halter top. When she took a drag, her arm arced out sideways and the cigarette became a sort of lit baton, punctuating the highlights of her conversation.

Similarly, in the nonfiction essay "The Old School Bell," Lynnae again wished to remember some of the more vibrant women in her family, but this time she added her own interpretations. Here, she discovered that her tendency toward conversational voice did not allow her to create the wise authorial commentary she felt the piece needed. Notice the formality and distance in this piece, and how the greater distance and formalized language makes this "voice," describing the history of Great Grandmother Annie Mae, different from the voice which describes Aunt Lee above. This first-person-narrative position is definitely in and of the story being told, but the more formalized voice makes the narration seem farther from the events as it comments on them.

> These days I am a little mystified at the discrepancy between how unceremoniously I received the old bell, and the almost sacred importance it now has in my life . . . . It is this very touching of lives which makes me wonder about the old bell. For the most part, in our natural world, the old bell is now silent. But there are times when I wonder. Could it be possible that the old bell's clang was transformed into a serene call? Could sound have filtered through the many years that have passed since Annie Mae's hand wrapped around its handle and her arm swung up and down to ring the students into the school house? Could she and the bell have been unknowingly calling me to school before I was even born, its harsh clang necessary to break through the generational barriers of resistance I would encounter and my ensuing lack of confidence? Could she and the bell have even been calling other women in our family to teach for generations to come?

Think of how different the latter example, in first person narration, would have sounded with the voice of the former example, and vice versa. The difference is not necessarily a function of the narration, but the tone of language that narration uses. In both these essays, Lynnae modified her own voice, maintaining the conversational, mostly in-character perspective, and seeking for her historical/authorial voice something more formalized. She read essayists such as Barry Lopez and Edward Abbey to learn how they approached their subject matter in terms of voice. From Lopez she discovered a high seriousness, and from Abbey an ironic insight. She allowed herself to try on the voices of Romantic-era authors such as Nathaniel Hawthorne because such language lent itself to formal interpretation and commentary. In the end, Lynnae found that she was able to contemporize some of the formal language of other writing and eras with her own voice. She wanted more characterization than an essayist such as Annie Dillard would create, but less than would be apparent in a real fiction story. In this way, Lynnae created not just one, but *two* of her own nonfiction voices, both drawing from the voices of others to tell these stories.

It may seem that I am advocating a copy-cat approach to writing, and this is, in part, true. Every author we read teaches us something about the dilemma of writing. From our reading, we get a sense of the scope of language, and the ways other authors have employed it to create the tone of their best works, and, over time, the body of works which comprises what we know as an author's voice. Discovering voice is not as simple as grafting technique, however. As we read, we take in to our original perspective the play of another's language, and when we apply it to our own work, it becomes something altogether different, something at once traditional in tone and structure, and absolutely new, because it is filtered through our perspective. Herein, I believe, lies the magic of what we know as authorial voice. It is more than simply the language we bring, initially, to a piece. Voice is a function of an author's reading and study, her apprenticeship to the *right* language for a story's tone and purpose. Just as we move from one social context to another, employing a language slightly different at work from that which we use at home, we must move from one story to the next, employing the language we think will best highlight the story we wish to tell. Both languages are ours. Both are learned. In both cases, too, an original magic takes place which is a function of the author's creativity. If genius is, as it has so often been defined, the ability to hold two seemingly contradictory ideas in tandem without confusion, then this thing we call the writer's voice may be a function of genius, for it is there that the author pieces together the seemingly disparate voices of her reading in order to create the new voice which is her own, a supple thing which bends and shapes itself to each story so artfully that, in the words of Coleridge, we "suspend our disbelief," and allow ourselves to be caught by and transported into the world of each new story, knowing all the while who has brought us there.

NOTES FOR SELECTED READINGS

Note the lyrical voice in James Joyce's "Araby."

Exercises

1. As a young and aspiring writer, W. Somerset Maugham used to copy the work of writers he admired. This increased his facility with language. Take a couple of pages of a writer whose work you admire—Faulkner, for example or Flannery O'Connor, especially if you are not from the South—and copy the work verbatim until you begin to hear and feel the writer's voice supersede your own.
2. When you get together with a small group of friends some evening, tape record the conversations. Be sure to inform everyone of this, however. At first, your friends will be self-conscious, but eventually they will forget about the tape recorder (be sure to place it out of sight), and they will speak in their own voices. Listen to how varied the individual voices are and notice the idiomatic speech.
3. In the first person pov of a wealthy 40-year-old man who was educated at Harvard, describe an autumn day of picking apples with his 10-year-old daughter. Then, describe the same scene in the first person pov of a laid-off steel worker picking apples with his daughter. Note the different style, tone, and voice in each piece.

CHAPTER

21

CREDIBLE SURPRISE ON THE PATH TO RESONANCE

As an editor of *Clackamas Literary Review,* a semi-annual national literary journal, I read hundreds of fiction submissions each year, and it was disappointing how similar in topic and utterly predictable so many of these stories were. I probably received forty stories each year of professors who are having affairs with graduate students and another twenty stories of graduate students who are having affairs with the students they teach in their capacity as Teaching Assistants. It would seem that life in graduate school is one big game we might call the "Sexual Chain of Command." Each year I received another twenty or thirty stories about parents who do not understand their teenage children and about the same number of stories of parents who are misunderstood. From the preponderance of these submissions, it would seem that everyone is either misunderstood or sexually promiscuous (it may be that when we are misunderstood we have affairs, or is it that when we have an affair we become misunderstood due to the necessity of lying?).

My point is that many of these stories are so haggard that in themselves they have become clichés. But is it possible to take one of these topics and breathe new life into it by making the conflict at least seem new and unique? By raising the

Without this playing with fantasy no creative work has ever yet come to birth. The debt we owe to the play of imagination is incalculable.

Carl Gustav Jung

stakes and escalating the conflict? By layering vibrant resonance in their end-ings? Yes, to all three.

To take such a tired topic and make it seem new greatly depends on the nature of *credible surprise*. Take a story of a mundane couple living in an apartment building and then throw in a radio that picks up and transmits all the conversations of the neighboring tenants, with the owner of the radio listening to them daily, and what you have added is a credible surprise. John Cheever does exactly that in his story "The Enormous Radio," and he does so in such a realistic and credible fashion—by staying in the concrete and physical world—that the radio itself essentially disappears from the story as we begin to listen to the sad lives inhabiting the building. It is not the *transmitter* that we focus on; it is what is *transmitted*. And that is the nature of good stories.

We all want to read something new, but essentially all of our plots have been exhausted. I tell my creative writing students that what we are doing as writers is telling the same stories again and again, and I add that there is nothing wrong with that. Because our plot supply has become exhausted, does that mean there is no longer a need to write a story, a play, a novel, or a poem? Of course not. As has been mentioned again and again, writing is a process of discovery for the writer as well as for the reader, and that alone makes the practice of writing worthwhile. With each story we write, we gain more human empathy just as we do with each story we read. But if we are to have readers, we had better make the story of unrequited love or betrayal or first love or revenge new and fresh so as to engage our reader. We can do so by offering some small but credible surprise, like the peacock that enters the dining room as two couples eat dinner in Raymond Carver's story "Feathers" or as when Kenny shoots the dog in Tobias Wolff's story "Hunter's in the Snow." As a reader, your mouth drops and you turn the page to read on, for the writer has given you something you did not expect, and oh, how we love the unexpected as long as it is not a **red herring**.

In the chapter on plot, we discussed the arc of a story and the need to establish conflict and escalate it before realizing a climax and a denouement, but we did not discuss **resonance**. Resonance is that vibration a reader feels, that chill on the spine, that hair bristling on the back of the neck. Do not confuse credible surprise with the resonance at the end of the story, however. Unearned surprise endings are cheap and facile. What we want is an ending with resonance that is credible due to the evidence inventoried earlier in the story. In Mary Robison's very short short story "Yours," it is autumn and a woman dying of cancer returns home to her husband with a car laden with pumpkins. They carve the pumpkins and then go to bed. In bed, she seems to be dying as her "pulse cords were fluttering under his fingers." And the story ends:

> At the telephone, Clark had a clear view out back and down to the porch. He wanted to get drunk with his wife once more. He wanted to tell her, from the greater perspective he had, that to own only a little talent, like his, was an awful,

plaguing thing; that being only a little special meant you expected too much, most of the time, and liked yourself too little. He wanted to assure her that she had missed nothing.

He was speaking into the phone now. He watched the jack-o'-lanterns. The jack-o'-lanterns watched him.

With that haunting image of the pumpkins within which votive candles burn in the night, the resonance is as palpable as fingernails dragged across a chalkboard.

Finding the right place to open a story is difficult, and sometimes that opening is not found until page two, three, or four. Escalating conflict in the middle of the story and incorporating credible surprise is also a challenge but finding the right ending where the resonance rings true may be the most difficult task of all. Sometimes your ending will come from some physical object found earlier in the story, such as the jack-o'-lanterns in "Yours."

MYSTERY AND SURPRISE

Craig Lesley

"Surprise me," I frequently suggest to workshop participants. Try creating a character who is both original and mysterious, one who displays power and is capable of surprising both the reader (and the writer) after we discover all the facts. Spare me the hackneyed middle-aged professor churning through a midlife crisis with a tawdry affair. Stay away from spinsters in purple who "discover" rather late in life that their ennui resulted from being molested. If you must, pitch those sorry tales to Drs. Ruth or Laura. Consider writing for television where all improbably-loose ends get wrapped up in a single hour.

Also bear in mind that real mystery and surprise have nothing to do with characters who are also witches, vampires, warlocks, or werewolves. King and Rice do it more successfully (at least commercially) than you ever will. Their pale imitators have gotten to be rather tiresome. Nor is surprise a masked misfit springing from the closet with a snarling chainsaw. When I want drive-in movie fare, I'll drive to one and stuff myself with hotdogs and greasy popcorn.

I'm asking for original, believable, and human characters tinged with mystery and capable of surprise. Geronimo Tagatac has given the reader exactly that kind of character in Augustine, the Filipino godfather of the young narrator in his story named for the mysterious fieldworker. Mr. Tagatac begins his narrative: "One Sunday a month, when the men slaughtered a pig, Augustine would fry the chopped intestines, garlic and vinegar, with the pig's blood, to make the black *deneguan* which we ate over rice. In the evenings I would hear the lisp of steel sharpened on stone coming through the darkness from his shack. When I thought of him, I thought of blood, earth and steel."

From the beginning, Augustine and submerged violence become associated in the narrator's and reader's minds, yet one of the surprises in the story is that no violence actually occurs on the page. In addition to violence, Augustine, a cropworker who came to California after the Asian exclusion laws were dropped following World War II, has an association with the earth and crops. The narrator recalls, "He was at the far edge of my sight and hearing, walking down the rows of a field, the whispering leaves and stalks brushing against the stiff twill of his khaki workpants, his boots making marks in the soft earth between the rows of squash and beans."

Part of Augustine's mystery arises from the camp stories circulating about his past. "Stories about Augustine, about fights and killings were whispered out of his hearing. More than one killing." These rumors have the force of scripture for the young narrator, especially when his Uncle Valeriano tells of a time he witnessed Augustine's power. On that occasion Augustine accidentally ran over lettuce crates with a tractor and the boss called him a "stupid, slant-eyed, black, son of a bitch" in front of the other men. As a result, according to Valeriano, Augustine's face became like "dark metal," resembling the "thick coarse steel that goes into the heavy blades of bolo knives."

Here, a less talented writer than Mr. Tagatac might choose to follow the bolo knife imagery with a physical attack on the boss. However, instead, the author presents a fine surprise that heightens Augustine's aura of mystery:

> That same afternoon, all of the lettuce leaves in the field began to turn brown at the edges. The next day, the crop, all nineteen acres, had begun to wither and was useless. By the third day, the whole field looked as though it had been burned black, and the men who had to walk its dying rows spoke in whispers. On the afternoon of the third day, Augustine turned to Valeriano and said in his quiet, accented English, "The boss don't need those crates now."
>
> "Plant disease," the boss said.
>
> "Augustine," said Valeriano, smiling.

Augustine's mysterious powers are further suggested by the fact that he always wears a long-sleeved workshirt and never washes with the other men in the bathhouse. He always washed "alone, late at night, and no one dared intrude on his privacy." Camp rumors claim he'd been badly scarred with knives and bullets, so badly scarred that his wife left him, and he had to pay women to sleep with him.

Mysterious rumors have enormous force in our own lives and in our fiction, an idea Mr. Tagatac applies in his story. Thinking of Augustine caused me to recall the stories I heard about the solitary men who roomed in my grandparents' house where I grew up. Reuben, a heavy smoker, had recurring tuberculosis and had spent six years in a sanitarium before being released. Whenever I had to change his bedsheets, I looked for bright spots of blood and covered my mouth with a bandanna so I wouldn't inhale "toxic spores." Dalton had killed dozens of enemy soldiers in Korea and had lost his toes due to frostbite. Sometimes, I'd open his closet, smelling cold steel and gun oil, then touch his rifles for a terrible thrill. I also carefully inspected his shoes and socks to see if they'd been altered in any way to accommodate his stumpy feet. Everett had robbed several banks in Tennessee and spent time in Leavenworth. All his visitors were shadowy suspects, and I camped outside his room, hoping to catch word of the next big heist. Once in a while, I'll employ one of my grandparents' roomers (or his close cousin) in a story.

When Mr. Tagatac's narrator is nine, he learns Augustine's power first-hand after a violent argument between Valeriano and one of the new men in camp. Furious, the new man retreats momentarily to the bunkhouse, then returns with a pistol:

> Everyone stood in the thick, red light and listened to the quick sound of the new man's footsteps coming out of the bunkhouse. His revolver's blue cylinder snapped closed as he walked toward Valeriano. Everyone stood frozen, waiting for the crack of the gun, waiting for the hard sound of Valeriano's body hitting the ground.
>
> Then, "Hssst!" Everyone's head turned, knowing that the shape coming out of the fading light was Augustine, drawn from across the field into the lethal vacuum. I remember seeing the stillness in Augustine's face. I saw his eyes, looking into the new man's face, his presence blotting out Valeriano and the other men, until I could see nothing but Augustine's face and eyes. Augustine's dark hand, with its hard, blue-black veins, reached out to the man. The man's gun hand rose to meet Augustine's as though drawn by the gold ring on his finger, and then the new man's hand was empty. Augustine held the revolver, then turned and was gone. He went into the new darkness so swiftly and quietly that I thought I could hear the air sliding into the space behind him as he strode across the field.

Augustine's intervention is especially remarkable as the reader recalls the stories of his scars from knife- and bullet-wounds. In this episode, he creates an uneasy peace. However, the displaced violence emerges in the new man's screaming nightmares, horrible dreams that infect the entire camp: The narrator's father believes his own father is whipping him for spilling a sack of rice. Valeriano dreams he's being bayoneted by Japanese soldiers. The narrator dreams Augustine's ring bites him as he tries it on.

After ten days, when the new man's dreams become unbearable, he leaps from bed one morning and drives away, naked and screaming, in an old green Hudson.

That car is a great detail because its specificity makes the surrounding events all the more probable. I've discovered that one way to convince readers as to the authenticity of a mystery or surprise is to link that event to a specific, concrete detail or place. If we believe in a Ford Taurus, we more readily accept the bizarre contents of its trunk. If we see the attractive young widow across the street wearing a Kansas State sweatshirt, we accept the rumor that both her husbands committed suicide.

Part of Augustine's power lies in his visionary storytelling. On the surface, he seems a simple fieldworker who drinks boiled coffee and eats beans and rice. However, on several occasions, he reveals a poetic imagination as he tells the narrator his versions of the natural world:

> Sometimes, after dinner, I would walk across the freshly plowed fields with Augustine. Once, he told me that the stars were fires in the mouths of faraway caves and that, if I looked carefully enough, I might see the faces of the people who lived in those sky shelters. He said that if I were ever lost in the forest and knew how to sing a special song, they would take me up into their caves and keep me safe for the night. But he never taught me the song.

When Augustine takes the boy to the beach, the powerful waves remind the narrator of Augustine's coffeepot coming to a boil, and the older man explains that the ocean's sounds come from "all the souls in heaven."

In addition, Augustine's power results in his always getting what he wants. He asks the narrator's father to be the boy's godfather and gets his request. Years earlier, when the father was courting the narrator's mother, Augustine made the father return with him to the Philippines, to the little village of Bataac. Both the reader and the narrator are left to speculate as to the sources of Augustine's power over people (everyone except his former wife) and events.

Mr. Tagatac leaves Augustine's greatest surprises until after his death. The narrator, now a young man, learns the details of Augustine's death from his father, who informs him that the old man had thousands of dollars in a savings account and that when he went to the morgue to identify the body, it bore no scars.

Much of Augustine's life has to be rethought, in the light of this new information. How much of his mystique was the force of rumor, gossip, perhaps superstition from the old country? Why did Augustine and the father journey back to the Philippines and why did the father go away from his bride-to-be? One of my students offered the left-field suggestion that perhaps the men had a sexual relationship or even that Augustine was a woman—hence the desire to always wash alone. That's pushing the edge perhaps, but the story is so rich with possibility, even that theory has a sliver of credulity. Of course only the father has seen Augustine's body, and he may not be telling all he knows.

One surprise remains. When the narrator receives Augustine's ring in the mail, he shows it to a woman friend. As she examines the face on the ring, she notes, "It's your face. But then you know that, don't you?"

As a reader and editor, I'm thankful to Mr. Tagatac for creating such a vivid and memorable character, and I'll remember Augustine's mystery, as well as the surprises in this fine story for a long time. Like the remarkable story telling itself, the character at first seems simple, but when we're finished, he's as elusive and awe-inspiring as those star-dwellers in the fiery mouths of their faraway caves.

NOTES FOR SELECTED READINGS

Note how Gabriel Garcia Marquez uses specific detail to create a magical world the reader can believe in his story "A Very Old Man With Enormous Wings."

Exercises

1. Look at a story you have written and ask yourself a question: Wherein lies the resonance in the ending and what accomplishes that resonance? For example, in the aforementioned story "Yours," the resonance is derived from the haunting image of the jack-o'-lanterns, with the burning votive candles connecting the reader to the wife's death. Could a physical object (such as the jack-o'-lanterns) be incorporated in your ending to amplify the resonance?
2. Make a chronological list of all of a character's actions in a story. For example, first she arrives home with the pumpkins; second, she suggests that she and her husband carve them; third, they carve the pumpkins; fourth, they go to bed. Then ask yourself if you could insert a more surprising action into the story that would heighten the reader's awareness without being a red herring.
3. In workshops, we often ask our students if we can "up the stakes" by increasing the tension, by raising the sense of risk the characters face. Read through one of your own stories and see if you can find a situation wherein you could raise the stakes. Continuing with this metaphor, if the story has a poker game and your character has twenty dollars left, and he bets twenty dollars, that is relatively safe. But what if he bets thirty dollars? That is upping the stakes.

CHAPTER

22

THEME

When someone speaks of *theme*, I think of bearded men in tweed jackets smoking pipes, black berets atilt, in mad and pedantic discussion. Sadly, *theme* is one of the most loaded words in literature, yet it does not have to be, for theme is really the simplest element of fiction and is the element that demands the least discussion in a book such as this. Here, then, is the definition of theme: *what the story means*.

Should a writer embark upon a story knowing its theme? No, almost always not. As the reader is given the sweet opportunity to learn something new, to be fair, the writer should have that same opportunity. Remember that writing is a process of discovery, and if the writer learns nothing new, chances are the reader will not either. Another reason I say *"almost always not"* is that if you go into a story knowing its theme, chances are the story will come out as a didactic treatise devoid of subtext. If you have so little trust in your readers as to hammer them with overt theme, turn your efforts to nonfiction. Fiction is a much more subtle art, one that demands the reader to experience what the characters experience and thereby gain empathy for them, and it is from this human empathy that the readers learn of the story's thematic concern.

The truth about any subject only comes when all the sides of the story are put together, and all their different meanings make one new one.

Alice Walker

Once the writer finishes several drafts of a story she may come to learn what her story means, and this knowledge allows her to clarify this meaning in subsequent drafts if the meaning is too mute. But with this said, sometimes a story's theme is too amorphous a matter to extract and define in a limited number of words. This is what Flannery O'Connor was alluding to in "Writing Short Stories" when she wrote:

> Meaning is what keeps the short story from being short. I prefer to talk about the meaning in a story rather than the theme of a story. People talk about the theme of a story as if the theme were like the string that a sack of chicken feed is tied with. They think that if you can pick out the theme, the way you pick the right thread in the chicken-feed sack, you can rip the story open and feed the chickens. But this is not the way meaning works in fiction.
>
> When you can state the theme of a story, when you can separate it from the story itself, then you can be sure the story is not a very good one. The meaning of a story has to be embodied in it, has to be made concrete in it. A story is a way to say something that can't be said any other way, and it takes every word in the story to say what the meaning is. You tell a story because a statement would be inadequate. When anybody asks what a story is about, the only proper thing is to tell him to read the story. The meaning of fiction is not abstract meaning but experienced meaning, and the purpose of making statements about the meaning of a story is only to help you to experience that meaning more fully.

O'Connor is correct in saying that the meaning of a story permeates the entire story from the first word to the last, but she is being somewhat disingenuous as well, for in her essay "The Element of Suspense in 'A Good Man is Hard to Find,'" she writes that the story is about a person's ability to personify grace. Yet, even though slightly contradictory, her point is useful: The theme of a story, its meaning, is not something as easily extracted as a tooth. It is like water beneath the surface that flows throughout, and trying to distinguish it from the water that rides above it is no easy task. The key is to jump in and get wet.

As a writer, I would never embark on writing a new story overly concerned about theme. You will discover what your story means. Allow yourself that pleasure, because to deny yourself that pleasure is to dilute one of the greatest joys of writing, and that is the discovery of what it is you are really writing about.

There will be occasions when you know exactly what you want to expose in your writing, which is fine, but pay close attention to how you relay that message to the reader, for you are in danger of waxing didactic as did Upton Sinclair in his novel *The Jungle*. Much of the book is good, but in the last third or so, Sinclair gets on the pulpit and preaches to the reader about the sins of the meatpacking industry, all the while greatly detracting from what art he had created earlier in the novel.

Remember that writing fiction is creating a subtle art of experiential participation: The reader is to walk in the shoes of your characters, go where they go, see what they see, do what they do, and through this vicarious action the reader should be allowed to proceed unfettered by your overt manipulation.

So, keep your hands off the readers. Leave them alone. Don't worry about theme. Just tell a good story and theme will take care of itself.

NOTES FOR SELECTED READINGS

Note the resonant ending in Louise Erdrich's "The Red Convertible."

Exercise

1. When you have finished a story, complete the following sentence: This story means . . . Have friends and classmates read your story and have them complete the same sentence. It is not important that all the answers be the same, of course, but they should be in the same ballpark. For example, it would be disconcerting to the author of a story about lost childhood if one person wrote "This story means the transition from childhood to adulthood is difficult at best" and another person wrote "This story means that choosing a major is difficult and counselors should be more helpful."

CHAPTER

23

REVISION

The word *revise*, along with the word *visit*, came to English from the Latin *videre*, meaning *to see*, and the Latin *visitare*, meaning *to go to see*. In that context, then, to revise a story is to go back to visit it and see it again. I mention this because all too often we think of revision as changing something when we must first realize that to revise is to pay another visit to the story wherein we will see it again, and in that sense it is entirely and literally possible that we could revise an entire draft without changing a single word.

The key to writing, any writing, is revision. Certainly, writing that first draft is an exhilarating process, but it is just the beginning of a much longer process. A first draft is only the first leg of the journey. If our destination is a story as finely polished as we can possibly make it, then each draft we write is a step toward that destination.

When I was much younger, I loved writing first drafts to the exclusion of revising them. Thus, I started many journeys, but I never arrived anywhere. Several years later I learned to love revision as well; it is an entirely different process, but when you realize how playful a process it can be, then you will enjoy it as well.

It has been said that time is a luxury, and it is, but in writing it is also a necessity. One must take

Perhaps if writers enjoyed a fuller experience of the private gratifications of artmaking, we would be less intimidated by the rigors of revision.

Valerie Miner

time off between drafts. If I finish a first draft on Tuesday and try to revise it on Wednesday, I will make a muddle of things; I cannot "re-see" my story so soon after having written that first draft because it is still in my head as well as on the page. If, however, I take a week away from the story, perhaps working on another project, then when I revisit the story I will see it with fresh eyes and with those new eyes I will see areas that are unclear. Thus, leave a draft alone for at least a few days before going back to revise.

Whenever I do a public reading, whether a reading of a published or an unpublished piece of fiction, I can hear areas that need to be revised. Reading my work aloud alone, however, is less effective because there is some connection between the audience and me that allows me to hear the work with new ears; it is almost as if I am hearing the work for the first time with *their* ears, seeing it for the first time with *their* eyes. If you have no one to read your work to, try reading before a mirror with pencil in hand. For some reason, that also seems to work. Be sure to make plenty of eye contact with that face staring you in the eyes; besides helping you hear your story—where it rings true and where it hits a sour note—reading aloud before a mirror is good practice for reading before an audience. Words are meant to be heard, after all, and when you have composed particularly beautiful sentences and paragraphs, reading them aloud allows you the full pleasure they afford as the words roll off your tongue to be retrieved by your ears. Reading silently is something akin to standing in the kitchen of Maxim's in Paris with your nostrils pinched shut.

Rewriting a story without a specific sense of direction can get you lost in the woods. You may not know where to go, but if you go into a new draft knowing that you are only going to rewrite for one thing—temperature, for example—then you will avoid the pitfalls of trying to do everything at once. For example, if you are writing a story set in Alaska in midwinter, you may devote an entire draft to lowering the temperature wherever possible. That's what Ron Carlson did in his story "Blazo." If you are in Phoenix, Arizona, some hot August afternoon, reading this story will ice you down.

You might write another draft focusing on the dialogue of one particular character, and another focusing on a heightened sense of setting, and another on tone, and another on language. Gustave Flaubert coined the term *Le mot juste*, meaning the exact word, and in rewriting for the exact, the precise, word, you may spend countless—yet enjoyable—hours. There is the story of Flaubert having met a friend at lunch who asked him how he had spent his morning. Flaubert told him he spent the entire morning trying to decide whether to keep or delete a comma. The friend asked what he finally decided, and Flaubert told him that he took the comma out. Later that evening, they met for dinner and this same friend asked Flaubert how he had spent the afternoon. Flaubert asked him if he remembered that comma he had taken out in the morning and the friend said yes, he did. "Well," Flaubert said. "I decided to put it back in."

Apocryphal or not, the story illustrates how careful we need be as writers. It sounds daunting, but if you enjoy the process of writing, this slow and painstaking revision is great fun. And as you can see, it is no surprise that a writer may go through twenty or thirty drafts before he feels he has arrived at the destination he sought from the beginning: the polished story.

As writers, we use different mediums: some of us use pencils and yellow legal pads, some of us use pens, others use typewriters, and still others of us use computers, as do I. Before I begin a revision, I always print a hard copy on which I can take notes as I read. In this first reading, I am not revising for anything specific such as temperature; rather, I am looking for any problems in any element of the story. Maybe I have changed a character's name in one area but not in another; maybe I have the time of day wrong in another area; maybe I have a character say something she need not say. In this first step of revision, I use black ink with which to make marginalia, on the second reading I use red ink, and the third I use green ink. In this fashion, I can see how my decisions have been changed with subsequent readings. Next, I go back to the computer, and as I refer to my hard copy and all the notes I have made in three different colors of ink, I begin to make changes. Once I have done this I print another hard copy and take the story before the mirror where I read it aloud with pen in hand, making changes on the manuscript as I read.

After making any changes on the hard copy during my "public reading," I go back to the computer and type those changes in, and then I begin the process of rewriting for a single aspect of the story I feel is weak. For example, I may feel that I have not quite clarified an individual character, so I go back through the hard copy and make notes where I feel I can heighten that character. Once I am done, I go back to the computer and type in the new changes. Next, I print another hard copy and begin the process again, this time focusing on a different element.

As one can see, I am probably going to make more changes in the earlier drafts. By the time I am on the fifteenth draft, it is not unusual that I may be making only one or two changes before I feel the story is as polished as I can make it. Then I leave the story alone for a week, print a new hard copy, and read it again. If I still feel the story is as polished as I can make it, then I consider it done.

Once I am at this stage, I give the story to friends and colleagues whose opinions I value. In the event that they suggest changes, and I agree with them, I go back and do another draft.

Finally, I *think* that I am done with the story, but the fact of the matter is that I may not be done. At this point I'll submit the story to a magazine. It may be that the editor will suggest changes, and again, if I agree with him, I will make the changes. If the editor accepts the story, he accepts it because I *am* done. If the editor rejects the story, I'll send it somewhere else until some other editor does accept it—or until I realize the need to revisit the story and see it again through fresh eyes.

The process I have outlined may or may not work for you. If it does not, fine; you will come up with your own. What is important is that you have your own process of revision. And I promise you this: If you don't already, you will learn to love the art of revision.

Exercises

1. Read your most recent story aloud before a mirror as if you were reading it before an audience. As you read, circle words, phrases, and clauses that do not sound as pleasing as they might. When you are finished, go back and rewrite those areas that sounded "off" and repeat the process.

2. Read your most recent story just before going to bed. Make sure it is the last thing you do before turning off the lights. This exercise will allow your subconscious to "work" on the story as you sleep. If there were an area in the story where you were stuck, this exercise will often help you come up with new ideas during your writing session the following day.

3. To revise for sentence level problems such as faulty grammar, poor punctuation, and spelling errors, read your story backwards starting with the last sentence, continuing with the penultimate sentence, and working all the way to the beginning of the story. The reason this works is because, when reading the story from front to back, your brain is considering content as well as grammar, punctuation, and spelling. This exercise allows the brain to focus on the sentence level without being concerned with meaning.

CHAPTER

24

PARTICIPATING IN THE WORKSHOP

There are many ways to orchestrate a writing workshop, but no matter how the instructor handles it, it can be quite daunting for the student writer the first time she is "on the block"—a rather disheartening metaphor for having your story critiqued by your instructor and fellow students. If the class meets weekly, you have provided enough copies of your story to the instructor, who then distributes them to the other students; they take them home and read them and write critiques of them. The next week you walk into class both excited and horrified: excited that your instructor and your fellow student writers will have loved your story; horrified that they will have hated it.

However, if the instructor has prepared the students in the proper decorum of the workshop, it does not have to be this way. In this chapter, I will explain how I conduct a workshop and what I expect from the student writers.

First of all, I explain that every story we workshop had better have some problems, because if the stories are perfect, then the student writers should be teaching the class and I should be out playing golf. When we go to the doctor because of an ache in the knee, we expect a diagnosis of what is wrong with suggestions of how to cure the problem. The same goes for a writing workshop:

People ask you for criticism, but they only want praise.

W. Somerset
Maugham

If we are realistic, we know that there will be problems with the stories we have written, no matter how slight or large, and we expect a diagnosis from the instructor and the student writers so that we can fix the problem and learn how to avoid it in the future. Thus, if we are going into the workshop with this attitude, we will be less likely to have our feelings hurt. I do not believe the workshop should be a place of unmitigated nurturing. Unconditional love is something your family can provide. The workshop is where we come to learn about problems in our writing and to learn how to avoid them in the future. And it is a place to learn of new possibilities. If you write a story based on your personal experience of having been codependent with someone suffering from something, you will have my sympathy, but if it does not carry on the page as a story should, I'll tell you why.

The student writers are required to do their best to leave their personal likes and dislikes at home. Admittedly, this is hard to do, but if you are against abortion and we are critiquing a story wherein the protagonist has an abortion, and you can't keep your feelings out of the discussion, then you might as well stay home.

I ask the student writers to read each story at least twice before coming to the workshop. They may make notes in the margins and correct punctuation mistakes and errors in spelling and the like, but we will not discuss those matters. After they have read the story twice, they write a critique of the story focusing on the elements of fiction as they have been discussed in this book. Thus, if there is a shift in pov on page six of the story we are workshopping, I would expect that many of the students would spot it and mention it in their critiques. Remember, the effort here is to help the writer. If I have shifted points of view in a story—and I have—and do not notice having done so, I hope someone would come to my aid by pointing out my error.

During the workshop we do not critique the story haphazardly with anyone speaking up about anything at any time. Rather, I conduct the workshop as a conductor of an orchestra: I decide what we will focus on and then ask different students what they feel about it. For example, I might say that story A is told in the first person and then I would ask a student what the effect would be of changing the point of view to the third person limited. Or, I might ask a student whether we needed all five characters in a particular story, and what would happen if we eliminated the character *Dolores* completely.

In this fashion, there is a sense of direction in the workshop. The writer of the story we are workshopping is not allowed to talk. He must remain silent and take notes. I tell him that we are editors at Harper's and that he has submitted the story and is presently in Paris sipping an espresso in a sidewalk café on the Rue de Vaugerard, and that his emissary is in the room to take notes on our discussion. The reason he is not allowed to talk is that inevitably someone will say that something is not working in the story and he will want to say, "But that's the way it really happened!" We don't care if that's the way it happened. What matters is how it happens on the page. In other words, it has to *carry on the page.*

After we have finished the discussion, we give the stories to the writer, along with the critiques we have written—me included—and the student writer takes them home and studies them. Of course, not everything we write will work or necessarily be "correct," but we have diagnosed some problems in his story that should help him in the rewrite. We will start the next class with him being able to ask us questions about what we wrote in our critiques of his story, and he may want to sound us out on new ideas for the story. Then he will be on his own to work on a rewrite.

At this point, I always collect the critiques so that I can evaluate them (later I will give them all to the writer for his keeping). If I feel a student writer is being mean-spirited in her critique—and I have had students like that, though not many—I will have a talk with her and thus endeavor to resolve the problem.

The reason a workshop is such a good learning tool is twofold. One: You, the student writer, are getting direct criticism of your work. In other words, you have worked hard and written a story in which inevitably you will have made some mistakes, and it is from mistakes that we learn and grow as writers. Two: You are being asked to write direct criticism of your fellow writers' work. Undoubtedly, it is easier to see a flaw in someone else's writing than it is to see one in your own. This is because in our own writing we have the story in two places; in our head and on the page—and sometimes we get the two places confused. In looking at the story on the page, the perfect story in our head gets in the way and we cannot see where we have erred on the page. Thus, in seeing a problem in a shift in pov in another student writer's story, you may learn how to avoid doing the same in your own work.

We do not focus only on the negative, of course, but that is our main concern; if I have cancer, I don't want the doctor telling me what a great personality I have and how fine my hair looks. Still, we can learn from where a writer succeeds. For example, if we see a student writer make great use of a flashforward when no one else in the class has tried the technique, we will stop and discuss why and how it is being used so successfully, then consider when we might use it as well.

So, remember, we are here to work together and to learn from each other, and there is nothing personal involved when we discuss each other's work. After all, we are crafting art, and crafting art is not a competition like the one-hundred-meter dash. Instead, we are all moving forward together one step at a time. If we remembered what literature was all about, creating human empathy and clarifying this human condition of ours, we would more clearly see the irony in acting as though a workshop were some kind of contest where there were winners and losers. The only losers will be people who embrace such an inane attitude towards the noble effort of creating art where there had been none before.

25

WORKSHOPPING A STORY IN THE FIRST PERSON

As you read the first draft of Toni Morgan's story "Benedictions," consider the following:

1. The setting: Do you feel as if you are there? Why or why not? Where do you think the setting is most clearly drawn? How does she achieve that? To what senses does she appeal? Where is the setting undeveloped?
2. The characters: How well do you come to know them? Which do you feel you know best? Whose story is it? What do the characters want? Can any of the characters be eliminated?
3. The plot: What is at stake for whom? Can the stakes be raised? How is the pacing?
4. The dialogue: Is it a close approximation of how these people would speak? Are idioms appropriately used? Is it sufficiently embodied?
5. The point of view: How would the story be different in another pov? What is the narrative distance? How does that affect the story?
6. Voice: What is the narrator's voice? Is it affected by the time in which the story takes place?

There is then creative reading as well as creative writing.

Ralph Waldo Emerson

BENEDICTIONS

Toni Morgan

Here we are the four of us, bouncing along a dirt and gravel road, in Mexico to show Jack the cotton growing potential of the western and central regions. Tucker is driving. His bald head is pink and peeling despite the sun lotion he rubs into it every morning. I'm always amazed that he burns so easily since he was born in Tucson and raised on the desert. Wouldn't you think the skin would eventually build up a tolerance? But there it is in front of me, looking more like an onion than ever. Tucker procures for the Army what the Army needs to feed and clothe its soldiers. The Army needs cotton for uniforms.

Dust rolls out from beneath the station wagon like a tail dragging along behind us. It lies thick on the dashboard, over the seats, and coats our luggage and the extra fuel cans piled up in the back. My lips are dry and chapped and all I want at the moment is a long soak in a hot tub with plenty of soap. I wonder again why I agreed to come on this trip. Tucker seemed indifferent when he'd first mentioned it, appearing not to care if I came along or stayed home. We've been together for six months, but I'm not sure we'll ever have a permanent relationship. Or if I want one. My mother, who lives with me, was dead set against my coming. We argued for days.

"I just don't understand you, Virginia. I'm going to ignore the fact that you'll obviously be sleeping with that man," she never refers to Tucker by name. He's been married twice before and she views him with suspicion and some scorn. "But how can you go off and leave Richie for six weeks? He's only five. What if he gets sick? What if I need to contact you?" But the trip sounded like a lark, and Jack and Kay can be fun, so I promised I'd call frequently. Besides, Richie loves being with her. He probably doesn't even notice I'm not there.

Northeast of us is a range of mountains. San Ignatio, where we plan to spend the night, is located in the foothills. The last village we passed was three hours back and there is no sign of a village or even a house ahead of us. As far as I can see in all directions are sage and mesquite. The mountains are the only things that interrupt the flat landscape under its azure blue dome.

"According to the map there's another road we have to take to get to San Ignatio," says Tucker. "It can't be too much further."

"Let's roll up the windows," Kay says. "The dust is so thick in here I can hardly breathe."

Kay is from Texas. "Amarillo, Honey," she tells people in her flat, nasal drawl. We all met in Phoenix where so many people have moved since the war started, looking for excitement or jobs. Jack comes from the

Central Valley of California. His family owns a large cattle operation there. He came to Phoenix partly for business opportunities and partly to get away from his wife. I'm from a small town in Nevada nobody's ever heard of. The only thing different about me is they were born rich.

"It's too hot," Jack says.

"Well, I'd rather be hot than choke to death, Sugar."

"Put out your cigarette. Maybe that will help." Jack is always complaining about Kay's chain-smoking. Kay ignores him, but she doesn't say any more about putting up the windows.

"This must be the turn off," says Tucker. He pulls to a stop and we all look at the words *"San Ignatio"* with an arrow painted on a piece of wood nailed to a stake that has been pounded into the ground, pointing to the mountains.

"Jesus, that road looks worse than the one we're on."

"I knew we should have stayed nearer the coast."

"Well, what do you all think? Should we turn off here or keep going?"

Kay is for keeping to the road we're on, but the rest of us vote for the turn off, so Tucker puts the car into gear and points it toward the mountains. After a while the road begins to climb into hills that are rounded and undulating. The land is still covered in sage and mesquite, but now there is an occasional solitary juniper. I can see the road in front of us go up one side of a hill, disappear at the top, reappear on the hill beyond and again beyond that. When we reach the top of the last hill I look down at a valley below. At its bottom is a dry creek bed strewn with rocks and boulders, with clumps of oak and willow along its edges. On the other side of the creek I can make out tracks leading up the side of yet another hill and again disappearing over the top. The car grinds down to where the road runs into the creek bed. Tucker drives slowly forward maneuvering around the boulders. I hang onto the door handle to keep from being pitched sideways into Kay. When we reach the other side Tucker stops the car and we all climb out.

"Well, what do you think, Folks?"

"I think we're fuckin' lost, Honey," Kay says.

Jack pulls out the map and lays it across the hood of the car. Kay wanders over to a large boulder, sits down and lights another cigarette. Her sleek brown hair falls forward as she leans into the match, cupping the flame with carmine tipped fingers. She blows out a long stream of smoke and ignores the two men arguing over the map.

My blouse is sticking to my back, and my linen shorts have ridden up in a bunch between my legs. I am stiff from sitting in the car all day. I start to follow the tracks up the hill, partly to work out the kinks and partly to get away from everyone for at least a few minutes. When I reach the top I yell back to the rest. "There's a town. I can see it."

A church and several small buildings are silhouetted against the sky as we approach, dark against lavender, and lights are beginning to flicker in the windows of houses scattered down the hillside. We enter by one of what we later learn are two roads leading to San Ignatio. The back one, which we took, is seldom used. "The creek crossing is not dependable, Señora," our landlady tells me. The other road leads from the coast, crosses the road we'd traveled much of the day, passes through San Ignatio and continues over the mountains, eventually leading to the Gulf.

We have no trouble finding rooms. Apparently it is not unusual for motorists to be stranded here during the winter when the road through the mountains becomes impassable, although there are fewer travelers these days, they say, with the war going on and fuel harder to come by. But most everything is available in Mexico if you have the money to pay for it, and the industrious villagers are happy to care for unexpected guests.

The room Tucker and I are offered is nearly bare. There is a double bed with a bright magenta blanket covering it. The intertwining roses and vines on the wooden headboard are delicate but crudely carved, and I think of the unknown, unskilled artist who carved them and wonder if he thought about the people who might eventually sleep in his bed. Above it, as though in blessing, a cross hangs on the wall. Under the single window is a carved and painted chest. There is no rug on the smooth, wood planked floor and no curtains hang at the window. The simple beauty of the room appeals to me. Tucker appears not to notice.

"Let's go find a bar and get a drink."

"I want to see if I can find someplace to take a bath."

"You can do that later. Right now I want a drink."

Jack and Kay are already sitting at a table when we walk into the cantina. Drinks are in front of them along with a plate of sliced lemons and a dish of peppers. They look to be arguing when Jack sees us and waves us over.

"The tequila isn't bad," Jack says.

A woman comes to take our order. She's wearing a black cotton, gathered skirt and a white blouse. Her dusty, bare feet are thrust into leather sandals. She doesn't smile, but stands silent, waiting. Tucker orders a beer for himself and a glass of tequila for me. The ceiling is low and a single bulb dangling on a short, black cord at the center of the room casts a weak light that doesn't quite reach into the corners. Besides the smell of beer and cigarette smoke, the air is rich with cooking odors.

There are two men sitting at a nearby table. The ashtray between them is overflowing with stubbed out cigarettes and there is a bottle of beer and a glass in front of each man. One man is wearing a dark suit. His thin black tie hangs loose at the collar of his white shirt, but otherwise he looks tidy, as though someone who cares about his appearance has tended him. His companion is thin and dark, with pockmarked skin drawn tight over his narrow face. His dark eyes stare out from under thick bushy brows. The two men are speaking so quickly and softly I can't follow their Spanish, but the thin one is drawing lines in some beer spilled on the table and in between is jabbing his finger at the man in the suit.

The waitress brings our drinks. I sip the tequila and enjoy the sharp taste on my tongue and the spreading warmth as it hits my belly. Jack pulls the map out of his pocket, unfolds it and lays it out on the table, the plate of lemon slices and the dish of peppers pushing up the paper in the middle like small mountains. Jack and Tucker discuss the next day's route. I try to make conversation with Kay. She answers my questions in one or two words, lighting one cigarette from the end of another.

Suddenly Kay sits back in her chair and folds her arms across her chest. "Well, you'll know soon enough. I'm pregnant."

"Oh, for Christ's sake, Kay. Do you have to blab everything you know?" Jack looks disgusted and takes another swallow of tequila.

"Well, I think it's important for our friends to know that I'm knocked up, Sugar. Aren't you just thrilled for me, Honey?" she asks me. "What do you suppose it is, a boy or a girl? I'd love to have a little girl, I think. But then, again, a little boy would be nice, too." She lights another cigarette then quickly stubs it out and starts to cry.

"Just shut-up, Kay," says Jack. "God dammit, can't we just finish this trip and think about our problem later? Where's the waitress? Let's see if we can get something to eat."

"I don't want anything to eat. Besides, it isn't your problem, it's my problem. You already have a wife and son." Kay pushes herself back from the table and stands up. "I'm going back to our room," she says.

"Go ahead, then. Go," says Jack. Kay turns and, as she hurries past his table, stumbles against the man in the suit. He stands up and grabs Kay's elbow, steadying her. He looks at her and then at Jack before sitting back down and letting Kay pass.

"I'm going with Kay," I say to Tucker. "I'll see you later." I turn and follow after Kay, running a few steps before I catch up with her on the road outside the cantina. She doesn't stop walking.

"He wants me to have an abortion."

"An abortion. How? Where?"

"Oh, Jack will arrange something. Tucker probably knows somebody. They perform abortions all the time in the border towns. It's just that it's so squalid and lower class."

As I lie under the magenta blanket thinking about Kay I hear Tucker and Jack coming up the stairs, bumping into walls.

"Shit."

"Shhh."

The door opens and closes and I hear footsteps going down the hall and then another door opens and closes. Tucker sits down heavily on the bed. I pull my feet back just in time. Shoes fall to the floor one by one. Tucker mutters under his breath as he struggles to pull off his slacks and shirt. When he climbs into bed he pulls me to him. His arms and face are cold and there is the smell of stale beer and tequila on his breath. I turn my head and pull back. He pulls me to him again and thrusts his hips against me. I can feel it poking my thigh. He thrusts at me again and his shiny bald head hits me on the cheek bringing a stinging pain and tears to my eyes.

"Quit it, Tucker. I'm not in the mood."

"Too bad. I am."

"I mean it, Tucker. I'm tired. It's been a long day. Let's get some sleep."

"I mean it, Tucker," he mimics.

The foul smell of his breath nauseates me and I pull away from him again.

"Come here, dammit. I didn't bring you along to tell me you're not in the mood. I'm in the mood and that'll have to be enough." He grabs my arms and rolls on top of me.

I slip off the bed and search along the floor for my nightgown. I pull it on and tie the straps where they're torn. I roll a snoring Tucker over and wrap myself in the magenta blanket. Toward dawn I fall asleep.

Tucker is ignoring me this morning as he re-packs the small suitcase he brought from the car yesterday. After a while he leaves the room. When I come downstairs he's sitting at the table with Kay and Jack. The three of them are laughing about something. There's a hammered silver coffeepot and several ceramic mugs on a small table near a door I think leads to the kitchen. Next to the coffeepot is a tray of rolls and a pot of butter. I pour a cup of coffee and go over and sit down.

"Where's your bag?" says Tucker. "Aren't you packed yet? We want to leave here right after we pay the bill."

"I'm not going," I say.

"What do you mean, you're not going?"

"I mean I'm not going with you. I'm staying here."

"Don't be ridiculous. Of course you're not staying here. Now go get your things together and stop playing games."

"I'm not playing games with you, Tucker." Kay and Jack are watching us, but neither of them says a word.

"How are you going to get back to Phoenix then? We're not coming back here for you."

"I don't know. I'll find something. A bus maybe." I have no idea, but surely there must be busses that go through this town to somewhere I can get transportation.

"You're crazy. I mean it now. Are you coming with us or not?"

"I'm not."

"Suit yourself then." He stands up, pushes the chair back and walks away. Neither Kay nor Jack look at me, but stand and follow Tucker.

Immediately I want to say "Wait, I've changed my mind," but I don't. I go back up to the room and wait for them to leave.

"There is a bus to Leone on Wednesday, Señora, but it is not so nice. Maybe you can hire Mr. Lopez to drive you in his auto." I'm surprised to find the waitress at the cantina is so helpful. Her name is Otilia, and she serves me a breakfast of fresh melon and the most delicious oatmeal I've ever tasted.

"Who is Mr. Lopez?"

"He was here last night sitting at that table over there with his brother-in-law."

"I remember the two men. Which one is Mr. Lopez?" If he's the thin pock-faced man I'll take the bus.

As though she can read my mind she says, "Mr. Lopez is the mayor of San Ignatio, Señora. He always wears a fine suit." She tells me he comes to the cantina every afternoon and she will tell him about me. She knows where I am staying and she will send him to me.

I finish the melon and decide to spend the rest of the morning exploring San Ignatio. By the time I've climbed the hill to the church I'm sweating and out of breath. The church stands at the top of the hill, the rough stone roads of the town leading out from it like spokes. It has a rounded dome, stained glass windows and whitewashed adobe walls, and I guess it's more like a cathedral than a church. I peer through the wide opened carved wooden doors. After the bright sunlight, it's hard to make out anything except for splashes of colored light that fall on the stone floor and the rows of wooden benches. As my eyes begin to adjust I see a crucifix hanging on the wall at the front of the church above a tall altar. The thin body and face of Christ look sad and tormented, and I wonder how this figure brings comfort to so many. In several niches along the walls there are carved figures painted in vivid blues, yellows, reds and gold, as though drenched in the colors from the glass in the windows. I recognize one of the figures as Mary and another as Jesus, his arms outstretched, but I have no idea which saints the rest of the figures represent. I see no one inside the church, but still I sense a presence. Perhaps it's all the statues. Or perhaps it's the ghosts of the hundreds of petitioners who have knelt before Mary's statue, seeking her intervention to solve the problems in their lives.

The shade offered by the spreading branches of ancient oak trees in the park across from the church draws me to it. There is a large fountain in the center of the park and water cascades into a rough stone bowl surrounding its base. Tables piled with fruits and vegetables and other tables of merchandise line three sides of the park. I stroll around to examine what is for sale. I am offered an embroidered tablecloth, dishes, cooking pots, tortillas, shoes, brooms, gum, magazines, cigarettes, a silver framed mirror, belts, beans, aprons, lace, pencils, pens, scissors, knives, gloves, hats, hoes, picks, shovels, barbecued chicken, chickens live and squawking, a pig with a rope tied around its neck, squash, lemons, oranges, leather purses, wallets, balls, rings, books and ball bats. Each item is offered with an eager smile and soft words assuring me of its value and uniqueness as I make my way around the tables. There are children playing and several young babies are in baskets near their mothers' stalls. Dogs dart in and out and dodge half-hearted kicks as they nose around the tables with food. Two small boys run up to me. One elbows the other who says, "You Norte Americano?" I say yes and they both laugh and run off.

The oleanders at the foot of my garden sway in the late evening breeze sweeping down off Camelback Mountain, over the manicured gardens of the hotels and resorts, over the stuccoed walls of the newly rich and the old rich, on its way to the desert stretching east of Scottsdale. I sit on the still warm patio, an old woman now, watching the sky turn from pink to lavender to gray and remember the colors of the sky in Mexico that summer.

Mr. Lopez did drive me to Leone. On the way he told me about his brother-in-law and their dispute over some property left to Mr. Lopez and his sister by their parents. The problem was irrigation. Mr. Lopez said his brother-in-law was a good man, but wretched in his luck and had little skill as a farmer. In Leone I caught a bus to Guadalajara, then another that traveled up along the Sea of Cortez, turned inland to Nogales, Tucson and home to Phoenix.

Jack finally divorced his wife, I heard, and married Kay. After the war they spent time in Saudi Arabia, where Jack did something with the government and growing cotton, then they moved to California. There were never any children though, and when Jack died his son by his first wife inherited everything. Tucker and I ran into each other from time to time, but after a while I didn't see him any more.

The End

Before continuing, consider the following questions once again:

1. The setting: Do you feel as if you are there? Why or why not? Where do you think the setting is most clearly drawn? How does she achieve that? To what senses does she appeal? Where is the setting undeveloped?

2. The characters: How well do you come to know them? Which do you feel you know best? Whose story is it? What do the characters want? Can any of the characters be eliminated?

3. The plot: What is at stake for whom? Can the stakes be raised? How is the pacing?
4. The dialogue: Is it a close approximation of how these people would speak? Is it sufficiently embodied?
5. The point of view: How would the story be different in another pov? What is the narrative distance? How does that affect the story?
6. Voice: What is the narrator's voice? Is it affected by the time in which the story takes place?

When you have finished, look at this same draft with marginalia, and then the critique that follows the draft.

BENEDICTIONS

by Toni Morgan

Here we are the four of us, bouncing along a dirt and gravel road in Mexico to show Jack the cotton growing potential of the western and central regions. Tucker is driving. His bald head is pink and peeling despite the sun lotion he rubs into it every morning. I'm always amazed that he burns so easily since he was born in Tucson and raised on the desert. Wouldn't you think the skin would   Pov? eventually build up a tolerance? But there it is in front of me, looking more like an onion than ever. Tucker procures for the Army what the Army   Time? needs to feed and clothe its soldiers. The Army needs cotton for uniforms.

Dust rolls out from beneath the station wagon like a tail dragging along behind us. It lies thick on the dashboard, over the seats, and coats our luggage and the extra fuel cans piled up in the back. My lips are dry and chapped and all I want at the moment is a long soak in a hot tub with plenty of soap. I wonder again why I agreed to come on this trip. Tucker seemed indifferent when he'd first mentioned it, appearing not to care if I came along or stayed home. We've been together for six months, but I'm not sure we'll ever have a permanent relationship. Or if I want one. My mother, who lives with me, was dead set against my coming. We argued for days.

"I just don't understand you, Virginia. I'm going to ignore the fact that you'll obviously be   Nice transition.

sleeping with that man," she never refers to Tucker by name. He's been married twice before and she views him with suspicion and some scorn. "But how can you go off and leave Richie for six weeks? He's only five. What if he gets sick? What if I need to contact you?" But the trip sounded like a lark, and Jack and Kay can be fun, so I promised I'd call frequently. Besides, Richie loves being with her. He probably doesn't even notice I'm not there.

Northeast of us is a range of mountains. San Ignatio, where we plan to spend the night, is located in the foothills. The last village we passed was three hours back and there is no sign of a village or even a house ahead of us. As far as I can see in all directions are sage and mesquite. The mountains are the only things that interrupt the flat landscape under its azure blue dome.

"According to the map there's another road we have to take to get to San Ignatio," says Tucker. "It can't be too much further."

"Let's roll up the windows," Kay says. "The dust is so thick in here I can hardly breathe."

Kay is from Texas. "Amarillo, Honey," she tells people in her flat, nasal drawl. We all met in Phoenix where so many people have moved since the war started, looking for excitement or jobs. Jack comes from the Central Valley of California. His family owns a large cattle operation there. He came to Phoenix partly for business opportunities and partly to get away from his wife. I'm from a small town in Nevada nobody's ever heard of. The only thing different about me is they were born rich.

Why not name town?

"It's too hot," Jack says.

"Well, I'd rather be hot than choke to death, Sugar."

"Put out your cigarette. Maybe that will help." Jack is always complaining about Kay's chain-smoking. Kay ignores him, but she doesn't say any more about putting up the windows.

"This must be the turn off," says Tucker. He pulls to a stop and we all look at the words "*San Ignatio*" with an arrow painted on a piece of wood nailed to a stake that has been pounded into the ground, pointing to the mountains.

"Jesus, that road looks worse than the one we're on."

"I knew we should have stayed nearer the coast."

"Well, what do you all think? Should we turn off here or keep going?"

Who is speaking?

Kay is for keeping to the road we're on, but the rest of us vote for the turn off, so Tucker puts the car into gear and points it toward the mountains. After a while the road begins to climb into hills that are rounded and undulating. The land is still covered in sage and mesquite, but now there is an occasional solitary juniper. I can see the road in front of us go up one side of a hill, disappear at the top, reappear on the hill beyond and again beyond that. When we reach the top of the last hill I look down at a valley below. At its bottom is a dry creek bed strewn with rocks and boulders, with clumps of oak and willow along its edges. On the other side of the creek I can make out tracks leading up the side of yet another hill and again disappearing over the top. The car grinds down to where the road runs into the creek bed. Tucker drives slowly forward maneuvering around the boulders. I hang onto the door handle to keep from being pitched sideways into Kay. When we reach the other side Tucker stops the car and we all climb out.

There would be more tension with two men and one woman.

"Well, what do you think, Folks?"

"I think we're fuckin' lost, Honey," Kay says.

Jack pulls out the map and lays it across the hood of the car. Kay wanders over to a large boulder, sits down and lights another cigarette. Her sleek brown hair falls forward as she leans into the match, cupping the flame with carmine tipped fingers. She blows out a long stream of smoke and ignores the two men arguing over the map.

Too eloquent for our 1st person narrator.

My blouse is sticking to my back, and my linen shorts have ridden up in a bunch between my legs. I am stiff from sitting in the car all day. I start to follow the tracks up the hill, partly to work out the kinks and partly to get away from everyone for at least a few minutes. When I reach the top I yell back to the rest. "There's a town. I can see it."

A church and several small buildings are silhouetted against the sky as we approach, dark against lavender, and lights are beginning to flicker in the windows of houses scattered down the hillside. We enter by one of what we later learn are two roads leading to San Ignatio. The back one, which we took, is seldom used. "The creek crossing is not dependable, Señora," our landlady tells me. The other road leads from the coast, crosses the road we'd traveled much of the day, passes through San Ignatio and continues over the mountains, eventually leading to the Gulf.

Narrator speaks Spanish?

More tension if she has limited ability.

We have no trouble finding rooms. Apparently it is not unusual for motorists to be stranded here during the winter when the road through the mountains becomes impassable, although there are fewer travelers these days, they say, with the war going on and fuel harder to come by. But most everything is available in Mexico if you have the money to pay for it, and the industrious villagers are happy to care for unexpected guests.

Chronology.

The room Tucker and I are offered is nearly bare. There is a double bed with a bright magenta blanket covering it. The intertwining roses and vines on the wooden headboard are delicate but crudely carved, and I think of the unknown, unskilled artist who carved them and wonder if he thought about the people who might eventually sleep in his bed. Above it, as though in blessing, a cross hangs on the wall. Under the single window is a carved and painted chest. There is no rug on the smooth, wood planked floor and no curtains hang at the window. The simple beauty of the room appeals to me. Tucker appears not to notice.

More description of cross— one more beat—it will be important later.

"Let's find a bar and get a drink."

"I want to see if I can find someplace to take a bath."

"You can do that later. Right now I want a drink."

Keep bar in same building— we gain nothing by shifting locales.

Jack and Kay are already sitting at a table when we walk into the cantina. Drinks are in front of them along with a plate of sliced lemons and a dish of peppers. They look to be arguing when Jack sees us and waves us over.

"The tequila isn't bad," Jack says.

A woman comes to take our order. She's wearing a black cotton, gathered skirt and a white blouse. Her dusty, bare feet are thrust into leather sandals. She doesn't smile, but stands silent, waiting. Tucker orders a beer for himself and a glass of tequila for me. The ceiling is low and a single bulb dangling on a short, black cord at the center of the room casts a weak light that doesn't quite reach into the corners. Besides the smell of beer and cigarette smoke, the air is rich with cooking odors.

Make her the landlady— same as before. The fewer the characters the better.

There are two men sitting at a nearby table. The ashtray between them is overflowing with stubbed out cigarettes and there is a bottle of beer and a glass in front of each man. One man is wearing a dark suit. His thin black tie hangs loose at the collar of his white shirt, but otherwise he looks tidy, as though someone who cares about his appearance has tended him. His companion is thin and dark, with pockmarked skin drawn tight over his narrow face. His dark eyes stare out from under thick bushy brows. The two men are speaking so quickly and softly I can't follow their Spanish, but the thin one is drawing lines in some beer spilled on the table and in between is jabbing his finger at the man in the suit.

Narrator should have only rudimentary knowledge of Spanish.

The waitress brings our drinks. I sip the tequila and enjoy the sharp taste on my tongue and the spreading warmth as it hits my belly. Jack pulls the map out of his pocket, unfolds it and lays it out on the table, the plate of lemon slices and the dish of peppers pushing up the paper in the middle like small mountains. Jack and Tucker discuss the next day's route. I try to make conversation with Kay. She answers my questions in one or two words, lighting one cigarette from the end of another.

Suddenly Kay sits back in her chair and folds her arms across her chest. "Well, you'll know soon enough. I'm pregnant."

Why would they wait until Mexico to discuss this?

"Oh, for Christ's sake, Kay. Do you have to blab everything you know?" Jack looks disgusted and takes another swallow of tequila.

"Well, I think it's important for our friends to know that I'm knocked up, Sugar. Aren't you just thrilled for me, Honey?" she asks me. "What do you suppose it is, a boy or a girl? I'd love to have a little girl, I think. But then, again, a little boy would be nice, too." She lights another cigarette then quickly stubs it out and starts to cry.

I like this, but it detracts from the narrator's story— whose story is this?

"Just shut-up, Kay," says Jack. "God dammit, can't we just finish this trip and think about our problem later? Where's the waitress? Let's see if we can get something to eat."

Wooden dialogue.

"I don't want anything to eat. Besides, it isn't your problem, it's my problem. You already have a wife and son." Kay pushes herself back from the table and stands up. "I'm going back to our room," she says.

"Go ahead, then. Go," says Jack. Kay turns and, as she hurries past his table, stumbles against the man in the suit. He stands up and grabs Kay's elbow, steadying her. He looks at her and then at Jack before sitting back down and letting Kay pass.

"I'm going with Kay," I say to Tucker. "I'll see you later." I turn and follow after Kay, running a few steps before I catch up with her on the road outside the cantina. She doesn't stop walking.

You'll change this if you locate bar in hotel.

"He wants me to have an abortion."

Clarify time of year.

"An abortion. How? Where?"

"Oh, Jack will arrange something. Tucker probably knows somebody. They perform abortions all the time in the border towns. It's just that it's so squalid and lower class."

As I lie under the magenta blanket thinking about Kay I hear Tucker and Jack coming up the stairs, bumping into walls.

"Shit."

"Shhh."

The door opens and closes and I hear footsteps going down the hall and then another door opens and closes. Tucker sits down heavily on the bed. I pull my feet back just in time. Shoes fall to the floor one by one. Tucker mutters under his breath as he struggles to pull off his slacks and shirt. When he climbs into bed he pulls me to him. His arms and face are cold and there is the smell of stale beer and tequila on his breath. I turn my head and pull back. He pulls me to him again and thrusts his hips against me. I can feel it poking my thigh. He thrusts at me again and his shiny bald head hits me on the cheek bringing a stinging pain and tears to my eyes.

"Quit it, Tucker. I'm not in the mood."

"Too bad. I am."

"I mean it, Tucker. I'm tired. It's been a long day. Let's get some sleep."

"*I mean it, Tucker,*" he mimics.

The foul smell of his breath nauseates me and I pull away from him again.

"Come here, dammit. I didn't bring you along to tell me you're not in the mood. I'm in the mood and that'll have to be enough." He grabs my arms and rolls on top of me.

I slip off the bed and search along the floor for my nightgown. I pull it on and tie the straps where they're torn. I roll a snoring Tucker over and wrap myself in the magenta blanket. Toward dawn I fall asleep.

Tucker is ignoring me this morning as he re-packs the small suitcase he brought from the car yesterday. After a while he leaves the room. When I come downstairs he's sitting at the table with Kay and Jack. The three of them are laughing about something. There's a hammered silver coffeepot and several ceramic mugs on a small table near a door I think leads to the kitchen. Next to the coffeepot is a tray of rolls and a pot of butter. I pour a cup of coffee and go over and sit down.

"Where's your bag?" says Tucker. "Aren't you packed yet? We want to leave here right after we pay the bill."

"I'm not going," I say.

"What do you mean, you're not going?"

"I mean I'm not going with you. I'm staying here."

"Don't be ridiculous. Of course you're not staying here. Now go get your things together and stop playing games."

What would she call it?

Nice!

Wrong mood—Kay would not laugh now. Have them sober.

"I'm not playing games with you, Tucker."
Kay and Jack are watching us, but neither of them
says a word.

"How are you going to get back to Phoenix
then? We're not coming back here for you."

"I don't know. I'll find something. A bus
maybe." I have no idea, but surely there must be
busses that go through this town to somewhere I
can get transportation.

"You're crazy. I mean it now. Are you coming
with us or not?"

"I'm not."

"Suit yourself then." He stands up, pushes
the chair back and walks away. Neither Kay nor
Jack look at me, but stand and follow Tucker.

Immediately I want to say "Wait, I've changed
my mind," but I don't. I go back up to the room
and wait for them to leave.

"There is a bus to Leone on Wednesday,
Señora, but it is not so nice. Maybe you can hire
Mr. Lopez to drive you in his auto." I'm surprised
to find the waitress at the cantina is so helpful.
Her name is Otilia, and she serves me a breakfast
of fresh melon and the most delicious oatmeal
I've ever tasted.

"Who is Mr. Lopez?"

"He was here last night sitting at that table
over there with his brother-in-law."

"I remember the two men. Which one is Mr.
Lopez?" If he's the thin pock-faced man I'll take
the bus.

As though she can read my mind she says,
"Mr. Lopez is the mayor of San Ignatio, Señora.
He always wears a fine suit." She tells me he
comes to the cantina every afternoon and she will
tell him about me. She knows where I am staying
and she will send him to me.

I finish the melon and decide to spend the
rest of the morning exploring San Ignatio. By the
time I've climbed the hill to the church I'm sweating and out of breath. The church stands at the
top of the hill, the rough stone roads of the town
leading out from it like spokes. It has a rounded
dome, stained glass windows and whitewashed

[handwritten margin note:] Kay or Jack or both would say something.

[handwritten margin note:] Use a little Spanish in following dialogue—Have the narrator a bit confused as to what is being said—and the reader, too.

[handwritten margin note:] Same hotel.

adobe walls, and I guess it's more like a cathedral than a church. I peer through the wide opened carved wooden doors. After the bright sunlight, it's hard to make out anything except for splashes of colored light that fall on the stone floor and the rows of wooden benches. As my eyes begin to adjust I see a crucifix hanging on the wall at the front of the church above a tall altar. The thin body and face of Christ look sad and tormented, and I wonder how this figure brings comfort to so many. In several niches along the walls there are carved figures painted in vivid blues, yellows, reds and gold, as though drenched in the colors from the glass in the windows. I recognize one of the figures as Mary and another as Jesus, his arms outstretched, but I have no idea which saints the rest of the figures represent. I see no one inside the church, but still I sense a presence. Perhaps it's all the statues. Or perhaps it's the ghosts of the hundreds of petitioners who have knelt before Mary's statue, seeking her intervention to solve the problems in their lives.

The shade offered by the spreading branches of ancient oak trees in the park across from the church draws me to it. There is a large fountain in the center of the park and water cascades into a rough stone bowl surrounding its base. Tables piled with fruits and vegetables and other tables of merchandise line three sides of the park. I stroll around to examine what is for sale. I am offered an embroidered tablecloth, dishes, cooking pots, tortillas, shoes, brooms, gum, magazines, cigarettes, a silver framed mirror, belts, beans, aprons, lace, pencils, pens, scissors, knives, gloves, hats, hoes, picks, shovels, barbecued chicken, chickens live and squawking, a pig with a rope tied around its neck, squash, lemons, oranges, leather purses, wallets, balls, rings, books and ball bats. Each item is offered with an eager smile and soft words assuring me of its value and uniqueness as I make my way around the tables. There are children playing and several young babies are in baskets near their mothers' stalls. Dogs dart in and out and dodge half-hearted kicks as they nose

> Here's the key to your story—make it look like it was carved by the same guy as the one above the bed.

around the tables with food. Two small boys run up to me. One elbows the other who says, "You Norte Americano?" I say yes and they both laugh and run off.

The oleanders at the foot of my garden sway in the late evening breeze sweeping down off Camel-back Mountain, over the manicured gardens of the hotels and resorts, over the stuccoed walls of the newly rich and the old rich, on its way to the desert stretching east of Scottsdale. I sit on the still warm patio, an old woman now, watching the sky turn from pink to lavender to gray and remember the colors of the sky in Mexico that summer.

Mr. Lopez did drive me to Leone. On the way he told me about his brother-in-law and their dispute over some property left to Mr. Lopez and his sister by their parents. The problem was irrigation. Mr. Lopez said his brother-in-law was a good man, but wretched in his luck and had little skill as a farmer. In Leone I caught a bus to Guadalajara, then another that traveled up along the Sea of Cortez, turned inland to Nogales, Tucson and home to Phoenix.

Jack finally divorced his wife, I heard, and married Kay. After the war they spent time in Saudi Arabia, where Jack did something with the government and growing cotton, then they moved to California. There were never any children though, and when Jack died his son by his first wife inherited everything. Tucker and I ran into each other from time to time, but after a while I didn't see him any more.

Marginalia:

Have a man who carries crucifixes here i.e., T.S. Eliot's objective correlative.

Big jump! End the story in Mexico.

No, not after rape. You are trying to tie up everything too neatly.

Critique

Dear Toni,

There is a lot to like in this draft. You do a good job of capturing much of the setting here so that we get a sense of Mexico, and you do a good job of establishing conflict early on and then raising the tension right away. And the flashback to the narrator's mother on page two is handled very smoothly; the reader rides right back in time with the narrator without a bump in the road. Good work in that.

What I want to do here is go through this page by page, drawing attention to my marginalia, and then I want to focus on some of the bigger issues that you may want to address in your next draft.

In the first two words, you have established the point of view. Great. Sometimes we will read the first two pages of a story and think that it is in the third person, and then the word *I* magically appears and we feel either dumb or duped. So good work, here. But in the same paragraph, you write *Wouldn't you think the skin would eventually build up a tolerance?* I realize this to be a rhetorical thought on the narrator's part, but it is also jarring to see the word *you* as if the narrator were addressing the reader and thus, I would eliminate that.

On this same page, we are told that they are on the trip to show Jack the "cotton growing potential" of the area, yet it never becomes clear why Jack wants to grow cotton in the area; it is Tucker, we are told, who procures supplies for the army. I would clarify just why they are all on this trip together.

On page two, you slide into the aforementioned flashback smoothly. To help you leave it and reenter story time just as smoothly, I would include a space break before starting the paragraph *Northeast of us . . .*

On page three, I do not know why the narrator would not name the town in Nevada where she is from. Place names are great for grounding the reader in a story, and *Elko* is far better than *a small town in Nevada nobody's ever heard of.* Farther down on this page, I am confused as to who is speaking in those three lines of dialogue I marked. A couple of tag lines with attribution will clear that up.

On page four, two large issues occur to me. First, I wonder if we could eliminate Kay. I wonder about this for several reasons, not the least of which is that the fewer characters you have in a story, the less confusing it is. Before we get to the end of this story, we wonder whose story it is. At one point, it seems to be Kay's story as she is discovered to be pregnant. At this point, we consider this possibility and conclude that the narrator is a detached observer. Of course, by the time the narrator is raped by Tucker, we realize that we were wrong and that this is, indeed, the narrator's story, but you do not want the reader to be confused to that extent.

Eliminating Kay would certainly raise the stakes, increase the tension, in that there now would be three characters—two men and a woman—traveling in Mexico where she would not have any resources for "escaping" from these men. Thus, I would suggest that you consider eliminating Kay.

My other concern on page four is one of point of view. I like the first person narrator's voice here, but I wonder about her describing Kay as *Her sleek brown hair falls forward as she leans into the match, cupping the flame with carmine tipped fingers.* Of course, that is beautiful writing, Toni, but (1) would the narrator have that ability in using such language; and (2) would she take the time to make such descriptions considering the circumstances? Thus, I am wondering if a change to a third person limited point of view might be more appropriate (by the way, I would mention the narrator's name more than once in the story; the only place I recall seeing her name was in the flashback, and by the end, I couldn't remember that her name was Virginia).

On page five, you have a minor problem with chronology in that you have the narrator speaking to the landlady and then the narrator makes the statement "We have no trouble finding rooms."

I would work on clarifying the setting here so that we see the church as they enter town. Then, I would make it clear that there is but one hotel in the town where they can find rooms. And then we can meet the landlady. I make these suggestions because the smaller the town, the fewer the resources for the narrator, and this raises the tension when we see her left behind.

On this same page, the landlady speaks to the narrator, but in which language? I would suggest that our narrator have only the most rudimentary knowledge of Spanish, again raising the stakes when she is left behind. The reader will wonder how she will ever get along. This can be clarified when they are in the *cantina*, drinking. And I would make the *cantina* in the same building as the inn with the landlady serving as hostess. Again, we don't gain anything by having them go to a *cantina* that is not in the hotel where they are staying (and having Tucker and Jack getting drunk in such close proximity to where our narrator is sleeping raises the tension as well).

You help yourself as a writer in inventorying the hotel room, and it is wise to have that cross above the bed in that the church will come into the story later, and the bed itself is where the rape occurs—directly beneath the cross. I would add one more beat to the description of the cross here on page five, however. Later in this critique, I will mention the cross again and it will be important to have this cross clearly described. It would probably be a good idea to give the carving one odd twist that the reader will recall. Physical objects can carry a terrific emotional weight, and this cross could do so and thereby be of more significance in the story than it is at present. (For further reading, see T. S. Eliot's "Hamlet and his Problems" in *The Sacred Wood*, wherein he coins the term "objective correlative," meaning a set of actions or objects that when seen by the reader evoke an emotion.)

If you agree that the bar should be in the hotel, you'll have to change the dialogue on page six. Maybe: "Let's go downstairs and get a drink." And again, I would have the waitress be the landlady whom we have met before. Give her some feature on first reference that we will see again here on page six, thus helping us recall her image. It could be something as simple as a slight limp.

I like the tension on page seven with Kay and the pregnancy, but as I indicated earlier, I think we should eliminate Kay because now it seems that this might be Kay's story. In other words, you have Kay's pregnancy competing with the narrator's rape, and the reader must decide where to vest his focus. (This also seems an odd place for Kay to discover she is pregnant; and if she already knew, why does it seem that this is the first time it has been discussed?)

Earlier on this page, I'd have the narrator struggle with some broken Spanish when she orders drinks (italicize the Spanish as we do with all foreign languages). This will increase the tension when she is left behind, stranded in Mexico with an inability to communicate.

If you have agreed to the suggestion of putting the bar in the hotel, then you'll have to make the necessary changes on page eight.

Page nine is certainly the pivotal point in the story. You do an excellent job at understating the rape. The mistake would be to draw it out with graphic detail. That last paragraph before the space break is just stunning and the reader is left shuddering. Earlier on the page, however, I would use whatever word our narrator would use for penis instead of using *it*. And italicize "*I mean it, Tucker*" when he mimics her. By the way, that mimicking is terrific characterization.

On page ten, I believe the mood has undeservedly shifted with the three of them laughing at the table when the narrator arrives. I do not believe they would be so happy with Kay in or not in the story. Instead, I would have the two men hung over and taciturn as they drink their coffee.

At the top of page eleven, I believe Jack would say something (as would Kay if she were to remain in the story) when Tucker leaves the *cantina* after the narrator says that she is not going with them.

On the same page, use a space break to indicate a temporal (time) and spatial (space) shift when she is talking to the landlady about transportation (the landlady if you take my suggestion of reducing the number of characters and places in the story by having the *cantina* in the hotel). And when the narrator is speaking to her about Mr. Lopez on this page, I would insert some Spanish and break up the speech more so that we can see she is having trouble communicating with the woman. As it is, she seems to be perfectly fluent which reduces the tension; again, if she is left behind and knows very little of the language, the tension is magnified. Tension, tension, tension.

Page twelve has huge potential for resonance, and that potential lies in the crucifix in the church which will remind us why she is here, so I would give the crucifix in the church the same malformation as the one in the hotel so that the reader will connect the two. Maybe the local crucifix carver has a trademarked scar on Christ's forehead that the narrator first notices in the bedroom and then notices again here in the church. Something like that to connect the two, so the reader will go back to that horrible moment in the bedroom.

Still on the same page: the narrator goes outside to a market of sorts where you have inventoried many, many items. I would reduce the number of items, thereby giving more weight to each, and—you can see where I am going now—have a table where a craftsman is busy carving various figures, and on his table the narrator sees the crucifixes with the same malformation. What would she do? Would she stop and touch one? Would she buy one?

In the ending you have here, you are trying to wrap everything up too neatly, I think. And having the story end back in Arizona so many years later when she is an old woman is a problematic **narrative distance** in its enormity. If we end our stay in Mexico at the market and then jump to Arizona many, many years later, one wonders what it was at the market that caused such reflection, and frankly, as it is, I don't know. Thus, I would greatly reduce the narrative distance. (And with the narrative distance that you do have, I would write this in the past tense. Notice that you shift from present tense to past tense when the narrator is an old woman back in Arizona. The present tense, by the way, slows down the action as we wait for events to unfold.)

I think you need to end the story in Mexico with her waiting for a bus or whatever transportation it is that will take her out of Mexico. This story needs to be more open-ended. Your last line is a throw-away line: *Tucker and I ran into each other from time to time, but after a while I didn't see him anymore.* So what? I think you were just looking for a way out here, Toni, and although you didn't find a plausible way out, you broke out just the same.

The key to the story is the undercurrent in the narrator that is not yet here. What was it that happened to her husband? Why would she go on this adventure with a man like Tucker? Why leave her son behind? In other words, I don't think you know enough about your narrator to provide the subtext to the story that would make the ending resonate for the reader. And the key question is why she would abandon the safety of Arizona for the dangers of traveling with a man like Tucker. Clarify that in your own mind and we will find a good ending in Mexico.

As I get to the end of this critique, Toni, I realize that I did not comment on the time. We are told that the story is taking place during the war—presumably World War II—but there is little evidence of the time in the story. In other words, it could be contemporary from the evidence in this draft. Is it important that the story take place during World War II? Why? How? How would it be different—to the narrator—if it were set in the same town today? Not very different, I would say.

The setting is stronger in the beginning, when they are traveling, than when they arrive. I would rewrite one or two drafts just for setting. Make it more Mexico.

O.K., Toni. Enough. This is a very good draft, one full of potential. In your next draft, rewrite for one thing. The key to the story is Virginia. Just who is this woman?

I look forward to seeing what decisions you will have made in rewriting the next draft.

—Tim

Revision

BENEDICTIONS

Toni Morgan

Here we are the three of us, bouncing along a dirt and gravel road in Mexico to show Jack the cotton-growing potential of the western and central regions. Tucker is driving. His bald head is pink and peeling despite the sun lotion he rubs into it every morning. I'm always amazed that he burns so easily since he was born in Tucson and raised in the desert. But there it is in front of me, looking more like an onion than ever. Tucker procures for the Army what the Army needs to feed and clothe its soldiers. The Army needs cotton for uniforms.

Dust rolls out from beneath the station wagon like a tail dragging along behind us. It lies thick on the dashboard, over the seats, and it coats our luggage and the extra fuel cans piled up in the back. My lips are dry and chapped and all I want at the moment is a long soak in a hot tub with plenty of soap. I wonder again why I agreed to come on this trip. Tucker seemed indifferent when he'd first mentioned it, appearing not to care if I came along or stayed home. We've been together for six months, but I'm not sure we'll ever have a permanent relationship. Or if I want one. My mother, who lives with me, was dead set against my coming. We argued for days.

"I just don't understand you, Virginia. I'm going to ignore the fact that you're obviously sleeping with that man." She never refers to Tucker by name. He's been married twice before and she views him with suspicion and some scorn. "But how can you go off and leave Richie for six weeks? He's only five. What if he gets sick? What if I need to contact you?" But the trip sounded like a lark, so I promised I'd call frequently. Besides, Richie loves being with her. He probably doesn't even notice I'm not there.

*   *   *

Northeast of us is a range of mountains. The town where we plan to spend the night is located in the foothills. The last village we passed was three hours back and there is no sign of a village or even a house ahead of us. As far as I can see in all directions are sage and mesquite. The mountains are the only things that interrupt the flat landscape under its azure blue dome.

"According to the map there's another road we have to take to get to San Ignacio," says Tucker. "It can't be too much further."

The three of us met in Phoenix where so many people have moved since Pearl Harbor, looking for jobs or excitement. Excitement mostly. Practically as soon as war was declared, Tucker came up from Tucson. Jack comes from the Central Valley of California. His family owns a large cattle operation there. He moved to Phoenix partly for business opportunities and partly to get away from his wife. I'm from a small town nobody's heard of. Elko, Nevada. A ranch town in the Ruby Valley. My father worked in the Elko Pharmacy. There was never enough money. Jack and Tucker were born rich.

"Let's roll up the windows," I say. "The dust is so thick in here I can hardly breathe."

"It's too hot," Jack says.

"Well, I'd rather be hot than choke to death," I tell him.

"Put out your cigarette. Maybe that will help." Tucker is always complaining about me smoking. I ignore him and roll up my window. It doesn't help.

"This must be the turn off," says Tucker. He pulls to a stop and we all look at the words "*San Ignacio*" with an arrow painted on a piece of wood nailed to a stake that has been pounded into the ground, pointing to the mountains.

"Jesus, that road looks worse than the one we're on," says Jack.

"I knew we should have stayed nearer the coast."

"Well, what do you all think?" Tucker says. "Should we turn off here or keep going?"

I'm for keeping to the road we're on, but Jack and Tucker vote for the turn off, so Tucker puts the car into gear and points it toward the mountains. After a while the road begins to climb into low, rolling hills. The land is still covered in sage and mesquite, but now there is an occasional solitary juniper. I can see the road in front of us go up one side of a hill, disappear at the top, reappear on the hill beyond and again beyond that. When we reach the top of the last hill, I look down at a valley below. At its bottom is a dry creek bed strewn with rocks and boulders, with clumps of oak and willow along its edges. On the other side of the creek I can make out tracks leading up the side of yet another hill and again disappearing over the top. The car grinds down to where the road runs into the creek bed. Tucker drives slowly forward maneuvering around the boulders. I hang onto the door handle to keep from being pitched sideways. When we reach the other side, Tucker stops the car and we all climb out.

"Well, what do you think, folks?"

"I think we're fuckin' lost," says Jack.

Jack pulls out the map and lays it across the hood of the car.

My blouse is sticking to my back, and my linen shorts have ridden up in a bunch between my legs. I'm stiff from sitting in the car all day. I wander over to a large boulder, sit down and light another cigarette, knowing I should try to cut down. I blow out a long stream of smoke and try to ignore the two men arguing over the map.

The sound of their voices is getting on my nerves. I stub out my cigarette and go back to the car to get a drink of water from the sweating, canvas bag hanging off the driver's outside mirror. I can tell Tucker is getting angry, and I decide to follow the tracks up the hill. When I reach the top I yell down to them. "There's a town. I can see it."

It's dusk. A church and several small buildings are silhouetted against the sky as we approach, dark against lavender, and lights flicker in the windows of houses scattered down the hillside. We enter by one of what we learn are two roads leading to San Ignacio. The back one, which we took, is seldom used. "The creek crossing is not dependable, Señora," our landlady later tells me. The other road leads from the coast, crosses the road we'd traveled much of the day, passes through San Ignacio and continues over the mountains, eventually leading to the Gulf.

We have no trouble finding rooms. Apparently it is not unusual for motorists to be stranded here during the winter when the road through the mountains becomes impassable, although there are fewer travelers these days, they say, with the war going on and fuel harder to come by. But most everything is available in Mexico if you have the money to pay for it, and the industrious residents of San Ignacio are happy to care for unexpected guests.

The room Tucker and I are offered is nearly bare. There is a double bed with a bright magenta blanket covering it. The intertwining roses and vines on the wooden headboard are delicate but crudely carved, and I think of the unknown, unskilled artist who carved them and wonder if he thought about the people who might eventually sleep in his bed. Above it, as though in blessing, a cross hangs on the wall. Under the single window is a carved and painted chest. There is no rug on the smooth, wood-planked floor and no curtains hang at the window. The simplicity of the room appeals to me. Tucker appears not to notice.

"Let's go find a bar and get a drink."

"I want to see if I can find someplace to take a bath and I need to call home."

"You can do that later. Right now I want a drink."

Jack is already sitting at a table when we walk into the cantina. A drink is in front of him along with a plate of sliced lemons and a dish of peppers. He sees us and waves us over.

"The tequila isn't bad."

A woman comes to take our order. She's wearing a black, gathered skirt and a white blouse. Her dusty, bare feet are thrust into leather sandals. She doesn't smile, but stands silent, waiting. Tucker orders a beer for himself and a glass of tequila for me. He grew up speaking Spanish.

The ceiling is low and a single bulb dangling on a short, black cord at the center of the room casts a weak light that doesn't quite reach into the corners. Besides the smell of beer and cigarette smoke, the air is rich with cooking odors.

There are two men sitting at a nearby table. The ashtray between them is overflowing with stubbed out cigarettes and there is a bottle of beer and a glass in front of each man. One man is wearing a dark suit. His thin black tie hangs loose at the collar of his white shirt, but otherwise he looks tidy, as though someone who cares about his appearance has tended him. His companion is thin and dark, with pockmarked skin drawn tight over his narrow face. His dark eyes stare out from under thick bushy brows. The two men are speaking so quickly and softly I can't follow their Spanish, but the thin one is drawing lines in some beer spilled on the table and in between is jabbing his finger at the man in the suit.

The waitress brings our drinks. I sip the tequila and enjoy the sharp taste on my tongue and the spreading warmth as it hits my belly. Jack pulls the map out of his pocket, unfolds it and lays it out on the table, the plate of lemon slices and the dish of peppers pushing up the paper in the middle like small mountains. Jack and Tucker discuss some property they plan to see the next day.

"The problem will be getting water to it," Tucker says.

"I have a little experience with that," says Jack. "We've done some irrigating on the ranch. This is the eastern edge of the three parcels, right?" He taps a spot on the map with his finger. "And the river is here at its closest point. That's what, five miles? It shouldn't be too hard to lay pipe that far. Mostly it'll depend on the terrain."

"If we could," says Tucker, "I think we'd produce as much cotton here, in one spot, as all the fields they've put in around Phoenix. And a lot cheaper." The two of them continue talking about their plans for the next day and the route we will take.

I turn to watch the two men at the other table, wondering if there will be a fight. But they seem to have calmed down, and the man in the suit stands. I hear him tell the other man goodnight. As he turns to leave he nods to me and says "Buenas noches, Señora."

"I'm ready to go back to the room, Tucker," I say. "I still want to get a bath and wash my hair tonight."

Tucker looks at me and then at the back of the man in the suit who is near the door, then he looks back at me, his eyebrow raised. "Lowering your standards a bit, aren't you?"

"That doesn't deserve an answer, Tucker."

I turn and walk out.

The landlady has told me I can go to the town hall tomorrow to make my phone call. There is only one telephone in town and it works between ten and twelve o'clock, she says. As I lie under the magenta blanket, wondering if Richie is missing me and picturing him asleep in his bed, little fingers still pinching the faded silk binding of his old baby blanket, I hear Tucker and Jack coming up the stairs. One of them trips and falls against the wall.

"Shit."

"Shhh."

The door opens and closes and I hear footsteps going down the hall and then another door opens and closes. Tucker sits down heavily on the bed. I pull my feet back just in time. Shoes fall to the floor one by one. Tucker mutters under his breath as he struggles to pull off his trousers and shirt. When he climbs into bed he pulls me to him. His arms and face are cold and there is the smell of stale beer and tequila on his breath. I turn my head and pull back. He pulls me to him again and thrusts his hips against me. I can feel it poking my thigh. He thrusts at me again and his shiny bald head hits me on the cheek bringing a stinging pain and tears to my eyes.

"Quit it, Tucker. I'm not in the mood."

"What's the matter? Your little Mexican bandito wear you out?"

"I mean it, Tucker. You're drunk. I'm tired. It's been a long day. Let's get some sleep."

"I mean it, Tucker," he mimics.

The foul smell of his breath nauseates me and I pull away from him again.

"Come here, dammit. I didn't bring you along to tell me you're not in the mood. I'm in the mood and that'll have to be enough." He grabs my arms and rolls on top of me.

I slip off the bed and search along the floor for my nightgown. I pull it on and tie the straps where they're torn. I roll a snoring Tucker over and wrap myself in the magenta blanket. Toward dawn I fall asleep.

*   *   *

Tucker is ignoring me this morning as he re-packs the small suitcase he brought from the car yesterday. After a while he leaves the room. When I come downstairs he's sitting at the table with Jack. Neither of them looks very happy. I think they may have been arguing. There's a hammered silver coffeepot and several earthenware mugs on a small table near a door I think leads to the kitchen. Next to the coffeepot are a tray of rolls and a pot of butter. I pour a cup of coffee and go over and sit down.

"Where's your bag?" says Tucker. "Aren't you packed yet? We want to leave here right after we pay the bill."

"I'm not going," I say.

"What do you mean, you're not going?"

"I mean I'm not going with you. I'm staying here."

"You can't stay in this God forsaken place," says Jack.

"Of course she's not staying here," says Tucker. "Now get your things together, Virginia, and stop playing games."

"I'm not playing games with you, Tucker." I light a cigarette, hoping they don't notice my hands are shaking.

"How are you going to get back to Phoenix then? We're not coming back here for you."

"I don't know. I'll find something. A bus maybe." I have no idea, but surely there must be busses that go through this town to somewhere I can get transportation.

"You're crazy. I mean it now. Are you coming with us or not?"

"I'm not."

"Suit yourself then." He stands up, pushes the chair back and walks out of the room.

"Virginia, why are you doing this?" Jack asks. "I know Tucker can be a total prick when he wants to, but we can all get separate rooms after this if you want. You don't have to stay here. Your Spanish is no better than mine is, and it won't be easy getting back to Phoenix."

I tell him I've thought about it and I won't go on with them. He doesn't press me any further, but asks if I have enough money to get home. I tell him yes.

"Here's some extra, just in case." He hands me some folded bills and turns to go.

I want to say wait, I've changed my mind. But I don't. I go back up to the room and wait for them to leave.

"Virginia, I can't hear you. What did you say?" My mother's voice is faint and tinny.

"I said how is Richie?" I shout to be heard over the pops and crackles.

"When will you be home?"

"Soon. Maybe next week. How is Richie?" I hear more wheezes. The lady behind the desk looks up at me, then down again at the ledger opened in front of her.

"What? What did you say? Virginia, I can't hear you. You need to come home. Richie misses you, and he's started . . . " The line goes dead.

"The line went dead," I tell the woman.

"I'm sorry, Señora. Let me try again." After forty minutes without success, the woman tells me the switchboard is closed for the day. Frustrated, I walk up the road to the cantina.

"There is a bus to Leone on Wednesday, Señora, but it is not so nice. Maybe you can hire Mr. Lopez to drive you in his auto." I'm surprised to find the waitress is so helpful. Her name is Otilia, and she serves me fresh melon and rolls.

"Who is Mr. Lopez?"

"He was here last night sitting at that table over there with Pedro Gutierrez."

"I remember the two men. Which one is Mr. Lopez?" If he's the thin pock-faced man I'll take the bus.

As though she can read my mind she says, "Mr. Lopez is the mayor of San Ignacio, Senora. He always wears a fine suit."

"And the other man?"

"He's Mr. Lopez' brother-in-law. They always argue, those two." Otilia tells me that Mr. Lopez and his sister inherited property from their parents. It is a very small holding, she says. "The brother-in-law, he is a good man, I think, but it is well known he has little skill as a farmer. Mr. Lopez, he worries about his sister."

She tells me Mr. Lopez comes to the cantina every day at two o'clock, and if I want to speak to him I should return at that time.

I finish the melon and decide to spend the time until two exploring. I awakened this morning to the clamoring of bells, and when I looked from the window I could see the dome of the church. I'm curious to see inside. As I climb the hill there are some shops, the doors opened and inviting, but I pass them by. I must watch where I step on the uneven stones, as there is evidence of the dogs that run free, darting here and there, nosing around wherever there is food. I look inside an opened gate set into a high wall and see a courtyard and a house with a long, covered patio. Bright red bougainvillea climb up the posts. I hear water tinkling somewhere.

When I reach the church, I'm out of breath and sweating. The church stands squarely at the top of the hill, the rough stone roads of San Ignacio leading out from it like spokes. Across from the church there is a plaza surrounded by ancient oak trees. The sounds of birds fill the air, but I don't see them. Then, as though one of the trees explodes, hundreds of birds fly up, only to disappear again into the branches of another tree. Their noise doesn't diminish. In the center of the plaza is a large fountain, and water cascades into a rough stone bowl surrounding its base. In my mind young courting couples stroll along the walkways on Sunday afternoons under the watchful eyes of duennas who sit on benches in the shade of the oak trees, gossiping. Do they still do this, I wonder?

The church has two bell towers, a rounded dome and whitewashed adobe walls, and I guess it's more like a cathedral than a church. I peer through the wide opened carved wooden doors. After the bright sunlight, it's hard to make out anything except for splashes of colored light that fall from the stained glass windows onto the stone floor and the rows of wooden benches. As my eyes begin to adjust, I see a crucifix hanging on the wall at the front of the church above a tall altar. The thin body and face of Christ looks sad and tormented, and I wonder how this figure brings comfort to so many. In several niches along the walls, there are carved figures painted in vivid blues, yellows, reds and gold, as though drenched in the colors from the glass in the windows. I recognize one of the figures as Mary and another as Jesus, his arms outstretched, but I have no idea which saints the rest of the figures represent. I see no one inside the church, but still I sense a presence. Perhaps it's all the statues. Or perhaps it's the ghosts of the hundreds of petitioners who have knelt before Mary's statue, seeking her intervention.

The interior is cool. I sit down on one of the worn benches and let the quiet wash over me. It is so very quiet. And peaceful. I wonder why I'm not frightened of being on my own in a foreign country. I told Jack I had enough money to get home. In truth, it will be close. I wonder what I'll do for money when I do get home. Without Tucker to pay the bills. And I think about Richie. What was my mother trying to tell me? I can't try calling again until tomorrow, and by ten o'clock I'm hoping I'll be on my way to Leone. I remember when Richie was born. I can almost smell his sweet, milky breath and feel the weight of him wrapped up and tucked in the corner of my arm. I'd planned to be a good mother. When did I stop trying? Was it after the divorce? Before? When my mother came to live with me, I guess it was just easier to let her take over. Little by little I turned the raising of my son over to her while I took up with people like Tucker.

A woman enters the church. As I pick up my things and prepare to leave, I watch her as she bends her knee, genuflects and crosses to the statue of Mary. The sound of a coin as it falls into the collection box echoes across the space that separates us.

When I step out of the church's shadow, I am again momentarily blinded and put my hand up to shield my eyes. The sun is white-hot and the heat nearly takes my breath away. There is no one else in sight except two small boys. They run up to me. One elbows the other who says, "You Norte Americano?" I say yes and they both laugh and run off.

I look at my watch. There is just time to reach the cantina and Mr. Lopez.

Critique of Revision

Toni,

You've done some very good work in this revision. First, the elimination of Kay has given us much more focus on Virginia, Tucker, and Jack. Kay may have her own story in the future. Sometimes we have peripheral characters in a story who have stories of their own and it will be up to us to write them.

I have some small concerns throughout the story such as more embodiment of dialogue—see page two, for example—but most of these concerns are relatively minor. As you focused on the elimination of Kay and a new ending in this draft, there are still some concerns that I mentioned in my last critique—moving the cantina into the hotel, for example—that you may want to consider addressing in your subsequent drafts.

What I would like to focus on here is Virginia's character and the ending.

You have given Virginia a clearer sense of character here by mentioning the divorce and how she has given up being a mother. I think you will have to go a couple of steps more to really draw her out, however. I wonder why she got divorced. Divorces were certainly rarer then, so I wonder what happened. That might bring some bearing on her present circumstances. Still, you have done a better job with her in this draft.

The ending is much better in this draft, but I don't think it is quite there. I think you are right in leaving out the market scene—that was a distraction. I don't know what we gain by having her exit the church to be addressed by a couple of boys, however. (I suppose it is possible that having one boy address her could remind her of her own son and her own maternal obligation, but that is not evident in this draft.) The boy asking if she is North American does not carry any weight. I think the weight we are looking for in the ending will be found back in the church. The title of the story is "Benedictions" after all. As you know, a benediction is a prayer for protection. What is it she needs protection *from?* Herself, it seems. But why?

Your last two sentences read: *I look at my watch. There is just time to reach the cantina and Mr. Lopez.* I am curious about your choice of having her appear to be almost late. I understand why you have made the decision—that time is running out for her, for all of us, and we better get on the straight and narrow and make some good decisions. But in the story, it doesn't work because she has no idea how long Mr. Lopez will stay at the cantina. He arrives at 2 P.M. He could stay until three. Or four. And the reader does not know what time it is when she looks at her watch.

I think a preferable ending would be inside the church, where you could illustrate the same thematic concern by having Virginia reflecting in the quiet solitude only to be interrupted by a woman who comes in and kneels beneath the crucifix—make it the crucifix—and begins to pray. That may be enough. The reader will see Virginia watching this woman pray for protection, and maybe the reader will wonder why Virginia doesn't pray as well. She sure does need the help.

O.K. Enough. You have greatly improved the story in this draft. I think you are just a few drafts away from finishing this. Then you might go find Kay and write a story about her.

—Tim

C H A P T E R

26

WORKSHOPPING A STORY IN THE THIRD PERSON

As you read the first draft of Ken Olsen's "Spending Azalea's Inheritance," consider the following:

1. The setting: Do you feel as if you are there? Why or why not? Where do you think the setting is most clearly drawn? How does he achieve that? To what senses does he appeal? Where is the setting undeveloped?

2. The characters: How well do you come to know them? Which do you feel you know best? Whose story is it? What do the characters want? Can any of the characters be eliminated?

3. The plot: What is at stake for whom? Can the stakes be raised? How is the pacing?

4. The dialogue: Is it a close approximation of how these people would speak? Are idioms appropriately used? Is it sufficiently embodied?

5. The point of view: How would the story be different in another pov? What is the narrative distance? How does that affect the story?

6. Voice: What is the narrator's voice? Is it affected by the time in which the story takes place?

Books must be read as deliberately and reservedly as they were written.

Henry David Thoreau

SPENDING AZALEA'S INHERITANCE

Ken Olsen

Kyle Sandvig lost control on a left-hand curve snaking through Washakie River Canyon on U.S. Highway 687.

His alarmed "son-of-a-bitch" joined shrieking tires and the metallic report of a handyman jack ricocheting around the back of his careening pickup. Belongings sluiced around the cab. A long white envelope whipped off the dash and, corner first, stabbed Kyle's right eye.

He erupted into more expletives.

Highway 687 long had been "Lucky 87" among bentonite haulers who plied its curves and, wired on speed or stupid from sleep deprivation, spilled their tractor-trailers trying to overachieve on these turns. The distressed semis slid into a guardrail if the drivers were lucky, into the canyon if they weren't, and almost always threw part of their gray-brown loads of powdery clay—used in oil-well drilling—into the Washakie River. Experienced drivers knew you couldn't make enough time on this road to squeeze an extra daily run between Grass Creek and Marlton. Newcomers learned the hard way. Or by seeing fresh remains of a mishap.

Kyle knew all this and still pushed the pickup. He ran all out in the straight stretches, jammed on the brakes just before the curves, pulled the truck down a gear and crammed the gas pedal to the floor to get maximum acceleration as he came out of the turns. All of which might have been fine, might have allowed him to successfully flirt with the odds, had it not been for two things:

The letter.

And the sudden appearance of a mule deer.

The letter was an attempt to address his father about the delicate subject of his father's new wife and his father's new will. Attempt. His father was a full-blooded Scandinavian who considered "how are you" complete emotional disclosure and welcomed feedback with the warmth of someone invited to share a case of amoebic dysentery. Never mind that Kyle's father had practically dictated every detail of Grandma Sandvig's will, even deciding how much of her sheep ranch she should gift to each of her children in the years before she died—an inheritance tax dodge.

Kyle also was afraid to express what he was feeling, knowing emotion would overwhelm him and he'd error on the side of bluntness. Simultaneously, anger and his mother's memory fought against letting the events of the last year and a half slide.

Less than two months after they had buried his mother, Kyle's father called to announce he'd married Azalea Barnaby Schule (pronounced 'School,' she demanded).

Kyle went out of his way not to be a jerk about this sudden intrusion into the void of his mother's death. He and his wife, Charley, sent a commanding bouquet of congratulatory flowers, flew home the first weekend possible, treated the newlyweds to dinner at the Deer Creek Inn and graciously agreed to Azalea's suggestion they anoint the occasion from the upper end of the wine list.

Everything about the meal was memorable. The new Mrs. Barnaby Schule Sandvig presented herself in blue silk pants suit, Clairol-dark hair in rigid order, makeup as careful as heart surgery and perfume demur. She stood nearly eye-to-eye with Kyle's father, a handsome compliment to his tall frame. She kept Peter close, sure to touch his lanky arm, pat his knee, or grab his long, spatulated fingers in hers. Peter's blue eyes waltzed. He'd give her a boyish smile and smooth the waves of his gray hair with his free hand. Being in love agreed with his health.

When she spoke, Kyle noticed the rightward offset of Azalea's lower jaw. And noticed she moved it in a circle after she finished speaking, as if chewing the last stray vowels.

Azalea left her light-blue blouse open well into the zone where some could have claimed cleavage. Instead she displayed purple-blue veins fanning out as if a road map were tattooed across her translucent skin.

Practically the only discourse during the top-drawer meal was a ninety-three-minute homily by Azalea on the wonders of Azalea and the Barnaby Schule clan (that's School, she reminded often, the rasp of her top denture dragging against the bottom denture). She somehow worked in a rant against the school lunch program as an appalling example of government waste, which particularly struck Kyle given that his mother had grown up extremely poor through no fault of laziness, drunkenness or other offenses Azalea mentioned.

Azalea asked a single question from fresh oyster appetizers through filet mignon and chocolate-raspberry torte with snifter of port. She leaned into the table, icy glare burning deep, and asked Kyle's wife, "what *is* your name?"

Charley, thinking Azalea wanted to know if she'd kept her last name when she married Kyle, replied "Guinn. Charley Guinn. It's Engli . . ."

"Charlie?" Azalea said.

"Oh, sorry. It's Charlene. My dad was counting on a son, after five daughters. So I've always been Charley."

Azalea stared a moment, then launched into the details of her father's career as a town councilman during World War II.

Next morning, Kyle and Charley took the early puddle-jumper to Denver and relayed back to Spokane by jet. Kyle stared out the window nearly the entire trip. Charley respected his need to brood and pulled out a sheaf of legal briefs. Kyle eventually noticed Charley hadn't turned a single page, no doubt lost in her own deliberations over keeping him from sucking them both into a multi-month dark mood. He couldn't figure a way to reassure her and lapsed back into his funk.

Charley finally probed Kyle over waffles after another twenty-four hours of silence.

"Your father seems happy."

"Azalea's pretty," Kyle conceded. "He's lonely. He hasn't fended for himself on the domestic front for something like four decades. They both cared for life-long mates who suffered long, difficult illnesses. He deserves happiness . . . companionship . . . after all he did those last six years for Mom."

Kyle grabbed a handful of fresh raspberries, dropped them on his waffle and vigorously put his fork to work.

"And you?" Charley asked.

"Mom's dead something over six weeks. He marries a woman he met while retrieving his car from the Ford shop."

"And?" Charley reached for Kyle's hand across the breakfast table, green eyes pouring into his, a strand of long blonde hair falling forward as she leaned toward him.

"She's not exactly father's type. Lake cabin. Boating. He throws up at the thought of water."

"She possesses some level of self-conferred pedigree," Charlie said with a nod. "Not the sort of thing I'd expect your father to seek out socially. Much less in marriage. How Scandanavian is that?"

"Azalea likes to RV. Mom hated to climb into that land barge. Dad had to sell his last Winnebago during the real estate bust in the early '80s and she was plenty riled when he bought an even bigger one the moment things turned around. Refused to go anywhere in it. Told him if he could afford an RV as big as a warehouse, he could afford to remodel her kitchen."

Kyle dropped his forehead onto Charley's hand and sighed.

"Azalea doesn't need a kitchen as long as Safeway sells deli platters," he said, looking up again. "She'd rather spend her time getting father to cart her around to see her friends than scaring up home-cooked food. And there's nothing like pulling up in your new husband's six-figure motorhome for making an impression."

Two months later Kyle and Charley returned to eastern Wyoming after receiving Peter's terse note about "removing your mother's excess belongings." Kyle took the occasion to ask his father to share the details of his new will.

Kari, his older sister, had pushed the idea. Living just 90 miles from Peter, she visited frequently and thought she'd overheard Azalea and Peter talking about making new wills during an impromptu appearance to drop off shirts she'd mended.

"You are really good at talking to him about these things," Kari said when she called to find out Kyle and Charley's travel plans. "You were the executor on his last will, so you've got the perfect entree."

"Translation: the Scandanavian convention forbids conversations about such personal topics but if anyone can get away with it, it's the male child?" Kyle said.

"Well, basically," Kari said. "I can't do it."

And probably shouldn't, Kyle thought, realizing his sister was too wrung out from running a preschool to engage Peter, even if she could violate tradition. And knowing that the task would fall to him preschool or not. She sewed up shirts, he mediated touchy family topics.

"There's no pretty version of this," Kyle said. "Peter Ander Sandvig, by Gum, earned every penny himself. No matter what's in the will, we can expect some sort of homily just for asking. Whatever. I'll run it up the flag pole."

Kyle saw Charley off on an early spring hike and he and Kari settled into deep high-backed chairs around the oblong conference table in Peter's home real estate office—panoramic views of the blue-green Big Horn range filling the picture windows. Peter dealt Kari and Kyle each a single page titled "Last Will and Testament of Peter Ander Sandvig."

The destiny of his moderately successful estate was mapped out in three clipped points. Any heir who challenged his will automatically inherited nothing. His personal possessions were for Azalea's use as long as she desired. The division of his assets were covered in a trust dated soon after Peter and Azalea's marriage.

"Trust?" Kyle said, running his hands through his wind-rumpled blondish hair. Except for height and age, he looked identical to his father, down to the Norse-blue eyes.

"Correct," Peter said.

"Do we get a look?" Kyle asked, glancing at Kari, who drew her five-foot, two-inch frame up to the table and nodded.

Peter put his hands on the edge of the table, looked at them for a moment, reluctantly shoved back, got up, and walked into the adjoining room. A file cabinet drawer opened and slammed. He strode back in and laid a copy of "Agreement for Establishment of Trust and Disbursement of Assets of Peter Ander Sandvig" in front of each of them.

Peter walked to the window and stared at the Big Horn Mountains. Financial success had come late in his career. His habit of throwing every dollar he could at a real estate venture had left him broke plenty of times but Peter just dug in and somehow pulled together another deal. He finally sold out at the right time and for once sat on the profits. Peter prized this three-hundred-thousand dollar view as just reward for his enterprise and tenacity. He always squared his shoulders as he gazed across the foothills from this vantage.

Kari gasped, diverting Kyle's eyes from his father's station at the window to the paper in front of him. The bulk of Peter's estate would go into a trust to provide for Azalea's needs. Distribution from the trust should be "generous." In the event that this wasn't sufficient, his house and his share of the Big Horn cabin—the only remnant of Grandma Sandvig's ranch still in the family—were to be sold. Once Azalea died, his children would split the remainder of the trust. After funeral expenses.

Kyle and Kari, meanwhile, would split a $12,487 retirement savings account and become joint owners of the "Yacht Club," a defunct seven-unit trailer court without occupants or—contrary to Peter's claim since obtaining it years earlier—"unlimited potential."

"Mom's estate?" Kyle said. "Didn't she have a little bit of stock in pharmaceuticals and something in savings?"

Peter turned from the window, came back to the table and dropped into his chair.

"It was, in its entirety, left to me."

"And?"

"That's the sum of the matter."

Kyle's raked his fingers through his hair and stammered stubbornly ahead.

"How?"

"Your mother bequeathed her assets to me," Peter said, pulling off his bifocals and discarding them on the table with an irritable clatter. "I am charged to do with them as I see best."

"Best?"

"This," Peter replied, pointing toward the trust.

"Huh. Guess I'm blind. Didn't see anything here about Mom's estate."

"It's covered. There."

Peter came out of his chair, leaned toward Kyle, and tapped on a particular paragraph with a fat black-and-gold fountain pen.

"This says Azalea gets a trust. The trust receives pretty much everything but that one IRA left over from your stint with Rogsdale Realty and the family's most glorious real estate holding . . ." Kyle stopped, noticing the tempo of his father's affirmative nod and the vein bulging in his father's neck.

"Forty-five years of marriage and Mom's contribution doesn't even get a cameo here?" Kyle asked. "What the . . ."

"Nursing homes are expensive," Peter said, clasping his hands together and looking down them like a gun sight. "Azalea's husband was ill for a long time. A very long time. She has nothing set aside and little retirement income."

"Screw this nursing home bullshit. I'm talking about Mom. My mother. The other Mrs. Sandvig. What's up with her stuff?"

"And for God sakes," Kari interjected. "Exactly when did Azalea's house in the heights and cabin at the lake become 'nothing set aside?'"

Peter ignored them, grabbed the bow of his gold-framed glasses, thrust them back on his face, stood and reached for the copies of the trust.

Kyle slammed his hand down on the papers. Peter stepped back.

"Take Mom's estate and establish a scholarship fund for poor kids like her from Ty Siding. Set up a fund to buy children's library books. Give something in her memory to the 'Save Cloud Peak Coalition.' Azalea still ought to get the queen's suite at Golden Crest Assisted Living."

"Exactly," Kari said.

Peter cleared his throat. "Azalea's situation left her with nothing. I have chosen to provide a trust to ensure her long-term care."

"Care? Nursing home? The way this reads she could build a swimming pool or go bake in the Caribbean," Kyle said. "She could give her children an allowance; she could take up with someone else on your dime."

"It is," Peter said, reaching over and jerking the copy of the trust out from under Kyle's hand "her affair."

Kyle, Charley and Kari took refuge in the least smoky bar in Marlton after Peter and Azalea retired for the night. Kyle fumed his way through straight shots of Maker's Mark.

"Mom gives up her career as an engraver—damn talented one at that—to bear his children, scrub his floors, even starch his dress shirts on the kitchen stove when he was losing his ass so bad they couldn't afford the dry cleaners."

"She gives him her pitiful savings when they married, gives him her meager inheritance so he can keep his real estate genius funded. Hell, she even patched pillow cases and sewed up the holes in our socks to keep us getting by."

"Here's Mom, who pulled together fine meals in that bachelor's kitchen—fickle oven, refrigerator you wedged closed with a chunk of wood jammed between the bottom of the door and the floor . . . barely enough counter space for a coffee pot. And her labor and sacrifice become Azalea's sweepstakes."

Kyle tipped back the last of the amber in his glass and looked around for a cocktail waitress. She arrived with a recharge. He took a long pull of bourbon.

Kari pushed her mug of coffee away, reached across the table and stole Kyle's glass. She sampled the drink, studied the glass and handed it back.

"That's slightly less shitty," Kari said, resuming her efforts to tie a plastic coffee stirring straw into a knot.

"You guys loved your mother very much," Charley said. "She'd be proud of you."

Charley offered her glass to Kari. Kari refused.

"One sip of a gin martini and I'd be asleep. Which I should get around to doing fairly soon."

Kyle and Charley loaded the pickup with mementos because U-Haul had misplaced their reservation and had only super-size trucks available for one-way rentals. They pulled out well into the night, unwilling to face the new administration in light of the new information. Once back in Spokane, Kyle spent months trying to write his father a letter. One that would explain his outrage, keep his father's jugular from bursting, and still stand up for the memory of his mother.

Kyle found it difficult to get the "dear asshole" flavor out of his repeated attempts. He tore up or tossed aside draft after draft.

Then Peter sent his own terse note:

Kyle:
The truck seems long overdue.
Love,
Father

"Jesus," Kyle said.

"Hon?" Charley called from the kitchen. "News from your dad?"

Kyle walked from the study to the stove, where Charley stirred potato-leek-cheddar soup in a stainless-steel pot.

"Eight words in four months. No return telephone calls. No other letters. Silence as cold as Azalea's stare."

"What did he say?" Charley asked.

"Bring back the truck."

"Like right now?"

"Like months ago."

Kyle hadn't rushed to return the midnight blue, four-wheel drive '89 Ford. It wasn't particularly comfortable and, because it was a diesel, clattered more than ran. At twelve feet long—a friend measured it as a joke—it handled like a pig in traffic. So Kyle and Charley used it to go fishing in places reachable only by muffler-robbing back roads when Kyle could sneak a summer weekend away from his newspaper photography job.

"Let's get a bumper sticker," Kyle said to Charley as a piece of chrome trim jiggled loose on the dusty August washboard and, with a metallic twing, went winging off into the dense stands of scraggly Douglas fir. "We're spending Azalea's inheritance."

His father's note came at an impossible time, a week before Kyle and Charley were scheduled for their first non-family vacation in four years—a long backpacking trip in the Cabinet-Yaak Wilderness. Peter knew when they were going. Kyle had written him about the trip—a letter actually mailed.

"What are you going to tell him?" Charley said, putting her hands on Kyle's waist, and leaning against him.

"I'll take off for his place Friday. Drive straight through. Grab a plane back."

"The letter?" she asked.

Kyle shrugged. "And tell him what?"

"What's brewing in there," Charley said, tapping Kyle's chest. "You can't just pack it around. It wears on both of us."

"Thanks for erasing mother from our lives? I appreciate you checking out before we had the chance to sort out her loss together? I didn't lose one parent, Charley, I lost two," Kyle said, shaking his head. "And you don't tell my father things. He has to osmosis them—well after the fact, when even regret feels like a cop out."

Charley turned back to the stove. "Give it another try," she said.

A smoldering Kyle jumped in the truck with a new letter two days later, intending to drive the 1,300 miles to his father's house in one shot, leave the truck in the driveway with the letter on the seat and disappear into the night. Or shove the letter in the mail slot. Or duct tape it to the windshield or dashboard. Or leave the truck in Meeteetse, catch a Greyhound back to the airport in Billings and call just before he boarded to say, "the keys are under the floor mat."

He'd replayed the possibilities a million ways. And was replaying them when the deer materialized feet from the left headlight. He jerked the truck hard right and immediately started to lose control.

Kyle fought the truck's slide, more by instinct from years of driving on snow and ice, than conscious effort.

"Get this under control," he cursed to himself, clipping a delineator post but mostly keeping the truck on the road. "Then what?"

A guardrail grabbed the right rear fender and, though Kyle had slowed the truck to under 50, sucked the entire vehicle into its embrace.

Kyle awoke in the medical/surgical wing of Northcentral Wyoming Medical Center at a day and an hour unknown to him. His sternum, abdomen and shoulder throbbed from the long bruise the shoulder and lap-belts had inflicted. The prickly, burning feeling came from the bits of glass launched into his face "upon impact," in the vernacular of the Highway Patrol. He felt relieved to wiggle his toes, to see his limbs weren't trussed up in traction.

Across the room, Peter Sandvig sat by the window, eye glasses perched pensively on his nose, his right fist grasping the letter, his left drumming the long, white envelope against his leg. The sight of his father in a hospital room alone was alarming. Peter crumpled at the sight of a bleeding finger. Having photographed more than his share of accident victims, Kyle knew the sight of his swollen face—much less camping here with the lacerated living image—would set his father to chewing the inside of his cheek.

If the letter didn't spark a something worse.

"I no longer feel welcome in your home or your heart," Peter read aloud, his voice grinding through the lines. "You pretend as if mother never existed and I . . ."

The door cracked opened. Azalea's head appeared.

"Peter?" she whispered. "Peter?" with more urgency.

Peter turned and gave a wave. "A few more minutes."

Kyle searched the room and confronted a potted miniature palm, endorsed with a "Speedy recovery, Love Azalea" card and parked with unmistakable purpose directly at his bedside. He groaned and rolled his head back toward the ceiling.

Peter slowly folded the letter and returned it to the envelope.

"Kyle," he started hoarsely as he rose from his seat, pulled off his glasses and made a gesture toward the door. "Charley's at the airport. Your sister's off to get her."

Kyle nodded, keeping his eyes on the letter.

"Rough landing, I guess?" Peter said.

Kyle gave a raspy "Yep."

"Seat belt's a great thing," Peter said, cocking an eye at his watch and glancing back at the door.

"What about the . . . sorry about the truck," Kyle offered.

Peter shrugged. "Somebody will buy it for parts." He sucked his cheek between his teeth for a slow moment, then continued. "The patrol-man said there was a bit of your personal stuff spread across the road. Little they could easily recover. This was addressed to me so I . . ."

Azalea cracked the door open again and called "Peter?"

Peter turned and gave a more brusque "in a few minutes." She withdrew.

"She doesn't know what your mother knew about patience," Peter said.

The two men looked past each other. Then Peter shook the letter.

"Family history isn't written or rewritten in a single letter, Kyle. Here you . . ."

"Just forget it," Kyle said, shrugging his shoulders and then grimacing from the pain. "Forget it. Let's not bother."

Peter cleared his throat.

Kyle face and neck throbbed. He settled back into the pillows and momentarily shut his eyes. He opened them again as he heard his father's quiet footsteps cross the room. The door opened and then softly closed.

The End

Before continuing, consider the following questions once again:

1. The setting: Do you feel as if you were there? Why or why not? Where do you think the setting is most clearly drawn? How does he

achieve that? To what senses does he appeal? Where is the setting undeveloped?

2. The characters: How well do you come to know them? Which do you feel you know best? Whose story is it? What do the characters want? Can any of the characters be eliminated?

3. The plot: What is at stake for whom? Can the stakes be raised? How is the pacing?

4. The dialogue: Is it a close approximation of how these people would speak? Are idioms appropriately used? Is it sufficiently embodied?

5. The point of view: How would the story be different in another pov? What is the narrative distance? How does that affect the story?

6. Voice: What is the narrator's voice? Is it affected by the time in which the story takes place?

When you have finished, look at this same draft with marginalia, and then the critique that follows the draft.

SPENDING AZALEA'S INHERITANCE

Ken Olsen

Kyle Sandvig lost control on a left-hand curve snaking through Washakie River Canyon on U.S. Highway 687.   Clarify time of day

His alarmed "son-of-a-bitch" joined shrieking tires and the metallic report of a handyman jack ricocheting around the back of his careening pickup. Belongings sluiced around the cab. A long white envelope whipped off the dash and, corner first, stabbed Kyle's right eye.

He erupted into more expletives.

Highway 687 long had been "Lucky 87" among bentonite haulers who plied its curves and, wired on speed or stupid from sleep deprivation, spilled their tractor-trailers trying to overachieve on these turns. The distressed semis slid into a guardrail if the drivers were lucky, into the canyon if they weren't, and almost always threw part of their gray-brown loads of powdery clay—used in oil-well drilling—into the Washakie River. Experienced drivers knew you couldn't make enough time on this road to squeeze an extra daily run between Grass Creek and Marlton. Newcomers learned the hard way. Or by seeing fresh remains of a mishap.

Kyle knew all this and still pushed the pickup. He ran all out in the straight stretches, jammed on the brakes just before the curves, pulled the truck down a gear and crammed the gas pedal to the floor to get maximum acceleration as he came out of the turns. All of which might have been fine, might have allowed him to successfully flirt with the odds, had it not been for two things:

The letter.

And the sudden appearance of a mule deer.

The letter was an attempt to address his father about the delicate subject of his father's new wife and his father's new will. Attempt. His father was a full-blooded Scandinavian who considered "how are you" complete emotional disclosure and welcomed feedback with the warmth of someone invited to share a case of amoebic dysentery. Never mind that Kyle's father had practically dictated every detail of Grandma Sandvig's will, even deciding how much of her sheep ranch she should gift to each of her children in the years before she died—an inheritance tax dodge.

Kyle also was afraid to express what he was feeling, knowing emotion would overwhelm him and he'd error on the side of bluntness. Simultaneously, anger and his mother's memory fought against letting the events of the last year and a half slide.

Less than two months after they had buried his mother, Kyle's father called to announce he'd married Azalea Barnaby Schule (pronounced 'School,' she demanded).

Kyle went out of his way not to be a jerk about this sudden intrusion into the void of his mother's death. He and his wife, Charley, sent a commanding bouquet of congratulatory flowers, flew home the first weekend possible, treated the newlyweds to dinner at the Deer Creek Inn and graciously agreed to Azalea's suggestion they anoint the occasion from the upper end of the wine list.

Marginal notes:

Authorial intrusion

Be specific i.e. Norwegian

Distracting image

Everything about the meal was memorable. The new Mrs. Barnaby Schule Sandvig presented herself in blue silk pants suit, Clairol-dark hair in rigid order, makeup as careful as heart surgery and perfume demur. She stood nearly eye-to-eye with Kyle's father, a handsome compliment to his tall frame. She kept Peter close, sure to touch his lanky arm, pat his knee, or grab his long, spatulated fingers in hers. Peter's blue eyes waltzed. He'd give her a boyish smile and smooth the waves of his gray hair with his free hand. Being in love agreed with his health.

Kyle's POV

When she spoke, Kyle noticed the rightward offset of Azalea's lower jaw. And noticed she moved it in a circle after she finished speaking, as if chewing the last stray vowels.

Azalea left her light-blue blouse open well into the zone where some could have claimed cleavage. Instead she displayed purple-blue veins fanning out as if a road map were tattooed across her translucent skin.

too long

Practically the only discourse during the top-drawer meal was a ninety-three-minute homily by Azalea on the wonders of Azalea and the Barnaby Schule clan (that's School, she reminded often, the rasp of her top denture dragging against the bottom denture). She somehow worked in a rant against the school lunch program as an appalling example of government waste, which particularly struck Kyle given that his mother had grown up extremely poor through no fault of laziness, drunkenness or other offenses Azalea mentioned.

Azalea asked a single question from fresh oyster appetizers through filet mignon and chocolate-raspberry torte with snifter of port. She leaned into the table, icy glare burning deep, and asked Kyle's wife, "what *is* your name?"

Charley, thinking Azalea wanted to know if she'd kept her last name when she married Kyle, replied "Guinn. Charley Guinn. It's Engli. . ."

Be consistent in spelling of charley

"Charlie?" Azalea said.

"Oh, sorry. It's Charlene. My dad was counting on a son, after five daughters. So I've always been Charley."

Azalea stared a moment, then launched into the details of her father's career as a town councilman during World War II.

Next morning, Kyle and Charley took the early puddle-jumper to Denver and relayed back to Spokane by jet. Kyle stared out the window nearly the entire trip. Charley respected his need to brood and pulled out a sheaf of legal briefs. Kyle eventually noticed Charley hadn't turned a single page, no doubt lost in her own deliberations over keeping him from sucking them both into a multi-month dark mood. He couldn't figure a way to reassure her and lapsed back into his funk.

Charley finally probed Kyle over waffles after another twenty-four hours of silence.

Need a Transition

"Your father seems happy."

"Azalea's pretty," Kyle conceded. "He's lonely. He hasn't fended for himself on the domestic front for something like four decades. They both cared for life-long mates who suffered long, difficult illnesses. He deserves happiness . . . companionship . . . after all he did those last six years for Mom."

Kyle grabbed a handful of fresh raspberries, dropped them on his waffle and vigorously put his fork to work.

Vigorously?

"And you?" Charley asked.

Embody the dialogue and clarify the setting

"Mom's dead something over six weeks. He marries a woman he met while retrieving his car from the Ford shop."

"And?" Charley reached for Kyle's hand across the breakfast table, green eyes pouring into his, a strand of long blonde hair falling forward as she leaned toward him.

"She's not exactly father's type. Lake cabin. Boating. He throws up at the thought of water."

"She possesses some level of self-conferred pedigree," Charlie said with a nod. "Not the sort of thing I'd expect your father to seek out socially. Much less in marriage. How Scandanavian is that?"

"Azalea likes to RV. Mom hated to climb into that land barge. Dad had to sell his last Winnebago during the real estate bust in the early '80s and she was plenty riled when he bought an even bigger one the moment things turned around. Refused to go anywhere in it. Told him if he could afford an RV as big as a warehouse, he could afford to remodel her kitchen."

Kyle dropped his forehead onto Charley's hand and sighed.

"Azalea doesn't need a kitchen as long as Safeway sells deli platters," he said, looking up again. "She'd rather spend her time getting father to cart her around to see her friends than scaring up home-cooked food. And there's nothing like pulling up in your new husband's six-figure motorhome for making an impression."

Two months later Kyle and Charley returned to eastern Wyoming after receiving Peter's terse note about "removing your mother's excess belongings." Kyle took the occasion to ask his father to share the details of his new will.

Kari, his older sister, had pushed the idea. Living just 90 miles from Peter, she visited frequently and thought she'd overheard Azalea and Peter talking about making new wills during an impromptu appearance to drop off shirts she'd mended.

"You are really good at talking to him about these things," Kari said when she called to find out Kyle and Charley's travel plans. "You were the executor on his last will, so you've got the perfect entree."

"Translation: the Scandanavian convention forbids conversations about such personal topics but if anyone can get away with it, it's the male child?" Kyle said.   Norwegian

"Well, basically," Kari said. "I can't do it."

And probably shouldn't, Kyle thought, realizing his sister was too wrung out from running a preschool to engage Peter, even if she could violate tradition. And knowing that the task would fall to him preschool or not. She sewed up shirts, he mediated touchy family topics.

"There's no pretty version of this," Kyle said. "Peter Ander Sandvig, by Gum, earned every penny himself. No matter what's in the will, we can expect some sort of homily just for asking. Whatever. I'll run it up the flag pole."

Kyle saw Charley off on an early spring hike and he and Kari settled into deep high-backed chairs around the oblong conference table in Peter's home real estate office—panoramic views of the blue-green Big Horn range filling the picture windows. Peter dealt Kari and Kyle each a single page titled "Last Will and Testament of Peter Ander Sandvig."

The destiny of his moderately successful estate was mapped out in three clipped points. Any heir who challenged his will automatically inherited nothing. His personal possessions were for Azalea's use as long as she desired. The division of his assets were covered in a trust dated soon after Peter and Azalea's marriage.

"Trust?" Kyle said, running his hands through his wind-rumpled blondish hair. Except for height and age, he looked identical to his father, down to the Norse-blue eyes.

"Correct," Peter said.

"Do we get a look?" Kyle asked, glancing at Kari, who drew her five-foot, two-inch frame up to the table and nodded.

Peter put his hands on the edge of the table, looked at them for a moment, reluctantly shoved back, got up, and walked into the adjoining room. A file cabinet drawer opened and slammed. He strode back in and laid a copy of "Agreement for Establishment of Trust and Disbursement of Assets of Peter Ander Sandvig" in front of each of them.

Peter walked to the window and stared at the Big Horn Mountains. Financial success had come late in his career. His habit of throwing every dollar he could at a real estate venture had left him broke plenty of times but Peter just dug in and somehow pulled together another deal. He finally sold out at the right time and for once sat on the profits. Peter prized this three-hundred-thousand dollar view as just reward for his enterprise and tenacity. He always squared his shoulders as he gazed across the foothills from this vantage.

Kari gasped, diverting Kyle's eyes from his father's station at the window to the paper in front of him. The bulk of Peter's estate would go into a trust to provide for Azalea's needs. Distribution from the trust should be "generous." In the event that this wasn't sufficient, his house and his share of the Big Horn cabin—the only remnant of Grandma Sandvig's ranch still in the family— were to be sold. Once Azalea died, his children would split the remainder of the trust. After funeral expenses.

Kyle and Kari, meanwhile, would split a $12,487 retirement savings account and become joint owners of the "Yacht Club," a defunct seven-unit trailer court without occupants or—contrary to Peter's claim since obtaining it years earlier— "unlimited potential."

"Mom's estate?" Kyle said. "Didn't she have a little bit of stock in pharmaceuticals and something in savings?"

Peter turned from the window, came back to the table and dropped into his chair.

"It was, in its entirety, left to me."

"And?"

"That's the sum of the matter."

Kyle's raked his fingers through his hair and stammered stubbornly ahead.

"How?"

"Your mother bequeathed her assets to me," Peter said, pulling off his bifocals and discarding them on the table with an irritable clatter. "I am charged to do with them as I see best."

"Best?"

"This," Peter replied, pointing toward the trust.

"Huh. Guess I'm blind. Didn't see anything here about Mom's estate."

"It's covered. There."

Peter came out of his chair, leaned toward Kyle, and tapped on a particular paragraph with a fat black-and-gold fountain pen.

"This says Azalea gets a trust. The trust receives pretty much everything but that one IRA left over from your stint with Rogsdale Realty and the family's most glorious real estate holding

. . ." Kyle stopped, noticing the tempo of his father's affirmative nod and the vein bulging in his father's neck.

"Forty-five years of marriage and Mom's contribution doesn't even get a cameo here?" Kyle asked. "What the . . ."

"Nursing homes are expensive," Peter said, clasping his hands together and looking down them like a gun sight. "Azalea's husband was ill for a long time. A very long time. She has nothing set aside and little retirement income."

"Screw this nursing home bullshit. I'm talking about Mom. My mother. The other Mrs. Sandvig. What's up with her stuff?"

"And for God sakes," Kari interjected. "Exactly when did Azalea's house in the heights and cabin at the lake become 'nothing set aside?'"

Peter ignored them, grabbed the bow of his gold-framed glasses, thrust them back on his face, stood and reached for the copies of the trust.

Kyle slammed his hand down on the papers. Peter stepped back.

"Take Mom's estate and establish a scholarship fund for poor kids like her from Ty Siding. Set up a fund to buy children's library books. Give something in her memory to the 'Save Cloud Peak Coalition.' Azalea still ought to get the queen's suite at Golden Crest Assisted Living."

"Exactly," Kari said.

Peter cleared his throat. "Azalea's situation left her with nothing. I have chosen to provide a trust to ensure her long-term care."

"Care? Nursing home? The way this reads she could build a swimming pool or go bake in the Caribbean," Kyle said. "She could give her children an allowance; she could take up with someone else on your dime."

"It is," Peter said, reaching over and jerking the copy of the trust out from under Kyle's hand "her affair."

Kyle, Charley and Kari took refuge in the least smoky bar in Marlton after Peter and Azalea retired for the night. Kyle fumed his way through straight shots of Maker's Mark.

do we need "least smoky"?

"Mom gives up her career as an engraver—damn talented one at that—to bear his children, scrub his floors, even starch his dress shirts on the kitchen stove when he was losing his ass so bad they couldn't afford the dry cleaners."

"She gives him her pitiful savings when they married, gives him her meager inheritance so he can keep his real estate genius funded. Hell, she even patched pillow cases and sewed up the holes in our socks to keep us getting by."

"Here's Mom, who pulled together fine meals in that bachelor's kitchen—fickle oven, refrigerator you wedged closed with a chunk of wood jammed between the bottom of the door and the floor . . . barely enough counter space for a coffee pot. And her labor and sacrifice become Azalea's sweepstakes."

Clarify who is speaking and embody

Kyle tipped back the last of the amber in his glass and looked around for a cocktail waitress. She arrived with a recharge. He took a long pull of bourbon.

Kari pushed her mug of coffee away, reached across the table and stole Kyle's glass. She sampled the drink, studied the glass and handed it back.

"That's slightly less shitty," Kari said, resuming her efforts to tie a plastic coffee stirring straw into a knot.

"You guys loved your mother very much," Charley said. "She'd be proud of you."

Charley offered her glass to Kari. Kari refused.

"One sip of a gin martini and I'd be asleep. Which I should get around to doing fairly soon."

Kyle and Charley loaded the pickup with mementos because U-Haul had misplaced their reservation and had only super-size trucks available for one-way rentals. They pulled out well into the night, unwilling to face the new administration in light of the new information. Once back in Spokane, Kyle spent months trying to write his father a letter. One that would explain his outrage, keep his father's jugular from bursting, and still stand up for the memory of his mother.

awkward sentence

Kyle found it difficult to get the "dear ass-hole" flavor out of his repeated attempts. He tore up or tossed aside draft after draft.

Then Peter sent his own terse note:

Kyle:
The truck seems long overdue.
Love,
Father

"Jesus," Kyle said.

"Hon?" Charley called from the kitchen. "News from your dad?"

Kyle walked from the study to the stove, where Charley stirred potato-leek-cheddar soup in a stainless-steel pot.

"Eight words in four months. No return telephone calls. No other letters. Silence as cold as Azalea's stare."

"What did he say?" Charley asked.

"Bring back the truck."

"Like right now?"

"Like months ago."

Kyle hadn't rushed to return the midnight blue, four-wheel drive '89 Ford. It wasn't particularly comfortable and, because it was a diesel, clattered more than ran. At twelve feet long—a friend measured it as a joke—it handled like a pig in traffic. So Kyle and Charley used it to go fishing in places reachable only by muffler-robbing back roads when Kyle could sneak a summer weekend away from his newspaper photography job.

"Let's get a bumper sticker," Kyle said to Charley as a piece of chrome trim jiggled loose on the dusty August washboard and, with a metallic twing, went winging off into the dense stands of scraggly Douglas fir. "We're spending Azalea's inheritance."

His father's note came at an impossible time, a week before Kyle and Charley were scheduled for their first non-family vacation in four years—a long backpacking trip in the Cabinet-Yaak Wilderness. Peter knew when they were going. Kyle had written him about the trip—a letter actually mailed.

"What are you going to tell him?" Charley said, putting her hands on Kyle's waist, and leaning against him.

"I'll take off for his place Friday. Drive straight through. Grab a plane back."

"The letter?" she asked.

Kyle shrugged. "And tell him what?"

"What's brewing in there," Charley said, tapping Kyle's chest. "You can't just pack it around. It wears on both of us."

"Thanks for erasing mother from our lives? I appreciate you checking out before we had the chance to sort out her loss together? I didn't lose one parent, Charley, I lost two," Kyle said, shaking his head. "And you don't tell my father things. He has to osmosis them—well after the fact, when even regret feels like a cop out."

Charley turned back to the stove. "Give it another try," she said.

A smoldering Kyle jumped in the truck with a new letter two days later, intending to drive the 1,300 miles to his father's house in one shot, leave the truck in the driveway with the letter on the seat and disappear into the night. Or shove the letter in the mail slot. Or duct tape it to the windshield or dashboard. Or leave the truck in Meeteetse, catch a Greyhound back to the airport in Billings and call just before he boarded to say, "the keys are under the floor mat."

He'd replayed the possibilities a million ways. And was replaying them when the deer materialized feet from the left headlight. He jerked the truck hard right and immediately started to lose control.

Kyle fought the truck's slide, more by instinct from years of driving on snow and ice, than conscious effort.

"Get this under control," he cursed to himself, clipping a delineator post but mostly keeping the truck on the road. "Then what?"

A guardrail grabbed the right rear fender and, though Kyle had slowed the truck to under 50, sucked the entire vehicle into its embrace.

Kyle awoke in the medical/surgical wing of Northcentral Wyoming Medical Center at a day and an hour unknown to him. His sternum, abdomen and shoulder throbbed from the long bruise the shoulder and lap-belts had inflicted. The prickly, burning feeling came from the bits of glass launched into his face "upon impact," in the vernacular of the Highway Patrol. He felt relieved to wiggle his toes, to see his limbs weren't trussed up in traction.

Across the room, Peter Sandvig sat by the window, eye glasses perched pensively on his nose, his right fist grasping the letter, his left drumming the long, white envelope against his leg. The sight of his father in a hospital room alone was alarming. Peter crumpled at the sight of a bleeding finger. Having photographed more than his share of accident victims, Kyle knew the sight of his swollen face—much less camping here with the lacerated living image—would set his father to chewing the inside of his cheek.

If the letter didn't spark a something worse.

"I no longer feel welcome in your home or your heart," Peter read aloud, his voice grinding through the lines. "You pretend as if mother never existed and I . . ."

The door cracked opened. Azalea's head appeared.

"Peter?" she whispered. "Peter?" with more urgency.

Peter turned and gave a wave. "A few more minutes."

Kyle searched the room and confronted a potted miniature palm, endorsed with a "Speedy recovery, Love Azalea" card and parked with unmistakable purpose directly at his bedside. He groaned and rolled his head back toward the ceiling.

Peter slowly folded the letter and returned it to the envelope.

"Kyle," he started hoarsely as he rose from his seat, pulled off his glasses and made a gesture toward the door. "Charley's at the airport. Your sister's off to get her."

Kyle nodded, keeping his eyes on the letter.

"Rough landing, I guess?" Peter said.

Kyle gave a raspy "Yep."

"Seat belt's a great thing," Peter said, cocking an eye at his watch and glancing back at the door.

"What about the . . . sorry about the truck," Kyle offered.

Peter shrugged. "Somebody will buy it for parts." He sucked his cheek between his teeth for a slow moment, then continued. "The patrolman said there was a bit of your personal stuff spread across the road. Little they could easily recover. This was addressed to me so I . . ."

Azalea cracked the door open again and called "Peter?"

Peter turned and gave a more brusque "in a few minutes." She withdrew.

"She doesn't know what your mother knew about patience," Peter said.

The two men looked past each other. Then Peter shook the letter.

"Family history isn't written or rewritten in a single letter, Kyle. Here you . . ."

"Just forget it," Kyle said, shrugging his shoulders and then grimacing from the pain. "Forget it. Let's not bother."

Peter cleared his throat.

Kyle's face and neck throbbed. He settled back into the pillows and momentarily shut his eyes. He opened them again as he heard his father's quiet footsteps cross the room. The door opened and then softly closed.

cut the last 2 sentences

Critique

Ken,

This is a very good draft with a lot of potential. You do a good job of revealing the inner conflict Ken faces without ever telling us how he feels—in other words, you do a good job of showing and not telling here.

I'm going to go through this draft page by page before discussing the ending, and it is the ending that needs the most work.

First, take out that appositive set off by dashes on page one ("used in oil drilling"). While it is useful information, the way it is imparted is what we call authorial intrusion. We can see the heavy hand of the author there, and that should not be apparent. You have awakened the reader from what John Gardner called the "fictional dream."

Later in the story, we see that it is night, that Kyle is driving with his headlights on. However, we do not get a sense of it being night on page one. Clarify the darkness of night on page one not only for consistency, but driving fast on a dangerous road at night raises the tension.

You mention that his father is Scandinavian, but why not be specific and call him Norwegian or Swedish? Be specific. You have a great line in that paragraph where you write " . . . who considered "How are you?" complete emotional disclosure . . ." but stop there. The rest of that line detracts from what you have already completed, and "amoebic dysentery" is a distracting image here. This is a good example of where less is more.

In the paragraph where you describe "the new Mrs. Barnaby Schule" you have a slight, very slight shift in point of view. You have established that this story is of the third person limited point of view (limited to Kyle), and at the end of this paragraph you write, *Being in love agreed with his health.* This sounds like it comes from a third person omniscient narrator rather than an observation of Kyle's, but you can mitigate the statement by adding the words *seemed to* and then there is no shift. *Being in love seemed to agree with his health.*

You need a transition between the paragraphs where Charley and Kyle return home, and the one where they are eating waffles. A couple of paragraphs down, remove the adverb *vigorously* because it focuses the reader's attention on the act of eating with no apparent reason.

In that same scene, embody the dialogue and give the reader a better sense of the physical world, in this case, the kitchen. What objects are in this room? What is the morning light like? The way it is, we could be anywhere. Are there objects here that would reveal something about Kyle's character? Are there pictures on the refrigerator?

Is there a picture of Kyle and his dad holding a string of trout taken when Kyle was a little boy? Something like this could help create some resonance in the ending.

When Kyle, Charley and Kari (these names all seem a bit too similar) got to the bar in Marlton, embody that dialogue and clarify *who* is speaking. Then clarify the passage of time. Do they leave that night right after having been drinking in the bar? Then fix that sentence that ends *face the new administration in light of new information*—again, we can feel the author's presence here and this pulls us out of the fictional dream you have created.

Okay, the pacing of the story has been very good. Now we are back to the accident. While this is not quite a framed story (because you don't end with the accident that you began with), it is pretty close to being one. You end with Kyle closing his eyes on his father, and then opening them as his father walks out. Better to end it by cutting the last two sentences so Kyle remains in control, so that he closes his eyes on his dad. Apparently he has given up in his efforts to have his dad recognize the importance his deceased mother had in both of their lives, and in that, he is giving up on a future with his father, but because we never knew what their relationship was as Kyle grew up, there is no resonance here. I would feel something, however, if there were earlier allusions to Kyle and his father doing something together in the long ago past. Little League? Boy Scouts? Fishing? Something to show that Kyle always hoped they would have the relationship that he wanted, that he pretended they had during a baseball game or a camping trip, but now, finally, he realizes all his efforts have been futile and that he is finally giving up. If you do that, Ken, then you will have the resonance you need in this final scene.

Good work here. I enjoyed this.

—Tim

Revision

SPENDING AZALEA'S INHERITANCE

Ken Olsen

Kyle Sandvig lost control on a left-hand curve snaking through Washakie River Canyon on U.S. Highway 687.

His alarmed "son-of-a-bitch" joined shrieking tires and the metallic report of a handyman jack ricocheting around the back of his careening pickup. Belongings sluiced around the cab. A long white envelope—with a ballpoint pen clipped to one end—whipped off the dash and, corner first, hit Kyle's right eye.

He erupted into more expletives.

Highway 687 long had been "Lucky 87" among bentonite haulers who plied its curves and, wired on speed or stupid from sleep deprivation, spilled their tractor-trailers trying to overachieve on these turns. The distressed semis slid into a guardrail if the drivers were lucky, into the canyon if they weren't, and almost always threw part of their gray-brown loads of powdery clay into the Washakie River. Experienced drivers knew you couldn't make enough time on this road to squeeze an extra daily run between Grass Creek and Marlton. Newcomers learned the hard way. Or by seeing fresh remains of a mishap.

Kyle knew all this from years of driving these roads and two summer stints loading bentonite trucks to make college tuition money. And still pushed the pickup despite it being night. He ran all out in the straight stretches, jammed on the brakes just before the curves, pulled the truck down a gear and crammed the gas pedal to the floor to get maximum acceleration as he came out of the turns. All of which might have been fine, might have allowed him to successfully flirt with the odds, had it not been for two things:

The letter.

And the sudden appearance of a mule deer.

The letter was an attempt to address his father about the delicate subject of his father's new wife and his father's new will. Attempt. His father was a full-blooded Norwegian who considered "how are you" complete emotional disclosure and advice an affront. Never mind that Kyle's father had practically dictated every detail of Grandma Sandvig's will, even deciding how much of her sheep ranch she should gift to each of her children in the years before she died—an inheritance tax dodge.

Kyle also was afraid to express what he was feeling, knowing emotion would overwhelm him and he'd error on the side of bluntness. Simultaneously, anger and his mother's memory fought against letting the events of the last year and a half slide.

Less than two months after they had buried his mother, Kyle's father called to announce he'd married Azalea Barnaby Schule (pronounced 'School,' she demanded).

Kyle went out of his way not to be a jerk about this sudden intrusion into the void of his mother's death. He and his wife, Charley, sent a commanding bouquet of congratulatory flowers, flew home the first weekend possible, treated the newlyweds to dinner at the Deer Creek Inn and graciously agreed to Azalea's suggestion they anoint the occasion from the upper end of the wine list.

Everything about the meal was memorable. The new Mrs. Barnaby Schule Sandvig presented herself in blue silk pants suit, Clairol-dark hair in rigid order, makeup as careful as heart surgery and perfume demur. She stood nearly eye-to-eye with Kyle's father, a handsome compliment to his tall frame. She kept Peter close, sure to touch his lanky arm, pat his knee, or grab his long, spatulated fingers in hers. Peter's blue eyes waltzed. He'd give her a boyish smile and smooth the waves of his gray hair with his free hand. Being in love agreed with his health.

When she spoke, Kyle noticed the rightward offset of Azalea's lower jaw. And noticed she moved it in a circle after she finished speaking, as if chewing the last stray vowels.

Azalea left her light-blue blouse open well into the zone where some could have claimed cleavage. Instead she displayed purple-blue veins fanning out as if a road map were tattooed across her translucent skin.

Practically the only discourse during the top-drawer meal was a hour-long homily by Azalea on the wonders of Azalea and the Barnaby Schule clan (that's School, she reminded often, the rasp of her top denture dragging against the bottom denture). She somehow worked in a rant against the school lunch program as an appalling example of government waste, which particularly struck Kyle given that his mother had grown up extremely poor through no fault of laziness, drunkenness or other offenses Azalea mentioned.

Azalea asked a single question from fresh oyster appetizers through filet mignon and chocolate-raspberry torte with snifter of port. She leaned into the table, icy glare burning deep, and asked Kyle's wife, "what *is* your name?"

Charley, thinking Azalea wanted to know if she'd kept her last name when she married Kyle, replied "Guinn. Charley Guinn. It's Engli. . ."

"Charlie?" Azalea said.

"Oh, sorry. It's Charlene. My dad was counting on a son, after five daughters. So I've always been Charley."

Azalea stared a moment, then launched into the details of her father's career as a town councilman during World War II.

Next morning, Kyle and Charley took the early puddle-jumper to Denver and relayed back to Spokane by jet. Kyle stared out the window nearly the entire trip. Charley respected his need to brood and pulled out a sheaf of legal briefs. Kyle eventually noticed Charley hadn't turned a single page, no doubt lost in her own deliberations over keeping him from miring both of them in a multi-month dark mood. He couldn't figure a way to reassure her and lapsed back into his funk.

Charley finally probed Kyle over waffles after another twenty-four hours of silence.

"Your father seems happy."

"Azalea's pretty and intelligent," Kyle conceded. "He's lonely. He hasn't fended for himself on the domestic front for something like four decades. They both cared for life-long mates who suffered long, difficult illnesses. He deserves happiness . . . companionship . . . after all he did those last six years for Mom."

Kyle grabbed a handful of fresh raspberries, dropped them on his waffle and put his fork to work.

"And you?" Charley asked.

"Mom's dead something over six weeks. He marries a woman he met while retrieving his car from the Ford shop."

"And?" Charley reached for Kyle's hand across the breakfast table, a strand of long brown hair falling forward as she leaned toward him.

"She's not exactly father's type. Lake front cabin. Boating. He throws up at the thought of water."

"She possesses some level of self-conferred pedigree," Charlie said with a nod. "Not the sort of thing I'd expect your father to seek out socially. Much less in marriage. How Norwegian is that?"

"Azalea likes to RV. Mom hated to climb into that land barge. Dad had to sell his last Winnebago during the real estate bust in the early '80s and she was plenty riled when he bought an even bigger one the moment things turned around. Refused to go anywhere in it. Told him if he could afford an RV as big as a warehouse, he could afford to remodel her kitchen."

Kyle dropped his forehead onto Charley's hand and sighed.

"Azalea doesn't need a kitchen as long as Safeway sells deli platters," he said, looking up again. "She'd rather spend her time getting Father to cart her around to see her friends than scaring up home-cooked food.

And there's nothing like pulling up in your new husband's six-figure motor home for making an impression."

Two months later Kyle and Charley returned to eastern Wyoming after receiving Peter's terse note about "removing your mother's excess belongings." Kyle took the occasion to ask his father to share the details of his new will.

Kari, his older sister, had pushed the idea. Living just 90 miles from Peter, she visited frequently and thought she'd overheard Azalea and Peter talking about making new wills during an impromptu appearance to drop off shirts she'd mended.

"You are really good at talking to him about these things," Kari said when she called to find out Kyle and Charley's travel plans. "You were the executor on his last will, so you've got the perfect entree."

"There's no pretty version of this," Kyle said. "Peter Ander Sandvig, by gum, earned every penny himself. No matter what's in the will, we can expect some sort of homily just for asking. Whatever. I'll run it up the flag pole."

Kyle saw Charley off on an early spring hike and he and Kari settled into deep high-backed chairs around the oblong conference table in Peter's home real estate office—panoramic views of the blue-green Big Horn range filling the picture windows. Peter dealt Kari and Kyle each a single page titled "Last Will and Testament of Peter Ander Sandvig."

The destiny of his moderately successful estate was mapped out in three clipped points. Any heir who challenged his will automatically inherited nothing. His personal possessions were for Azalea's use as long as she desired. The division of his assets was covered in a trust dated soon after Peter and Azalea's marriage.

"Trust?" Kyle said, running his hands through his wind-rumpled blondish hair. Except for height and age, he looked identical to his father, down to the Norse-blue eyes.

"Correct," Peter said.

"Do we get a look?" Kyle asked, glancing at Kari, who drew her five-foot, two-inch frame up to the table and nodded.

Peter put his hands on the edge of the table, looked at them for a moment, reluctantly shoved back, got up, and walked into the adjoining room. A file cabinet drawer opened and slammed. He strode back in and laid a copy of "Agreement for Establishment of Trust and Disbursement of Assets of Peter Ander Sandvig" in front of each of them.

Peter walked to the window and stared at the mountains. Financial success had come late in his career and his endless scramble left him unable or unwilling to respond to Kyle's childhood pestering to go fishing, hunting or practice baseball. His habit of throwing every dollar he could at a real estate venture left him broke plenty of times but Peter just dug in and somehow pulled together another deal. He finally sold out at the right time and for once sat on the profits. Peter prized this three-hundred-thousand dollar view as just reward for his enterprise and tenacity. He always squared his shoulders as he gazed across the foothills from this vantage.

Kyle heard Kari gasp and shifted his eyes from his father's station at the window to the paper in front of him. The bulk of Peter's estate would go into a trust to provide for Azalea's needs. Distribution from the trust should be "generous." In the event that this wasn't sufficient, his house and his share of the Big Horn cabin—the only remnant of Grandma Sandvig's ranch still in the family—were to be sold. Once Azalea died, his children would split the remainder of the trust. After funeral expenses.

Kyle and Kari, meanwhile, would split a $12,487 retirement savings account and become joint owners of the "Yacht Club," a defunct seven-unit trailer court without occupants or—contrary to Peter's claim since obtaining it years earlier—"unlimited potential."

"And Mom's estate?" Kyle said. "Didn't she have a little bit of stock in pharmaceuticals and something in savings?"

Peter turned from the window, came back to the table and dropped into his chair.

"It was, in its entirety, left to me."

"And?"

"That's the sum of the matter."

Kyle's raked his fingers through his hair and stammered stubbornly ahead.

"How?"

"Your mother bequeathed her assets to me," Peter said, pulling off his bifocals and discarding them on the table with an irritated clatter. "I am charged to do with them as I see best."

"Best?"

"This," Peter replied, pointing toward the trust.

"Huh. Guess I'm blind. Didn't see anything here about Mom's estate."

"It's covered. There."

Peter came out of his chair, leaned toward Kyle, and tapped on a particular paragraph with a fat black-and-gold fountain pen.

"This says Azalea gets a trust. The trust receives pretty much everything but that IRA left over from your stint with Rogsdale Realty and the family's most glorious real estate holding . . ." Kyle stopped, noticing the tempo of his father's affirmative nod and the vein bulging in his father's neck.

"Forty-five years of marriage and Mom's contribution doesn't even get a cameo here?" Kyle asked. "What the . . ."

"Nursing homes are expensive," Peter said, clasping his hands together and looking down them like a gun sight. "Azalea's husband was ill for a long time. A very long time. She has nothing set aside and little retirement income."

"Screw this nursing home bullshit. I'm talking about Mom. My mother. The other Mrs. Sandvig. What's up with her stuff?"

"And for God sakes," Kari interjected. "Exactly when did Azalea's house in the heights and cabin at the lake become 'nothing set aside?'"

Peter ignored them, grabbed the bow of his gold-framed glasses, thrust them back on his face, stood and reached for the copies of the trust.

Kyle slammed his hand down on the papers. Peter stepped back.

"Take Mom's estate and establish a scholarship fund for poor kids like her from Ty Siding. Set up a fund to buy children's library books. Give something in her memory to the 'Save Cloud Peak Coalition.' Azalea still ought to get the queen's suite at Golden Crest Assisted Living."

"Exactly," Kari said.

Peter cleared his throat. "Azalea's situation left her with nothing. I have chosen to provide a trust to ensure her long-term care."

"Care? Nursing home? The way this reads she could build a swimming pool or go bake in the Caribbean," Kyle said. "She could give her children an allowance; she could take up with someone else on your dime."

"It is," Peter said, reaching over and jerking the copy of the trust out from under Kyle's hand "her affair."

Kyle, Charley and Kari took refuge in the least smoky bar in Marlton after Peter and Azalea retired for the night. Kyle fumed his way through straight shots of Maker's Mark.

"Mom gives up her career as an engraver—damn talented one at that—to bear his children, scrub his floors, even hand starch his dress shirts when he was losing his ass so bad they couldn't afford the dry cleaners," Kyle said, slamming his empty glass on the table.

"She gives him her pitiful savings when they get married, gives him her meager inheritance so he can keep his real estate genius funded. Hell, she even patched pillow cases and sewed up the holes in our socks to keep us getting by."

Kyle picked up his glass, recentered it on the well-stained coaster several times, looked back at his sister and continued.

"Here's Mom, who pulled together fine meals in that bachelor's kitchen—fickle oven, refrigerator you wedged closed with a chunk of wood jammed between the bottom of the door and the floor . . . barely enough counter space for a coffee pot. And her labor and sacrifice become Azalea's sweepstakes."

Kyle turned in his seat and waved at the cocktail waitress with exasperation. She trotted over with a recharge. He took a long pull of bourbon.

Kari pushed her mug of coffee away, reached across the table and stole Kyle's glass. She sampled the drink and handed it back.

"This is slightly less awful than what they call coffee," Kari said, scowling at her barely touched mug.

Charley offered her glass to Kari to no avail.

"One sip of a gin martini and I'd be asleep," Kari said with a weary smile. "Which I should do fairly soon."

Kyle and Charley stayed up long enough to load the pickup with mementos after returning from the bar. Peter had offered it after they learned U-Haul had misplaced their reservation and had only super-size trucks available for one-way rentals. Kyle quickly accepted, sensing the pickup loan carried complications, but more anxious to end the visit than worry about future details.

They pulled out before anyone else was awake the next morning, unwilling to face the new administration in light of Peter's revelations. Once back in Spokane, Kyle spent months trying to write his father a letter. One that would explain his outrage, keep his father's jugular from bursting, and still stand up for the memory of his mother.

Kyle found it difficult to get the "dear asshole" flavor out of his repeated attempts. He tore up or tossed aside draft after draft.

Then Peter sent his own terse note:

Kyle:
The truck seems long overdue.
Love,
Father

"Jesus," Kyle said.

"Hon?" Charley called from the kitchen. "News from your dad?"

Kyle walked from the study to the stove, where Charley stirred potato-leek-cheddar soup in a stainless-steel pot.

"Eight words in four months. No return telephone calls. No other letters. Silence as cold as Azalea's stare."

"What did he say?" Charley asked.

"Bring back the truck."

"Like right now?"

"Like months ago."

Kyle hadn't rushed to return the midnight blue, four-wheel drive '89 Ford. It wasn't particularly comfortable and, because it was a diesel, clattered more than ran. At twelve feet long—a friend measured it as a joke—it handled like a pig in traffic. So Kyle and Charley used it to go fishing in places reachable only by muffler-robbing back roads when Kyle could sneak a summer weekend away from his newspaper photography job.

"Let's get a bumper sticker," Kyle said to Charley as a piece of chrome trim jiggled loose on the dusty August washboard and went winging off into the dense stands of scraggly Douglas fir with a metallic twing. "We're spending Azalea's inheritance."

302 PART TWO **Fiction**

His father's note came at an impossible time, a week before Kyle and Charley were scheduled for their first non-family vacation in four years—a long backpacking trip in the Cabinet-Yaak Wilderness. Peter knew when they were going. Kyle had written him about the trip—a letter actually mailed.

"What are you going to tell him?" Charley said, putting her hands on Kyle's waist, and leaning against him.

"I'll take off for his place Friday. Drive straight through. Grab a plane back."

"The letter?" she asked.

Kyle shrugged. "And tell him what?"

"What's brewing in there," Charley said, tapping Kyle's chest. "You can't just pack it around. It wears on both of us."

"Thanks for erasing mother from our lives? I appreciate you checking out before we had the chance to sort out her loss together? I didn't lose one parent, Charley, I lost two," Kyle said, shaking his head. "And you don't tell my father things. He has to osmosis them—well after the fact, when even regret feels like a copout."

Charley turned back to the stove. "Give it another try," she said.

A smoldering Kyle jumped in the truck with a new letter two days later, intending to drive the 1,300 miles to his father's house in one shot, leave the truck in the driveway with the letter on the seat and disappear into the night. Or shove the letter in the mail slot. Or duct tape it to the windshield or dashboard. Or leave the truck in Meeteetse, catch a Greyhound back to the airport in Billings and call just before he boarded to say, "the keys are under the floor mat."

He'd replayed the possibilities a million ways. And was replaying them when the deer materialized feet from the left headlight. He jerked the truck hard right and immediately started to lose control.

Kyle fought the truck's slide, more by instinct from years of driving on snow and ice, than conscious effort.

"Get this under control," he cursed to himself, clipping a delineator post but mostly keeping the truck on the road. "Then what?"

A guardrail grabbed the right rear fender and, though Kyle had slowed the truck to under 50, sucked the entire vehicle into its embrace.

Kyle awoke in the medical/surgical wing of Northcentral Wyoming Medical Center at a day and an hour unknown to him. His sternum, abdomen and shoulder throbbed from the long bruise the shoulder and lap-belts had inflicted. The prickly, burning feeling came from the bits of glass launched into his face "upon impact," in the vernacular of the Highway Patrol. He felt relieved to wiggle his toes, to see his limbs weren't trussed up in traction.

Across the room, Peter Sandvig sat by the window, eye glasses perched pensively on his nose, his right fist grasping the letter, his left drumming the long, white envelope against his leg. The sight of his father in a hospital room alone was alarming. Peter crumpled at the sight of a bleeding finger. Having photographed more than his share of accident victims, Kyle knew the sight of his swollen face would set his father to chewing the inside of his cheek.

If the letter didn't spark something worse.

"I no longer feel welcome in your home or your heart," Peter read aloud, his voice grinding through the lines. "You pretend as if mother never existed and I. . ."

The door cracked opened. Azalea's head appeared.

"Peter?" she whispered. "Peter?" with more urgency.

Peter turned and gave a wave. "A few more minutes."

Kyle searched the room, confronted a potted miniature palm—endorsed with a "Speedy recovery, Love Azalea" card—and parked with unmistakable purpose directly at his bedside. He groaned and rolled his head back toward the ceiling.

Peter slowly folded the letter and returned it to the envelope.

"Kyle," he started hoarsely as he rose from his seat, pulled off his glasses and made a gesture toward the door. "Charley's at the airport. Your sister's off to get her."

Kyle nodded, keeping his eyes on the letter.

"Rough landing, I guess?" Peter said.

Kyle gave a raspy "Yep."

"Seat belt's a great thing," Peter said, cocking an eye at his watch and glancing back at the door.

"What about the . . . sorry about the truck," Kyle offered.

Peter shrugged. "Somebody will buy it for parts." He pinched his cheek between his teeth for a slow moment, then continued. "The patrolman said there was a bit of your personal stuff spread across the road. Little they could easily recover. This was addressed to me so I . . ."

Azalea cracked the door open again and called "Peter?"

Peter turned and gave a more brusque "in a few minutes." She withdrew.

"She doesn't know what your mother knew about patience," Peter said.

The two men looked past each other. Then Peter shook the letter.

"Family history isn't written or rewritten in a single letter, Kyle. Here you . . ."

Peter's voice settled into a businesslike tone, mindful of his trademark lectures about the ups and downs of real estate, and life's "big picture."

Kyle's face and neck started throbbing again.

"Forget it, dad," he finally said, wishing bruises and bandages didn't prevent him from rolling the other direction. "Just forget it. Let's not bother."

Peter stopped.
Kyle settled back into the pillows and closed his eyes.

Critique of Revision

This is a good rewrite, Ken, although we have pretty much the same problem with the ending as in the earlier draft. I like the way you have established it being night as he drives on that dangerous road, and as I said in the first critique, this helps raise the tension, but now I see it also adds to the credibility of the accident itself.

That space break between their return and breakfast the next morning was all you needed. Something so simple works wonders. A few pages later, however, I indicated that you needed to clarify who is speaking in the bar. You did show us that Kyle speaks first, but I still don't know who is speaking the next line (it's either Kari or Charley). Anyway, if it is only Kyle who is speaking, that seems a bit strange. Even though he is angry and on a bit of a tirade, there still would be interjections by the other two women. This scene could be developed in such a way as to create more resonance in the ending, too. For example, his sister could remember something from their childhood and they could reminisce about it with Charley asking questions. It might be something that Charely never knew. Maybe Kari says something like, "Kyle, remember that day when you came home with your report card with straight A's? And how mom made lasagna, your favorite, for dinner?"

"I remember sitting on the sofa looking out the front window for dad. I couldn't wait for him to come home, so I could show him."

"He must have been proud of you," Charley said.

"He came in the door, and I ran up to him and handed him the report card. He looked at it, handed it back and said, 'That's what your grades should be. You're a Sandvig.' Then he went into the kitchen and told mom about some land he was acquiring, and he never mentioned the report card again."

This is just an example of what you could do earlier in the story so that the reader will recall this in the end when Kyle closes his own eyes and shuts out the father he kept longing for but never got. Obviously, you can do a better job than the example I provided here, but something like this will really help your ending. Too often, writers feel that to improve their ending, they must literally work on it when sometimes the best work one can do for an ending is to work on the beginning and middle of the story.

Good work here, Ken. I'll look forward to seeing another draft.

—Tim

STORIES FOR FURTHER READING

On Reading Fiction

Reading is, of course, a great pleasure for all us. When an author spirits us away in her story so that we fall into what John Gardner called the "fictional dream," we unwittingly travel to new places wherein we meet new people with whom we share new experiences, all of this while sitting at home before a fire on a rainy Sunday afternoon. If the story is good enough, if the setting is rendered so real with specific detail that we feel the day fall into evening, as we do when we read Raymond Carver's "What We Talk About When We Talk About Love," we stay in the dream until the last word of the story, and when we awaken, when we put the book down, we arrive back home slightly altered, somehow larger than we were before.

But as writers, we read differently than those who read only for pleasure, and if we are to learn to write better, we must learn to read better by being alert and awake and thus outside of the dream. Certainly we read for pleasure, but we also read to learn: how to write a better scene, how to create a clearer setting, how to write stronger dialogue, how to clarify our characters and make them three dimensional, and how to advance a well-paced plot. To some extent, we reduce our pleasure when analyzing the stories we read, but if we can learn how Raymond Carver marks the passage of time with the changing of light through the kitchen window in the aforementioned story, then it will have been worth the loss. If we can learn how to create the arc of a story in just a few pages by analyzing Mary Robison's story "Yours," the knowledge gained will outweigh the pleasure the story would have given us without analysis.

Not only do we examine the elements of fiction—point of view, plot, character, setting, dialogue, style, tone and voice—but we must be on high alert for detecting objects in the fiction that signify meanings other than their own. Sometimes these symbols are clearly indicated as are the vigil candles burning inside the pumpkins during the woman's last night alive in the Robison story included here, and sometimes they are more subtle as is the chalice the narrator imagines he is carrying in James Joyce's story "Araby," or as is the very setting described in the first paragraph of John Steinbeck's "The Chrysanthemums." As one can see, if a writer is going to learn anything from reading, he cannot allow himself to be lulled into the dream the writer is trying to hypnotize him into with an engaging plot and fascinating characters.

When we have finished reading a story, it is useful to answer the following questions:

1. Whose story is it? In other words, who is the main character (the protagonist)?
2. Into whose life did this story come? In other words, just *who* is this protagonist and how does the author develop him or her?
3. What is the point of view? Is the pov effective? Were there any shifts in pov, for example, from third person limited to third person multiple?
4. Where is the story set, and which of our five senses does the writer appeal to in the reader? In other words, is the setting rendered mostly visually? Is there a dominant impression? How does the writer make you feel like you are there?
5. What do we learn about the characters through their dialogue? Does the dialogue approximate the way these people would speak?
6. Is the author employing any symbols in the story? What is their meaning and why did the author choose to use them?
7. What is the percentage of scene as opposed to exposition? Can you identify each scene and do the scenes rise to form an arc in that the writer starts with conflict and moves on by increasing the tension until the story arrives at a climax before the final denouement?

The casual reader ensconced in "Gardner's Fictional Dream" will no doubt consider some of these questions subconsciously, but he will not learn as much about the careful craft of fiction unless he is awake and outside the dream posing questions such as these. So, yes, enjoy the following stories, but be alert and learn from them as well, for as you read them you take on the role of apprentice to these masters. If you let them, they will teach you much.

THE ORDINARY SON

Ron Carlson (b. 1947)

The story of my famous family is a story of genius and its consequences, I suppose, and I am uniquely and particularly suited to tell the story since genius avoided me—and I it—and I remain an ordinary man, if there is such a thing, calm in all weathers, aware of event, but uninterested and generally incapable of deciphering implication. As my genius brother Garrett used to say, "Reed, you're not screwed too tight like the rest of us, but you're still screwed." Now, there's a definition of the common man you can trust, and further, you can trust me. There's no irony in that or deep inner meaning or Freudian slips, any kind of slip really, simply what it says. My mother told me many times I have a good heart, and of course, she was a genius, and that heart should help with this story, but a heart, as she said so often, good as it may be, is always trouble.

Part of the reason this story hasn't come together before, the story of my famous family, is that no one remembers they were related. They all had their own names. My father was Duncan Landers, the noted NASA physicist, the man responsible for every facet of the photography of the first moon landing. There is still camera gear on the moon inscribed with this name. That is, Landers. He was born Duncan Lrsdyksz, which was changed when NASA began their public-relations campaigns in the mid-sixties: the space agency suggested that physicists who worked for NASA should have more vowels in their names. They didn't want their press releases to seem full of typographical errors or foreigners. Congress was reading this stuff. So Lrsdyksz became Landers. (My father's close associate Igor Oeuroi didn't get just vowels; his name became LeRoy Rodgers. After le Cowboy Star, my mother quipped.)

My mother was Gloria Rainstrap, the poet who spent twenty years fighting for workers' rights from Texas to Alaska; in one string she gave four thousand consecutive lectures in her travels, not missing a night as she drove from village to village throughout the country. It still stands as some kind of record.

Wherever she went, she stirred up the best kind of trouble, reading her work and then spending hours in whatever guest house or spare bedroom she was given, reading the poems and essays of the people who had come to see her. She was tireless, driven by her overwhelming sense of fairness, and she was certainly the primary idealist to come out of twentieth-century Texas. When she started leaving home for months, years at a time, I was just a lad, but I remember her telling my father, Duncan, one night, "Texas is too small for what I have to do."

This was not around the dinner table. We were a family of geniuses and did not have a dinner table. In fact, the only table we did have was my father's drafting table, which was in the entry so that you had to squeeze sideways to even get into our house. "It sets the tone," Duncan used to say. "I want anyone coming into our home to see my work. That work is the reason we have a roof, anyway." He said that one day after my friend Jeff Shreckenbah and I inched past him on the way to my room. "And who are these people coming in the door?"

"It is your son and his friend," I told him.

"Good," he said, his benediction, but he said it deeply into his drawing, which is where he spent his time at home. He wouldn't have known if the Houston Oilers had arrived, because he was about to invent the modern gravity-free vacuum hinge that is still used today.

Most of my father, Duncan Landers's, work was classified, top-secret, eyes only, but it didn't matter. No one except Jeff Shreckenbah came to our house. People didn't come over.

We were geniuses. We had no television, and we had no telephone. "What should I do," my father would say from where he sat in the entry, drawing, "answer some little buzzing device? Say hello to it?" NASA tried to install phones for us. Duncan took them out. It was a genius household and not to be diminished by primitive electronic foo-fahs.

My older sister was named Christina by my father and given the last name Rossetti by my mother. When she finally fled from M.I.T. at nineteen, she gave herself a new surname: Isotope. There had been some trouble, she told me, personal trouble, and she needed the new name to remind herself she wouldn't last long—and then she asked me how I liked my half-life. I was twelve then, and she laughed and said, "I'm kidding, Reed. You're not a genius; you're going to live forever." I was talking to her on the "hot line," the secret phone our housekeeper, Clovis Armandy, kept in a kitchen cupboard.

"Where are you going?" I asked her.

"West with Mother," she said. Evidently, Gloria Rainstrap had driven up to Boston to rescue Christina from some sort of meltdown. "A juncture of some kind," my father told me. "Not to worry."

Christina said, "I'm through with theoretical chemistry, but chemistry isn't through with me. Take care of Dad. See you later."

We three children were eight years apart; that's how geniuses plan their families. Christina had been gone for years, it seemed, from our genius household; she barely knew our baby brother, Garrett.

Garrett and I took everything in stride. We accepted that we were a family of geniuses and that we had no telephone or refrigerator or proper beds. We thought it was natural to eat crackers and sardines months on end. We thought the front yard was supposed to be a jungle of overgrown grass, weeds, and whatever reptiles would volunteer to live there. Twice a year the City of Houston street crew came by and mowed it all down, and daylight would pour in for a month or two. We had no cars. My father was always climbing into white Chevrolet station wagons, unmarked, and going off to the NASA Space Center south of town. My mother was always stepping up into orange VW buses driven by other people and driving off to tour. My sister had been the youngest student at M.I.T. My brother and I did our own laundry for years and walked to school, where by about seventh grade, we began to see the differences between the way ordinary people lived and the way geniuses lived. Other people's lives, we learned, centered fundamentally on two things: television and soft foods rich with all the versions of sugar.

By the time I entered junior high school, my mother's travels had kicked into high gear, and she hired a woman we came to know well, Clovis Armandy, to live in and to assist with our corporeal care. Gloria Rainstrap's parental theory and practice could be summed up by the verse I heard her say a thousand times before I reached the age of six: "Feed the soul, the body finds a way." And she fed our souls with a groaning banquet of iron ethics at every opportunity. She wasn't interested in sandwiches or casseroles. She was the kind of person who had a moral motive for her every move. We had no refrigerator because it was simply the wrong way to prolong the value of food, which had little value in the first place. We had no real furniture because furniture became the numbing insulation of drones for the economy, an evil in itself. If religion was the opiate of the masses, then home furnishings were the Novocain of the middle class. Any small surfeit of comfort undermined our moral fabric. *We live for the work we can do, not for things,* she told us. I've met and heard lots of folks who shared Gloria's posture toward life on this earth, but I've never found anyone who put it so well, presented her ideas so convincingly, beautifully, and so insistently. They effectively seduced you into wanting to go without. I won't put any of her poems in this story, but they were transcendent. The *Times* called her "Buddha's angry daughter." My mother's response to people who were somewhat shocked at our empty house and its unkempt quality was, "We're ego distant. These little things," she'd say, waving her hand over the litter of the laundry, discarded draft paper, piles of top-secret documents in the hallway, various toys, the odd empty tin of sardines, "don't bother us in the least. We aren't even here for them." I always loved that last and still use it when a nuisance arises: I'm not even here for it. "Ego distant," my friend Jeff Shreckenbah used to say, standing in our empty house, "which means your ma doesn't sweat the small stuff."

My mother's quirk, and one she fostered, was writing on the bottom of things. She started it because she was always gone, away for months at a time, and she wanted us to get her messages throughout her absence and thereby be reminded again of making correct decisions and ethical choices. It was not unusual to find ballpoint-pen lettering on the bottom of our shoes, and little marker messages on the bottom of plates (where she wrote in a tiny script), and anywhere that you could lift up and look under, she would have left her mark. These notes primarily confused us. There I'd be in math class and cross my legs and see something on the edge of my sneaker and read, "Your troubles, if you stay alert, will pass very quickly away."

I'm not complaining. I never, except once or twice, felt deprived. I like sardines, still. It was a bit of a pinch when we got to high school, and I noted with new poignancy that I didn't quite have the wardrobe to keep up. Geniuses dress plain but clean, and not always as clean as their ordinary counterparts, who have nothing better to do with their lives than buy and sort and wash clothes.

Things were fine. I turned seventeen. I was hanging out sitting around my bare room, reading books, the History of This, the History of That, dry stuff, waiting for my genius to kick in. This is what had happened to Christina. One day when she was ten, she was having a tea party with her dolls, which were two rolled pink towels, the next day she cataloged and diagrammed the amino acids, laying the groundwork for two artificial sweeteners and a mood elevator. By the time my mother, Gloria Rainstrap, returned from the Northwest and my father looked up from his table, the State Department "mentors" had been by and my sister, Christina, was on her way to the inner sanctums of the Massachusetts Institute of Technology. I remember my mother standing against my father's drafting table, her hands along the top. Her jaw was set and she said. "This is meaningful work for Christina, her special doorway."

My father dragged his eyes up from his drawings and said, "Where's Christina now?"

So the day I went into Garrett's room and found him writing equations on a huge scroll of butcher paper, which he had used until that day to draw battle re-creations of the French and Indian War, was a big day for me. I stood there in the gloom, watching him crawl along the paper, reeling out figures of which very few were numbers I recognized, most of the symbols being Xs and Ys and the little twisted members of the Greek alphabet, and I knew that it had skipped me. Genius had cast its powerful, clear eye on me and said. "No thanks." At least I was that smart. I realized that I was not going to get to be a genius.

The message took my body a piece at a time, loosening each joint and muscle on the way up and then filling my face with a strange warmth, which I knew immediately was relief.

I was free.

I immediately took a job doing landscaping and general cleanup and maintenance at the San Jacinto Resort Motel on the old Hempstead Highway. My friend Jeff Shreckenbah worked next door at Alfredo's American Cafe, and he had told me that the last guy doing handiwork at the motel had been fired for making a holy mess of the parking lot with a paintbrush, and when I applied, Mr. Rakkerts, the short little guy who owned the place, took me on. These were the days of big changes for me.

I bought a car, an act that would have at one time been as alien for me as intergalactic travel or applying to barber college. I bought a car. It was a four-door lime-green Plymouth Fury III, low miles. I bought a pair of chinos. These things gave me exquisite pleasure. I was seventeen and I had not known the tangible pleasure of having things. I bought three new shirts and a wristwatch with a leather strap, and I went driving in the evenings, alone, south from our subdivision of Spring Woods with my arm on the green sill of my lime-green Plymouth Fury III through the vast spaghetti bowl of freeways and into the mysterious network of towers that was downtown Houston. It was my dawning.

Late at night, my blood rich with wonder at the possibilities of such a vast material planet, I would return to our tumbledown genius ranch house, my sister off putting new legs on the periodic table at M.I.T., my mother away in Shreveport showing the seaport workers there the way to political and personal power, my brother in his room edging closer to new theories of rocket reaction and thrust, my father sitting by the entry, rapt in his schematics. As I came in and sidled by his table and the one real light in the whole front part of the house, his pencilings on the space station hinge looking as beautiful and inscrutable to me as a sheet of music, he'd say my name as simple greeting. "Reed."

"Duncan," I'd say in return.

"How goes the metropolis?" he'd add, not looking up. His breath was faintly reminiscent of sardines: in fact, I still associate that smell, which is not as unpleasant as it might seem, with brilliance. I know he said *metropolis* because he didn't know for a moment which city we were in.

"It teems with industrious citizenry well into the night," I'd answer.

Then he'd say it, "Good," his benediction, as he'd carefully trace his lead holder and its steel-like wafer of 5H pencil-lead along a precise new line deep into the vast white space. "That's good."

The San Jacinto Resort Motel along the Hempstead Highway was exactly what you might expect a twenty-unit motel to be in the year 1966. The many bright new interstates had come racing to Houston and collided downtown in a maze, and the old Hempstead Highway had been supplanted as a major artery into town. There was still a good deal of traffic on the four-lane, and the motel was always about half full, and as you would expect, never the same half. There were three permanent occupants, including a withered old man named Newcombe Shinetower, who was a hundred years old that summer and who had no car, just a room full of magazines with red and yellow covers, stacks of these things with titles like *Too Young for Comfort* and *Treasure Chest*. There were other titles. I was in Mr. Shinetower's room only on two occasions. He wore the same flannel shirt every day of his life and was heavily gone to seed. Once or twice a day I would see him shuffling out toward Alfredo's

American Cafe, where Jeff told me he always ate the catfish. "You want to live to be a hundred," Jeff said, "eat the catfish." I told him I didn't know about a hundred and that I generally preferred smaller fish. I was never sure if Mr. Shinetower saw me or not as I moved through his line of sight. He might have nodded; it was hard to tell. What I felt was that he might exist on another plane, the way rocks are said to: they're in there but in a rhythm too slow for humans to perceive.

It was in his room, rife with the flaking detritus of the ages, that Jeff tried to help me reckon with the new world. "You're interested in sex, right?" he asked me one day as I took my break at the counter of Alfredo's. I told him I was, but that wasn't exactly the truth. I was indifferent. I understood how it was being packaged and sold to the American people, but it did not stir me, nor did any of the girls we went to school with, many of whom were outright beauties and not bashful about it. This was Texas in the sixties. Some of these buxom girls would grow up and try to assassinate their daughters' rivals on the cheerleading squad. If sex was the game, some seemed to say, deal me in. And I guess I felt it was a game, too, one I could sit out. I had begun to look a little closer at the ways I was different from my peers, worrying about anything that might be a genius tendency. And I took great comfort in the unmistakable affection I felt for my Plymouth Fury III.

"Good," he said. "If you're interested, then you're safe; you're not a genius. Geniuses"—here he leaned closer to me and squinted his eyes up to let me know this was a ground-breaking postulate—"have a little trouble in the sex department."

I liked Jeff: he was my first "buddy." I sat on the round red Naugahyde stool at Alfredo's long Formica counter and listened to his speech, including, "sex department," and I don't know, it kind of made sense to me. There must have been something on my face, which is a way of saying there must have been nothing on my face, absolutely nothing, a blank blank, because Jeff pulled his apron off his head and said, "Meet me out back in two minutes." He looked down the counter to where old Mr. Shinetower sucked on his soup. "We got to get you some useful information."

Out back, of course, Jeff led me directly around to the motel and Mr. Shinetower's room, which was not unlocked, but opened when Jeff gave the doorknob a healthy rattle. Inside in the sour dark, Jeff lit the lamp and picked up one of the old man's periodicals.

Jeff held the magazine and thumbed it like a deck of cards, stopping finally at a full-page photograph that he presented to me with an odd kind of certainty. "There," he said. "This is what everybody is trying for. This is the goal." It was a glossy color photograph, and I knew what it was right away, even in the poor light, a shiny shaved pubis, seven or eight times larger than life size. "This makes the world go round."

I was going along with Jeff all the way on this, but that comment begged for a remark, which I restrained. I could feel my father in me responding about the forces that actually caused and maintained the angular momentum of the earth. Instead I looked at the picture, which had its own lurid beauty. Of course, what it looked like was a landscape, a barren but promising promontory in not this but another world, the seam too perfect a fold for anything but ceremony. I imagined landing a small aircraft on the tawny slopes and approaching the entry, stepping lightly with a small party of explorers, alert for the meaning of such a place. The air would be devoid of the usual climatic markers (no clouds or air pressure), and in the stillness we would be silent and reverential. The light in the photograph captivated me in that it seemed to come from everywhere, a flat, even twilight that would indicate a world with one or maybe two distant polar suns. There was an alluring blue shadow that ran along the cleft the way a footprint in snow holds its own blue glow, and that aberration affected and intrigued me.

Jeff had left my side and was at the window, on guard, pleased that I was involved in my studies. "So," he said. "It's really something, isn't it?" He came to me, took the magazine and took one long look at the page the way a thirsty man drinks from a jug, and he set it back on the stack of Old Man Shinetower's magazines.

"Yes," I said. "It certainly is." Now that it was gone, I realized I had memorized the photograph, that place.

"Come on. Let's get out of here before he gets back." Jeff cracked the door and looked out, both ways. "Whoa," he said, setting the door closed again. "He's coming back. He's on the walk down about three rooms." Jeff then did an amazing thing: he dropped like a rock to all fours and then onto his stomach and slid under the bed. I'd never seen anyone do that I've never seen it since. I heard him hiss: "Do something. Hide."

"Again I saw myself arriving in the photograph. Now I was alone. I landed carefully and the entire venture was full of care, as if I didn't want to wake something. I had a case of instruments and I wanted to know about that light, that shadow. I could feel my legs burn as I climbed toward it step by step.

What I did in the room was take two steps back into the corner and stand behind the lamp. I put my hands at my side and my chin up. I stood still. At that moment we heard a key in the lock and daylight spilled across the ratty shag carpet. Mr. Shinetower came in. He was wearing the red-and-black plaid shirt that he wore every day. It was like a living thing; someday it would go to lunch at Alfredo's without him.

He walked by me and stopped for a moment in front of the television to drop a handful of change from his pocket into a mason jar on top, turn on the television until it lit and focused, and then he continued into the little green bathroom, and I saw the door swing halfway closed behind him.

Jeff slid out from the bed, stood hastily, his eyes whirling, and opened the door and went out. He was closing it behind him when I caught the

edge and followed him into the spinning daylight. When I pulled the
door, he gasped, so I shut it and we heard it register closed, and then we
slipped quickly through the arbor to the alley behind the units and then
ran along the overgrown trail back to the bayou and sat on the weedy
slope. Jeff was covered with clots of dust and hairy white goo-gah. It was
thick in his hair and I moved away from him while he swatted at it for a
while. Here we could smell the sewer working at the bayou, an odd, rich
industrial silage, and the sky was gray, but too bright to look at, and I went
back to the other world for a moment, the cool perfect place I'd been tour-
ing in Mr. Shinetower's magazine, quiet and still, and offering that light.
Jeff was spitting and pulling feathers of dust from his collar and sleeves. I
wanted so much to be stirred by what I had seen; I had stared at it and I
wanted it to stir me, and it had done something. I felt something. I wanted
to see that terrain, chart it, understand where the blue glow arose and how
it lay along the juncture, and how that light, I was certain, interfered with
the ordinary passage of time. Time? I had a faint headache.

"That was close," Jeff said finally. He was still cloaked with flotsam
from under Mr. Shinetower's bed. "But it was worth it. Did you get a
good look? See what I'm talking about?"

"It was a remarkable photograph," I said.

"Now you know. You've seen it, you know. I've got to get back to work.
Let's go fishing this weekend, eh?" He rose and, still whacking soot and
ashes and wicked whatevers from his person, ran off toward Alfredo's.

"I've seen it," I said, and I sat there as the sadness bled through me.
Duncan would have appreciated the moment and corrected Jeff the way
he corrected me all those years. "Seeing isn't knowing," he would say.
"To see something is only to establish the first terms of your misunder-
standing." That I remembered him at such a time above the rife bayou
moments after my flight over the naked photograph made me sad. I was
not a genius, but I would be advised by one forevermore.

Happily, my work at the motel was straightforward and I enjoyed it
very much. I could do most of it with my shirt off, cutting away the tena-
cious vines from behind each of the rooms so that the air-conditioning
units would not get strangled, and I sweated profusely in the sweet
humid air. I painted the pool fence and enameled the three metal tables a
kind of turquoise blue, a fifties turquoise that has become tony again just
this year, a color that calls to the passer by: Holiday! We're on holiday!

Once a week I poured a pernicious quantity of lime into the two man-
holes above the storm sewer, and it fell like snow on the teeming backs
of thousands of albino waterbugs and roaches that lived there. This did
not daunt them in the least. I am no expert on any of the insect tribes
nor do I fully understand their customs, but my association with those
subterranean multitudes showed me that they looked forward to this
weekly toxic snowfall.

Twice a week I pressed the enormous push broom from one end of the driveway to the other until I had a wheelbarrow full of gravel and the million crushed tickets of litter people threw from their moving vehicles along the Hempstead Highway. It was wonderful work. The broom alone weighed twenty pounds. The sweeping, the painting, the trimming braced me; work that required simply my back, both my arms and both my legs, but neither side of my brain.

Mr. Leeland Rakkerts lived in a small apartment behind the office and could be summoned by a bell during the night hours. He was just sixty that June. His wife had passed away years before and he'd become a reclusive little gun nut, and had a growing gallery of hardware on a peg-board in his apartment featuring long-barreled automatic weaponry and at least two dozen huge handguns. But he was fine to me, and he paid me cash every Friday afternoon. When he opened the cash drawer, he always made sure that be you friend or foe, you saw the .45 pistol that rested there, too. My mother would have abhorred me working for him, a man she would have considered the enemy, and she would have said as much, but I wasn't taking the high road, nor the low road, just a road. That summer, the upkeep of the motel was my job, and I did it as well as I could. I'd taken a summer job and was making money. I didn't weigh things on my scale of ethics every ten minutes, because I wasn't entirely sure I had such a scale. I certainly didn't have one as fully evolved as my mother's.

It was a bit like being in the army: when in doubt, paint something. I remeasured and overpainted the parking lot where the last guy had drunkenly painted a wacky series of parentheses where people were supposed to park, and I did a good job with a big brush and five gallons of high mustard yellow, and when I finished I took the feeling of satisfaction in my chest to be simply that: satisfaction. Even if I was working for the devil, the people who put their cars in his parking lot would be squared away.

Getting in my Plymouth Fury III those days with a sweaty back and a pocketful of cash, I knew I was no genius, but I felt—is this close?—like a great guy, a person of some command.

That fall my brother, Garrett Lrsdyksz (he'd changed his name back with a legal kit that Baxter, our Secret Service guy, had got him through the mail), became the youngest student to matriculate at Rice University. He was almost eleven. And he didn't enter as a freshman; he entered as a junior. In physics, of course. There was a little article about it on the wire services, noting that he had, without any assistance, set forward the complete set of equations explaining the relationship between the rotation of the earth and "special atmospheric aberrations most hospitable to exit trajectories of ground-fired propulsion devices." You can look it up and all you'll find is the title because the rest, like all the work he did his cataclysmic year at Rice, is classified, top-secret, eyes-only. Later he explained his research this way to me: "There are storms and then there are storms, Reed. A high-pressure area is only a high-pressure area down here on earth; it has a different pressure on the other side."

I looked at my little brother, a person forever in need of a haircut, and I thought: He's mastered the other side, and I can just barely cope with this one.

That wasn't exactly true, of course, because my Plymouth Fury III and my weekly wages from the San Jacinto Resort Motel allowed me to start having a little life, earthbound as it may have been. I started hanging out a little at Jeff Shreckenbah's place, a rambling hacienda out of town with two outbuildings where his dad worked on stock cars. Jeff's mother called me Ladykiller, which I liked, but which I couldn't hear without imagining my mother's response; my mother who told me a million times, "Morality commences in the words we use to speak of our next act."

"Hey, Ladykiller," Mrs. Shreckenbah would say to me as we pried open the fridge looking for whatever we could find. Mr. Shreckenbah made me call him Jake, saying we'd save the last names for the use of the law-enforcement officials and members of the Supreme Court. They'd let us have Lone Star long-necks if we were staying, or Coca-Cola if we were hitting the road. Some nights we'd go out with Jake and hand him wrenches while he worked on his cars. He was always asking me, "What's the plan?" an opening my mother would have approved of.

"We're going fishing," I told him, because that's what Jeff and I started doing. I'd greet his parents, pick him up, and then Jeff and I would cruise hard down Interstate 45 fifty miles to Galveston and the coast of the warm Gulf of Mexico, where we'd drink Lone Star and surf-cast all night long, hauling in all sorts of mysteries of the deep. I loved it.

Jeff would bring along a pack of Dutch Masters cigars and I'd stand waist deep in the warm water, puffing on the cheap cigar, throwing a live shrimp on a hook as far as I could toward the equator, the only light being the stars above us, the gapped two-story skyline of Galveston behind us, and our bonfire on the beach, tearing a bright hole in the world.

When fish struck, they struck hard, waking me from vivid daydreams of Mr. Leeland Rakkerts giving me a bonus for sweeping the driveway so thoroughly, a twenty so crisp it hurt to fold it into my pocket. My dreams were full of crisp twenties. I could see Jeff over there, fifty yards from me, the little orange tip of his cigar glowing, starlight on the flash of his line as he cast. I liked having my feet firmly on the bottom of the ocean standing in the night. My brother and sister and my mother and father could shine their lights into the elemental mysteries of the world; I could stand in the dark and fish. I could feel the muscles in my arm as I cast again; I was stronger than I'd been two months ago, and then I felt the fish strike and begin to run south.

Having relinquished the cerebral, not that I ever had it in my grasp, I was immersing myself in the real world the same way I was stepping deeper and deeper into the Gulf, following the frenzied fish as he tried to take my line. I worked him back, gave him some, worked him back. Though I had no idea what I would do with it, I had decided to make a lot of money, and as the fish drew me up to my armpits and the bottom grew irregular, I thought about the ways it might be achieved. Being no genius, I had few ideas.

I spit out my cigar after the first wavelet broke over my face, and I called to Jeff, "I got one."

He was behind me now, backing toward the fire, and he called, "Bring him up here and let's see."

The top half of my head, including my nose and my two hands and the fishing pole were all that were above sea level when the fish relented and I began to haul him back. He broke the surface several times as I backed out of the ocean, reeling as I went. Knee deep, I stopped and lifted the line until a dark form lifted into the air. I ran him up to Jeff by the fire and showed him there, a two-pound catfish. When I held him, I felt the sudden shock of his gaffs going into my finger and palm.

"Ow!" Jeff said. "Who has got whom?" He took the fish from me on a gill stick.

I shook my stinging hand.

"It's all right," he assured me, throwing another elbow of driftwood onto the fire and handing me an icy Lone Star. "Let's fry this guy up and eat him right now. I'm serious. This is going to be worth it. We're going to live to be one hundred years old, guaranteed."

We'd sit, eat, fish some more, talk, and late we'd drive back, the dawn light gray across the huge tidal plain, smoking Dutch Masters until I was queasy and quiet, dreaming about my money, however I would make it.

Usually this dream was interrupted by my actual boss, Mr. Leeland Rakkerts, shaking my shoulder as I stood sleeping on my broom in the parking lot of the hot and bothered San Jacinto Resort Motel, saying, "Boy! Hey! Boy! You can take your zombie fits home or get on the stick here." I'd give him the wide-eyed nod and continue sweeping, pushing a thousand pounds of scraggly gravel into a conical pile and hauling it in my wheelbarrow way out back into the thick tropical weeds at the edge of the bayou and dumping it there like a body. It wasn't a crisp twenty-dollar bill he'd given me, but it was a valuable bit of advice for a seventeen-year-old, and I tried to take it as such.

Those Saturdays after we'd been to the Gulf beat in my skull like a drum, the Texas sun a thick pressure on my bare back as I moved through the heavy humid air skimming and vacuuming the pool, rearranging the pool furniture though it was never, ever moved because no one ever used the pool. People hadn't come to the San Jacinto Resort Motel to swim. Then standing in the slim shade behind the office, trembling under a sheen of sweat, I would suck on a tall bottle of Coca-Cola as if on the very nectar of life, and by midafternoon as I trimmed the hedges along the walks and raked and swept, the day would come back to me, a pure pleasure, my lime-green Plymouth Fury III parked in the shady side of Alfredo's American Cafe, standing like a promise of every sweet thing life could offer.

These were the days when my brother, Garrett, was coming home on weekends, dropped at our curb by the maroon Rice University van after a week in the research dorms, where young geniuses from all over the world lived in bare little cubicles, the kind of thing somebody with an I.Q. of 250 apparently loves. I had been to Garrett's room on campus and it was perfect for him. There was a kind of pad in one corner surrounded by a little bank of his clothing and the strip of butcher paper running the length of the floor, covered with numbers and letters and tracked thoroughly with the faint gray intersecting grid of sneaker prints. His window looked out onto the pretty green grass quad.

It was the quietest building I have ever been in, and I was almost convinced that Garrett might be the only inmate, but when we left to go down to the cafeteria for a sandwich, I saw the other geniuses in their rooms, lying on their stomachs like kids drawing with crayons on a rainy day. Then I realized that they were kids and it was a rainy day and they were working with crayons, the only difference was that they were drawing formulas for how many muons could dance on a quark.

Downstairs there were a whole slug of the little people in the dining hall sitting around in the plastic chairs, swinging their feet back and forth six inches off the floor, ignoring their trays of tuna fish sandwiches and tomato soup, staring this way and then that as the idea storms in their brains swept through. You could almost see they were thinking by how their hair stood in fierce clusters.

There was one adult present, a guy in a blue sweater vest who went from table to table urging the children to eat: Finish that sandwich, drink your milk, go ahead, use your spoon, try the soup, it's good for you. I noticed he was careful to register and gather any of the random jottings the children committed while they sat around doodling in spilled milk. I guess he was a member of the faculty. It would be a shame for some nine-year-old to write the key to universal field theory in peanut butter and jelly and then eat the thing.

"So," I said as we sat down, "Garrett. How's it going?"

Garrett looked at me, his trance interrupted, and as it melted away and he saw me and the platters of cafeteria food before us, he smiled. There he was, my little brother, a sleepy-looking kid with a spray of freckles up and over his nose like the crab nebula, and two enthusiastic front teeth that would be keeping his mouth open for decades. "Reed," he said. *"How's it going?"* I love that. I've always liked your acute sense of narrative. So linear and right for you." His smile, which took a moment and some force to assemble, was ancient, beneficent, as if he both envied and pitied me for something, and he shook his head softly. "But things here aren't going, kid." He poked a finger into the white bread of his tuna sandwich and studied the indentation like a man finding a footprint on the moon. "Things here *are*. This is it. Things. . ." He started again. "Things aren't bad, really. It's kind of a floating circle. That's close. Things aren't going; they float in the circle. Right?"

We were both staring at the sandwich; I think I might have been waiting for it to float, but only for a second. I understood what he was saying. Things existed. I'm not that dumb. Things, whatever they might be, and that was a topic I didn't even want to open, had essence, not process. That's simple; that doesn't take a genius to decipher. "Great," I said. And then I said what you say to your little brother when he sits there pale and distracted and four years ahead of you in school. "Why don't you eat some of that, and I'll take you out and show you my car."

It wasn't as bad a visit as I'm making it sound. We were brothers; we loved each other. We didn't have to say it. The dining room got me a little until I realized I should stop worrying about these children and whether or not they were happy. Happiness wasn't an issue. The place was clean; the food was fresh. Happiness, in that cafeteria, was simply beside the point.

On the way out, Garrett introduced me to his friend Donna Li, a ten-year-old from New Orleans, whom he said was into programming. She was a tall girl with shiny hair and a ready smile, eating alone by the window. This was 1966 and I was certain she was involved somehow in television. You didn't hear the word *computer* every other sentence back then. When she stood to shake my hand, I had no idea of what to say to her and it came out, "I hope your programming is floating in the circle."

"It is," she said.

"She's written her own language," Garrett assured me, "and now she's on the applications."

It was my turn to speak again and already I couldn't touch bottom, so I said. "We're going out to see my car. Do you want to see my car?"

Imagine me in the parking lot then with these two little kids. On the way out I'd told Garrett about my job at the motel and that Jeff Shreckenbah and I had been hanging out and fishing on the weekends and that Jeff's dad raced stock cars, and for the first time all day Garrett's face filled with a kind of wonder, as if this were news from another world, which I guess it was. There was a misty rain with a faint petrochemical smell in it, and we approached my car as if it were a sleeping Brontosaurus. They were both entranced and moved toward it carefully, finally putting their little hands on the wet fender in unison. "This is your car," Garrett said, and I wasn't sure if it was the *your* or the *car* that had him in awe.

I couldn't figure out what floats in the circle or even where the circle was, but I could rattle my keys and start that Plymouth Fury III and listen to the steady sound of the engine, which I did for them now. They both backed away appreciatively.

"It's a large car," Donna Li said.

"Reed," Garrett said to me. "This is really something. And what's that smell?"

I cocked my head, smelling it, too, a big smell, budging the petrocarbons away, a live, salty smell, and then I remembered: I'd left half a bucket of bait shrimp in the trunk, where they'd been ripening for three days since my last trip to Galveston with Jeff.

"That's rain in the bayou, Garrett."

"Something organic," Donna Li said, moving toward the rear of the vehicle.

"Here, guys," I said, handing Garrett the bag of candy, sardine tins, and peanut-butter-and-cheese packs I'd brought him. I considered for half a second showing him the pile of rotting crustaceans; it would have been cool and he was my brother. But I didn't want to give the geniuses the wrong first impression of the Plymouth.

"Good luck with your programming," I told Donna Li, shaking her hand. "And Garrett, be kind to your rocketry."

Garrett smiled at that again and said to Donna, "He's my brother."

And she added, "And he owns the largest car in Texas."

I felt bad driving my stinking car away from the two young people, but it was that or fess up. I could see them standing in my rearview mirror for a long time. First they watched me, then they looked up, both of them for a long time. They were geniuses looking into the rain; I counted on their being able to find a way out of it.

SHILOH

Bobbie Ann Mason (b. 1940)

Leroy Moffitt's wife, Norma Jean, is working on her pectorals. She lifts three-pound dumbbells to warm up, then progresses to a twenty-pound barbell. Standing with her legs apart, she reminds Leroy of Wonder Woman.

"I'd give anything if I could just get these muscles to where they're real hard," says Norma Jean. "Feel this arm. It's not as hard as the other one."

"That's 'cause you're right-handed," says Leroy, dodging as she swings the barbell in an arc.

"Do you think so?"

"Sure."

Leroy is a truckdriver. He injured his leg in a highway accident four months ago, and his physical therapy, which involves weights and a pulley, prompted Norma Jean to try building herself up. Now she is attending a body-building class. Leroy has been collecting temporary disability since his tractor-trailer jackknifed in Missouri, badly twisting his left leg in its socket. He has a steel pin in his hip. He will probably not be able to drive his rig again. It sits in the backyard, like a gigantic bird that has flown home to roost. Leroy has been home in Kentucky for three months, and his leg is almost healed, but the accident frightened him and he does not want to drive any more long hauls. He is not sure what to do next. In the meantime, he makes things from craft kits. He started by building a miniature log cabin from notched Popsicle sticks. He varnished it and placed it on the TV set, where it remains. It reminds him of a rustic Nativity scene. Then he tried string art (sailing ships on black velvet), a macrame owl kit, a snap-together B-17 Flying Fortress, and a lamp made out of a model truck, with a light fixture screwed in the top of the cab. At first the kits were diversions, something to kill time, but now he is thinking about building a full-scale log house from a kit. It would be considerably cheaper than building a regular house, and besides, Leroy has grown to appreciate how things are put together. He has begun to realize that in all the years he was on the road he never took time to examine anything. He was always flying past scenery.

"They won't let you build a log cabin in any of the new subdivisions," Norma Jean tells him.

"They will if I tell them it's for you," he says, teasing her. Ever since they were married, he has promised Norma Jean he would build her a new home one day. They have always rented, and the house they live in is small and nondescript. It does not even feel like a home, Leroy realizes now.

Norma Jean works at the Rexall drugstore, and she has acquired an amazing amount of information about cosmetics. When she explains to Leroy the three stages of complexion care, involving creams, toners, and moisturizers, he thinks happily of other petroleum products—axle grease, diesel fuel. This is a connection between him and Norma Jean. Since he has been home, he has felt unusually tender about his wife and guilty over his long absences. But he can't tell what she feels about him. Norma Jean has never complained about his traveling; she has never made hurt remarks, like calling his truck a "widow-maker." He is reasonably certain she has been faithful to him, but he wishes she would celebrate his permanent homecoming more happily. Norma Jean is often startled to find Leroy at home, and he thinks she seems a little disappointed about it. Perhaps he reminds her too much of the early days of their marriage, before he went on the road. They had a child who died as an infant, years ago. They never speak about their memories of Randy, which have almost faded, but now that Leroy is home all the time, they sometimes feel awkward around each other, and Leroy wonders if one of them should mention the child. He has the feeling that they are waking up out of a dream together—that they must create a new marriage, start afresh. They are lucky they are still married. Leroy has read that for most people losing a child destroys the marriage—or else he heard this on *Donahue*. He can't always remember where he learns things anymore.

At Christmas, Leroy bought an electric organ for Norma Jean. She used to play the piano when she was in high school. "It don't leave you," she told him once. "It's like riding a bicycle."

The new instrument had so many keys and buttons that she was bewildered by it at first. She touched the keys tentatively, pushed some buttons, then pecked out "Chopsticks." It came out in an amplified fox-trot rhythm, with marimba sounds.

"It's an orchestra!" she cried.

The organ had a pecan-look finish and eighteen preset chords, with optional flute, violin, trumpet, clarinet, and banjo accompaniments. Norma Jean mastered the organ almost immediately. At first she played Christmas songs. Then she bought *The Sixties Songbook* and learned every tune in it, adding variations to each with the rows of brightly colored buttons.

"I didn't like these old songs back then," she said. "But I have this crazy feeling I missed something."

"You didn't miss a thing," said Leroy.

Leroy likes to lie on the couch and smoke a joint and listen to Norma Jean play "Can't Take My Eyes Off You" and "I'll Be Back." He is back again. After fifteen years on the road, he is finally settling down with the woman he loves. She is still pretty. Her skin is flawless. Her frosted curls resemble pencil trimmings.

Now that Leroy has come home to stay, he notices how much the town has changed. Subdivisions are spreading across western Kentucky like an oil slick. The sign at the edge of town says "Pop: 11,500"—only seven hundred more than it said twenty years before. Leroy can't figure out who is living in all the new houses. The farmers who used to gather around the courthouse square on Saturday afternoons to play checkers and spit tobacco juice have gone. It has been years since Leroy has thought about the farmers, and they have disappeared without his noticing.

Leroy meets a kid named Stevie Hamilton in the parking lot at the new shopping center. While they pretend to be strangers meeting over a stalled car, Stevie tosses an ounce of marijuana under the front seat of Leroy's car. Stevie is wearing orange jogging shoes and a T-shirt that says CHATTAHOOCHEE SUPER-RAT. His father is a prominent doctor who lives in one of the expensive subdivisions in a new white-columned brick house that looks like a funeral parlor. In the phone book under his name there is a separate number, with the listing "Teenagers."

"Where do you get this stuff?" asks Leroy. "From your pappy?"

"That's for me to know and you to find out," Stevie says. He is slit-eyed and skinny.

"What else you got?"

"What you interested in?"

"Nothing special. Just wondered."

Leroy used to take speed on the road. Now he has to go slowly. He needs to be mellow. He leans back against the car and says, "I'm aiming to build me a log house, soon as I get time. My wife, though, I don't think she likes the idea."

"Well, let me know when you want me again." Stevie says. He has a cigarette in his cupped palm, as though sheltering it from the wind. He takes a long drag, then stomps it on the asphalt and slouches away.

Stevie's father was two years ahead of Leroy in high school. Leroy is thirty-four. He married Norma Jean when they were both eighteen, and their child Randy was born a few months later, but he died at the age of four months and three days. He would be about Stevie's age now. Norma Jean and Leroy were at the drive-in, watching a double feature (*Dr. Strangelove* and *Lover Come Back*), and the baby was sleeping in the back seat. When the first movie ended, the baby was dead. It was the sudden infant death syndrome. Leroy remembers handing Randy to a nurse at the emergency room, as though he were offering her a large doll as a present. A dead baby feels like a sack of flour. "It just happens sometimes," said the doctor, in what Leroy always recalls as a nonchalant tone. Leroy can hardly remember the child anymore, but he still sees vividly a scene from *Dr. Strangelove* in which the President of the United States was talking in a folksy voice on the hot line to the Soviet premier about the bomber accidentally headed toward Russia. He was in the War Room, and the world map was lit up. Leroy remembers Norma Jean standing catatonically beside him in the hospital and himself thinking: Who is this strange girl? He had forgotten who she was. Now scientists are saying that crib death is caused by a virus. Nobody knows anything, Leroy thinks. The answers are always changing.

When Leroy gets home from the shopping center, Norma Jean's mother, Mabel Beasley, is there. Until this year, Leroy has not realized how much time she spends with Norma Jean. When she visits, she inspects the closets and then the plants, informing Norma Jean when a plant is droopy or yellow. Mabel calls the plants "flowers," although there are never any blooms. She always notices if Norma Jean's laundry is piling up. Mabel is a short, overweight women whose tight, brown-dyed curls look more like a wig than the actual wig she sometimes wears. Today she has brought Norma Jean an off-white dust ruffle she made for the bed; Mabel works in a custom-upholstery shop.

"This is the tenth one I made this year," Mabel says. "I got started and couldn't stop."

"It's real pretty," says Norma Jean.

"Now we can hide things under the bed," says Leroy, who gets along with his mother-in-law primarily by joking with her. Mabel has never really forgiven him for disgracing her by getting Norma Jean pregnant. When the baby died, she said that fate was mocking her.

"What's that thing?" Mabel says to Leroy in a loud voice, pointing to a tangle of yarn on a piece of canvas.

Leroy holds it up for Mabel to see. "It's my needlepoint," he explains. "This is a *Star Trek* pillow cover."

"That's what a woman would do," says Mabel. "Great day in the morning!"

"All the big football players on TV do it," he says.

"Why, Leroy, you're always trying to fool me. I don't believe you for one minute. You don't know what to do with yourself—that's the whole trouble. Sewing!"

"I'm aiming to build us a log house," says Leroy. "Soon as my plans come."

"Like *heck* you are," says Norma Jean. She takes Leroy's needlepoint and shoves it into a drawer. "You have to find a job first. Nobody can afford to build now anyway."

Mabel straightens her girdle and says, "I still think before you get tied down y'all ought to take a little run to Shiloh."

"One of these days, Mama," Norma Jean says impatiently.

Mabel is talking about Shiloh, Tennessee. For the past few years, she has been urging Leroy and Norma Jean to visit the Civil War battleground there. Mabel went there on her honeymoon—the only real trip she ever took. Her husband died of a perforated ulcer when Norma Jean was ten, but Mabel, who was accepted into the United Daughters of the Confederacy in 1975, is still preoccupied with going back to Shiloh.

"I've been to kingdom come and back in that truck out yonder," Leroy says to Mabel, "but we never yet set foot in that battleground. Ain't that something? How did I miss it?"

"It's not even that far," Mabel says.

After Mabel leaves, Norma Jean reads to Leroy from a list she has made. "Things you could do," she announces. "You could get a job as a guard at Union Carbide, where they'd let you set on a stool. You could get on at the lumberyard. You could do a little carpenter work, if you want to build so bad. You could—"

"I can't do something where I'd have to stand up all day."

"You ought to try standing up all day behind a cosmetics counter. It's amazing that I have strong feet, coming from two parents that never had strong feet at all." At the moment Norma Jean is holding on to the kitchen counter, raising her knees one at a time as she talks. She is wearing two-pound ankle weights.

"Don't worry," says Leroy. "I'll do something."

"You could truck calves to slaughter for somebody. You wouldn't have to drive any big old truck for that."

"I'm going to build you this house," says Leroy. "I want to make you a real home."

"I don't want to live in any log cabin."

"It's not a cabin. It's a house."

"I don't care. It looks like a cabin."

"You and me together could lift those logs. It's just like lifting weights."

Norma Jean doesn't answer. Under her breath, she is counting. Now she is marching through the kitchen. She is doing goose steps.

Before his accident, when Leroy came home he used to stay in the house with Norma Jean, watching TV in bed and playing cards. She would cook fried chicken, picnic ham, chocolate pie—all his favorites. Now he is home alone much of the time. In the mornings, Norma Jean disappears, leaving a cooling place in the bed. She eats a cereal called Body Buddies, and she leaves the bowl on the table, with the soggy tan balls floating in a milk puddle. He sees things about Norma Jean that he never realized before. When she chops onions, she stares off into a corner, as if she can't bear to look. She puts on her house slippers almost precisely at nine o'clock every evening and nudges her jogging shoes under the couch. She saves bread heels for the birds. Leroy watches the birds at the feeder. He notices the peculiar way goldfinches fly past the window. They close their wings, then fall, then spread their wings to catch and lift themselves. He wonders if they close their eyes when they fall. Norma

Jean closes her eyes when they are in bed. She wants the lights turned out. Even then, he is sure she closes her eyes.

He goes for long drives around town. He tends to drive a car rather carelessly. Power steering and an automatic shift make a car feel so small and inconsequential that his body is hardly involved in the driving process. His injured leg stretches out comfortably. Once or twice he has almost hit something, but even the prospect of an accident seems minor in a car. He cruises the new subdivisions, feeling like a criminal rehearsing for a robbery. Norma Jean is probably right about a log house being inappropriate here in the new subdivisions. All the houses look grand and complicated. They depress him.

One day when Leroy comes home from a drive he finds Norma Jean in tears. She is in the kitchen making a potato and mushroom-soup casserole, with grated-cheese topping. She is crying because her mother caught her smoking.

"I didn't hear her coming. I was standing here puffing away pretty as you please," Norma Jean says, wiping her eyes.

"I knew it would happen sooner or later," says Leroy, putting his arm around her.

"She don't know the meaning of the word 'knock,'" says Norma Jean. "It's a wonder she hadn't caught me years ago."

"Think of it this way," Leroy says. "What if she caught me with a joint?"

"You better not let her!" Norma Jean shrieks. "I'm warning you, Leroy Moffitt!"

"I'm just kidding. Here, play me a tune. That'll help you relax."

Norma Jean puts the casserole in the oven and sets the timer. Then she plays a ragtime tune, with horns and banjo, as Leroy lights up a joint and lies on the couch, laughing to himself about Mabel's catching him at it. He thinks of Stevie Hamilton—a doctor's son pushing grass. Everything is funny. The whole town seems crazy and small. He is reminded of Virgil Mathis, a boastful policeman Leroy used to shoot pool with. Virgil recently led a drug bust in a back room at a bowling alley, where he seized ten thousand dollars' worth of marijuana. The newspaper had a picture of him holding up the bags of grass and grinning widely. Right now, Leroy can imagine Virgil breaking down the door and arresting him with a lungful of smoke. Virgil would probably have been alerted to the scene because of all the racket Norma Jean is making. Now she sounds like a hard-rock band. Norma Jean is terrific. When she switches to a Latin-rhythm version of "Sunshine Superman," Leroy hums along. Norma Jean's foot goes up and down, up and down.

"Well, what do you think?" Leroy says, when Norma Jean pauses to search through her music.

"What do I think about what?"

His mind has gone blank. Then he says, "I'll sell my rig and build us a house." That wasn't what he wanted to say. He wanted to know what she thought—what she *really* thought—about them.

"Don't start in on that again," says Norma Jean. She begins playing "Who'll Be the Next in Line?"

Leroy used to tell hitchhikers his whole life story—about his travels, his hometown, the baby. He would end with a question: "Well, what do you think?" It was just a rhetorical question. In time, he had the feeling that he'd been telling the same story over and over to the same hitchhikers. He quit talking to hitchhikers when he realized how his voice sounded— whining and self-pitying, like some teenage-tragedy song. Now Leroy has the sudden impulse to tell Norma Jean about himself, as if he had just met her. They have known each other so long they have forgotten a lot about each other. They could become reacquainted. But when the oven timer goes off and she runs to the kitchen, he forgets why he wants to do this.

The next day, Mabel drops by. It is Saturday and Norma Jean is cleaning. Leroy is studying the plans of his log house, which have finally come in the mail. He has them spread out on the table—big sheets of stiff blue paper, with diagrams and numbers printed in white. While Norma Jean runs the vacuum, Mabel drinks coffee. She sets her coffee cup on a blueprint.

"I'm just waiting for time to pass," she says to Leroy, drumming her fingers on the table.

As soon as Norma Jean switches off the vacuum, Mabel says in a loud voice, "Did you hear about the datsun dog that killed the baby?"

Norma Jean says, "The word is 'dachshund.'"

"They put the dog on trial. It chewed the baby's legs off. The mother was in the next room all the time." She raises her voice. "They thought it was neglect."

Norma Jean is holding her ears. Leroy manages to open the refrigerator and get some Diet Pepsi to offer Mabel. Mabel still has some coffee and she waves away the Pepsi.

"Datsuns are like that," Mabel says. "They're jealous dogs. They'll tear a place to pieces if you don't keep an eye on them."

"You better watch out what you're saying, Mabel," says Leroy.

"Well, facts is facts."

Leroy looks out the window at his rig. It is like a huge piece of furniture gathering dust in the backyard. Pretty soon it will be an antique. He hears the vacuum cleaner, Norma Jean seems to be cleaning the living room rug again.

Later, she says to Leroy, "She just said that about the baby because she caught me smoking. She's trying to pay me back."

"What are you talking about?" Leroy says, nervously shuffling blueprints.

"You know good and well," Norma Jean says. She is sitting in a kitchen chair with her feet up and her arms wrapped around her knees. She looks small and helpless. She says, "The very idea, her bringing up a subject like that! Saying it was neglect."

"She didn't mean that," Leroy says.

"She might not have *thought* she meant it. She always says things like that. You don't know how she goes on."

"But she didn't really mean it. She was just talking."

Leroy opens a king-sized bottle of beer and pours it into two glasses, dividing it carefully. He hands a glass to Norma Jean and she takes it from him mechanically. For a long time, they sit by the kitchen window watching the birds at the feeder.

Something is happening. Norma Jean is going to night school. She has graduated from her six-week body-building course and now she is taking an adult-education course in composition at Paducah Community College. She spends her evenings outlining paragraphs.

"First you have a topic sentence," she explains to Leroy. "Then you divide it up. Your secondary topic has to be connected to your primary topic."

To Leroy, this sounds intimidating. "I never was any good in English," he says.

"It makes a lot of sense."

"What are you doing this for, anyhow?"

She shrugs. "It's something to do." She stands up and lifts her dumbbells a few times.

"Driving a rig, nobody cared about my English."

"I'm not criticizing your English."

Norma Jean used to say, "If I lose ten minutes' sleep, I just drag all day." Now she stays up late, writing compositions. She got a B on her first paper—a how-to theme on soup-based casseroles. Recently Norma Jean has been cooking unusual foods—tacos, lasagna, Bombay chicken. She doesn't play the organ anymore, though her second paper was called "Why Music Is Important to Me." She sits at the kitchen table, concentrating on her outlines, while Leroy plays with his log house plans, practicing with a set of Lincoln Logs. The thought of getting a truckload of notched, numbered logs scares him, and he wants to be prepared. As he and Norma Jean work together at the kitchen table, Leroy has the hopeful thought that they are sharing something, but he knows he is a fool to think this. Norma Jean is miles away. He knows he is going to lose her. Like Mabel, he is just waiting for time to pass.

One day, Mabel is there before Norma Jean gets home from work, and Leroy finds himself confiding in her. Mabel, he realizes, must know Norma Jean better than he does.

"I don't know what's got into that girl," Mabel says. "She used to go to bed with the chickens. Now you say she's up all hours. Plus her a-smoking. I like to died."

"I want to make her this beautiful home," Leroy says, indicating the Lincoln Logs. "I don't think she even wants it. Maybe she was happier with me gone."

"She don't know what to make of you, coming home like this."

"Is that it?"

Mabel takes the roof off his Lincoln Log cabin. "You couldn't get *me* in a log cabin," she says. "I was raised in one. It's no picnic, let me tell you."

"They're different now," says Leroy.

"I tell you what," Mabel says, smiling oddly at Leroy.

"What?"

"Take her on down to Shiloh. Y'all need to get out together, stir a little. Her brain's all balled up over them books."

Leroy can see traces of Norma Jean's features in her mother's face. Mabel's worn face has the texture of crinkled cotton, but suddenly she looks pretty. It occurs to Leroy that Mabel has been hinting all along that she wants them to take her with them to Shiloh.

"Let's all go to Shiloh," he says. "You and me and her. Come Sunday."

Mabel throws up her hands in protest. "Oh, no, not me. Young folks want to be by theirselves."

When Norma Jean comes in with groceries, Leroy says excitedly, "Your mama here's been dying to go to Shiloh for thirty-five years. It's about time we went, don't you think?"

"I'm not going to butt in on anybody's second honeymoon," Mabel says.

"Who's going on a honeymoon, for Christ's sake?" Norma Jean says loudly.

"I never raised no daughter of mine to talk that-a-way," Mabel says.

"You ain't seen nothing yet," says Norma Jean. She starts putting away boxes and cans, slamming cabinet doors.

"There's a log cabin at Shiloh," Mabel says. "It was there during the battle. There's bullet holes in it."

"When are you going to *shut up* about Shiloh, Mama?" asks Norma Jean.

"I always thought Shiloh was the prettiest place, so full of history," Mabel goes on. "I just hoped y'all could see it once before I die, so you could tell me about it." Later, she whispers to Leroy, "You do what I said. A little change is what she needs."

"Your name means 'the king,'" Norma Jean says to Leroy that evening. He is trying to get her to go to Shiloh, and she is reading a book about another century.

"Well, I reckon I ought to be right proud."

"I guess so."

"Am I still king around here?"

Norma Jean flexes her biceps and feels them for hardness. "I'm not fooling around with anybody, if that's what you mean," she says.

"Would you tell me if you were?"

"I don't know."

"What does *your* name mean?"

"It was Marilyn Monroe's real name."

"No kidding!"

"Norma comes from the Normans. They were invaders," she says. She closes her book and looks hard at Leroy. "I'll go to Shiloh with you if you'll stop staring at me."

On Sunday, Norma Jean packs a picnic and they go to Shiloh. To Leroy's relief, Mabel says she does not want to come with them. Norma Jean drives, and Leroy, sitting beside her, feels like some boring hitch-hiker she has picked up. He tries some conversation, but she answers him in monosyllables. At Shiloh, she drives aimlessly through the park, past bluffs and trails and steep ravines. Shiloh is an immense place, and Leroy cannot see it as a battleground. It is not what he expected. He thought it would look like a golf course. Monuments are everywhere, showing through the thick clusters of trees. Norma Jean passes the log cabin Mabel mentioned. It is surrounded by tourists looking for bullet holes.

"That's not the kind of log house I've got in mind," says Leroy apologetically.

"I know *that*."

"This is a pretty place. Your Mama was right."

"It's O.K.," says Norma Jean. "Well, we've seen it. I hope she's satisfied."

They burst out laughing together.

At the park museum, a movie on Shiloh is shown every half hour, but they decide that they don't want to see it. They buy a souvenir Confederate flag for Mabel, and then they find a picnic spot near the cemetery. Norma Jean has brought a picnic cooler, with pimiento sandwiches, soft drinks, and Yodels. Leroy eats a sandwich and then smokes a joint, hiding it behind the picnic cooler. Norma Jean has quit smoking altogether. She is picking cake crumbs from the cellophane wrapper, like a fussy bird.

Leroy says, "So the boys in gray ended up in Corinth. The Union soldiers zapped 'em finally. April 7, 1862."

They both know that he doesn't know any history. He is just talking about some of the historical plaques they have read. He feels awkward, like a boy on a date with an older girl. They are still just making conversation.

"Corinth is where Mama eloped to," says Norma Jean.

They sit in silence and stare at the cemetery for the Union dead and, beyond, at a tall cluster of trees. Campers are parked nearby, bumper to bumper, and small children in bright clothing are cavorting and squealing. Norma Jean wads up the cake wrapper and squeezes it tightly in her hand. Without looking at Leroy, she says, "I want to leave you."

Leroy takes a bottle of Coke out of the cooler and flips off the cap. He holds the bottle poised near his mouth but cannot remember to take a drink. Finally he says, "No, you don't."

"Yes, I do."

"I won't let you."

"You can't stop me."

"Don't do me that way."

Leroy knows Norma Jean will have her own way. "Didn't I promise to be home from now on?" he says.

"In some ways, a woman prefers a man who wanders," says Norma Jean. "That sounds crazy, I know."

"You're not crazy."

Leroy remembers to drink from his Coke. Then he says, "Yes, you *are* crazy. You and me could start all over again. Right back at the beginning."

"We *have* started all over again," says Norma Jean. "And this is how it turned out."

"What did I do wrong?"

"Nothing."

"Is this one of those women's lib things?" Leroy asks.

"Don't be funny."

The cemetery, a green slope dotted with white markers, looks like a subdivision site. Leroy is trying to comprehend that his marriage is breaking up, but for some reason he is wondering about white slabs in a graveyard.

"Everything was fine till Mama caught me smoking," says Norma Jean, standing up. "That set something off."

"What are you talking about?"

"She won't leave me alone—*you* won't leave me alone." Norma Jean seems to be crying, but she is looking away from him. "I feel eighteen again. I can't face that all over again." She starts walking away. "No, it *wasn't* fine. I don't know what I'm saying. Forget it."

Leroy takes a lungful of smoke and closes his eyes as Norma Jean's words sink in. He tries to focus on the fact that thirty-five hundred soldiers died on the grounds around him. He can only think of that war as a board game with plastic soldiers. Leroy almost smiles, as he compares the Confederates' daring attack on the union camps and Virgil Mathis's raid on the bowling alley. General Grant, drunk and furious, shoved the Southerners back to Corinth, where Mabel and Jet Beasley were married years later, when Mabel was still thin and good-looking.

The next day, Mabel and Jet visited the battleground, and then Norma Jean was born, and then she married Leroy and they had a baby, which they lost, and now Leroy and Norma Jean are here at the same battleground. Leroy knows he is leaving out a lot. He is leaving out the insides of history. History was always just names and dates to him. It occurs to him that building a house out of logs is similarly empty—too simple. And the real inner workings of a marriage, like most of history, have escaped him. Now he sees that building a log house is the dumbest idea he could have had. It was clumsy of him to think Norma Jean would want a log house. It was a crazy idea. He'll have to think of something else, quickly. He will wad the blueprints into tight balls and fling them into the lake. Then he'll get moving again. He opens his eyes. Norma Jean has moved away and is walking through the cemetery, following a serpentine brick path.

Leroy gets up to follow his wife, but his good leg is asleep and his bad leg still hurts him. Norma Jean is far away, walking rapidly toward the bluff by the river, and he tries to hobble toward her. Some children run past him, screaming noisily. Norma Jean has reached the bluff, and she is looking out over the Tennessee River. Now she turns toward Leroy and waves her arms. Is she beckoning to him? She seems to be doing an exercise for her chest muscles. The sky is unusually pale—the color of the dust ruffle Mabel made for their bed.

WHAT WE TALK ABOUT WHEN WE TALK ABOUT LOVE

Raymond Carver (1939–1988)

My friend Mel McGinnis was talking. Mel McGinnis is a cardiologist, and sometimes that gives him the right.

The four of us were sitting around his kitchen table drinking gin. Sunlight filled the kitchen from the big window behind the sink. There were Mel and me and his second wife, Teresa—Terri, we called her—and my wife, Laura. We lived in Albuquerque then. But we were all from somewhere else.

There was an ice bucket on the table. The gin and the tonic water kept going around, and we somehow got on the subject of love. Mel thought real love was nothing less than spiritual love. He said he'd spent five years in a seminary before quitting to go to medical school. He said he still looked back on those years in the seminary as the most important years in his life.

Terri said the man she lived with before she lived with Mel loved her so much he tried to kill her. Then Terri said, "He beat me up one night. He dragged me around the living room by my ankles. He kept saying, 'I love you, I love you, you bitch.' He went on dragging me around the living room. My head kept knocking on things." Terri looked around the table. "What do you do with love like that?"

She was a bone-thin woman with a pretty face, dark eyes, and brown hair that hung down her back. She liked necklaces made of turquoise, and long pendant earrings.

"My God, don't be silly. That's not love, and you know it," Mel said. "I don't know what you'd call it, but I sure know you wouldn't call it love."

"Say what you want to, but I know it was," Terri said. "It may sound crazy to you, but it's true just the same. People are different, Mel. Sure, sometimes he may have acted crazy. Okay. But he loved me. In his own way maybe, but he loved me. There was love there, Mel. Don't say there wasn't."

Mel let out his breath. He held his glass and turned to Laura and me. "The man threatened to kill me," Mel said. He finished his drink and reached for the gin bottle. "Terri's a romantic. Terri's of the kick-me-so-I'll-know-you-love-me school. Terri, hon, don't look that way." Mel reached across the table and touched Terri's cheek with his fingers. He grinned at her.

"Now he wants to make up," Terri said.

"Make up what?" Mel said. "What is there to make up? I know what I know. That's all."

"How'd we get started on this subject, anyway?" Terri said. She raised her glass and drank from it. "Mel always has love on his mind," she said. "Don't you, honey?" She smiled, and I thought that was the last of it.

"I just wouldn't call Ed's behavior love. That's all I'm saying, honey," Mel said. "What about you guys?" Mel said to Laura and me. "Does that sound like love to you?"

"I'm the wrong person to ask," I said. "I didn't even know the man. I've only heard his name mentioned in passing. I wouldn't know. You'd have to know the particulars. But I think what you're saying is that love is an absolute."

Mel said, "The kind of love I'm talking about is. The kind of love I'm talking about, you don't try to kill people."

Laura said, "I don't know anything about Ed, or anything about the situation. But who can judge anyone else's situation?"

I touched the back of Laura's hand. She gave me a quick smile. I picked up Laura's hand. It was warm, the nails polished, perfectly manicured. I encircled the broad wrist with my fingers, and I held her.

"When I left, he drank rat poison," Terri said. She clasped her arms with her hands. "They took him to the hospital in Santa Fe. That's where we lived then, about ten miles out. They saved his life. But his gums went crazy from it. I mean they pulled away from his teeth. After that, his teeth stood out like fangs. My God," Terri said. She waited a minute, then let go of her arms and picked up her glass.

"What people won't do!" Laura said.

"He's out of the action now," Mel said. "He's dead."

Mel handed me the saucer of limes. I took a section, squeezed it over my drink, and stirred the ice cubes with my finger.

"It gets worse," Terri said. "He shot himself in the mouth. But he bungled that too. Poor Ed," she said. Terri shook her head.

"Poor Ed nothing," Mel said. "He was dangerous."

Mel was forty-five years old. He was tall and rangy with curly soft hair. His face and arms were brown from the tennis he played. When he was sober, his gestures, all his movements, were precise, very careful.

"He did love me though, Mel. Grant me that," Terri said. "That's all I'm asking. He didn't love me the way you love me. I'm not saying that. But he loved me. You can grant me that, can't you?"

"What do you mean, he bungled it?" I said.

Laura leaned forward with her glass. She put her elbows on the table and held her glass in both hands. She glanced from Mel to Terri and waited with a look of bewilderment on her open face, as if amazed that such things happened to people you were friendly with.

"How'd he bungle it when he killed himself?" I said.

"I'll tell you what happened," Mel said. "He took this twenty-two pistol he'd bought to threaten Terri and me with. Oh, I'm serious, the man was always threatening. You should have seen the way we lived in those days. Like fugitives, I even bought a gun myself. Can you believe it? A guy like me? But I did, I bought one for self-defense and carried it in the glove compartment. Sometimes I'd have to leave the apartment in the middle of the night. To go to the hospital, you know? Terri and I weren't married then, and my first wife had the house and kids, the dog, everything, and Terri and I were living in this apartment here. Sometimes, as I say, I'd get a call in the middle of the night and have to go in to the hospital at two or three in the morning. It'd be dark out there in the parking lot, and I'd break into a sweat before I could even get to my car. I never knew if he was going to come up out of the shrubbery or from behind a car and start shooting. I mean, the man was crazy. He was capable of wiring a bomb, anything. He used to call my service at all hours and say he needed to talk to the doctor, and when I'd return the call, he'd say, 'Son of a bitch, your days are numbered.' Little things like that. It was scary, I'm telling you."

"I still feel sorry for him," Terri said.

"It sounds like a nightmare," Laura said. "But what exactly happened after he shot himself?"

Laura is a legal secretary. We'd met in a professional capacity. Before we knew it, it was a courtship. She's thirty-five, three years younger than I am. In addition to being in love, we like each other and enjoy one another's company. She's easy to be with.

"What happened?" Laura said.

Mel said, "He shot himself in the mouth in his room. Someone heard the shot and told the manager. They came in with a passkey, saw what had happened, and called an ambulance. I happened to be there when they brought him in, alive but past recall. The man lived for three days. His head swelled up to twice the size of a normal head. I'd never seen anything like it, and I hope I never do again. Terri wanted to go in and sit with him when she found out about it. We had a fight over it. I didn't think she should see him like that. I didn't think she should see him, and I still don't."

"Who won the fight?" Laura said.

"I was in the room with him when he died," Terri said. "He never came up out of it. But I sat with him. He didn't have anyone else."

"He was dangerous," Mel said. "If you call that love, you can have it."

"It was love," Terri said. "Sure, it's abnormal in most people's eyes. But he was willing to die for it. He did die for it."

"I sure as hell wouldn't call it love," Mel said. "I mean, no one knows what he did it for. I've seen a lot of suicides, and I couldn't say anyone ever knew what they did it for."

Mel put his hands behind his neck and tilted his chair back. "I'm not interested in that kind of love," he said. "If that's love, you can have it."

Terri said, "We were afraid. Mel even made a will out and wrote to his brother in California who used to be a Green Beret. Mel told him who to look for if something happened to him."

Terri drank from her glass. She said, "But Mel's right—we lived like fugitives. We were afraid. Mel was, weren't you, honey? I even called the police at one point, but they were no help. They said they couldn't do anything until Ed actually did something. Isn't that a laugh?" Terri said.

She poured the last of the gin into her glass and waggled the bottle. Mel got up from the table and went to the cupboard. He took down another bottle.

"Well, Nick and I know what love is," Laura said. "For us, I mean," Laura said. She bumped my knee with her knee. "You're supposed to say something now," Laura said, and turned her smile on me.

For an answer, I took Laura's hand and raised it to my lips. I made a big production out of kissing her hand. Everyone was amused.

"We're lucky," I said.

"You guys," Terri said. "Stop that now. You're making me sick. You're still on the honeymoon, for God's sake. You're still gaga, for crying out loud. Just wait. How long have you been together now? How long has it been? A year? Longer than a year?"

"Going on a year and a half," Laura said, flushed and smiling.

"Oh, now," Terri said. "Wait awhile."

She held her drink and gazed at Laura.

"I'm only kidding," Terri said.

Mel opened the gin and went around the table with the bottle.

"Here, you guys," he said. "Let's have a toast. I want to propose a toast. A toast to love. To true love," Mel said.

We touched glasses.

"To love," we said.

Outside in the backyard, one of the dogs began to bark. The leaves of the aspen that leaned past the window ticked against the glass. The afternoon sun was like a presence in this room, the spacious light of ease and generosity. We could have been anywhere, somewhere enchanted. We raised our glasses again and grinned at each other like children who had agreed on something forbidden.

"I'll tell you what real love is," Mel said. "I mean, I'll give you a good example. And then you can draw your own conclusions." He poured more gin into his glass. He added an ice cube and a sliver of lime. We waited and sipped our drinks. Laura and I touched knees again. I put a hand on her warm thigh and left it there.

"What do any of us really know about love?" Mel said. "It seems to me we're just beginners at love. We say we love each other and we do, I don't doubt it. I love Terri and Terri loves me, and you guys love each other too. You know the kind of love I'm talking about now. Physical love, that impulse that drives you to someone special, as well as love of the other person's being, his or her essence, as it were. Carnal love and, well, call it sentimental love, the day-to-day caring about the other person. But sometimes I have a hard time accounting for the fact that I must have loved my first wife too. But I did, I know I did. So I suppose I am like Terri in that regard. Terri and Ed." He thought about it and then he went on. "There was a time when I thought I loved my first wife more than life itself. But now I hate her guts. I do. How do you explain that? What happened to that love? What happened to it, is what I'd like to know. I wish someone could tell me. Then there's Ed. Okay, we're back to Ed. He loves Terri so much he tries to kill her and he winds up killing himself." Mel stopped talking and swallowed from his glass. "You guys have been together eighteen months and you love each other. It shows all over you. You glow with it. But you both loved other people before you met each other. You've both been married before, just like us. And you probably loved other people before that too, even. Terri and I have been together five years, been married for four. And the terrible thing, the terrible thing is, but the good thing too, the saving grace, you might say, is that if something happened to one of us—excuse me for saying this—but if something happened to one of us tomorrow, I think the other one, the other person, would grieve for a while, you know, but then the surviving party would go out and love again, have someone else soon enough. All this, all of this love we're talking about, it would just be a memory. Maybe not even a memory. Am I wrong? Am I way off base? Because I want you to set me straight if you think I'm wrong. I want to know. I mean, I don't know anything, and I'm the first one to admit it."

"Mel, for God's sake," Terri said. She reached out and took hold of his wrist. "Are you getting drunk? Honey? Are you drunk?"

"Honey, I'm just talking," Mel said. "All right? I don't have to be drunk to say what I think. I mean, we're all just talking, right?" Mel said, He fixed his eyes on her.

"Sweetie, I'm not criticizing," Terri said.

She picked up her glass.

"I'm not on call today," Mel said. "Let me remind you of that. I am not on call," he said.

"Mel, we love you," Laura said.

Mel looked at Laura. He looked at her as if he could not place her, as if she was not the woman she was.

"Love you too, Laura," Mel said. "And you, Nick, love you too. You know something?" Mel said. "You guys are our pals," Mel said.

He picked up his glass.

Mel said, "I was going to tell you about something. I mean, I was going to prove a point. You see, this happened a few months ago, but it's still going on right now, and it ought to make us feel ashamed when we talk like we know what we're talking about when we talk about love."

"Come on now," Terri said. "Don't talk like you're drunk if you're not drunk."

"Just shut up for once in your life," Mel said very quietly. "Will you do me a favor and do that for a minute? So as I was saying, there's this old couple who had this car wreck out on the interstate. A kid hit them and they were all torn to shit and nobody was giving them much chance to pull through."

Terri looked at us and then back at Mel. She seemed anxious, or maybe that's too strong a word.

Mel was handing the bottle around the table.

"I was on call that night," Mel said. "It was May or maybe it was June. Terri and I had just sat down to dinner when the hospital called. There'd been this thing out on the interstate. Drunk kid, teenager, plowed his dad's pickup into this camper with this old couple in it. They were up in their mid-seventies, that couple. The kid—eighteen, nineteen, something—he was DOA. Taken the steering wheel through his sternum. The old couple, they were alive, you understand. I mean, just barely. But they had everything. Multiple fractures, internal injuries, hemorrhaging, contusions, lacerations, the works, and they each of them had themselves concussions. They were in a bad way, believe me. And, of course, their age was two strikes against them. I'd say she was worse off than he was. Ruptured spleen along with everything else. Both kneecaps broken. But they'd been wearing their seatbelts and, God knows, that's what saved them for the time being."

"Folks, this is an advertisement for the National Safety Council," Terri said. "This is your spokesman, Dr. Melvin R. McGinnis, talking." Terri laughed. "Mel," she said, "sometimes you're just too much. But I love you, hon," she said.

"Honey, I love you," Mel said.

He leaned across the table. Terri met him halfway. They kissed.

"Terri's right," Mel said as he settled himself again. "Get those seatbelts on. But seriously, they were in some shape, those oldsters. By the time I got down there, the kid was dead, as I said. He was off in a corner, laid out on a gurney. I took one look at the old couple and told the ER nurse to get me a neurologist and an orthopedic man and a couple of surgeons down there right away."

He drank from his glass. "I'll try to keep this short," he said. "So we took the two of them up to the OR and worked like fuck on them most of the night. They had these incredible reserves, those two. You see that once in a while. So we did everything that could be done, and toward morning we're giving them a fifty-fifty chance, maybe less than that for her. So here they are, still alive the next morning. So, okay, we move them into the ICU, which is where they both kept plugging away at it for two weeks, hitting it better and better on all the scopes. So we transfer them out to their own room."

Mel stopped talking. "Here," he said, "let's drink this cheapo gin the hell up. Then we're going to dinner, right? Terri and I know a new place. That's where we'll go, to this new place we know about. But we're not going until we finish up this cut-rate, lousy gin."

Terri said, "We haven't actually eaten there yet. But it looks good. From the outside, you know."

"I like food," Mel said. "If I had it to do all over again, I'd be a chef, you know? Right, Terri?" Mel said.

He laughed. He fingered the ice in his glass.

"Terri knows," he said. "Terri can tell you. But let me say this. If I could come back again in a different life, a different time and all, you know what? I'd like to come back as a knight. You were pretty safe wearing all that armor. It was all right being a knight until gunpowder and muskets and pistols came along."

"Mel would like to ride a horse and carry a lance," Terri said.

"Carry a woman's scarf with you everywhere," Laura said.

"Or just a woman," Mel said.

"Shame on you," Laura said.

Terri said, "Suppose you came back as a serf. The serfs didn't have it so good in those days," Terri said.

"The serfs never had it good," Mel said. "But I guess even the knights were vessels to someone. Isn't that the way it worked? But then everyone is always a vessel to someone. Isn't that right, Terri? But what I liked about knights, besides their ladies, was that they had that suit of armor, you know, and they couldn't get hurt very easy. No cars in those days, you know? No drunk teenagers to tear into your ass."

"Vassals," Terri said.

"What?" Mel said.

"Vassals," Terri said. "They were called vassals, not vessels."

"Vassals, vessels," Mel said, "what the fuck's the difference? You knew what I meant anyway. All right," Mel said. "So I'm not educated. I learned my stuff. I'm a heart surgeon, sure, but I'm just a mechanic. I go in and I fuck around and I fix things. Shit," Mel said.

"Modesty doesn't become you," Terri said.

"He's just a humble sawbones," I said. "But sometimes they suffocated in all that armor, Mel. They'd even have heart attacks if it got too hot and they were too tired and worn out. I read somewhere that they'd fall off their horses and not be able to get up because they were too tired to stand with all that armor on them. They got trampled by their own horses sometimes."

"That's terrible," Mel said. "That's a terrible thing, Nicky. I guess they'd just lay there and wait until somebody came along and made a shish kebab out of them."

"Some other vessel," Terri said.

"That's right," Mel said. "Some vassal would come along and spear the bastard in the name of love. Or whatever the fuck it was they fought over in those days."

"Same things we fight over these days," Terri said.

Laura said, "Nothing's changed."

The color was still high in Laura's cheeks. Her eyes were bright. She brought her glass to her lips.

Mel poured himself another drink. He looked at the label closely as if studying a long row of numbers. Then he slowly put the bottle down on the table and slowly reached for the tonic water.

"What about the old couple?" Laura said. "You didn't finish that story you started."

Laura was having a hard time lighting her cigarette. Her matches kept going out.

The sunshine inside the room was different now, changing, getting thinner. But the leaves outside the window were still shimmering, and I stared at the pattern they made on the panes and on the Formica counter. They weren't the same patterns, of course.

"What about the old couple?" I said.

"Older but wiser," Terri said.

Mel stared at her.

Terri said, "Go on with your story, hon. I was only kidding. Then what happened?"

"Terri, sometimes," Mel said.

"Please, Mel," Terri said. "Don't always be so serious, sweetie. Can't you take a joke?"

"Where's the joke?" Mel said.

He held his glass and gazed steadily at his wife.

"What happened?" Laura said.

Mel fastened his eyes on Laura. He said, "Laura, if I didn't have Terri and if I didn't love her so much, and if Nick wasn't my best friend, I'd fall in love with you. I'd carry you off, honey," he said.

"Tell your story," Terri said. "Then we'll go to that new place, okay?"

"Okay," Mel said. "Where was I?" he said. He stared at the table and then he began again.

"I dropped in to see each of them every day, sometimes twice a day if I was up doing other calls anyway. Casts and bandages, head to foot, the both of them. You know, you've seen it in the movies. That's just the way they looked, just like in the movies. Little eye-holes and nose-holes and mouth-holes. And she had to have her legs slung up on top of it. Well, the husband was very depressed for the longest while. Even after he found out that his wife was going to pull through, he was still very depressed. Not about the accident, though. I mean, the accident was one thing, but it wasn't everything. I'd get up to his mouth-hole, you know, and he'd say no, it wasn't the accident exactly but it was because he couldn't see her through his eye-holes. He said that was what was making him feel so bad. Can you imagine? I'm telling you, the man's heart was breaking because he couldn't turn his goddamn head and *see* his goddamn wife."

Mel looked around the table and shook his head at what he was going to say.

"I mean, it was killing the old fart just because he couldn't *look* at the fucking woman."

We all looked at Mel.

"Do you see what I'm saying?" he said.

Maybe we were a little drunk by then. I know it was hard keeping things in focus. The light was draining out of the room, going back through the window where it had come from. Yet nobody made a move to get up from the table to turn on the overhead light.

"Listen," Mel said. "Let's finish this fucking gin. There's about enough left here for one shooter all around. Then let's go eat. Let's go to the new place."

"He's depressed," Terri said. "Mel, why don't you take a pill?"

Mel shook his head. "I've taken everything there is."

"We all need a pill now and then," I said.

"Some people are born needing them," Terri said.

She was using her finger to rub at something on the table. Then she stopped rubbing.

"I think I want to call my kids," Mel said. "Is that all right with everybody? I'll call my kids," he said.

Terri said, "What if Marjorie answers the phone? You guys, you've heard us on the subject of Marjorie? Honey, you know you don't want to talk to Marjorie. It'll make you feel even worse."

"I don't want to talk to Marjorie," Mel said. "But I want to talk to my kids."

"There isn't a day goes by that Mel doesn't say he wishes she'd get married again. Or else die," Terri said. "For one thing," Terri said, "she's bankrupting us. Mel says it's just to spite him that she won't get married again. She has a boyfriend who lives with her and the kids, so Mel is supporting the boyfriend too."

"She's allergic to bees," Mel said. "If I'm not praying she'll get married again, I'm praying she'll get herself stung to death by a swarm of fucking bees."

"Shame on you," Laura said.

"Bzzzzzzz," Mel said, turning his fingers into bees and buzzing them at Terri's throat. Then he let his hands drop all the way to his sides.

"She's vicious," Mel said. "Sometimes I think I'll go up there dressed like a beekeeper. You know, that hat that's like a helmet with the plate that comes down over your face, the big gloves, and the padded coat? I'll knock on the door and let loose a hive of bees in the house. But first I'd make sure the kids were out, of course."

He crossed one leg over the other. It seemed to take him a lot of time to do it. Then he put both feet on the floor and leaned forward, elbows on the table, his chin cupped in his hands.

"Maybe I won't call the kids, after all. Maybe it isn't such a hot idea. Maybe we'll just go eat. How does that sound?"

"Sounds fine to me," I said. "Eat or not eat. Or keep drinking. I could head right on out into the sunset."

"What does that mean, honey?" Laura said.

"It just means what I said," I said. "It means I could just keep going. That's all it means."

"I could eat something myself," Laura said. "I don't think I've ever been so hungry in my life. Is there something to nibble on?"

"I'll put out some cheese and crackers," Terri said.

But Terri just sat there. She did not get up to get anything.

Mel turned his glass over. He spilled it out on the table.

"Gin's gone," Mel said.

Terri said, "Now what?"

I could hear my heart beating. I could hear everyone's heart. I could hear the human noise we sat there making, not one of us moving, not even when the room went dark.

ARABY

James Joyce (1882–1941)

North Richmond Street, being blind, was a quiet street except at the hour when the Christian Brothers' School set the boys free. An uninhabited house of two storeys stood at the blind end, detached from its neighbours in a square ground. The other houses of the street, conscious of decent lives within them, gazed at one another with brown imperturbable faces.

The former tenant of our house, a priest, had died in the back drawing-room. Air, musty from having been long enclosed, hung in all the rooms, and the waste room behind the kitchen was littered with old useless papers. Among these I found a few paper-covered books, the pages of which were curled and damp: *The Abbot*, by Walter Scott, *The Devout Communicant* and *The Memoirs of Vidocq*. I liked the last best because its leaves were yellow. The wild garden behind the house contained a central appletree and a few straggling bushes under one of which I found the late tenant's rusty bicycle-pump. He had been a very charitable priest; in his will he had left all his money to institutions and the furniture of his house to his sister.

When the short days of winter came dusk fell before we had well eaten our dinners. When we met in the street the houses had grown sombre. The space of sky above us was the colour of ever-changing violet and towards it the lamps of the street lifted their feeble lanterns. The cold air stung us and we played till our bodies glowed. Our shouts echoed in the silent street. The career of our play brought us through the dark muddy lanes behind the houses where we ran the gauntlet of the rough tribes from the cottages, to the back doors of the dark dripping gardens where odours arose from the ashpits, to the dark odorous stables where a coachman smoothed and combed the horse or shook music from the buckled harness. When we returned to the street, light from the kitchen windows had filled the areas. If my uncle was seen turning the corner we hid in the shadow until we had seen him safely housed. Or if Mangan's sister came out on the doorstep to call her brother in to his tea we watched her from our shadow peer up and down the street. We waited to see whether she would remain or go in and, if she remained, we left our shadow and walked up to Mangan's steps resignedly. She was waiting for us, her figure defined by the light from the half-opened door. Her brother always teased her before he obeyed and I stood by the railings looking at her. Her dress swung as she moved her body and the soft rope of her hair tossed from side to side.

Every morning I lay on the floor in the front parlour watching her door. The blind was pulled down to within an inch of the sash so that I could not be seen. When she came out on the doorstep my heart leaped. I ran to the hall, seized my books and followed her. I kept her brown figure always in my eye and, when we came near the point at which our ways diverged, I quickened my pace and passed her. This happened morning after morning. I had never spoken to her, except for a few casual words, and yet her name was like a summons to all my foolish blood.

Her image accompanied me even in places the most hostile to romance. On Saturday evenings when my aunt went marketing I had to go to carry some of the parcels. We walked through the flaring streets, jostled by drunken men and bargaining women, amid the curses of labourers, the shrill litanies of shop-boys who stood on guard by the barrels of pigs' cheeks, the nasal chanting of street-singers, who sang a *come-all-you* about O'Donovan Rossa, or a ballad about the troubles in our native land. These noises converged in a single sensation of life for me: I imagined that I bore my chalice safely through a throng of foes. Her name sprang to my lips at moments in strange prayers and praises which I myself did not understand. My eyes were often full of tears (I could not tell why) and at times a flood from my heart seemed to pour itself out into my bosom. I thought little of the future. I did not know whether I would ever speak to her or not or, if I spoke to her, how I could tell her of my confused adoration. But my body was like a harp and her words and gestures were like fingers running upon the wires.

One evening I went into the back drawing-room in which the priest had died. It was a dark rainy evening and there was no sound in the house. Through one of the broken panes I heard the rain impinge upon the earth, the fine incessant needles of water playing in the sodden beds. Some distant lamp or lighted window gleamed below me. I was thankful that I could see so little. All my senses seemed to desire to veil themselves and, feeling that I was about to slip from them, I pressed the palms of my hands together until they trembled, murmuring: "O love! O love!" many times.

At last she spoke to me. When she addressed the first words to me I was so confused that I did not know what to answer. She asked me was I going to *Araby*. I forgot whether I answered yes or no. It would be a splendid bazaar, she said she would love to go.

"And why can't you?" I asked.

While she spoke she turned a silver bracelet round and round her wrist. She could not go, she said, because there would be a retreat that week in her convent. Her brother and two other boys were fighting for their caps and I was alone at the railings. She held one of the spikes, bowing her head towards me. The light from the lamp opposite our door caught the white curve of her neck, lit up her hair that rested there and, falling, lit up the hand upon the railing. It fell over one side of her dress and caught the white border of a petticoat, just visible as she stood at ease.

"It's well for you," she said.

"If I go," I said, "I will bring you something."

What innumerable follies laid waste my waking and sleeping thoughts after that evening! I wished to annihilate the tedious intervening days. I chafed against the work of school. At night in my bedroom and by day in the classroom her image came between me and the page I strove to read. The syllables of the word *Araby* were called to me through the silence in which my soul luxuriated and cast an Eastern enchantment over me. I asked for leave to go to the bazaar on Saturday night. My aunt was surprised and hoped it was not some Freemason affair. I answered few questions in class. I watched my master's face pass from amiability to sternness; he hoped I was not beginning to idle. I could not call my wandering thoughts together. I had hardly any patience with the serious work of life which, now that it stood between me and my desire, seemed to me child's play, ugly monotonous child's play.

On Saturday morning I reminded my uncle that I wished to go to the bazaar in the evening. He was fussing at the hallstand, looking for the hatbrush, and answered me curtly:

"Yes, boy, I know."

As he was in the hall I could not go into the front parlour and lie at the window. I left the house in bad humour and walked slowly towards the school. The air was pitilessly raw and already my heart misgave me.

When I came home to dinner my uncle had not yet been home. Still it was early. I sat staring at the clock for some time and, when its ticking began to irritate me, I left the room. I mounted the staircase and gained the upper part of the house. The high cold empty gloomy rooms liberated me and I went from room to room singing. From the front window I saw my companions playing below in the street. Their cries reached me weakened and indistinct and, leaning my forehead against the cool glass, I looked over at the dark house where she lived. I may have stood there for an hour, seeing nothing but the brown-clad figure cast by my imagination, touched discreetly by the lamplight at the curved neck, at the hand upon the railings and at the border below the dress.

When I came downstairs again I found Mrs. Mercer sitting at the fire. She was an old garrulous woman, a pawnbroker's widow, who collected used stamps for some pious purpose. I had to endure the gossip of the tea-table. The meal was prolonged beyond an hour and still my uncle did not come. Mrs. Mercer stood up to go: she was sorry she couldn't wait any longer, but it was after eight o'clock and she did not like to be out late, as the night air was bad for her. When she had gone I began to walk up and down the room, clenching my fists. My aunt said:

"I'm afraid you may put off your bazaar for this night of Our Lord."

At nine o'clock I heard my uncle's latchkey in the halldoor. I heard him talking to himself and heard the hallstand rocking when it had received the weight of his overcoat. I could interpret these signs. When he was midway through his dinner I asked him to give me the money to go to the bazaar. He had forgotten.

"The people are in bed and after their first sleep now," he said.

I did not smile. My aunt said to him energetically:

"Can't you give him the money and let him go? You've kept him late enough as it is."

My uncle said he was very sorry he had forgotten. He said he believed in the old saying: "All work and no play makes Jack a dull boy." He asked me where I was going and, when I had told him a second time he asked me did I know *The Arab's Farewell to his Steed*. When I left the kitchen he was about to recite the opening lines of the piece to my aunt.

I held a florin tightly in my hand as I strode down Buckingham Street towards the station. The sight of the streets thronged with buyers and glaring with gas recalled to me the purpose of my journey. I took my seat in a third-class carriage of a deserted train. After an intolerable delay the train moved out of the station slowly. It crept onward among ruinous houses and over the twinkling river. At Westland Row Station a crowd of people pressed to the carriage doors; but the porters moved them back, saying that it was a special train for the bazaar. I remained alone in the bare carriage. In a few minutes the train drew up beside an improvised wooden platform. I passed out on to the road and saw by the lighted dial of a clock that it was ten minutes to ten. In front of me was a large building which displayed the magical name.

I could not find any sixpenny entrance and, fearing that the bazaar would be closed, I passed in quickly through a turnstile, handing a shilling to a weary-looking man. I found myself in a big hall girdled at half its height by a gallery. Nearly all the stalls were closed and the greater part of the hall was in darkness. I recognised a silence like that which pervades a church after a service. I walked into the centre of the bazaar timidly. A few people were gathered about the stalls which were still open. Before a curtain, over which the words *Café Chantant* were written in coloured lamps, two men were counting money on a salver. I listened to the fall of the coins.

Remembering with difficulty why I had come I went over to one of the stalls and examined porcelain vases and flowered tea-sets. At the door of the stall a young lady was talking and laughing with two young gentlemen. I remarked their English accents and listened vaguely to their conversation.

"O, I never said such a thing!"

"O, but you did!"

"O, but I didn't!"

"Didn't she say that?"

"Yes. I heard her."

"O, there's a . . . fib!"

Observing me the young lady came over and asked me did I wish to buy anything. The tone of her voice was not encouraging; she seemed to have spoken to me out of a sense of duty. I looked humbly at the great jars that stood like eastern guards at either side of the dark entrance to the stall and murmured:

"No, thank you."

The young lady changed the position of one of the vases and went back to the two young men. They began to talk of the same subject. Once or twice the young lady glanced at me over her shoulder.

I lingered before her stall, though I knew my stay was useless, to make my interest in her wares seem the more real. Then I turned away slowly and walked down the middle of the bazaar. I allowed the two pennies to fall against the sixpence in my pocket. I heard a voice call from one end of the gallery that the light was out. The upper part of the hall was now completely dark.

Gazing up into the darkness I saw myself as a creature driven and derided by vanity; and my eyes burned with anguish and anger.

SWEET FEED

Melissa Pritchard

> A little thing comforts us because
> a little thing afflicts us.
> —PASCAL

They were cooks, both crazy for food, they could have changed their minds a dozen times.

"What if it was today?"

"Me, I couldn't eat. I could maybe order, but I couldn't get the food down."

"What if he has a heart attack? Fatty dinner, no movement in the cell, stress. What stress!"

"Cooks Become Executioners."

"We'd be heroes."

Bald to the waist, massive as you'd want a cook, Moss had a bland noxious face, spongy hands, arms quivery like puddings when he pounded and cut. He spouted massive sweat, all his various bigness contrasting with a meager, puny attitude to cooking, like it was laundry, a thing he was hired to do. Fifteen years of his kettled cud had saved the prison money, unquestioned. He had no aesthete's eye, no feel for the possibilities, the uses, the salvation of food.

When he got the job, Grady hoped there'd be somebody to discuss cuisine with. He felt conspicuously let down. Moss was a bricklayer, a slabber, misleadingly obese—but what a zero, a collapse, in artistry.

Here it was, now here it came, Waller's Final Supper, with Moss at the dentist for an emergency root canal. He'd kept rolling his stubby finger along his gum yesterday, swearing. Grady knew how Moss intended microwaving Waller's last dinner—a man's final meal on earth—what was more poignant, more deserving of cautious, theologic ceremony? Grady's frustration of the past weeks, ladling splotchy stew, wan bumpy cereals, knifing up pans of nile green Jell-O, his repressed artistry clutched at this opportunity, with Moss home aching in the mouth, to outdo himself. The marketing he could do on his lunch hour; now he should meet Waller, get a better picture of his appetite.

A. B. C. Waller, Jr. had been in prison twenty-two years. He was about to be publicly executed. Waller's disposition, Grady felt, was comprehensible. His own less so.

First he smirked at the mustachio. Waller, a short, average-to-dumpy man, had a freakish mustache waxed out like fancy wrought iron. He diddled and petted alternate sides, spiraling them into horns, except the left side drooped, driving Grady nuts.

Then he started apologetic:

"Sorry to disturb you, Mr. Waller." (From what? contemplating his execution?) "I'm Grady Benson, filling in for the cook who has a toothache, root canal apparently." (Quit babbling . . .)

Grady sipped a breath. "At any rate, I'll be preparing your dinner tonight, so I kind of thought I'd stop by, go over some of the delicate points with you."

Silence.

"I'm something of a professional cook, graduated from cooking school and plan to maybe own a restaurant in five years. I can make you a supper you'll never forget. . ."

Silence.

Grady held up his clipboard. "Moss says you've asked for wild rabbit, black-pepper gravy, twenty buttermilk biscuits, and a blackberry pie. That right, sir?" The voice, since he'd expected silence, jumped him.

"That's right."

"Tricky, the wild part, sir. I can pick up some domestic rabbit over at the butcher shop, if that's acceptable to you."

"No taste to hutch rabbit."

"I could fix a mustard glaze."

"No sauce. Plain fried."

Waller turned. Grady could see his face close. The eyes, so far as Grady could tell, had practically no pupils.

"Rifle shop, somebody'd be likely to get a rabbit for you. They got a different taste, wild. Backyard rabbit's like chicken water."

"I see, thank you." Grady made a note next to wild rabbit—rifle shop, possibly feed store?

He bounced his pencil down the list but Waller shrugged, didn't matter to him, homemade or bakery on the biscuits, if a pie was homemade or store-bought. He was apathetic, enough to cause Grady, with his shopping list, to get frustrated. He would make him care, do up the finest biscuits, pie and pepper gravy Waller'd ever known, and herbs all over the rabbit.

"Well, guess that does it. You ask for milk or coffee?"

"Both."

"No problem. Ah. Pleased to meet you." The silliness of his reflexive politeness stopped him.

Waller, staring between his polished shoes, squinted up as if maybe he regretted Grady's leaving, the visit ending, though he'd acted grudging the whole time. This emboldened Grady, who had a degree of morbid gawker-on.

"Why rabbit, Mr. Waller?"

"Oh hell, probably because of my uncle, him and me used to hunt, he'd cook rabbit right over the fire. Get spin off a wild animal, he'd say.

Rub your nose on it, chew on it, you can get tough from its sliding down in you awhile."

The almost primitive poetry, the sadness, Grady couldn't believe it. What he said was "You hunt much before, Mr. Waller?"

"Every season. Some fishing in the summer. I liked it, not killing so much as waiting. Same with the fishing."

"I've had quail before."

"Yeah, quail's good tasting."

"Well, I'd better"—Grady lifted the clipboard—"get started."

Waller'd already turned away, busy with his hair ropes.

Goaded by the man's chilly apathy, Grady took two hours at lunch locating and buying what he needed.

The rabbit was late, making Grady crazy. His blackberry pie with its sparkling, crimped crust sat on the counter. The biscuits, rolled and cut, lay under a damp, striped towel. The rest of the prisoners would still be alive tomorrow; they could get by tonight on cold cuts and packaged cupcakes.

He skimmed the cleaning and jointing instructions: photographs showed yellow hands puppeting before a white drape of apron. The hands sexless, the butcher's apron monolithic. He fretted over the rattan tray, the green linen mat, napkin molded into a fan, the mossed basket of white violets, objects he had borrowed from his own apartment. The rabbit was late, really he should have bought some backyard chicken-water ex-Easter bunny. How could Waller tell the difference?

Then he had his rabbit. "Mature buck," the man from the gun shop classified, letting it sag off his shoulder, drop cloddish onto the stainless steel counter. "Know how to gut?"

Grady was prim. "Of course."

"Hey, this one stood up in the road a bull's-eye on it saying shootme, shootme, help somebody, shootme. Like a darn suicide."

He became grateful time was short; he could have stared at the rabbit a long, grievous while. Chef-like, he angled the shears and jointing knife alongside the plush, puddled body. His cookbook, a large fancy one from England, was propped against the rice canister.

Grady swore. The first photograph showed a hand with shears at a pretty angle slitting the belly, yet the first printed instruction said sever the head at the back of the neck, the feet at the first joint. There was no photograph of a beheading or befooting. He wondered if Waller couldn't be brought in, under guard, to do this first thing. He got the cleaver.

Cupping his left hand over the head and eye like a blessing, he hurled the cleaver in a shuttered motion from his right shoulder. Whack. Where to put the head. Queasy, he balled it up in paper toweling, letting it go with hasty ceremony into the rubber barrel under the counter. He had a hitchcock fear of that head, but one look at the clock sobered him, tethered him to the book's demands. Slit the belly to the vent. He tugged the flesh out from the fur, pulled at the hind legs until they popped loose, severed the tail. In step five, pry front legs free, draw the animal up out of its skin. Grady embarrassed himself by being sick. After hanging over the sink with the taps running, he returned to the skinned carcass, removed the entrails and jointed the body. This was easier. He'd done chickens. It was chicken now, raspberry flesh, the bluish glisten over it. Flipping the pieces in seasoned flour, he began frying them in peanut oil. Good smell, Grady sniffed, thumb-smoothing the white ball of tail, setting it on the ledge, a luck piece.

Two uniformed guards entered the enormous work kitchen while Grady fidgeted with matches and a white candle. Uncover the rabbit last, he told them. Pepper gravy's in this pewter boat. Awarded for his presentation in cooking schools, Grady half-wished for a camera.

"Pretty," one guard said, pinkie in the gravy and sucking.

"Waste of time," said the other.

He'd saved a bit of rabbit for himself on a plastic salad plate. About the time he pictured Waller receiving his meal, Grady took a small picky bite. He could identify the taste as rank, almost weedy, but couldn't swallow the meat, nipping it out of his mouth. He began mopping up blood, gristle, sinew.

And later, while Grady was gouging out flubby pale eyes of potatoes (the cruelties. . . slicing, chopping bits of animal, mute skinned vegetables—a series of kitchen horrors), one of the guards returned his tray, the Cynic who'd called Grady's effort a waste. Had it been the other, the appreciative one, he might have inquired how Waller'd acted, if he'd been pleased.

The two of them, however, both stared at the tray. A blot of blackberry, a faint swipe around Grady's Wedgwood plate where one of twenty biscuits had chased gravy. A circle of coffee in the saucer. Knife and fork laid in an X or a cross.

"Why didn't he just inhale the napkin?"

Grady was moved by this ravenous, defiant appetite. He decided to ask.

"Did he say anything?"

"What?"

"Didn't he say something about my dinner?"

"Nope. Just ate."

Grady pictured Waller eating, TV turned down, green napkin denting into the blue prison shirt. The mustachio, cliche of evil, bits of food sticking in it. Mouth methodically circling. Aware of its last bite. Petty, this feeling cheated of a doomed man's praise, but he wondered if it made a difference (imagine Moss trying to do that dinner!). Grady's reward would have to be evidential in the wiped-clean plates and nothing left over.

He carried the tray to the sink, swinging the plate to rinse it. A note lay under the plate. He clunked the plate in the sink, turned off the water, dried his fingers, picked up the note.

> It surely is better to step into the next world, tho I doubt there is one, on a full stomach. Rabbit was good, tho not the best. The best is first. P.S. Flowers nice. Yours in All Sincerity, A. B. C. Waller Jr.

"What in hell panty-waist thing is this?" Moss, groggy on painkillers, stared at the tray. "Sonabitch. Grady, this guy's an ice cold killer, a murderer, a no-soul, how come the flowers and doily shit?"

Grady couldn't speak to somebody like Moss about food, its seriousness, how he offered Waller this final vitality of rabbit. Waller's instincts had been perfect, his wish perfect. Grady couldn't explain any of it.

"Why are you back? Your face is still swollen."

"Execution. I could get a place for you."

Now he was staring at the tray. Grady wondered what Moss could be thinking.

"Got an idea for your restaurant."

"What's that?"

"Dead Man's Dinners. You get your menu from a bunch of last suppers. Photos and stories of the guys, what they did, what they ordered. Have people eating in little fake cells."

"Then the check kills them?" Grady snorted, but Moss had turned gray and grumpy so he stopped.

"Great idea, Moss. That is one big idea. Thanks."

"Nothin. Jesus, my face hurts. Feels walked on."

Moss was crammed with the others, face big and hurting watching Waller die. Grady skinned and diced potatoes, then onions, his eyes squeezing water. He couldn't go home. He decided to make sweet dough and freeze it. Five minutes to eleven. Wheeled in on the gurney. Trussed down. Everybody waiting for him to get the injection.

Grady stopped that picture, put in its place a rabbit bounding, springing whole around the woodsy insides of Waller, with violets fragrant, seeding.

In the prison kitchen then, punching gray, greasy dough, in a stink of yeast, Grady brought his forehead to the steel lip of the bowl, wanting comfort from his blind, little rise of bread.

THE CHRYSANTHEMUMS

John Steinbeck (1902–1968)

The high grey-flannel fog of winter closed off the Salinas Valley from the sky and from all the rest of the world. On every side it sat like a lid on the mountains and made of the great valley a closed pot. On the broad, level land floor the gang plows bit deep and left the black earth shining like metal where the shares had cut. On the foothill ranches across the Salinas River, the yellow stubble fields seemed to be bathed in pale cold sunshine, but there was no sunshine in the valley now in December. The thick willow scrub along the river flamed with sharp and positive yellow leaves.

It was a time of quiet and of waiting. The air was cold and tender. A light wind blew up from the southwest so that the farmers were mildly hopeful of a good rain before long; but fog and rain do not go together.

Across the river, on Henry Allen's foothill ranch there was little work to be done, for the hay was cut and stored and the orchards were plowed up to receive the rain deeply when it should come. The cattle on the higher slopes were becoming shaggy and rough-coated.

Elisa Allen, working in her flower garden, looked down across the yard and saw Henry, her husband, talking to two men in business suits. The three of them stood by the tractor shed, each man with one foot on the side of the little Fordson. They smoked cigarettes and studied the machine as they talked.

Elisa watched them for a moment and then went back to her work. She was thirty-five. Her face was lean and strong and her eyes were as clear as water. Her figure looked blocked and heavy in her gardening costume, a man's black hat pulled low down over her eyes, clodhopper shoes, a figured print dress almost completely covered by a big corduroy apron with four big pockets to hold the snips, the trowel and scratcher, the seeds and the knife she worked with. She wore heavy leather gloves to protect her hands while she worked.

She was cutting down the old year's chrysanthemum stalks with a pair of short and powerful scissors. She looked down toward the men by the tractor shed now and then. Her face was eager and mature and handsome; even her work with the scissors was over-eager, over-powerful. The chrysanthemum stems seemed too small and easy for her energy.

She brushed a cloud of hair out of her eyes with the back of her glove, and left a smudge of earth on her cheek in doing it. Behind her stood the neat white farm house with red geraniums close-banked around it as high as the windows. It was a hard-swept looking little house, with hard-polished windows, and a clean mud-mat on the front steps.

Elisa cast another glance toward the tractor shed. The strangers were getting into their Ford coupe. She took off a glove and put her strong fingers down into the forest of new green chrysanthemum sprouts that were growing around the old roots. She spread the leaves and looked down among the close-growing stems. No aphids were there, no sow-bugs or snails or cutworms. Her terrier fingers destroyed such pests before they could get started.

Elisa started at the sound of her husband's voice. He had come near quietly, and he leaned over the wire fence that protected her flower garden from cattle and dogs and chickens.

"At it again," he said. "You've got a strong new crop coming."

Elisa straightened her back and pulled on the gardening glove again. "Yes. They'll be strong this coming year." In her tone and on her face there was a little smugness.

"You've got a gift with things," Henry observed. "Some of those yellow chrysanthemums you had this year were ten inches across. I wish you'd work out in the orchard and raise apples that big."

Her eyes sharpened. "Maybe I could do it, too. I've a gift with things, all right. My mother had it. She could stick anything in the ground and make it grow. She said it was having planters' hands that knew how to do it."

"Well, it sure works with flowers," he said.

"Henry, who were those men you were talking to?"

"Why, sure, that's what I came to tell you. They were from the Western Meat Company. I sold those thirty head of three-year-old steers. Got nearly my own price, too."

"Good," she said. "Good for you."

"And I thought," he continued, "I thought how it's Saturday afternoon, and we might go into Salinas for dinner at a restaurant, and then to a picture show—to celebrate, you see."

"Good," she repeated. "Oh, yes. That will be good."

Henry put on his joking tone. "There's fights tonight. How'd you like to go to the fights?"

"Oh, no," she said breathlessly. "No, I wouldn't like fights."

"Just fooling, Elisa. We'll go to a movie. Let's see. It's two now. I'm going to take Scotty and bring down those steers from the hill. It'll take us maybe two hours. We'll go in town about five and have dinner at the Cominos Hotel. Like that?"

"Of course I'll like it. It's good to eat away from home."

"All right, then. I'll go get up a couple of horses."

She said, "I'll have plenty of time to transplant some of these sets, I guess."

She heard her husband calling Scotty down by the barn. And a little later she saw the two men ride up the pale yellow hillside in search of the steers.

There was a little square sandy bed kept for rooting the chrysanthemums. With her trowel she turned the soil over and over, and smoothed it and patted it firm. Then she dug ten parallel trenches to receive the sets. Back at the chrysanthemum bed she pulled out the little crisp shoots, trimmed off the leaves of each one with her scissors and laid it on a small orderly pile.

A squeak of wheels and plod of hoofs came from the road. Elisa looked up. The country road ran along the dense bank of willows and cottonwoods that bordered the river, and up this road came a curious vehicle, curiously drawn. It was an old spring-wagon, with a round canvas top on it like the cover of a prairie schooner. It was drawn by an old bay horse and a little grey-and-white burro. A big stubble-bearded man sat between the cover flaps and drove the crawling team. Underneath the wagon, between the hind wheels, a lean and rangy mongrel dog walked sedately. Words were painted on the canvas, in clumsy, crooked letters. "Pots, pans, knives, sisors, lawn mores, Fixed." Two rows of articles, and the triumphantly definitive "Fixed" below. The black paint had run down in little sharp points beneath each letter.

Elisa, squatting on the ground, watched to see the crazy, loose-jointed wagon pass by. But it didn't pass. It turned into the farm road in front of her house, crooked old wheels skirling and squeaking. The rangy dog darted from between the wheels and ran ahead. Instantly the two ranch shepherds flew out at him. Then all three stopped, and with stiff and quivering tails, with taut straight legs, with ambassadorial dignity, they slowly circled, sniffing daintily. The caravan pulled up to Elisa's wire fence and stopped. Now the newcomer dog, feeling out-numbered, lowered his tail and retired under the wagon with raised hackles and bared teeth.

The man on the wagon seat called out, "That's a bad dog in a fight when he gets started."

Elisa laughed. "I see he is. How soon does he generally get started?"

The man caught up her laughter and echoed it heartily. "Sometimes not for weeks and weeks," he said. He climbly stiffly down, over the wheel. The horse and the donkey drooped like unwatered flowers.

Elisa saw that he was a very big man. Although his hair and beard were greying, he did not look old. His worn black suit was wrinkled and spotted with grease. The laughter had disappeared from his face and eyes the moment his laughing voice ceased. His eyes were dark, and they were full of the brooding that gets in the eyes of teamsters and of sailors. The calloused hands he rested on the wire fence were cracked, and every crack was a black line. He took off his battered hat.

"I'm off my general road, ma'am," he said. "Does this dirt road cut over across the river to the Los Angeles highway?"

Elisa stood up and shoved the thick scissors in her apron pocket. "Well, yes, it does, but it winds around and then fords the river. I don't think your team could pull through the sand."

He replied with some asperity, "It might surprise you what them beasts can pull through."

"When they get started?" she asked.

He smiled for a second. "Yes. When they get started."

"Well," said Elisa, "I think you'll save time if you go back to the Salinas road and pick up the highway there."

He drew a big finger down the chicken wire and made it sing. "I ain't in any hurry, ma'am. I go from Seattle to San Diego and back every year. Takes all my time. About six months each way. I aim to follow nice weather."

Elisa took off her gloves and stuffed them in the apron pocket with the scissors. She touched the under edge of her man's hat, searching for fugitive hairs. "That sounds like a nice kind of a way to live," she said.

He leaned confidentially over the fence. "Maybe you noticed the writing on my wagon. I mend pots and sharpen knives and scissors. You got any of them things to do?"

"Oh, no," she said quickly. "Nothing like that." Her eyes hardened with resistance.

"Scissors is the worst thing," he explained. "Most people just ruin scissors trying to sharpen 'em, but I know how. I got a special tool. It's a little bobbit kind of thing, and patented. But it sure does the trick."

"No, My scissors are all sharp."

"All right, then. Take a pot," he continued earnestly, "a bent pot, or a pot with a hole. I can make it like new so you don't have to buy no new ones. That's a saving for you."

"No," she said shortly. "I tell you I have nothing like that for you to do."

His face fell to an exaggerated sadness. His voice took on a whining undertone. "I ain't had a thing to do today. Maybe I won't have no supper tonight. You see I'm off my regular road. I know folks on the highway clear from Seattle to San Diego. They save their things for me to sharpen up because they know I do it so good and save them money."

"I'm sorry," Elisa said irritably. "I haven't anything for you to do."

His eyes left her face and fell to searching the ground. They roamed about until they came to the chrysanthemum bed where she had been working. "What's them plants, ma'am?"

The irritation and resistance melted from Elisa's face. "Oh, those are chrysanthemums, giant whites and yellows. I raise them every year, bigger than anybody around here."

"Kind of a long-stemmed flower? Looks like a quick puff of colored smoke?" he asked.

"That's it. What a nice way to describe them."

"They smell kind of nasty till you get used to them," he said.

"It's a good bitter smell," she retorted, "not nasty at all."

He changed his tone quickly. "I like the smell myself."

"I had ten-inch blooms this year," she said.

The man leaned farther over the fence. "Look, I know a lady down the road a piece, has got the nicest garden you ever seen. Got nearly every kind of flower but no chrysanthemums. Last time I was mending a copper-bottom washtub for her (that's a hard job but I do it good), she said to me, 'If you ever run acrost some nice chrysantheums I wish you'd try to get me a few seeds.' That's what she told me."

Elisa's eyes grew alert and eager. "She couldn't have known much about chrysanthemums. You *can* raise them from seed, but it's much easier to root the little sprouts you see there."

"Oh," he said. "I s'pose I can't take none to her, then."

"Why yes you can," Elisa cried. "I can put some in damp sand, and you can carry them right along with you. They'll take root in the pot if you keep them damp. And then she can transplant them."

"She'd sure like to have some, ma'am. You say they're nice ones?"

"Beautiful," she said. "Oh, beautiful." Her eyes shone. She tore off the battered hat and shook out her dark pretty hair. "I'll put them in a flower pot, and you can take them right with you. Come into the yard."

While the man came through the picket gate Elisa ran excitedly along the geranium-bordered path to the back of the house. And she returned carrying a big red flower pot. The gloves were forgotten now. She kneeled on the ground by the starting bed and dug up the sandy soil with her fingers and scooped it into the bright new flower pot. Then she picked up the little pile of shoots she had prepared. With her strong fingers she pressed them into the sand and tamped around them with her knuckles. The man stood over her. "I'll tell you what to do," she said. "You remember so you can tell the lady."

"Yes, I'll try to remember."

"Well, look. These will take root in about a month. Then she must set them out, about a foot apart in good rich earth like this, see?" She lifted a handful of dark soil for him to look at. "They'll grow fast and tall. Now remember this: In July tell her to cut them down, about eight inches from the ground."

"Before they bloom?" he asked.

"Yes, before they bloom." Her face was tight with eagerness. "They'll grow right up again. About the last of September the buds will start."

She stopped and seemed perplexed. "It's the budding that takes the most care," she said hesitantly. "I don't know how to tell you." She looked deep into his eyes, searchingly. Her mouth opened a little, and she seemed to be listening. "I'll try to tell you," she said. "Did you ever hear of planting hands?"

"Can't say I have, ma'am."

"Well, I can only tell you what it feels like. It's when you're picking off the buds you don't want. Everything goes right down into your fingertips. You watch your fingers work. They do it themselves. You can feel how it is. They pick and pick the buds. They never make a mistake. They're with the plant. Do you see? Your fingers and the plant. You can feel that, right up your arm. They know. They never make a mistake. You can feel it. When you're like that you can't do anything wrong. Do you see that? Can you understand that?"

She was kneeling on the ground looking up at him. Her breast swelled passionately.

The man's eyes narrowed. He looked away self-consciously, "Maybe I know," he said. "Sometimes in the night in the wagon there—"

Elisa's voice grew husky. She broke in on him, "I've never lived as you do, but I know what you mean. When the night is dark—why, the stars are sharp-pointed, and there's quiet. Why, you rise up and up! Every pointed star gets driven into your body. It's like that. Hot and sharp and—lovely."

Kneeling there, her hand went out toward his legs in the greasy black trousers. Her hesitant fingers almost touched the cloth. Then her hand dropped to the ground. She crouched low like a fawning dog.

He said, "It's nice, just like you say. Only when you don't have no dinner, it ain't."

She stood up then, very straight, and her face was ashamed. She held the flower pot out to him and placed it gently in his arms. "Here. Put it in your wagon, on the seat, where you can watch it. Maybe I can find something for you to do."

At the back of the house she dug in the can pile and found two old and battered aluminum saucepans. She carried them back and gave them to him. "Here, maybe you can fix these."

His manner changed. He became professional. "Good as new I can fix them." At the back of his wagon he set a little anvil, and out of an oily tool box dug a small machine hammer. Elisa came through the gate to watch him while he pounded out the dents in the kettles. His mouth grew sure and knowing. At a difficult part of the work he sucked his under-lip.

"You sleep right in the wagon?" Elisa asked.

"Right in the wagon, ma'am. Rain or shine I'm dry as a cow in there."

"It must be nice," she said. "It must be very nice. I wish women could do such things."

"It ain't the right kind of a life for a woman."

Her upper lip raised a little, showing her teeth. "How do you know? How can you tell?" she said.

"I don't know, ma'am," he protested. "Of course I don't know. Now here's your kettles, done. You don't have to buy no new ones."

"How much?"

"Oh, fifty cents'll do. I keep my prices down and my work good. That's why I have all them satisfied customers up and down the highway."

Elisa brought him a fifty-cent piece from the house and dropped it in his hand. "You might be surprised to have a rival some time. I can sharpen scissors, too. And I can beat the dents out of little pots. I could show you what a woman might do."

He put his hammer back in the oily box and shoved the little anvil out of sight. "It would be a lonely life for a woman, ma'am, and a scarey life, too, with animals creeping under the wagon all night." He climbed over the singletree, steadying himself with a hand on the burro's white rump. He settled himself in the seat, picked up the lines. "Thank you kindly, ma'am," he said. "I'll do like you told me; I'll go back and catch the Salinas road."

"Mind," she called, "if you're long in getting there, keep the sand damp."

"Sand, ma'am? . . . Sand? Oh, sure. You mean around the chrysanthemums. Sure I will." He clucked his tongue. The beasts leaned luxuriously into their collars. The mongrel dog took his place between the back wheels. The wagon turned and crawled out the entrance road and back the way it had come, along the river.

Elisa stood in front of her wire fence watching the slow progress of the caravan. Her shoulders were straight, her head thrown back, her eyes half-closed, so that the scene came vaguely into them. Her lips moved silently, forming the words "Good-bye—good-bye." Then she whispered, "That's a bright direction. There's a glowing there." The sound of her whisper startled her. She shook herself free and looked about to see whether anyone had been listening. Only the dogs had heard. They lifted their heads toward her from their sleeping in the dust, and then stretched out their chins and settled asleep again. Elisa turned and ran hurriedly into the house.

In the kitchen she reached behind the stove and felt the water tank. It was full of hot water from the noonday cooking. In the bathroom she tore off her soiled clothes and flung them into the corner. And then she scrubbed herself with a little block of pumice, legs and thighs, loins and chest and arms, until her skin was scratched and red. When she had dried herself she stood in front of a mirror in her bedroom and looked at her body. She tightened her stomach and threw out her chest. She turned and looked over her shoulder at her back.

After a while she began to dress, slowly. She put on her newest underclothing and her nicest stockings and the dress which was the symbol of her prettiness. She worked carefully on her hair, penciled her eyebrows and rouged her lips.

Before she was finished she heard the little thunder of hoofs and the shouts of Henry and his helper as they drove the red steers into the corral. She heard the gate bang shut and set herself for Henry's arrival.

His step sounded on the porch. He entered the house calling, "Elisa, where are you?"

"In my room, dressing. I'm not ready. There's hot water for your bath. Hurry up. It's getting late."

When she heard him splashing in the tub, Elisa laid his dark suit on the bed, and shirt and socks and tie beside it. She stood his polished shoes on the floor beside the bed. Then she went to the porch and sat primly and stiffly down. She looked toward the river road where the willow-line was still yellow with frosted leaves so that under the high grey fog they seemed a thin band of sunshine. This was the only color in the grey afternoon. She sat unmoving for a long time. Her eyes blinked rarely.

Henry came banging out of the door, shoving his tie inside his vest as he came. Elisa stiffened and her face grew tight. Henry stopped short and looked at her. "Why—why, Elisa. You look so nice!"

"Nice? You think I look nice? What do you mean by 'nice'?"

Henry blundered on. "I don't know. I mean you look different, strong and happy."

"I am strong? Yes, strong. What do you mean 'strong'?"

He looked bewildered. "You're playing some kind of a game," he said helplessly. "It's a kind of a play. You look strong enough to break a calf over your knee, happy enough to eat it like a watermelon."

For a second she lost her rigidity. "Henry! Don't talk like that. You didn't know what you said." She grew complete again. "I'm strong," she boasted. "I never knew before how strong."

Henry looked down toward the tractor shed, and when he brought his eyes back to her, they were his own again. "I'll get out the car. You can put on your coat while I'm starting."

Elisa went into the house. She heard him drive to the gate and idle down his motor, and then she took a long time to put on her hat. She pulled it here and pressed it there. When Henry turned the motor off she slipped into her coat and went out.

The little roadster bounced along on the dirt road by the river, raising the birds and driving the rabbits into the brush. Two cranes flapped heavily over the willow-line and dropped into the river-bed.

Far ahead on the road Elisa saw a dark speck. She knew.

She tried not to look as they passed it, but her eyes would not obey. She whispered to herself sadly, "He might have thrown them off the road. That wouldn't have been much trouble, not very much. But he kept the pot," she explained. "He had to keep the pot. That's why he couldn't get them off the road."

The roadster turned a bend and she saw the caravan ahead. She swung full around toward her husband so she could not see the little covered wagon and the mismatched team as the car passed them.

In a moment it was over. The thing was done. She did not look back.

She said loudly, to be heard above the motor, "It will be good, tonight, a good dinner."

"Now you're changed again," Henry complained. He took one hand from the wheel and patted her knee. "I ought to take you in to dinner oftener. It would be good for both of us. We get so heavy out on the ranch."

"Henry," she asked, "could we have wine at dinner?"

"Sure we could. Say! That will be fine."

She was silent for a while; then she said, "Henry, those prize fights, do the men hurt each other very much?"

"Sometimes a little, not often. Why?"

"Well, I've read how they break noses, and blood runs down their chests. I've read how the fighting gloves get heavy and soggy with blood."

He looked around at her. "What's the matter, Elisa? I didn't know you read things like that." He brought the car to a stop, then turned to the right over the Salinas River bridge.

"Do any women ever go to the fights?" she asked.

"Oh, sure, some. What's the matter, Elisa? Do you want to go? I don't think you'd like it, but I'll take you if you really want to go."

She relaxed limply in the seat. "Oh, no. No. I don't want to go. I'm sure I don't." Her face was turned away from him. "It will be enough if we can have wine. It will be plenty." She turned up her coat collar so he could not see that she was crying weakly—like an old woman.

THE RED CONVERTIBLE

Lyman Lamartine

Louise Erdrich (b. 1954)

I was the first one to drive a convertible on my reservation. And of course it was red, a red Olds. I owned that car along with my brother Henry Junior. We owned it together until his boots filled with water on a windy night and he bought out my share. Now Henry owns the whole car, and his younger brother Lyman (that's myself), Lyman walks everywhere he goes.

How did I earn enough money to buy my share in the first place? My own talent was I could always make money. I had a touch for it, unusual in a Chippewa. From the first I was different that way, and everyone recognized it. I was the only kid they let in the American Legion Hall to shine shoes, for example, and one Christmas I sold spiritual bouquets for the mission door to door. The nuns let me keep a percentage. Once I started, it seemed the more money I made the easier the money came. Everyone encouraged it. When I was fifteen I got a job washing dishes at the Joliet Café, and that was where my first big break happened.

It wasn't long before I was promoted to busing tables, and then the short-order cook quit and I was hired to take her place. No sooner than you know it I was managing the Joliet. The rest is history. I went on managing. I soon became part owner, and of course there was no stopping me then. It wasn't long before the whole thing was mine.

After I'd owned the Joliet for one year, it blew over in the worst tornado ever seen around here. The whole operation was smashed to bits. A total loss. The fryalator was up in a tree, the grill torn in half like it was paper. I was only sixteen. I had it all in my mother's name, and I lost it quick, but before I lost it I had every one of my relatives, and their relatives, to dinner, and I also bought that red Olds I mentioned, along with Henry.

The first time we saw it! I'll tell you when we first saw it. We had gotten a ride up to Winnipeg, and both of us had money. Don't ask me why, because we never mentioned a car or anything, we just had all our money. Mine was cash, a big bankroll from the Joliet's insurance. Henry had two checks—a week's extra pay for being laid off, and his regular check from the Jewel Bearing Plant.

We were walking down Portage anyway, seeing the sights, when we saw it. There it was, parked, large as life. Really as *if* it was alive. I thought of the word *repose*, because the car wasn't simply stopped, parked, or whatever. That car reposed, calm and gleaming, a FOR SALE sign in its left front window. Then, before we had thought it over at all, the car belonged to us and our pockets were empty. We had just enough money for gas back home.

We went places in that car, me and Henry. We took off driving all one whole summer. We started off toward the Little Knife River and Mandaree in Fort Berthold and then we found ourselves down in Wakpala somehow, and then suddenly we were over in Montana on the Rocky Boy, and yet the summer was not even half over. Some people hang on to details when they travel, but we didn't let them bother us and just lived our everyday lives here to there.

I do remember this one place with willows. I remember I laid under those trees and it was comfortable. So comfortable. The branches bent down all around me like a tent or a stable. And quiet, it was quiet, even though there was a powwow close enough so I could see it going on. The air was not too still, not too windy either. When the dust rises up and hangs in the air around the dancers like that, I feel good. Henry was asleep with his arms thrown wide. Later on, he woke up and we started driving again. We were somewhere in Montana, or maybe on the Blood Reserve—it could have been anywhere Anyway it was where we met the girl.

All her hair was in buns around her ears, that's the first thing I noticed about her. She was posed alongside the road with her arm out, so we stopped. That girl was short, so short her lumber shirt looked comical on her, like a nightgown. She had jeans on and fancy moccasins and she carried a little suitcase.

"Hop on in," says Henry. So she climbs in between us.

"We'll take you home," I says. "Where do you live?"

"Chicken," she says.

"Where the hell's that?" I ask her.

"Alaska."

"Okay," says Henry, and we drive.

We got up there and never wanted to leave. The sun doesn't truly set there in summer, and the night is more a soft dusk. You might doze off, sometimes, but before you know it you're up again, like an animal in nature. You never feel like you have to sleep hard or put away the world. And things would grow up there. One day just dirt or moss, the next day flowers and long grass. The girl's name was Susy. Her family really took to us. They fed us and put us up. We had our own tent to live in by their house, and the kids would be in and out of there all day and night. They couldn't get over me and Henry being brothers, we looked so different. We told them we knew we had the same mother, anyway.

One night Susy came in to visit us. We sat around in the tent talking of this and that. The season was changing. It was getting darker by that time, and the cold was even getting just a little mean. I told her it was time for us to go. She stood up on a chair.

"You never seen my hair," Susy said.

That was true. She was standing on a chair, but still, when she unclipped her buns the hair reached all the way to the ground. Our eyes opened. You couldn't tell how much hair she had when it was rolled up so neatly. Then my brother Henry did something funny. He went up to the chair and said, "Jump on my shoulders." So she did that, and her hair reached down past his waist, and he started twirling, this way and that, so her hair was flung out from side to side.

"I always wondered what it was like to have long pretty hair," Henry says. Well we laughed. It was a funny sight, the way he did it. The next morning we got up and took leave of those people.

* * *

On to greener pastures, as they say. It was down through Spokane and across Idaho then Montana and very soon we were racing the weather right along under the Canadian border through Columbus, Des Lacs, and then we were in Bottineau County and soon home. We'd made most of the trip, that summer, without putting up the car hood at all. We got home just in time, it turned out, for the army to remember Henry had signed up to join it.

I don't wonder that the army was so glad to get my brother that they turned him into a Marine. He was built like a brick outhouse anyway. We liked to tease him that they really wanted him for his Indian nose. He had a nose big and sharp as a hatchet, like the nose on Red Tomahawk, the Indian who killed Sitting Bull, whose profile is on signs all along the North Dakota highways. Henry went off to training camp, came home once during Christmas, then the next thing you know we got an overseas letter from him. It was 1970, and he said he was stationed up in the northern hill country. Whereabouts I did not know. He wasn't such a hot letter writer, and only got off two before the enemy caught him. I could never keep it straight, which direction those good Vietnam soldiers were from.

I wrote him back several times, even though I didn't know if those letters would get through. I kept him informed all about the car. Most of the time I had it up on blocks in the yard or half taken apart, because that long trip did a hard job on it under the hood.

I always had good luck with numbers, and never worried about the draft myself. I never even had to think about what my number was. But Henry was never lucky in the same way as me. It was at least three years before Henry came home. By then I guess the whole war was solved in the government's mind, but for him it would keep on going. In those years I'd put his car into almost perfect shape. I always thought of it as his car while he was gone, even though when he left he said, "Now it's yours," and threw me his key.

"Thanks for the extra key," I'd said, "I'll put it up in your drawer just in case I need it." He laughed.

When he came home, though, Henry was very different, and I'll say this: the change was no good. You could hardly expect him to change for the better, I know. But he was quiet, so quiet, and never comfortable sitting still anywhere but always up and moving around. I thought back to times we'd sat still for whole afternoons, never moving a muscle, just shifting our weight along the ground, talking to whoever sat with us, watching things. He'd always had a joke, then, too, and now you couldn't get him to laugh, or when he did it was more the sound of a man choking, a sound that stopped up the throats of other people around him. They got to leaving him alone most of the time, and I didn't blame them. It was a fact: Henry was jumpy and mean.

I'd bought a color TV set for my mom and the rest of us while Henry was away. Money still came very easy. I was sorry I'd ever bought it though, because of Henry. I was also sorry I'd bought color, because with black-and-white the pictures seem older and farther away. But what are you going to do? He sat in front of it, watching it, and that was the only time he was completely still. But it was the kind of stillness that you see in a rabbit when it freezes and before it will bolt. He was not easy. He sat in his chair gripping the armrests with all his might, as if the chair itself was moving at a high speed and if he let go at all he would rocket forward and maybe crash right through the set.

Once I was in the room watching TV with Henry and I heard his teeth click at something. I looked over, and he'd bitten through his lip. Blood was going down his chin. I tell you right then I wanted to smash that tube to pieces. I went over to it but Henry must have known what I was up to. He rushed from his chair and shoved me out of the way, against the wall I told myself he didn't know what he was doing.

My mom came in, turned the set off real quiet, and told us she had made something for supper. So we went and sat down. There was still blood going down Henry's chin, but he didn't notice it and no one said anything, even though every time he took a bit of his bread his blood fell onto it until he was eating his own blood mixed in with the food.

While Henry was not around we talked about what was going to happen to him. There were no Indian doctors on the reservation, and my mom was afraid of trusting the old man, Moses Pillager, because he courted her long ago and was jealous of her husbands. He might take revenge through her son. We were afraid that if we brought Henry to a regular hospital they would keep him.

"They don't fix them in those places," Mom said; "they just give them drugs."

"We wouldn't get him there in the first place," I agreed, "so let's just forget about it."

Then I thought about the car.

Henry had not even looked at the car since he'd gotten home, though like I said, it was in tip-top condition and ready to drive. I thought the car might bring the old Henry back somehow. So I bided my time and waited for my chance to interest him in the vehicle.

One night Henry was off somewhere. I took myself a hammer. I went out to that car and I did a number on its underside. Whacked it up. Bent the tail pipe double. Ripped the muffler loose. By the time I was done with the car it looked worse than any typical Indian car that has been driven all its life on reservation roads, which they always say are like government promises—full of holes. It just about hurt me, I'll tell you that! I threw dirt in the carburetor and I ripped all the electric tape off the seats. I made it look just as beat up as I could. Then I sat back and waited for Henry to find it.

Still, it took him over a month. That was all right, because it was just getting warm enough, not melting, but warm enough to work outside.

"Lyman," he says, walking in one day, "that red car looks like shit."

"Well it's old," I says. "You got to expect that."

"No way!" says Henry. "That car's a classic! But you went and ran the piss right out of it, Lyman, and you know it don't deserve that. I kept that car in A-one shape. You don't remember. You're too young. But when I left, that car was running like a watch. Now I don't even know if I can get it to start again, let alone get it anywhere near its old condition."

"Well you try," I said, like I was getting mad, "but I say it's a piece of junk."

Then I walked out before he could realize I knew he'd strung together more than six words at once.

After that I thought he'd freeze himself to death working on that car. He was out there all day, and at night he rigged up a little lamp, ran a cord out the window, and had himself some light to see by while he worked. He was better than he had been before, but that's still not saying much. It was easier for him to do the things the rest of us did. He ate more slowly and didn't jump up and down during the meal to get this or that or look out the window. I put my hand in the back of the TV set, I admit, and fiddled around with it good, so that it was almost impossible now to get a clear picture. He didn't look at it very often anyway. He was always out with that car or going off to get parts for it. By the time it was really melting outside, he had it fixed.

I had been feeling down in the dumps about Henry around this time. We had always been together before. Henry and Lyman. But he was such a loner now that I didn't know how to take it. So I jumped at the chance one day when Henry seemed friendly. It's not that he smiled or anything. He just said, "Let's take that old shitbox for a spin." Just the way he said it made me think he could becoming around.

We went out to the car. It was spring. The sun was shining very bright. My only sister, Bonita, who was just eleven years old, came out and made us stand together for a picture. Henry leaned his elbow on the red car's windshield, and he took his other arm and put it over my shoulder, very carefully, as though it was heavy for him to lift and he didn't want to bring the weight down all at once.

"Smile," Bonita said, and he did.

That picture, I never look at it anymore. A few months ago, I don't know why, I got his picture out and tacked it on the wall. I felt good about Henry at the time, close to him. I felt good having his picture on the wall, until one night when I was looking at television. I was a little drunk and stoned. I looked up at the wall and Henry was staring at me. I don't know what it was, but his smile had changed, or maybe it was gone. All I know is I couldn't stay in the same room with that picture. I was shaking. I got up, closed the door, and went into the kitchen. A little later my friend Ray came over and we both went back into that room. We put the picture in a brown bag, folded the bag over and over tightly, then put it way back in a closet.

I still see that picture now, as if it tugs at me, whenever I pass that closet door. The picture is very clear in my mind. It was so sunny that day Henry had to squint against the glare. Or maybe the camera Bonita held flashed like a mirror, blinding him, before she snapped the picture. My face is right out in the sun, big and round. But he might have drawn back, because the shadows on his face are deep as holes. There are two shadows curved like little hooks around the ends of his smile, as if to frame it and try to keep it there—that one, first smile that looked like it might have hurt his face. He has his field jacket on and the worn-in clothes he'd come back in and kept wearing ever since. After Bonita took the picture, she went into the house and we got into the car. There was a full cooler in the trunk. We started off, east, toward Pembina and the Red River because Henry said he wanted to see the high water.

The trip over there was beautiful. When everything starts changing, drying up, clearing off, you feel like your whole life is starting. Henry felt it, too. The top was down and the car hummed like a top. He'd really put it back in shape, even the tape on the seats was very carefully put down and glued back in layers. It's not that he smiled again or even joked, but his face looked to me as if it was clear, more peaceful. It looked as though he wasn't thinking of anything in particular except the bare fields and windbreaks and houses we were passing.

The river was high and full of winter trash when we got there. The sun was still out, but it was colder by the river. There were still little clumps of dirty snow here and there on the banks. The water hadn't gone over the banks yet, but it would, you could tell. It was just at its limit, hard swollen glossy like an old gray scar. We made ourselves a fire, and we sat down and watched the current go. As I watched it I felt something squeezing inside me and tightening and trying to let go all at the same time. I knew I was not just feeling it myself; I knew I was feeling what Henry was going through at that moment. Except that I couldn't stand it, the closing and opening. I jumped to my feet. I took Henry by the shoulders and I started shaking him. "Wake up," I says, "wake up, wake up, wake up!" I didn't know what had come over me. I sat down beside him again.

His face was totally white and hard. Then it broke, like stones break all of a sudden when water boils up inside them.

"I know it," he says. "I know it. I can't help it. It's no use."

We start talking. He said he knew what I'd done with the car. It was obvious it had been whacked out of shape and not just neglected. He said he wanted to give the car to me for good now, it was no use. He said he'd fixed it just to give it back and I should take it.

"No way," I says, "I don't want it."

"That's okay," he says, "you take it."

"I don't want it, though," I says back to him, and then to emphasize, just to emphasize, you understand, I touch his shoulder. He slaps my hand off.

"Take that car," he says.

"No," I say. "Make me," I say, and then he grabs my jacket and rips the arm loose. That jacket is a class act, suede with tags and zippers. I push Henry backwards, off the log. He jumps up and bowls me over. We go down in a clinch and come up swinging hard, for all we're worth, with our fists. He socks my jaw so hard I feel like it swings loose. Then I'm at his rib cage and land a good one under his chin so his head snaps back. He's dazzled. He looks at me and I look at him and then his eyes are full of tears and blood and at first I think he's crying. But no, he's laughing. "Ha! Ha!" he says. "Ha! Ha! Take good care of it."

"Okay," I says, "okay, no problem. Ha! Ha!"

I can't help it, and I start laughing, too. My face feels fat and strange, and after a while I get a beer from the cooler in the trunk, and when I hand it to Henry he takes his shirt and wipes my germs off. "Hoof-and-mouth disease," he says. For some reason this cracks me up, and so we're really laughing for a while, and then we drink all the rest of the beers one by one and throw them in the river and see how far, how fast, the current takes them before they fill up and sink.

"You want to go on back?" I ask after a while. "Maybe we could snag a couple nice Kashpaw girls."

He says nothing. But I can tell his mood is turning again.

"They're all crazy, the girls up here, every damn one of them."

"You're crazy too," I say, to jolly him up. "Crazy Lamartine boys!"

He looks as though he will take this wrong at first. His face twists, then clears, and he jumps up on his feet. "That's right!" he says. "Crazier 'n hell. Crazy Indians!"

I think it's the old Henry again. He throws off his jacket and starts swinging his legs out from the knees like a fancy dancer. He's down doing something between a grass dance and a bunny hop, no kind of dance I ever saw before, but neither has anyone else on all this green growing earth. He's wild. He wants to pitch whoopee! He's up and at me and all over. All this time I'm laughing so hard, so hard my belly is getting tied up in a knot.

"Got to cool me off!" he shouts all of a sudden. Then he runs over to the river and jumps in.

There's boards and other things in the current. It's so high. No sound comes from the river after the splash he makes, so I run right over. I look around. It's getting dark. I see he's halfway across the water already, and I know he didn't swim there but the current took him. It's far. I hear his voice, though, very clearly across it.

"My boots are filling," he says.

He says this in a normal voice, like he just noticed and he doesn't know what to think of it. Then he's gone. A branch comes by. Another branch. And I go in.

By the time I get out of the river, off the snag I pulled myself onto, the sun is down. I walk back to the car, turn on the high beams, and drive it up the bank. I put it in first gear and then I take my foot off the clutch. I get out, close the door, and watch it plow softly into the water. The head-lights reach in as they go down, searching, still lighted even after the water swirls over the back end. I wait. The wires short out. It is all finally dark. And then there is only the water, the sound of it going and running and going and running and running.

A VERY OLD MAN WITH ENORMOUS WINGS

Gabriel García Márquez (b. 1928)

On the third day of rain they had killed so many crabs inside the house that Pelayo had to cross his drenched courtyard and throw them into the sea, because the newborn child had a temperature all night and they thought it was due to the stench. The world had been sad since Tuesday. Sea and sky were a single ash-gray thing and the sands of the beach, which on March nights glimmered like powdered light, had become a stew of mud and rotten shellfish. The light was so weak at noon that when Pelayo was coming back to the house after throwing away the crabs, it was hard for him to see what it was that was moving and groaning in the rear of the courtyard. He had to go very close to see that it was an old man, a very old man, lying face down in the mud, who, in spite of his tremendous efforts, couldn't get up, impeded by his enormous wings.

Frightened by that nightmare, Pelayo ran to get Elisenda, his wife, who was putting compresses on the sick child, and he took her to the rear of the courtyard. They both looked at the fallen body with mute stupor. He was dressed like a ragpicker. There were only a few faded hairs left on his bald skull and very few teeth in his mouth, and his pitiful condition of a drenched great-grandfather had taken away any sense of grandeur he might have had. His huge buzzard wings, dirty and half-plucked, were forever entangled in the mud. They looked at him so long and so closely that Pelayo and Elisenda very soon overcame their surprise and in the end found him familiar. Then they dared speak to him, and he answered in an incomprehensible dialect with a strong sailor's voice. That was how they skipped over the inconvenience of the wings and quite intelligently concluded that he was a lonely castaway from some foreign ship wrecked by the storm. And yet, they called in a neighbor woman who knew everything about life and death to see him, and all she needed was one look to show them their mistake.

"He's an angel," she told them. "He must have been coming for the child, but the poor fellow is so old that the rain knocked him down."

On the following day everyone knew that a flesh-and-blood angel was held captive in Pelayo's house. Against the judgment of the wise neighbor woman, for whom angels in those times were the fugitive survivors of a celestial conspiracy, they did not have the heart to club him to death. Pelayo watched over him all afternoon from the kitchen, armed with his bailiff's club, and before going to bed he dragged him out of the mud and locked him up with the hens in the wire chicken coop. In the middle of the night, when the rain stopped, Pelayo and Elisenda were still killing crabs. A short time afterward the child woke up without a fever and with a desire to eat. Then they felt magnanimous and decided to put the angel on a raft with fresh water and provisions for three days and leave him to his fate on the high seas. But when they went out into the courtyard with the first light of dawn, they found the whole neighborhood in front of the chicken coop having fun with the angel, without the slightest reverence, tossing him things to eat through the openings in the wire as if he weren't a supernatural creature but a circus animal.

Father Gonzaga arrived before seven o'clock, alarmed at the strange news. By that time onlookers less frivolous than those at dawn had already arrived and they were making all kinds of conjectures concerning the captive's future. The simplest among them thought that he should be named mayor of the world. Others of sterner mind felt that he should be promoted to the rank of five-star general in order to win all wars. Some visionaries hoped that he could be put to stud in order to implant on earth a race of winged wise men who could take charge of the universe. But Father Gonzaga, before becoming a priest, had been a robust woodcutter. Standing by the wire, he reviewed his catechism in an instant and asked them to open the door so that he could take a close look at that pitiful man who looked more like a huge decrepit hen among the fascinated chickens. He was lying in a corner drying his open wings in the sunlight among the fruit peels and breakfast leftovers that the early risers had thrown him. Alien to the impertinences of the world, he only lifted his antiquarian eyes and murmured something in his dialect when Father Gonzaga went into the chicken coop and said good morning to him in Latin. The parish priest had his first suspicion of an impostor when he saw that he did not understand the language of God or know how to greet His ministers. Then he noticed that seen close up he was much too human; he had an unbearable smell of the outdoors, the back side of his wings was strewn with parasites and his main feathers had been mistreated by terrestrial winds, and nothing about him measured up to the proud dignity of angels. Then he came out of the chicken coop and in a brief sermon warned the curious against the risks of being ingenuous. He reminded them that the devil had the bad habit of making use of carnival tricks in order to confuse the unwary. He argued that if wings were not the essential element in determining the difference between a hawk and an airplane, they were even less so in the recognition of angels. Nevertheless, he promised to write a letter to his bishop so that the latter would write to his primate so that the latter would write to the Supreme Pontiff in order to get the final verdict from the highest courts.

His prudence fell on sterile hearts. The news of the captive angel spread with such rapidity that after a few hours the courtyard had the bustle of a marketplace and they had to call in troops with fixed bayonets to disperse the mob that was about to knock the house down. Elisenda, her spine all twisted from sweeping up so much marketplace trash, then got the idea of fencing in the yard and charging five cents admission to see the angel.

The curious came from far away. A traveling carnival arrived with a flying acrobat who buzzed over the crowd several times, but no one paid any attention to him because his wings were not those of an angel but, rather, those of a sidereal bat. The most unfortunate invalids on earth came in search of health: a poor woman who since childhood had been counting her heartbeats and had run out of numbers; a Portuguese man who couldn't sleep because the noise of the stars disturbed him; a sleep-walker who got up at night to undo the things he had done while awake; and many others with less serious ailments. In the midst of that ship-wreck disorder that made the earth tremble, Pelayo and Elisenda were happy with fatigue, for in less than a week they had crammed their rooms with money and the line of pilgrims waiting their turn to enter still reached beyond the horizon.

The angel was the only one who took no part in his own act. He spent his time trying to get comfortable in his borrowed nest, befuddled by the hellish heat of the oil lamps and sacramental candles that had been placed along the wire. At first they tried to make him eat some mothballs, which, according to the wisdom of the wise neighbor woman, were the food prescribed for angels. But he turned them down, just as he turned down the papal lunches that the penitents brought him, and they never found out whether it was because he was an angel or because he was an old man that in the end he ate nothing but eggplant mush. His only supernatural virtue seemed to be patience. Especially during the first days, when the hens pecked at him, searching for the stellar parasites that proliferated in his wings, and the cripples pulled out feathers to touch their defective parts with, and even the most merciful threw stones at him, trying to get him to rise so they could see him standing. The only time they succeeded in arousing him was when they burned his side with an iron for branding steers, for he had been motionless for so many hours that they thought he was dead. He awoke with a start, ranting in his her-metic language and with tears in his eyes, and he flapped his wings a couple of times, which brought on a whirlwind of chicken dung and lunar dust and a gale of panic that did not seem to be of this world. Although many thought that his reaction had been one not of rage but of pain, from then on they were careful not to annoy him, because the majority understood that his passivity was not that of a hero taking his ease but that of a cataclysm in repose.

Father Gonzaga held back the crowd's frivolity with formulas of maid-servant inspiration while awaiting the arrival of a final judgment on the nature of the captive. But the mail from Rome showed no sense of urgency. They spent their time finding out if the prisoner had a navel, if his dialect had any connection with Aramaic, how many times he could fit on the head of a pin, or whether he wasn't just a Norwegian with wings. Those meager letters might have come and gone until the end of time if a providential event had not put an end to the priest's tribulations.

It so happened that during those days, among so many other carnival attractions, there arrived in town the traveling show of the woman who had been changed into a spider for having disobeyed her parents. The admission to see her was not only less than the admission to see the angel, but people were permitted to ask her all manner of questions about her absurd state and to examine her up and down so that no one would ever doubt the truth of her horror. She was a frightful tarantula the size of a ram and with the head of a sad maiden. What was most heart-rending, however, was not her outlandish shape but the sincere affliction with which she recounted the details of her misfortune. While still practically a child she had sneaked out of her parents' house to go to a dance, and while she was coming back through the woods after having danced all night without permission, a fearful thunderclap rent the sky in two and through the crack came the lightning bolt of brimstone that changed her into a spider. Her only nourishment came from the meatballs that charitable souls chose to toss into her mouth. A spectacle like that, full of so much human truth and with such a fearful lesson, was bound to defeat without even trying that of a haughty angel who scarcely deigned to look at mortals. Besides, the few miracles attributed to the angel showed a certain mental disorder, like the blind man who didn't recover his sight but grew three new teeth, or the paralytic who didn't get to walk but almost won the lottery, and the leper whose sores sprouted sunflowers. Those consolation miracles, which were more like mocking fun, had already ruined the angel's reputation when the woman who had been changed into a spider finally crushed him completely. That was how Father Gonzaga was cured forever of his insomnia and Pelayo's courtyard went back to being as empty as during the time it had rained for three days and crabs walked through the bedrooms.

The owners of the house had no reason to lament. With the money they saved they built a two-story mansion with balconies and gardens and high netting so that crabs wouldn't get in during the winter, and with iron bars on the windows so that angels wouldn't get in. Pelayo also set up a rabbit warren close to town and gave up his job as bailiff for good, and Elisenda bought some satin pumps with high heels and many dresses of iridescent silk, the kind worn on Sunday by the most desirable women in those times. The chicken coop was the only thing that didn't receive any attention. If they washed it down with creolin and burned tears of myrrh inside it every so often, it was not in homage to the angel but to drive away the dungheap stench that still hung everywhere like a ghost and was turning the new house into an old one. At first, when the child learned to walk, they were careful that he not get too close to the chicken coop. But then they began to lose their fears and got used to the smell, and before the child got his second teeth he'd gone inside the chicken coop to play, where the wires were falling apart. The angel was no less standoffish with him than with other mortals, but he tolerated the most ingenious infamies with the patience of a dog who had no illusions. They both came down with chicken pox at the same time. The doctor who took care of the child couldn't resist the temptation to listen to the angel's heart, and he found so much whistling in the heart and so many sounds in his kidneys that it seemed impossible for him to be alive. What surprised him most, however, was the logic of his wings. They seemed so natural on that completely human organism that he couldn't understand why other men didn't have them too.

When the child began school it had been some time since the sun and rain had caused the collapse of the chicken coop. The angel went dragging himself about here and there like a stray dying man. They would drive him out of the bedroom with a broom and a moment later find him in the kitchen. He seemed to be in so many places at the same time that they grew to think that he'd been duplicated, that he was reproducing himself all through the house, and the exasperated and unhinged Elisenda shouted that it was awful living in that hell full of angels. He could scarcely eat and his antiquarian eyes had also become so foggy that he went about bumping into posts. All he had left were the bare cannulae of his last feathers. Pelayo threw a blanket over him and extended him the charity of letting him sleep in the shed, and only then did they notice that he had a temperature at night, and was delirious with the tongue twisters of an old Norwegian. That was one of the few times they became alarmed, for they thought he was going to die and not even the wise neighbor woman had been able to tell them what to do with dead angels.

And yet he not only survived his worst winter, but seemed improved with the first sunny days. He remained motionless for several days in the farthest corner of the courtyard, where no one would see him, and at the beginning of December some large, stiff feathers began to grow on his wings, the feathers of a scarecrow, which looked more like another misfortune of decrepitude. But he must have known the reason for those changes, for he was quite careful that no one should notice them, that no one should hear the sea chanteys that he sometimes sang under the stars. One morning Elisenda was cutting some bunches of onions for lunch when a wind that seemed to come from the high seas blew into the kitchen. Then she went to the window and caught the angel in his first attempts at flight. They were so clumsy that his fingernails opened a furrow in the vegetable patch and he was on the point of knocking the shed down with the ungainly flapping that slipped on the light and couldn't get a grip on the air. But he did manage to gain altitude. Elisenda let out a sigh of relief, for herself and for him, when she saw him pass over the last houses, holding himself up in some way with the risky flapping of a senile vulture. She kept watching him even when she was through cutting the onions and she kept on watching until it was no longer possible for her to see him, because then he was no longer an annoyance in her life but an imaginary dot on the horizon of the sea.

THE LESSON

Toni Cade Bambara (1939–1995)

Back in the days when everyone was old and stupid or young and foolish and me and Sugar were the only ones just right, this lady moved on our block with nappy hair and proper speech and no makeup. And quite naturally we laughed at her, laughed the way we did at the junk man who went about his business like he was some big-time president and his sorry-ass horse his secretary. And we kinda hated her too, hated the way we did the winos who cluttered up our parks and pissed on our handball walls and stank up our hallways and stairs so you couldn't halfway play hide-and-seek without a goddamn gas mask. Miss Moore was her name. The only woman on the block with no first name. And she was black as hell, cept for her feet, which were fish-white and spooky. And she was always planning these boring-ass things for us to do, us being my cousin, mostly, who lived on the block cause we all moved North the same time and to the same apartment then spread out gradual to breathe. And our parents would yank our heads into some kinda shape and crisp up our clothes so we'd be presentable for travel with Miss Moore, who always looked like she was going to church, though she never did. Which is just one of the things the grownups talked about when they talked behind her back like a dog. But when she came calling with some sachet she'd sewed up or some gingerbread she'd made or some book, why then they'd all be too embarrassed to turn her down and we'd get handed over all spruced up. She'd been to college and said it was only right that she should take responsibility for the young ones' education, and she not even related by marriage or blood. So they'd go for it. Specially Aunt Gretchen. She was the main gofer in the family. You got some ole dumb shit foolishness you want somebody to go for, you send for Aunt Gretchen. She been screwed into the go-along for so long, it's a blood-deep natural thing with her. Which is how she got saddled with me and Sugar and Junior in the first place while our mothers were in a la-de-da apartment up the block having a good ole time.

So this one day Miss Moore rounds us all up at the mailbox and it's puredee hot and she's knockin herself out about arithmetic. And school suppose to let up in summer I heard, but she don't never let up. And the starch in my pinafore scratching the shit outta me and I'm really hating this nappy-head bitch and her goddamn college degree. I'd much rather go to the pool or to the show where it's cool. So me and Sugar leaning on the mailbox being surly, which is a Miss Moore word. And Flyboy checking out what everybody brought for lunch. And Fat Butt already wasting his peanut-butter-and-jelly sandwich like the pig he is. And Junebug punchin on Q.T.'s arm for potato chips. And Rosie Giraffe shifting from one hip to the other waiting for somebody to step on her foot or ask her if she from Georgia so she can kick ass, preferably Mercedes'. And Miss Moore asking us do we know what money is, like we a bunch of retards. I mean real money, she say, like it's only poker chips or monopoly papers we lay on the grocer. So right away I'm tired of this and say so. And would much rather snatch Sugar and go to the Sunset and terrorize the West Indian kids and take their hair ribbons and their money too. And Miss Moore files that remark away for next week's lesson on brotherhood, I can tell. And finally I say we oughta get to the subway cause it's cooler and besides we might meet some cute boys. Sugar done swiped her mama's lipstick, so we ready.

So we heading down the street and she's boring us silly about what things cost and what our parents make and how much goes for rent and how money ain't divided up right in this country. And then she gets to the part about we all poor and live in the slums, which I don't feature. And I'm ready to speak on that, but she steps out in the street and hails two cabs just like that. Then she hustles half the crew in with her and hands me a five-dollar bill and tells me to calculate 10 percent tip for the driver. And we're off. Me and Sugar and Junebug and Flyboy hangin out the window and hollering to everybody, putting lipstick on each other cause Flyboy a faggot anyway, and making farts with our sweaty armpits. But I'm mostly trying to figure how to spend this money. But they all fascinated with the meter ticking and Junebug starts laying bets as to how much it'll read when Flyboy can't hold his breath no more. Then Sugar lays bets as to how much it'll be when we get there. So I'm stuck. Don't nobody want to go for my plan, which is to jump out at the next light and run off to the first bar-b-que we can find. Then the driver tells us to get the hell out cause we there already. And the meter reads eighty-five cents. And I'm stalling to figure out the tip and Sugar say give him a dime. And I decide he don't need it bad as I do, so later for him. But then he tries to take off with Junebug foot still in the door so we talk about his mama something ferocious. Then we check out that we on Fifth Avenue and everybody dressed up in stockings. One lady in a fur coat, hot as it is. White folks crazy.

"This is the place," Miss Moore say, presenting it to us in the voice she uses at the museum. "Let's look in the windows before we go in."

"Can we steal?" Sugar asks very serious like she's getting the ground rules squared away before she plays. "I beg your pardon," say Miss Moore, and we fall out. So she leads us around the windows of the toy store and me and Sugar screamin, "This is mine, that's mine, I gotta have that, that was made for me, I was born for that," till Big Butt drowns us out.

"Hey, I'm goin to buy that there."

"That there? You don't even know what it is, stupid."

"I do so," he say punchin on Rosie Giraffe. "It's a microscope."

"Whatcha gonna do with a microscope, fool?"

"Look at things."

"Like what, Ronald?" ask Miss Moore. And Big Butt ain't got the first notion. So here go Miss Moore gabbing about the thousands of bacteria in a drop of water and the somethinorother in a speck of blood and the million and one living things in the air around us is invisible to the naked eye. And what she say that for? Junebug go to town on that "naked" and we rolling. Then Miss Moore ask what it cost. So we all jam into the window smudgin it up and the price tag say $300. So then she ask how long'd take for Big Butt and Junebug to save up their allowances. "Too long," I say. "Yeh," adds Sugar, "outgrown it by that time." And Miss Moore say no, you never outgrow learning instruments. "Why, even medical students and interns and," blah, blah, blah. And we ready to choke Big Butt for bringing it up in the first damn place.

"This here costs four hundred eighty dollars," says Rosie Giraffe. So we pile up all over her to see what she pointin out. My eyes tell me it's a chunk of glass cracked with something heavy, and different-color inks dripped into the splits, then the whole thing put into a oven or something. But for $480 it don't make sense.

"That's a paperweight made of semi-precious stones fused together under tremendous pressure," she explains slowly, with her hands doing the mining and all the factory work.

"So what's a paperweight?" asks Rosie Giraffe.

"To weigh paper with, dumbbell," say Flyboy, the wise man from the East.

"Not exactly," say Miss Moore, which is what she say when you warm or way off too. "It's to weigh paper down so it won't scatter and make your desk untidy." So right away me and Sugar curtsy to each other and then to Mercedes who is more the tidy type.

"We don't keep paper on top of the desk in my class," say Junebug, figuring Miss Moore crazy or lyin one.

"At home, then," she say. "Don't you have a calendar and pencil case and a blotter and a letter-opener on your desk at home where you do your homework?" And she know damn well what our homes look like cause she nosys around in them every chance she gets.

"I don't even have a desk," say Junebug. "Do we?"

"No And I don't get no homework neither," says Big Butt.

"And I don't even have a home," say Flyboy like he do at school to keep the white folks off his back and sorry for him. Send this poor kid to camp posters, is his specialty.

"I do," says Mercedes, "I have a box of stationery on my desk and a picture of my cat. My godmother bought the stationery and the desk. There's a big rose on each sheet and the envelopes smell like roses."

"Who wants to know about your smelly-ass stationery," say Rosie Giraffe fore I can get my two cents in.

"It's important to have a work area all your own so that . . ."

"Will you look at this sailboat, please," say Flyboy, cuttin her off and pointin to the thing like it was his. So once again we tumble all over each other to gaze at this magnificent thing in the toy store which is just big enough to maybe sail two kittens across the pond if you strap them to the posts tight. We all start reciting the price tag like we in assembly. "Hand-crafted sailboat of fiberglass at one thousand one hundred ninety-five dollars."

"Unbelievable," I hear myself say and am really stunned. I read it again for myself just in case the group recitation put me in a trance. Same thing. For some reason this pisses me off. We look at Miss Moore and she lookin at us, waiting for I dunno what.

"Who'd pay all that when you can buy a sailboat set for a quarter at Pop's, a tube of glue for a dime, and a ball of string for eight cents? It must have a motor and a whole lot else besides," I say. "My sailboat cost me about fifty cents."

"But will it take water?" say Mercedes with her smart ass.

"Took mine to Alley Pond Park once," say Flyboy. "String broke. Lost it. Pity."

"Sailed mine in Central Park and it keeled over and sank. Had to ask my father for another dollar."

"And you got the strap," laugh Big Butt. "The jerk didn't even have a string on it. My old man wailed on his behind."

Little Q.T. was staring hard at the sailboat and you could see he wanted it bad. But he too little and somebody'd just take it from him. So what the hell. "This boat for kids, Miss Moore?"

"Parents silly to buy something like that just to get all broke up," say Rosie Giraffe.

"That much money it should last forever," I figure.

"My father'd buy it for me if I wanted it."

"Your father, my ass," say Rosie Giraffe getting a chance to finally push Mercedes.

"Must be rich people shop here," say Q.T.

"You are a very bright boy," say Flyboy. "What was your first clue?" And he rap him on the head with the back of his knuckles, since Q.T. the only one he could get away with. Though Q.T. liable to come up behind you years later and get his licks in when you half expect it.

"What I want to know is," I says to Miss Moore though I never talk to her, I wouldn't give the bitch that satisfaction, "is how much a real boat costs? I figure a thousand'd get you a yacht any day."

"Why don't you check that out," she says, "and report back to the group?" Which really pains my ass. If you gonna mess up a perfectly good swim day least you could do is have some answers. "Let's go in," she say like she got something up her sleeve. Only she don't lead the way. So me and Sugar turn the corner to where the entrance is, but when we get there I kinda hang back. Not that I'm scared, what's there to be afraid of, just a toy store. But I feel funny, shame. But what I got to be shamed about? Got as much right to go in as anybody. But somehow I can't seem to get hold of the door, so I step away from Sugar to lead. But she hangs back too. And I look at her and she looks at me and this is ridiculous. I mean, damn, I have never ever been shy about doing nothing or going nowhere. But then Mercedes steps up and then Rosie Giraffe and Big Butt crowd in behind and shove, and next thing we all stuffed into the doorway with only Mercedes squeezing past us, smoothing out her jumper and walking right down the aisle. Then the rest of us rumble in like a glued-together jigsaw done all wrong. And people lookin at us. And it's like the time me and Sugar crashed into the Catholic church on a dare. But once we got in there and everything so hushed and holy and the candles and the bowin and the handkerchiefs on all the drooping heads, I just couldn't go through with the plan. Which was for me to run up to the altar and do a tap dance while Sugar played the nose flute and messed around in the holy water. And Sugar kept givin me the elbow. Then later teased me so bad I tied her up in the shower and turned it on and locked her in. And she'd be there till this day if Aunt Gretchen hadn't finally figured I was lyin about the boarder takin a shower.

Same thing in the store. We all walkin on tiptoe and hardly touchin the games and puzzles and things. And I watched Miss Moore who is steady watchin us like she waitin for a sign. Like Mama Drewery watches the sky and sniffs the air and takes note of just how much slant is in the bird formation. Then me and Sugar bump smack into each other, so busy gazing at the toys, specially the sailboat. But we don't laugh and go into our fat-lady bump-stomach routine. We just stare at that price tag. Then Sugar run a finger over the whole boat. And I'm jealous and want to hit her. Maybe not her, but I sure want to punch somebody in the mouth.

"Watcha bring us here for, Miss Moore?"

"You sound angry, Sylvia. Are you mad about something?" Givin me one of them grins like she tellin a grown-up joke that never turns out to be funny. And she's lookin very closely at me like maybe she planning to do my portrait from memory. I'm mad, but I won't give her that satisfaction. So I slouch around the store bein very bored and say, "Let's go."

Me and Sugar at the back of the train watchin the tracks whizzin by large then small then getting gobbled up in the dark. I'm thinkin about this tricky toy I saw in the store. A clown that somersaults on a bar then does chin-ups just cause you yank lightly at his leg. Cost $35. I could see me askin my mother for a $35 birthday clown. "You wanna who that costs what?" she'd say, cocking her head to the side to get a better view of the hole in my head. Thirty-five dollars could buy new bunk beds for Junior and Gretchen's boy. Thirty-five dollars and the whole household could go visit Granddaddy Nelson in the country. Thirty-five dollars would pay for the rent and the piano bill too. Who are these people that spend that much for performing clowns and $1000 for toy sailboats? What kinda work they do and how they live and how come we ain't in on it? Where we are is who we are, Miss Moore always pointin out. But it don't necessarily have to be that way, she always adds then waits for somebody to say that poor people have to wake up and demand their share of the pie and don't none of us know what kind of pie she talking about in the first damn place. But she ain't so smart cause I still got her four dollars from the taxi and she sure ain't gettin it. Messin up my day with this shit. Sugar nudges me in my pocket and winks.

Miss Moore lines us up in front of the mailbox where we started from, seem like years ago, and I got a headache for thinkin so hard. And we lean all over each other so we can hold up under the draggy-ass lecture she always finishes us off with at the end before we thank her for borin us to tears. But she just looks at us like she readin tea leaves. Finally she say, "Well, what did you think of F.A.O. Schwarz?"

Rosie Giraffe mumbles, "White folks crazy."

"I'd like to go there again when I get my birthday money," says Mercedes, and we shove her out the pack so she has to lean on the mailbox by herself.

"I'd like a shower. Tiring day," say Flyboy.

Then Sugar surprises me by sayin, "You know, Miss Moore, I don't think all of us here put together eat in a year what that sailboat costs." And Miss Moore lights up like somebody goosed her. "And?" she say, urging Sugar on. Only I'm standin on her foot so she don't continue.

"Imagine for a minute what kind of society it is in which some people can spend on a toy what it would cost to feed a family of six or seven. What do you think?"

"I think," say Sugar pushing me off her feet like she never done before, cause I whip her ass in a minute, "that this is not much of a democracy if you ask me. Equal chance to pursue happiness means an equal crack at the dough, don't it?" Miss Moore is besides herself and I am disgusted with Sugar's treachery. So I stand on her foot one more time to see if she'll shove me. She shuts up, and Miss Moore looks at me, sorrowfully I'm thinkin. And somethin weird is goin on, I can feel it in my chest.

"Anybody else learn anything today?" lookin dead at me. I walk away and Sugar has to run to catch up and don't even seem to notice when I shrug her arm off my shoulder.

"Well, we got four dollars anyway," she says.

"Uh hunh."

"We could go to Hascombs and get half a chocolate layer and then go to the Sunset and still have plenty money for potato chips and ice cream sodas."

"Un hunh."

"Race you to Hascombs," she say.

We start down the block and she gets ahead which is O.K. by me cause I'm going to the West End and then over to the Drive to think this day through. She can run if she want to and even run faster. But ain't nobody gonna beat me at nuthin.

YOURS

Mary Robison (b. 1949)

Allison struggled away from her white Renault, limping with the weight of the last of the pumpkins. She found Clark in the twilight on the twig- and leaf-littered porch behind the house.

He wore a wool shawl. He was moving up and back in a padded glider, pushed by the ball of his slippered foot.

Allison lowered a big pumpkin, let it rest on the wide floorboards.

Clark was much older—seventy-eight to Allison's thirty-five. They were married. They were both quite tall and looked something alike in their facial features. Allison wore a natural-hair wig. It was a thick blonde hood around her face. She was dressed in bright-dyed denims today. She wore durable clothes, usually, for she volunteered afternoons at a chil- dren's day-care center.

She put one of the smaller pumpkins on Clark's long lap. "Now, nothing surreal," she told him. "Carve just a *regular* face. These are for kids."

In the foyer, on the Hepplewhite desk, Allison found the maid's chore list with its cross-offs, which included Clark's supper. Allison went quickly through the day's mail: a garish coupon packet, a bill from Jamestown Liquors, November's pay-TV program guide, and the worst thing, the funniest, an already opened, extremely unkind letter from Clark's relations up North. "You're an old fool," Allison read, and, "You're being cruelly deceived." There was a gift check for Clark enclosed, but it was uncashable, signed, as it was, "Jesus H. Christ."

Late, late into this night, Allison and Clark gutted and carved the pumpkins together, at an old table set on the back porch, over newspaper after soggy newspaper, with paring knives and with spoons and with a Swiss Army knife Clark used for exact shaping of tooth and eye and nos- tril. Clark had been a doctor, an internist, but also a Sunday watercolorist. His four pumpkins were expressive and artful. Their carved features were suited to the sizes and shapes of the pumpkins. Two looked ferocious and jagged. One registered surprise. The last was serene and beaming.

Allison's four faces were less deftly drawn, with slits and areas of distortion. She had cut triangles for noses and eyes. The mouths she had made were just wedges—two turned up and two turned down.

By one in the morning they were finished. Clark, who had bent his long torso forward to work, moved back over to the glider and looked out sleepily at nothing. All the lights were out across the ravine.

Clark stayed. For the season and time, the Virginia night was warm. Most leaves had been blown away already, and the trees stood unboth- ered. The moon was round above them.

Allison cleaned up the mess.

"Your jack-o'-lanterns are much, much better than mine," Clark said to her.

"Like hell," Allison said.

"Look at me," Clark said, and Allison did.

She was holding a squishy bundle of newspapers. The papers reeked sweetly with the smell of pumpkin guts.

"Yours are *far* better," he said.

"You're wrong. You'll see when they're lit," Allison said.

She went inside, came back with yellow vigil candles. It took her a while to get each candle settled, and then to line up the results in a row on the porch railing. She went along and lit each candle and fixed the pumpkin lids over the little flames.

"See?" she said.

They sat together a moment and looked at the orange faces.

"We're exhausted. It's good-night time," Allison said. "Don't blow out the candles. I'll put in new ones tomorrow."

That night, in their bedroom, a few weeks earlier in her life than had been predicted, Allison began to die. "Don't look at me if my wig comes off," she told Clark. "Please."

Her pulse cords were fluttering under his fingers. She raised her knees and kicked away the comforter. She said something to Clark about the garage being locked.

At the telephone, Clark had a clear view out back and down to the porch. He wanted to get drunk with his wife once more. He wanted to tell her, from the greater perspective he had, that to own only a little talent, like his, was an awful, plaguing thing; that being only a little special meant you expected too much, most of the time, and liked yourself too little. He wanted to assure her that she had missed nothing.

He was speaking into the phone now. He watched the jack-o'-lanterns. The jack-o'-lanterns watched him.

Glossary

alliteration: the repetition of consonant sounds, usually occurring at the beginnings of words, which produces an echo effect and links words through their sounds.

ambiguity: open to more than one meaning.

antagonist: character who opposes or rivals the protagonist.

arc: the curved shape of a story—as opposed to the straight line of an anecdote—with its establishment of initial conflict followed by its rise in complication, its climax and its denouement.

assonance: the repetition of vowel sounds in the final syllables of words; it produces an effect similar to alliteration.

backstory: the history of the story prior to page one of the written text.

cacophony: the blending of sounds to produce a noisy or unpleasant effect on the ear—it has the opposite effect of **euphony.**

caesura: a pause within a line that usually occurs because of punctuation—maybe a comma. A caesura may also happen because of the way two words fall next to each other rhythmically.

character: the person or people of the story; greater than or equal to plot in importance.

cliché: phrase or image which is, and has been, so commonly used that it is not original at all.

connotation: the cultural and contextual definition of a word.

denotation: standard, or dictionary, definition.

dénouement: final resolution of the plot; follows the climax.

dialogue: verbal exchange between characters; **direct dialogue**—two or more people are speaking in a scene; **indirect dialogue**—speech that is reported, as in *John told him he could come.*

diction: word choice.

enjambment: (also known as the "run-on line") the line's grammatical sense and meaning carry over into the next. Hence, the line "runs on."

euphony: the blending of sounds to produce a pleasurable effect on the ear.

exposition: "telling" or "explaining," as differentiated from *scene,* which is "live" action.

extended or controlling metaphor: a metaphor which extends itself throughout an entire poem. It may control the entire poem, being the dominant image that drives the poem's meaning.

falling meter: stressed to unstressed syllables.

first person point of view: one of the characters narrates the story using the pronoun *I*.

flashback: narrator goes back in time to narrate some backstory. Sometimes a space-break is used to indicate this temporal and spatial shift.

flashforward: narrator goes forward in time to narrate some future story; rarer than a flashback.

foil: a character who, through contrast, heightens the distinctive characteristics of other characters.

foot: one measure of stressed and unstressed syllables.

futurestory: the future of the story after the last page of the written text.

image: picture created by words.

implied metaphor: implies rather than states, what main object is being compared to, usually through action or by ascribing attributes.

in medias res: in the middle of things; meant to instruct a writer to begin his story in the middle where the conflict exists.

irony: the use of events or conditions that produce unexpected outcomes or contradiction. Some event we (or a character) may think to be true but turns out otherwise may be ironic. Irony may be conveyed by an underlying voice or tone.

line: a line of text in a poem.

metadiscourse: The narrator announces his presence and enters the story by commenting on the story itself, as in *I am having trouble with the plot, but bear with me*. This can occur with an omniscient narrator.

metaphor: a comparison that says one thing *is* another.

meter: the arrangement of measured rhythm in poetry (*measured* is a key word here; think of how music is measured); based on the positions of the stressed and unstressed syllables in words.

mood: author's emotional and intellectual attitude toward a story as well as character's emotional and intellectual attitude in a story.

narrative distance: temporal (and spatial) distance from which a story is told. If a narrator is thirty-six years old and he is telling the story of an event that took place when he was twelve, the narrative distance is twenty-four years.

onomatopoeia: the sound or rhythm of a word mimicking the object or phenomenon to which it refers.

pacing: the speed in which events take place. Good pacing requires the writer to know what to leave in in exposition or scene, and what to leave out.

persona: the speaker of the poem (or story) and the one who takes on the point of view.

personification: giving a nonhuman object some human characteristic.

plot: the series of events in a story, no matter how those events are organized.

point of view: the stance taken by the persona—the attitude and the view of the world he imparts to the reader. Along with stance and attitude comes tone.

protagonist: literally "the first actor" but generally considered to be the chief character.

real subject, or generated subject: what the poem comes to say, ultimately the most powerful of the subjects in the poem. This is the subject that may be referred to as the core, the heart, or the kernel of the poem.

red herring: a false clue in a story wherein the reader has been duped to believe some object or action has an importance that it does not. This is something to avoid.

resonance: the emotional reverberation that a character in a story has caused the reader to feel, often occurring at the climax and/or the denouement of a story.

rhyme: an echoing produced by close placement of two or more words with similarly sounding final syllables. Types of rhyme: **masculine rhyme**, in which two words end with the same vowel-consonant combination (hand/band); **feminine rhyme**, in which two syllables rhyme (shiver/liver); **end-rhyme**, in which the rhyme comes at the ends of the lines (this is probably the most commonly used rhyme); **internal rhyme**, in which a word within a line rhymes with another word in that line, or rhymes with a word of similar placement in the following line; **slant rhyme**, in which the sounds nearly rhyme but do not form a "true rhyme" (land/lend).

rising meter: unstressed syllables to stressed syllables.

scene: "live action," in which the reader views events as they unfold. There is often dialogue in a scene.

sestina: a poem that comprises six stanzas, each with six lines, and a three-line stanza called an envoy. Hence there are always thirty-nine lines in a sestina. The last words of the first six lines of the poem are repeated as the end words of the following five stanzas, and all the words must be included in the envoy. It is a traditional French form that was used in writing love poetry in the thirteenth century.

shift in point of view: usually the error of leaving third person limited point of view for third person multiple, but may be the more egregious error of shifting from third person to first or second.

simile: a comparison using the words *like* or *as.*

stanza: a group of lines in a poem separated from another group of lines by a space break. In free verse, these groups of lines do not need to be the same in number, but a stanza usually signifies that there is some type of organizational structure to the poem. A writer often organizes lines into stanzas based on some conceptual coherence.

style: a writer's rhetorical strategy which includes her use of diction.

syntax: word order.

theme: the central meaning of the story derived from the characters' actions and reactions in relation to the plot.

third person limited: the point of view of "he" or "she," limited to one character in a story. In other words, if you limit the point of view to the character Susan, you cannot narrate a scene unless Susan is present.

third person multiple: the point of view of "he" or "she," not limited to one character. In other words, you may narrate a scene when Susan is present and then another scene when Susan is absent and other characters occupy the scene.

third person omniscient: the point of view which the narrator is all-knowing and that narrator may narrate any character's thoughts. The narrator may even interject thoughts that are not those of any of the characters; however, such interjection is rarely done and is often viewed as somewhat archaic.

tone: the emotional sense behind the voice of the persona sometimes communicated through the use of irony, hyperbole, and understatement.

triggering subject: the subject that causes the poem to come up in the first place, to be written. It's the subject that the reader first attaches to and that often guides them further into the poem.

voice: the expressive force and tone of the words spoken by the author and the **persona** in the poem; in the story, it is the combination of style and tone.

Contributors' Biographies

Diana Abu-Jaber is Writer-in-Residence at Portland State University and also writes for *The Oregonian* newspaper. Her first novel, *Arabian Jazz*, won the Oregon Book Award.

H. Lee Barnes teaches creative writing at the Community College of Southern Nevada. His fiction has appeared in numerous literary journals and *Gunning for Ho*, a collection of short stories, was published in 1999 (University of Nevada Press).

Ron Carlson is a professor of creative writing at Arizona State University. His most recent book is *At Bridger* (Picador), a collection of short stories.

Lisa Chavez is the author of *Destruction Bay* (West End Press, 1999) and *In An Angry Season* (U. of Arizona Press, 2001). She is an assistant professor of creative writing at the University of New Mexico.

Tracy Daugherty is an associate professor of English at Oregon State University. His most recent book is the novel *The Boy Orator* (SMU Press).

Beckian Fritz Goldberg teaches creative writing at Arizona State University. Her latest collection of poems is *Never Be the Horse* (University of Akron Press, 1999).

James Hoggard teaches literature and creative writing at Midwestern State University in Witchita Falls, Texas. His most recent collection of poems is *Medea in Taos* (Pecan Grove Press).

Lynn Hoggard is professor of French and English at Midwestern State University in Texas. She has translated collections of poetry by Paul Valery and Henri Michaux. She was a featured poet in *A Certain Attitude: Poems by Seven Texas Women* (Pecan Grove Press).

Craig Lesley teaches at Portland State University. His most recent novel is *Storm Riders* (Picador).

Valerie Miner teaches in the MFA program at the University of Minnesota. Her most recent book is the novel *Range of Light* (Zoland Press).

Ken Olsen is a newspaper reporter in Portland, Oregon.

Melissa Pritchard is the director of the MFA Program in Creative Writing at Arizona State University. Her most recent short story collection is *Disappearing Ingenue* (Doubleday).

Alberto Ríos is Regents' Professor of English at Arizona State University. He is the author of numerous books of poetry and stories. His latest, *Capirotada*, is a collection of personal essays (University of New Mexico Press).

Kevin Stein is professor of literature and creative writing at Bradley University. His latest collection of poems is *Chance Ransom* (University of Illinois Press).

Virgil Suarez teaches creative writing, and Latino/a and Caribbean Literature at Florida State University in Tallahassee. His most recent collections of poems are *You Come Singing* and *In The Republic of Longing*.

Gary Thompson has taught in the Creative Writing Program at California State University, Chico for twenty-five years. His poems have been published in many magazines and anthologies; his most recent collection is *On John Muir's Trail* (Bear Star Press).

Amy Sage Webb is an assistant professor of creative writing at Emporia State University. Her fiction has appeared in numerous literary journals.

Other Credits

Index